Dickens, Journalism, and Nationhood

Studies in Major Literary Authors

William E. Cain, *General Editor*

For a full list of titles in this series, please visit www.routledge.com

"Somewhat on the Community-System"
Fourierism in the Works of Nathaniel Hawthorne
Andrew Loman

Colonialism and the Modernist Moment in the Early Novels of Jean Rhys
Carol Dell'Amico

Melville's Monumental Imagination
Ian S. Maloney

Writing "Out of All the Camps"
J.M. Coetzee's Narratives of Displacement
Laura Wright

Here and Now
The Politics of Social Space in D. H. Lawrence and Virginia Woolf
Youngjoo Son

"Unnoticed in the Casual Light of Day"
Philip Larkin and the Plain Style
Tijana Stojković

Queer Times
Christopher Isherwood's Modernity
Jamie M. Carr

Edith Wharton's "Evolutionary Conception"
Darwinian Allegory in Her Major Novels
Paul J. Ohler

The End of Learning
Milton and Education
Thomas Festa

Reading and Mapping Hardy's Roads
Scott Rode

Creating Yoknapatawpha
Readers and Writers in Faulkner's Fiction
Owen Robinson

No Place for Home
Spatial Constraint and Character Flight in the Novels of Cormac McCarthy
Jay Ellis

The Machine that Sings
Modernism, Hart Crane, and the Culture of the Body
Gordon A. Tapper

Influential Ghosts
A Study of Auden's Sources
Rachel Wetzsteon

D.H. Lawrence's Border Crossing
Colonialism in His Travel Writings and "Leadership" Novels
Eunyoung Oh

Dorothy Wordsworth's Ecology
Kenneth R. Cervelli

Sports, Narrative, and Nation in the Fiction of F. Scott Fitzgerald
Jarom Lyle McDonald

Shelley's Intellectual System and its Epicurean Background
Michael A. Vicario

Modernist Aesthetics and Consumer Culture in the Writings of Oscar Wilde
Paul L. Fortunato

Milton's Uncertain Eden
Understanding Place in *Paradise Lost*
Andrew Mattison

Henry Miller and Religion
Thomas Nesbit

The Magic Lantern
Representation of the Double in Dickens
Maria Cristina Paganoni

The Environmental Unconscious in the Fiction of Don DeLillo
Elise A. Martucci

James Merrill
Knowing Innocence
Reena Sastri

Yeats and Theosophy
Ken Monteith

Pynchon and the Political
Samuel Thomas

Paul Auster's Postmodernity
Brendan Martin

Editing Emily Dickinson
The Production of an Author
Lena Christensen

Cormac McCarthy and the Myth of American Exceptionalism
John Cant

Our Scene is London
Ben Jonson's City and the Space of the Author
James D. Mardock

Poetic Language and Political Engagement in the Poetry of Keats
Jack Siler

Politics and Aesthetics in *The Diary of Virginia Woolf*
Joanne Campbell Tidwell

Homosexuality in the Life and Work of Joseph Conrad
Love Between the Lines
Richard J. Ruppel

Shakespeare in the Victorian Periodicals
Kathryn Prince

Shakespeare and the Economic Imperative
"What's aught but as 'tis valued?"
Peter F. Grav

Wallace Stevens and the Realities of Poetic Language
Stefan Holander

Milton and the Spiritual Reader
Reading and Religion in Seventeenth-Century England
David Ainsworth

Everybody's America
Thomas Pynchon, Race, and the Cultures of Postmodernism
David Witzling

Dickens, Journalism, and Nationhood
Mapping the World in *Household Words*
Sabine Clemm

Dickens, Journalism, and Nationhood

Mapping the World in *Household Words*

Sabine Clemm

Routledge
Taylor & Francis Group
New York London

First published 2009
by Routledge
270 Madison Ave, New York, NY 10016

Simultaneously published in the UK
by Routledge
2 Park Square, Milton Park, Abingdon, Oxon OX14 4RN

Routledge is an imprint of the Taylor & Francis Group, an informa business

Typeset in Sabon by IBT Global.

Library of Congress Cataloging in Publication Data

Clemm, Sabine, 1974-
Dickens, journalism, and nationhood : mapping the world in Household words / by Sabine Clemm.
p. cm. — (Studies in major literary authors)
Includes bibliographical references and index.
ISBN-13: 978-0-415-95846-2 (hbk.)
ISBN-10: 0-415-95846-6 (hbk.)
ISBN-13: 978-0-203-88775-2 (ebk.)
ISBN-10: 0-203-88775-1 (ebk.)
1. Household words. 2. Dickens, Charles, 1812–1870—Knowledge—National characteristics. 3. Dickens, Charles, 1812–1870—Knowledge—Journalism. 4. National characteristics in literature. 5. National characteristics in mass media. 6. Journalism—Great Britain—History—19th century. I. Title.
PR4592.P7C64 2009
828'.8—dc22
2008021084

ISBN10: 0-415-95846-6 (hbk)
ISBN10: 0-203-88775-1 (ebk)

ISBN13: 978-0-415-95846-2 (hbk)
ISBN13: 978-0-203-88775-2 (ebk)

Contents

Figures

Acknowledgments

My first and most heartfelt gratitude belongs to Cora Kaplan, without whom this book would never have been begun, let alone completed. I would also like to thank Sally Shuttleworth and Lucy Hartley for their valuable feedback and advice and John McGavin for his kind support. Further, I am indebted to my editors at Routledge for their patience and encouragement throughout.

Equally crucial to the completion of this project have been my friends and family, who bore countless rants with singular forbearance and freely provided moral and IT support, sympathetic ears, a few timely kicks in the backside, and an occasional stiff drink. My particular thanks go to John Armstrong, Heather Bourne, Oliver and Wolfgang Clemm, Ute and Paul Denkena, Maaten Furlong, Sue Kerr, Julia Köhler, Helen and Paul Lewis, Alexandra Mant, Sarah Mitchell, James Murrell, Moi Rickman, Doug Robinson, Barbara and Mathias Seiter, Howard Stone, Steve and Beth Taverner, Ivo Veldhuis, Melanie Wagner, Peter White, and Lu Shin Wong.

Introduction

> More than any other novelist of his century, [Dickens] understood and created the national character.[1]
>
> Peter Ackroyd, 'Dickens', BBC series

> 'A little of the genuine old English Bagstock stamina, Sir, would do all the good in the world to the human breed.' [. . .] The Major [. . .] was certainly true-blue, whatever other endowments he may have possessed or wanted, coming within the 'genuine old English' classification, which has never been exactly ascertained.[2]
>
> Charles Dickens, *Dombey and Son*

> Our Household Words will not [. . .] treat of the hopes, the enterprises, triumphs, joys and sorrows, of this country only, but, in some degree, of those of every nation upon earth. For nothing can be a source of real interest in one of them, without concerning all the rest.[3]
>
> Charles Dickens, 'A Preliminary Word'

This book examines the way in which Charles Dickens's weekly family journal *Household Words* imagines and structures the world. The complexities that this book will address are suggested in the three quotations above. Ackroyd's definition of Dickens as the 'most English' of writers is a commonplace today, yet Dickens himself repeatedly points out, as the extract from *Dombey and Son* shows, that it is virtually impossible to define what 'genuine English' characteristics actually are. *Household Words* forms an arena in which the complex and often contradictory strands of the question of national identity can be untangled or, indeed, knotted anew. As the quotation from Dickens's 'Preliminary Word' shows, the journal considers Britain as both isolated from and intertwined with other nations. Clearly, the relationship between Dickens's work and the English national character is more complicated than is usually expected of this 'most English' of writers.

In her discussion of Dickens's treatment of the English character in relation to Italy, Tore Rem asserts that 'however fascinating his letters, journalism and travel books may be, they are not the main reason for studying Dickens.'[4] It is true, of course, that Dickens's journals seem to have attracted scholars precisely because they were *his* journals. Most studies of Dickens, even of his relationship with Englishness, Europe, and the world at large, focus on one or two novels (or, less frequently, travel books) and one or two places respectively, using the journalism as secondary, incidental evidence. After a brief flurry of interest in Dickens's journalism in the late 1960s and early 1970s[5], its academic pursuit was largely limited to Anne Lohrli until quite recently, when researchers such as Lillian Nayder and John Drew have turned to it afresh.[6] However, most of these studies still focus either on Charles Dickens or on his relationship with individual authors, like Wilkie Collins, Elizabeth Gaskell, or George Augustus Sala.[7]

This book aims not to study Dickens through *Household Words* or to see the journal as a mere expression of its 'conductor' or a weaker shadow of his novels, but to consider *Household Words* as an independent and complex entity in its own right, a multifarious and often contradictory production of meaning. Margaret Beetham points out that 'a periodical is not a window on to the past or even a mirror of it' but 'a complex process in which writers, editors, publishers and readers engaged in [a struggle . . .] to make their world meaningful'.[8] Ostensibly self-sufficient articles reflect onto each other and acquire meaning from the context in which they appear. It is precisely this complexity and heterogeneity that makes the periodical genre so attractive, compared to single-authored works. Although the journal was Dickens's brainchild, and although he initially conceived of it, like Tore Rem, as an additional line of communication to the readers of his novels, the journal quickly outgrew this relatively restricted function and took on a life and shape of its own. Of course, Dickens remained the figurehead and central 'voice' in his journal to a higher degree than the editors of other journals did, but even he could not prevent contradictions, occasional falsehoods, and some topics he disapproved of from forcing their way into the journal.[9]

My particular focus lies on *Household Words*' treatment of nationhood and national identity because it is not only a central concern of *Household Words* but also has resounding implications for the media of the twenty-first as well as the nineteenth century. Most *Household Words* numbers feature at least one or two (often more) articles that relate stories, anecdotes, histories, customs, or economic, agricultural, and geological features of other countries and colonies, which rendered these locations more accessible and palatable to armchair travellers, investors, and even potential emigrants.

To take a random example: number 205, dated February 25, 1854, contains eight pieces: a short story, a book review, two travel reports, a poem, two informational articles, and the concluding part of a historical account. The opening story is set in 'one of those old fashioned winters in the day of the Georges, when [. . .] newspapers were devoid of all foreign intelligence'.[10] This sets off nicely the amount of 'foreign intelligence' that follows—clearly, newspapers and journals have moved on since. The second item, for instance, is a description of 'Modern Greek Songs', which describes in some detail the customs and traditions of contemporary Greece.[11] A short piece entitled 'Jack and the Union Jack' then discusses the excellent conditions of employment in the British navy and draws attention to the professional opportunities that Britannia's rule of the waves offers.[12] Counterbalancing the masculine business of travel and seafaring, the next item is a poem about a young Englishwoman who 'Died in India'.[13] It is followed by an account of travel in Eastern Germany and Bohemia.[14] The sixth item is a factual piece explaining the production and advantages of watered silk, which in turn is followed by the final chapter of a two-part history of 'Holland House' and its various occupants.[15] The number concludes with an article describing a fair in Paris.[16] In other words, four of these eight pieces are set in or describe life in countries other than Britain, while a fifth discusses the advantages of a professional career in seafaring.

Bound up with *Household Words'* interest in foreign places is an ever-present preoccupation with what it means to be English. This applies to the British colonies and to European countries alike, although I will show throughout that different degrees of 'foreignness' exist in both *Household Words* and other publications: while (Western) European nations are usually seen as partners (or indeed rivals) on a similar level to Britain itself, the relationship between Britain and its colonies is clearly hierarchical. Furthermore, the discourse about Europe tends to be more distanced and formal, whereas Britain felt fully in charge of the colonies, politically as well as discursively. Although the major events in the 1850s focused attention on Britain's empire or the European context, the shifts and opinions that these brought about were bound up with the current discourse on nationhood and Englishness. Moreover, *Household Words* writers directly question the nature of the English national character itself at several junctures, while the journal simultaneously endeavours to embody 'English' moralities and strives to unite its readers (and, arguably, writers and producers) as one community. Indeed, the moral code that many critics have identified in *Household Words* is intimately related to what it means to be English.

Although constructions of national character and race have received plenty of academic attention, they are rarely discussed in relation to the periodical genre. Yet the close affinity between the rise of the periodical press and the rise of the nation as a primary order of identity has been well-established since the publication of Benedict Anderson's *Imagined Communities*.[17] The readers of a newspaper or magazine form an 'imagined community', just as the subjects in a nation do. Although every individual reads their copy of a newspaper or periodical 'in silent privacy [. . .] each communicant is [nonetheless] aware that the ceremony he performs is being replicated simultaneously by thousands (or millions) of others of whose existence he is confident, yet of whose identity he has not the slightest notion'.[18] The masses of readers imagine themselves (and each other) as part of a community that, literally, buys into the same values as expressed in the publication of their choice.[19] To call this community 'imagined' is not to say that it is also *imaginary*—on the contrary, the very act of collectively imagining the community creates it.[20] In Antony Easthope's terms, this act of imagination exists side by side with the material manifestations of nationhood in a mutually dependent symbiosis:

> National cultures are material in that they are produced through institutions, practices and traditions which historians and sociologists can describe. But national cultures are also reproduced through narratives and discourses about which those social sciences feel inhibited but which recent work in theory makes a matter of coherent analysis.[21]

The periodical genre, then, not only reflects but actively participates in the production of a national identity. However, *Household Words* makes a particularly pertinent case study in this context not simply because it forms part of the genre—in fact, it actively and consciously endorses the idea of an imagined community between writers, editors, and readers in its quest to find a unified (and manifestly English) 'voice'.

THE HISTORICAL CONTEXT OF THE 1850s

Household Words spanned most of the 1850s (its first issue was dated Saturday, March 30, 1850, and its last May 28, 1859[22]), an interesting and in some ways pivotal period that has sometimes been misunderstood as uneventful.[23] Britain had come through the revolutions that had shaken much of Europe in 1848–9 relatively unscathed, and celebrated itself in the Great Exhibition of 1851, the first major world's fair. Technological advances such as the electric telegraph and the spread of the railway network brought the European nations closer together and seemed to ring the change for a future in which miscommunication between nations would become impossible and eternal peace the natural consequence. The two major armed conflicts in which Britain got involved in this decade both took place thousands of miles away, so Britain itself is often thought to have sailed through the period complacently and relatively undisturbed.

However, Britain was in significant turmoil for most of the decade, both internally and in its international relations. 1850 marked the final year of the Irish Famine, which had ravaged Ireland for five years running and caused immeasurable suffering and devastation, as well as diverse governmental headaches.[24] Politically, the 1850s were characterised by 'confusion' and saw no less than five governments overthrown (or undermined) as a result of internal divisions and shifting alliances in both Liberals and Conservatives.[25] Although the workers' movements appeared to have faded out and social balance returned after Chartism made its last stance in 1848, 'resentment was never far below the surface'.[26] Britain's economy experienced a massive boom between 1848 and 1857, but the wealth it generated was by no means distributed equally—the classes nearer the bottom of the social ladder got an ever-diminishing share of it and reacted accordingly.[27] Therefore

> to see the period 1850–75 as one of unusual industrial peace is misleading. That trade-union militancy was common is shown by the widespread engineering strikes and lockouts of 1851–2, the Preston textile dispute of 1853–4, bitter unrest in the building industry in 1859 [. . .] And if some disputes were the products of hard times or of attempts to cut wages [. . .], others took place during booms when workers felt able to act from a position of strength.[28]

On an international level, Britain fared no better. Relationships with its European neighbours were fraught and shaky throughout the decade, and opinions varied indecisively on whether Britain formed part of Europe or was aloof from (and superior to) the continent. France in particular was viewed with great suspicion. After the 1848 revolutions and the *coup d'état* of Napoleon III in December 1851, Britain saw itself under the threat of imminent invasion and in isolation from the rest of the continent, the sole and much envied stronghold of freedom and civilisation. In 1853, this reservation gradually gave way to an alliance with France against Russia, which led to the drawn-out Crimean War that killed far more British soldiers through illness, weather conditions, and mismanagement than in combat. By the time Britain and France jointly defeated Russia, there was little enthusiasm left for the war, and the victory came at a bitter price. Barely a year on, fresh conflict flared up in Britain's most valuable colonial possession, only recently celebrated as the most successful and beneficial imperial project for both natives and colonisers (at least, that was the view of the British media), when the so-called 'Indian Mutiny' began in May 1857. Having dispatched all its troops to India to subdue the potentially disastrous rebellion, Britain became deeply aware of its own vulnerability and came to regard its European neighbours with renewed suspicion. By the end of the decade, its relationship with France was once more riddled with fear, a fact that is amply testified in the rapid growth of the British Rifle Volunteers who hoped to repel the threat of French invasion.[29] Patrick Brantlinger summarises the period aptly:

> The Australian gold rush, the search for the Nile's sources, the Crimean War, and the Mutiny made that decade a turning point for imperialist ideology, long before the New Imperialism manifested itself in the Scramble for Africa and all the other parts of the world

that still remained to be overrun by European bearers of light and of Maxim guns.'[30]

All in all, Britain's position during this period, both on a national and international level, was much more turbulent and fragile than is usually assumed. Reading *Household Words* against this unsettled background throws a new light on its portrayal of other nations as well as on the journal itself.

THE PUBLICATION HISTORY OF *HOUSEHOLD WORDS*

The fact that the decade was marked not by tranquillity but by multiple tensions and conflicts smouldering under the surface may explain to some degree why Dickens wanted a journal that could reach across all social boundaries and unite his readers in a 'multitude moved by one sympathy'.[31] '*Household Words* was the fulfilment of Dickens's long-cherished wish to conduct a journal in which he could speak personally to the large circle of readers whom his novels had drawn to him'.[32] However, the founding of a periodical was not simply a consequence of his success as novelist. Dickens achieved his initial acclaim as an author not through his novels but as a journalist, and his entire career was punctuated with spells of journalistic work. He became parliamentary reporter for the *True Sun* when he was nineteen, then wrote for the *Mirror of Parliament*, and subsequently worked for the *Morning Chronicle*, contributing occasional pieces to Holland's *Monthly Magazine*.[33] Only five years into his journalistic career did his first novel begin serial publication. Tellingly, *The Pickwick Papers* leaned towards the format of a collection of miscellaneous writings that the author merely 'edited', as is indicated in its full title: *Posthumous Papers of the Pickwick Club, edited by Boz.*

Dickens first became editor of a journal in August 1836, when he took on the editorship of *Bentley's Miscellany*. From the beginning, his relationship with Richard Bentley, the publisher and owner of the magazine, was volatile, as they continually clashed in their views on editorship.[34] Bentley considered 'the magazine as a showcase for the notable gallery of writers he had attracted to his person and his enterprises' and envisaged the editor 'as a kind of manager and displayer of that talent'. In contrast, Dickens claimed a far more active and dominant role for himself and regarded the publication as a 'projection of his tastes and his abilities'.[35] Bentley's view emphasised the multifarious nature of a periodical with several different contributors and potentially differing opinions, whereas Dickens privileged the unity of the whole product under his command. In all his journalistic projects that were to follow, this view never changed, and it was largely responsible for the homogeneous nature that critics so often find in *Household Words*. After many threats, Dickens finally resigned from *Bentley's Miscellany* in early 1839, since 'he could not, in any of his endeavours, comfortably work for or capitulate to a superior' and was thoroughly frustrated with the degree of interference from Bentley himself.[36]

Bentley's Miscellany was followed by a second attempt at editorship only a few months later, *Master Humphrey's Clock*. This time the concept was Dickens's own: 'He would write the framework of the periodical, pursue certain recurrent themes and features, contribute occasional stories, but leave room for others' who 'would have to conform to the style and contents prescribed by the editor'.[37] Wary after his difficulties with Bentley, Dickens demanded and was contractually granted total control over the magazine's contents. The central persona or 'shadow', which kept the journal together, had been a popular notion in eighteenth-century journals that Dickens had read in his childhood.[38] This concept set such a narrow framework that Dickens ended up writing the entire journal himself.[39] When sales began to drop, Dickens expanded a few initial sketches into a serialised novel, *The Old Curiosity Shop*, which saved the journal for some time, but in the end *Master Humphrey's Clock* fell victim to 'the tyrannical pressure of taste and economics'.[40]

In 1845 Dickens entertained plans for yet another periodical, *The Cricket*, which he subsequently dropped in favour of 'two allied but very different projects later that year: a Christmas Book, *The Cricket on the Hearth* [. . .] and a new periodical, the *Daily News*, which Dickens founded and for a while edited'.[41] The *Daily News* was intended as a liberal newspaper rivalling the *Morning Chronicle* and *The Times*. Dickens was not best suited to the editorship of a newspaper, which pursued quite different goals than the mixture of light entertainment and companionship that he had aimed for in *Master Humphrey's Clock*. Furthermore, similar challenges to his editorial authority arose as he had experienced with *Bentley's Miscellany*. This time, Dickens resigned less than three weeks after the first issue's appearance on January 21st, 1846, and asked his friend John Forster to take over.[42]

By the time Dickens took on his next editorial project, *Household Words*, he was the celebrated author of seven novels, three Christmas stories, a travel book, and countless shorter texts. He shaped his plans for *Household Words* while working on his eighth and all-time favourite novel, *David Copperfield*, which—along with *Dombey and Son*—marked the beginning of his full literary maturity, producing darker novels of increased weight, structure, and discrimination, compared to the light-hearted, funny (though no less sentimental), and often rambling tales of his youth.

Despite the failure of the concept in *Master Humphrey's Clock*, Dickens originally proposed a central persona or 'shadow', 'a kind of semi-omniscient, omnipresent, intangible creature' who could 'bind all this together, and [. . .] get a character established as it were which any of the writers may maintain without difficulty'.[43] This shadow would 'represent common-sense and humanity' and expose any kind of public shortcoming.[44] John Forster advised against this concept, and the idea of the shadow was abandoned shortly after. Instead, *Household Words* was held together by a more subtle form of unity, which Dickens captured neatly when he played with possible titles for the journal: 'And here a strange idea, but with decided advantages. "CHARLES DICKENS. A WEEKLY JOURNAL DESIGNED FOR THE INSTRUCTION AND ENTERTAINMENT OF ALL CLASSES OF READERS. CONDUCTED BY HIMSELF."'[45] Although this may have been intended as a joke, *Household Words* finally did achieve 'its cohesiveness [. . .] through assimilation to a Dickensian vision of life' rather than an external framework such as the shadow would have offered: 'While employing a diversity of writers, while ranging over a multitude of subjects, *Household Words* would seem to speak with a single voice', and that voice Dickens's own.[46] *Household Words*, then, 'was to be the mouthpiece of its "Conductor", the embodiment of his "Household tenderness", his optimism, his humour, his indignation against social wrong. Such principles as it had were the opinions that Dickens held'.[47] This concept dispenses with any claims to neutrality or objectivity: *Household Words* has to be read as a highly subjective production notoriously edited and retouched by Dickens and the staff he employed for this purpose. Indeed, Stone labels *Household Words* as a 'personal instrument', implying an active purpose.[48] 'Dickens insisted [that articles . . .] were to be [. . .], in information and opinion, consistent with one another' and with his own beliefs.[49] My analysis will show, however, that Dickens did not always succeed in keeping such tight control over the journal—occasionally, *Household Words* undermines the purpose of its conductor.[50]

More than simply presenting a unified outlook, *Household Words* explicitly aimed to unite its readers in an 'imagined community'. This is nowhere clearer than in Dickens's 'Preliminary Word', which set out the goals for the journal:

> We hope to be the comrade and friend of many thousands of people, of both sexes, and of all ages and conditions, on whose faces we may never look. [*Household Words* is . . .] not calculated to render any of us less ardently persevering in ourselves, less tolerant of one another, less faithful in the progress of mankind, less thankful for the privilege of living in this summer-dawn of time. [. . .] We know the great responsibility of such a privilege; [. . .] the pictures that it conjures up, in hours of solitary labour, of a multitude moved by one sympathy [. . .].[51]

This brief passage expresses the journal's desire to transcend (if not dissolve) all social boundaries—even while upholding national ones—and to form a single, in some sense homogeneous community. This community is imagined, since the individual persons involved with the journal will never see each other's faces and merely dream, in solitude, that they are part of a community with shared objects and feelings.[52] In Harold Clark's pert phrase, *Household Words* thus presented 'a watered-down Christian morality which could be summarized as "love one another"'.[53]

Although many nineteenth-century periodicals open with a similar declaration of intent, *Household Words* stands out because of its high degree of self-awareness and the almost metaphysical nature of the community it intends to form. Instead of proclaiming specific interests, topics, or political credos, or simply giving a taste of the kind of material readers can expect to find in *Household Words*, 'A Preliminary Word' emphasises the spiritual benefits that readers will reap from buying into its community. This community, in turn, is bound up from the start not so much with the British nation but with Englishness, its emotive umbrella. The notorious twin aims that advertisements for *Household Words* pronounced, namely 'instruction and entertainment'[54], only feature marginally in the 'Preliminary Word', which emphasises its intention to nourish 'wonder' and 'fancy'—both relating less to the journal's actual content than to their effects on readers.

In comparison, *Bentley's Miscellany* announces in its opening number that it has no business with politics, science, sentiment, or serious drama, but will deliver merry songs and 'tale[s] of wit'.[55] It makes clear what contents readers can expect and effectively dares them to take it or leave it. Similarly, the initial 'Confession of Faith' in *Fraser's Magazine* states that the journal is to be a literary miscellany and then lays out in some detail the journal's political creed, nailing its colours to the mast of the British nation-state:

> Our creed is this—that if the Foreign Office were closed altogether, it would be so much better for the country; and that the policy of England should be insular, as she is an island, and colonial, as she is the queen of colonies, the nursing mother of empires.[56]

This is a straightforward political stance, concerned with policies and offices rather than feelings and friendship (though the fact that this is expressed in the language of religion is also interesting). Finally, *Chambers's Edinburgh Journal* bears more similarity to *Household Words* in its aims, but it stresses them far more bluntly. 'The Editor's Address to His Readers' announces that he hopes to bring cheap instruction and entertainment to '*every man in the British dominions*', to schoolboys, labourers, and teenage girls, and offers a taste of the reading matter they can expect (such as informational articles, advice on housekeeping, and adventure stories).[57] Moreover, the editor stands out as a single voice speaking to other individuals: 'I throw myself on the good sense of my countrymen for support'.[58] Thus, the element of communal fellowship is weakened—such 'fellow-feeling' as there is stems from the external cohesion of the British nation. In contrast, *Household Words*' 'Preliminary Word' uses the first person plural 'we', which shrinks or expands its scope throughout.[59] Even while appealing to readers across the 'British dominions', the framework and title of

Chambers's Edinburgh Journal emphasise its Scottishness.[60] For all their differences, all three journals' introductory articles state simply what they are going to offer to the audience; the roles of producers and consumers are clearly defined. *Household Words'* 'Preliminary Word', on the other hand, blurs the boundaries between them and emphasises the union between readers and writers in a common goal. This is especially important when, as I will argue, this union merges discursively with all that is considered as good in Englishness.[61]

To strengthen the impression of unity, most material in *Household Words* (even Dickens's own) appeared unsigned.[62] Although nearly four hundred writers contributed to *Household Words*, it attempted to present a unanimous, homogeneous front, as if all articles stemmed from the same pen.[63] The only name that appeared with any regularity was Dickens's own, proclaiming him the 'conductor' of *Household Words* on every other page.[64] His preference for the title of 'conductor' rather than 'editor' of *Household Words* suggests a sense of orchestrating a host of writers into a harmonious whole. Yet the omission of authors' names also created some resentment especially among the younger contributors such as Wilkie Collins or George Sala, who made their first serious entry onto the literary stage in *Household Words*:

> Objecting to the anonymity required of those whose works were published under Dickens's name, Collins expressed the discontent felt by such writers as Elizabeth Gaskell and George Augustus Sala, who came to believe that Dickens unfairly profited from the labors of unnamed subordinates. To these writers, it appeared that Dickens had created a class system in which contributors were the servants or hands and Dickens himself was the master.[65]

Ironically, Dickens thus incurred the same accusations of editorial tyranny and interference (albeit for different reasons[66]) that had caused him to break ranks with Bentley back in 1839.[67] Characteristically, disputes over control with his publishers were also behind Dickens's decision to kill off *Household Words* in 1859. When Bradbury and Evans refused to print Dickens's statement on the end of his marriage in their other publication *Punch* and simultaneously reminded him of his contractual obligations, Dickens, chafing against such a threat, determined to abandon *Household Words* and to replace it with another journal 'on the same plan as the first'.[68]

The sense of homogeneity that a modern reader of *Household Words* may experience is further intensified by the fact that the physical weekly numbers have all but disappeared, and most copies of the journal survive only in its bound volumes. The nineteenth-century tradition of binding periodicals in hardback volumes creates the impression that '*really* the periodical is a kind of book and the numbers are incomplete sections of the whole', which effectively denied the periodical its significance as a genre in its own right.[69] The 'particular relationship to time which gives the periodical its name and its distinctiveness' is thus retrospectively erased.[70] Moreover, advertisements and other accompanying material were usually left out of the bound volumes. Consequently, the translation 'from periodical to volume always involve[s] a redefinition of the text, even if [. . .] every word is the same in the two versions'.[71] In addition to the advertisements, *Household Words'* two supplements, the *Household Words Almanac* and the *Household Narrative of Current Events*, were also left out of the bound version. All these factors contribute to the difficulty of recreating and fully understanding the impact the journal must have had in its time.

Household Words soon attracted a steady though not colossal readership, selling about 40,000 copies each week and generating a continuous profit for Dickens and his publishers Bradbury & Evans.[72] The question emerges how it situated itself in a market that was already well supplied with similar publications. Merrill Distad calculates an 'estimated total of more than 50,000 Victorian periodicals' in addition to the spread of daily newspapers that had begun to emerge in the eighteenth century.[73] Even in the first half of the nineteenth century an astonishing number of periodicals existed. Cranfield states that 'the number of weekly periodicals (not newspapers) issued in London on a given Saturday in 1846 was about seventy-three', consisting of 'two literary papers, twelve economic and social journals, fourteen penny and halfpenny magazines, three tracts, five musicals, and thirty-seven weekly sheets forming separate books'.[74] The biggest of these, such as the *London Journal*, sold up to 400,000 copies a week.[75] In addition, '227 *monthly* periodical works were sent out on the last day of July 1846', and there were a further 'thirty-eight quarterlies'.[76] These periodicals represented sports, philosophical, religious, professional and social interests as well as a number of charitable societies.

The most immediate rival on the market that *Household Words* strove to enter was *Chambers's Edinburgh Journal*, a family journal owned by the Edinburgh publishers Robert and William Chambers. Although Dickens was 'desirous to avoid [. . .] imitation' in typographical and other matters[77], *Household Words* looked remarkably similar to *Chambers's Edinburgh Journal*.[78] This was probably no coincidence, since W.H. Wills, Dickens's subeditor, had been *Chambers's* assistant editor for three years in the 1840s, continued to write for it until 1849, and was married to the proprietors' younger sister Janet.[79] *Chambers's* was 'the successful staple product which Dickens deliberately ensured he could match' and the yardstick by which he measured 'the superiority, in imaginative appeal and journalistic impact, of his own offering.'[80] The key difference between the journals was Dickens's continual desire for imagination and 'fancy'.

Household Words intended to address a wide audience not merely for commercial reasons. One of its ideological purposes (which does briefly surface in the 'Preliminary Word') was to 'give the less educated classes a cheap but edifying alternative to their literary diet of crime, sensation, and marvels'; 'each number should amuse, teach, improve, arouse, and delight'.[81] The staple literary fare of the poor and uneducated at the time were cheap periodicals,

> almanacks [sic] [. . .] chapbooks and ballads, usually printed on poor paper, illustrated with crude woodcut, and selling at anything between a farthing and a shilling. They dealt largely with scandal, executions, natural disasters, and the more gory murders, and were heartily vulgar—and popular.[82]

Dickens wanted to replace these with a wholesome diet of 'entertainment and instruction'. He tried to achieve this by making *Household Words* lighter in its moral outlook than most current family journals and by emphasising humour and 'fancy' over their 'utilitarian tone' and blunt demand for reform.[83] *Household Words* published some articles that were of particular interest to the labouring classes and several more pleading for a better social structure, but the desire to provide light entertainment took priority throughout. Yet *Household Words'* implied audience was rather more narrowly defined than the all-inclusive, class-transcending community that Dickens's 'Preliminary Word' envisaged, since the journal often silently excluded certain groups from its imagined community of writers and readers. It vehemently 'espoused the cause of the poor and the working classes', but from a middle-class perspective: the poor were discussed in terms of charity but rarely addressed directly.[84] Overall, it targeted an audience that could afford to travel and to read for pleasure and was reasonably well educated.[85]

Household Words' contents generally consisted of informational material, of fiction and entertainment, and of commentary on social conditions and society in general. In all three categories, it embraced an astonishing variety, though often at the expense of depth and detail. Articles covered diverse aspects of national and imperial politics, current affairs, the law, history, physics, industry, agriculture, medicine, botany, zoology, literary reviews, and travel reports from all over the world, offering bite-sized information to its readers interspersed with fiction and poetry. While none of the

> abuses decried [. . .], reforms advocated, [and . . .] conditions criticized, were first brought to public attention by *Household Words* [. . .] the popular—'readable'—discussion of these matters in Dickens's widely read periodical brought them attention that their sober presentation in specialized journals and in upper-class journals did not give them.[86]

Thus, one purpose of *Household Words* 'was to *publicise* the causes of the day', and its individuality lay 'first, in its personal attitude, and, second, in its handling of non-fiction prose'.[87] Even such material as was intended to inform and instruct was presented 'not in literal, matter-of-fact, "encyclopaedical" fashion', but in a florid, embellished, and 'lively' manner.[88] This constant demand to be imaginative and entertaining led to some rather crude generalisations, especially with regard to the representation of other nations. An example is Grenville Murray's 'Roving Englishman', who caps his elaborate ridicule of the German people by translating German newspaper advertisements word for word, deliberately rendering them ungrammatical in English: '"To Emilie. Sad the heart! [. . .] Loves she me?" "Mademoiselle [. . .] is most humbly prayed to send a letter for her slave B. to the post office."'[89] This is quite a clumsy means of increasing the humour of these inappropriate advertisements, which had already been the subject of an earlier *Household Words* article.[90] It becomes problematic, however, when the same narrator then claims to give his readership an accurate idea of the places he visits and to be inspired by a desire to educate.[91] The double aims of instruction and entertainment thus led to considerable difficulties when the aim was to represent the world for the instruction of *Household Words'* readers.

MAPPING THE WORLD

The present study, then, will examine *Household Words* in the light of its sustained interest in Englishness, foreign nations, and nationhood in general, and it will tease out the structures into which *Household Words'* view of the world divides.[92] Its intention is to develop a coherent sense not only of *Household Words'* relationship with the world, but of the journal itself and the climate in which it existed. A close examination of selected material from *Household Words* and other contemporary publications will show that *Household Words* uses roughly the following categories to imagine and structure the world: England/Britain, Ireland, Europe, the colonies, and 'the world beyond'—China, 'savages', and other 'alien' cultures. Moving outwards from the metropolis of London, these could crudely be represented as a nest of concentric circles.[93]

My first chapter considers the Great Exhibition of 1851 as an event that appeared to bring the whole world together under one roof and provoked a large-scale reassessment of what it meant to be English, of different degrees of 'foreignness', and of the different dimensions, implications, and ambiguities of Britain's engagement with the world. I look at contemporary accounts from a range of sources to argue that the complex array of exhibits, exhibitors, and visitors that filled the Crystal Palace already contains the outlines of the concentric circles that subsequent chapters will trace in more detail. I shall show that the Great Exhibition imposed a number of exclusions on its representation of the world. These exclusions are mirrored in *Household Words'* own coverage of the event.

The second chapter looks at the innermost 'circles' of this model. *Household Words'* overall perspective is firmly anchored in London as the capital of England and the pinnacle of global civilisation, an assertion that creeps up repeatedly. I argue that *Household Words* frequently shows itself aware of the arbitrariness of national characteristics and its own struggle to define these. However, even the most astute writers never quite abandon the assumption that an essential Englishness does exist, even though *Household Words'* definitions of it are usually fairly feeble. Overall, the journal tends to concentrate on what is, in Dickens's phrase, 'un-English'.[94] The relationship between England and Britain is, however, somewhat fuzzy, as Scotland and Wales (never Ireland) are at times included in 'England'. Both receive very little attention in *Household Words'* nine years of publication, but a basic sense remains of Scotland as an independent, if not overly important, entity, whereas Wales is mostly submerged in 'England' and only excites comment as a curious and backward region.

The next category, Ireland, is the most volatile of all the countries that make up the United Kingdom and is therefore treated separately in the third chapter. Although a full part of the United Kingdom, *Household Words*—mirroring the British media at large—frequently views it as a colony, toying with ideas for large-scale resettlement and deciding on the values, virtues, and habits that need to be nurtured in the native population in order to solve the 'Irish difficulty'.[95] However, *Household Words* only considers Ireland in this light (or any other) in the immediate aftermath of the Irish famine. After 1854, hardly any articles focus on contemporary Ireland in its own right.[96] Ireland's propensity to change position in *Household Words'* (and British) view of the world means that it is the part in which the otherwise neat system of concentric circles is most likely to collapse.

Continuing outward, the next 'circle' is taken up by Europe. Although most of *Household Words'* attention is given to individual European countries (especially to France), a secondary notion of Europe as an entity beyond the sum of its parts is clearly detectable. I shall argue that two conflicting discourses exist during this period: one sees Britain as a full and leading member of 'the European powers', and the second views it as separate and isolated from 'the continent'. Other contemporary media veered wildly between the two views: starting as 'Eurosceptics' in the aftermath of the 1848 revolutions and the French *coup d'état*, most of Britain came to define itself as 'European' during the years of the Crimean War, only to fall back on its former distrust towards the end of the decade. *Household Words*, on the other hand, maintains a much more stable and open-minded view of Europe throughout and generally considers Europe on a similar level of worth as Britain itself.

My fifth chapter looks at *Household Words'* treatment of India. While places such as Australia or Canada are frequently imagined as empty or their native population easily dismissed as 'savage', the evident presence of India's peoples and their long-standing cultures poses a discursive difficulty for *Household Words* and other media, since they made it difficult to regard the country simply as a major resource of agricultural and mineral goods. The Sepoy Rebellion of 1857 radically challenged the stereotype of the 'mild Hindoo', which had hitherto justified Britain's exploitation of India. I argue that *Household Words* struggled to explain the Rebellion of 1857 and was, consequently, slow to respond to it. When it did respond, it was primarily with the series 'Wanderings in India', which is set in the India of the late 1840s and retrospectively seems to 'predict' and rationalise the events of 1857. Using a number of native and European 'witnesses', the series reassesses and readjusts conflicting contemporary images of Indian peoples and offers a critique of Empire while posing as a straightforward travel account.

I shall conclude my analysis with a brief consideration of what *Household Words* sees as the very edges of humanity, namely 'savages'. It is possible that we will be faced with the same fundamental question that the narrator asks in *Dombey and Son*:

> In this round world of many circles within circles, do we make a weary journey from the high grade to the low, to find at last that they lie close together, that the two extremes touch, and that our journey's end is but our starting place?[97]

1 'Amidst the heterogeneous masses'

Household Words and the Great Exhibition of 1851[1]

Ten months before the Great Exhibition of the Works of Industry of All Nations opened in Hyde Park, Richard Horne published an article entitled 'The Wonders of 1851' in Charles Dickens's weekly journal *Household Words*. In this article, Horne took issue with the debate about which system of classification the Committee of the Great Exhibition should adopt to order the mass of exhibits. There were two obvious choices: one was to sort them according to the different manufacturing processes to which they pertained, the other, to sort them by their place of origin. The former, 'a fusion of the productions of all nations', was the order favoured by Prince Albert, because it would 'amalgamate and fraternise one country with another'.[2] Moreover, it would also allow those visitors with a stake in manufacturing to compare different production methods directly.

Horne dryly comments that 'this feeling is excellent; but we fear it would cause an utter confusion, and amidst the heterogeneous masses, nobody would be able to make a study of the productions of any particular nation'. In his view, 'the natural arrangement' would be to keep 'the productions of each country [. . .] separate', even at the expense of those visitors whom this industrial Exhibition claimed to benefit the most. Clearly, the need for ordering and containing the heterogeneous masses of nations, cultures, peoples, and classes, and for keeping 'fraternisation' between them in check, superseded the advantages that 'horny-handed industry' might derive from a direct comparison.[3]

The debate about classification highlights the key contradictions that riddled both the Exhibition itself and *Household Words*' treatment of it. On the one hand, the Exhibition was publicised as a fair of universal harmony transcending national, social, geographical, religious, gender, and racial boundaries. On the other, it represented an arena for direct comparison and even competition between these. Precisely because the Exhibition aimed to 'fraternise' nations and thus posed a threat to national boundaries and the safeties that they suggested, it also provoked jingoistic responses. The same ambiguity is evident in terms of class: even while the Great Exhibition claimed to celebrate the 'dignity

1851.

Figure 1.1 '1851: Please, Sir, Shall I Hold your Horse?' in *Punch*, 20 (January—June, 1851), 60.

of labour'[4], it excluded labourers both from the exhibits themselves and from its implied audience.

This chapter argues that, rather than delivering a faithful representation of 'all nations', the Great Exhibition represented the psychological map of the world as it lived in the collective imagination of Victorian England. I will examine briefly who created the Great Exhibition's vision of the world, and who came to view it. I will then sketch what this vision looked like, particularly with reference to India and China, before turning to

Household Words' stance on the Exhibition and its surrounding questions of nationality and national character.

HISTORICAL CONTEXT AND CONTEMPORARY RECEPTION

The Great Exhibition took place soon after the troubled 'Hungry Forties' and within only three years of the European revolutions of 1848 and Chartist disquiet in Britain. These recent experiences lingered in the public memory and found expression in pessimistic predictions that the Exhibition would invite a Chartist rebellion or foreign invasion. When it turned out to be a peaceful event, many commentators expressed their exuberant hopes that it would ring in an 'era of peace and good will, of progress and amelioration'.[5] Indeed, many studies of the mid-Victorian years, understanding W.L. Burn's appellation of the 'Age of Equipoise' to mean a time of peace, prosperity, and stability, take the Exhibition as their starting point.[6] The Exhibition offered such an enormous 'heterogeneous mass' of material and meanings that it could be harnessed to almost any conviction or cause: 'All sorts of morals grow out of [the Exhibition] [. . .] The only fault we have to find with them is, that they cut each other's throats', *Punch* stated the case in a nutshell.[7] Recent works on the Great Exhibition, for instance, examine it in terms of commodity culture and consumerism, nationhood, empire, class, and gender.[8]

The Great Exhibition originally sprang from a series of national exhibitions organised by the Royal Society of Art from 1845 onwards. Their purpose was to 'improve general taste' in the design of 'useful objects'.[9] From this emerged the idea of a large-scale exhibition of industry, which was to take place in 1851. The body ultimately in charge of planning it was a group consisting of twenty-four men:

> As a group, [the Royal Commissioners] were wealthy and well educated [. . .] The vast majority had been supportive of political reform and were committed to free trade [. . .] these men believed in 'progress', and were deeply interested in science and technological innovation.[10]

In some ways, they represented a cross-section of society, including members of 'the aristocracy, the political establishment, science, industry, the arts, commerce and finance, agriculture, and the empire'. Only a quarter of the Royal Commission actually took an active role in organising the exhibition, which 'suggests that what many of them symbolized [. . .] was more important [than] what they actually contributed'. However, there were also exclusions: while Scotland had one representative, Ireland and Wales had none. Neither did the working classes, 'because anyone who could claim to speak for them [. . .] would probably have been seen as too radical, democratic, and threatening'.[11] This fear later recurred in the pessimistic expectations of unrest and rebellion on the shilling days, a legacy of Chartism and the 1848 European revolutions.

In order to counteract the omission of the working classes, Prince Albert and Henry Cole formed the Central Working Classes Committee (CWCC) in 1850, whose aim it was to enable and encourage members of the working class to attend the Exhibition, organise and monitor cheap accommodation, and facilitate orientation. The CWCC enlisted a number of famous names, such as Charles Dickens, Samuel Wilberforce (the Bishop of Oxford who had coined the phrase 'dignity of labour'), Arnold Thackeray[12], and John Forster. Furthermore, it featured 'several Protestant clergymen, four Members of Parliament, and three former Chartists [. . .] Given the elite composition of the Royal Commission, the CWCC must have appeared quite radical'.[13] Consequently, when the CWCC asked for the Royal Commission's approval of its work, it received a blanket rejection. At the proposal of Charles Dickens, 'the CWCC dissolved itself after being in existence for barely one month', since 'without official recognition, [it . . .] would be unable either to render efficiently the services it sought to perform or to command the confidence of the working classes'.[14] The reins of the Great Exhibition were thus very much in the hands of the elite, a group of powerful, wealthy men, some of whom had not only an ideological but also a commercial interest in the way in which the Exhibition represented the world.

The Royal Commission's refusal to acknowledge the Central Working Classes Committee's work is characteristic of the general emphasis that the Great Exhibition placed on the consuming rather than the producing end of the manufacturing process. In the months leading up to the Exhibition, the fear most persistently voiced was that of a Chartist or foreign rebellion, and the idea of shilling days, on which poorer citizens could enter the Great Exhibition, aroused significant opposition.[15] Although the shilling days were intended to make the Great Exhibition accessible and appealing across all sections of society, and to add to its inclusiveness, the responses they evoked in the media and urban, vocal public suggested that they had quite the opposite effect, bringing out the middle classes' intolerance or, at least, ambivalence.[16] Thus, *The Times* at first reassured its readers that, although the recent European revolutions had made the association of a large crowd of people with revolution inevitable, 'the unconstrained movements of a free people' were something to be proud of and look forward to as a manifestation of English liberty.[17] Less than three weeks later, before the first shilling day on May 26, *The Times* stated, with some distaste, its belief that 'the aristocratic element retires' before 'King Mob enters'.[18] Similarly, the *Illustrated London News* expected 'teeming myriads' to enter the Crystal Palace on shilling days. Although it reported this in positive terms, there is nonetheless some ambiguity in its voyeuristic attitude to these visitors:

> Among the many interesting spectacles which London will shortly offer to foreigners, none will be more interesting than the visits of

these hordes of working-men—the men who made the Exhibition what it is, and who, we fervently hope, will derive the greatest advantages from it.[19]

Figure 1.2 'Design for a Fountain: To Be Placed in the Transept on the Shilling Days', in *Punch*, 20 (January—June, 1851), 257.

Punch, meanwhile, ridiculed the fear of a drunken mob invading in a cartoon (fig. 3) and decried the decision not to serve alcohol in the Crystal Palace as condescending, since it indicated to foreigners that 'you poor, uncivilised English could not restrain your appetites [and would] make beasts of yourselves.'[20]

When the behaviour of the attending working classes turned out to be virtually impeccable, this surprising fact provoked much comment and praise in the contemporary press for several weeks, and their habits, manners, and the choices they made in viewing the Exhibition were analysed in detail—yet another curiosity on display inside the Crystal Palace.[21] *Punch* even proclaimed that the humble working classes had shown themselves 'superior' to their social betters:

> the high-paying portion of the public go to look at each other, and to be looked at, while the shilling visitors go to gain instruction from what they see; and the result is, they are far better behaved than the well-dressed promenaders who push each other about, and stare each other out of countenance.[22]

The working-class press, in the form of the *Northern Star*, hardly paid any attention to the shilling days themselves but registered its disapproval of the 'aristocratical [sic] *hauteur* and exclusiveness' of the opening ceremony on May 1, from which even season-ticket holders were excluded.[23] It chafed against 'the alarmists', who warned of Socialist and Red Republican violations, and 'persuade[d] the commissioners to give colour to these dastardly fabrications by the adoption of such a course.'[24] Simultaneously, however, it offered its regular subscribers a large steel print of the interior of the Crystal Palace as a reward for their custom. These engravings, of which thirty-four appeared in irregular intervals between 1837 and 1851, typically portrayed leaders and supporters of the working classes or important events in the labouring classes' history. The fact that the last two ever to appear were dedicated to the Great Exhibition indicates the importance that the *Northern Star* attributed to this event in general.[25]

The middle classes' concerns about the inclusion of the workers among the spectators were mirrored by the omission of labour from the spectacle itself. Although the Great Exhibition displayed modern machinery, the workers who operated the machines did not appear alongside them.[26] The production process thus appeared sanitised and dehumanised, as the poverty and suffering that often went hand in hand with it, were not shown. One source of this apparent contradiction in the professed and actual aims of the Exhibition was the ambiguous meaning of the term 'labour', which in 1851 signified 'anyone who was not idle' and could refer to the owners of factories as well as to those who worked in them or to independent artisans.[27] This is not to say that the omission of the working classes was merely an accident of semantics, however; on the contrary, some contemporary commentators

Figure 1.3 'Specimens from Mr. Punch's Industrial Exhibition of 1850. (To Be Improved in 1851)', in *Punch*, 18 (January—June, 1850), 145.

anticipated and drew attention to it. *Punch*, for instance, implored its readers to 'let the thought /Pass from the labour to the labourer pale' and rendered the conspicuous absence of workers visible in a prescient sketch a year prior to the Exhibition: it shows the labourers in glass cages, inspected with interest by a well-clad, marvelling visitor (fig.4).[28] The cartoon not only draws attention to the deletion of the labourers from the manufacturing process but also suggests that the wealthy spectators are as unfamiliar with the human dimension of industry as with the machinery on display, since they can afford to be interested only in the finished commodity.

The working classes were thus underrepresented at both the exhibiting and the visiting end of the Great Exhibition. This is not to say, however, that they did *not* visit the Exhibition. Gibbs-Smith records that out of a total of 6,039,195 visitors, nearly three quarters (4,439,419) bought shilling tickets, and at least a significant proportion of those must have been labourers and their families.[29] Thus, the actual audience of the Exhibition may have differed quite radically from the constructed one. Several manufacturers subsidised their workers with money or holidays to enable them to go to London.[30] Motivations for this generosity were manifold. A frequently held opinion was that the Great Exhibition would educate the labouring masses—although *Punch* pointed out that not everybody viewed this as a positive outcome:

The people's taste they may refine;
But, on the other hand, 'tis clear,
They'll cause the masses to repine,
And wish to live above their sphere.[31]

Many employers hoped that their workers would take pride at seeing the finished product on display, and feel that they were an important part of the process. Others commissioned their labourers to find out about rival products and their manufacture.[32] Once again, the contrasting elements of encompassing harmony and of direct competition manifested themselves together in the Great Exhibition.

A similar emphasis on consumption rather than manufacture existed in the way in which the international dimension of the Great Exhibition was marketed and justified to the British public. The Exhibition's initial purpose had been not so much to celebrate the achievements of British industry but to highlight its deficiencies and thus to inspire competition and improvement. This was the rationale behind the decision to invite international contributions.[33] Hence, one major selling strategy of the international exhibition was the claim that the inclusion of foreign exhibits would educate British manufacturers and thus directly benefit Britain. Auerbach sees this as symptomatic of the contradictory balance between the internationalism which members of the Royal Commission of the Exhibition held privately, and the need to 'present it in more nationalistic and commercially beneficial terms' in order to win public support for the Exhibition.[34] Both strands are once more clearly visible in the popular press of the time, as George Sala's *Household Words* article 'The Foreign Invasion' demonstrates. Sala expresses the hope that the Great Exhibition will dispel some of the worst national stereotypes and contribute to a mutual understanding between nations—after all, the foreigners 'paid for what they have had, like honest men', and thus benefited the British economy.[35]

A similar contradiction determined the debate about classification and representation, as Horne's article indicated. As it turned out, the Exhibition committee shared Horne's scepticism about the potential fraternisation of the 'heterogeneous masses' and adopted a primary order of state boundaries. Gibbs-Smith lists a total of 13,937 exhibitors, 7,381 of whom were British and 6,556 foreign.[36] These numbers may be misleading, however, as several 'foreign' exhibits belonged to British owners, such as the East India Company, who provided the exhibits for India and China. This circumstance alone raises objections to newspaper journalists' and exhibition writers' tendency to map the various national exhibits directly onto the countries they supposedly originated from, and to read the one as an 'encyclopaedic representation' of the other.[37] Far from being objective, exhaustive, or 'encyclopaedic' representations, some displays of other nations, especially of British colonies, were designed to get across a specific agenda. Several other countries did not appear at all. Consequently, the Exhibition's representation of the world was predominantly Euro- and Anglocentric. This explains why, for example, 'Sheffield' took up twice as much space as 'Africa'. The east wing of the Crystal Palace housed all 'foreign' countries, while the west wing accommodated Britain and its colonies. This distribution shows how much the Empire was at the heart of the British self-perception—it might otherwise seem odd that regions as large and diverse as India, the West Indies, Africa, and Canada appeared together with Wales and England, while culturally and geographically close nations such as France or Belgium were situated at the opposite end of the building. Within some sections belonging to particular countries or regions, thirty further subdivisions classed exhibits according to various branches of industry (such as raw materials, machines, fabric manufacture, stationery, iron and hardware etc.).[38] The result of this elaborate classification was that inside the Crystal Palace, the world appeared as a structured, compartmentalised space where the visitor could stroll and inspect at leisure whatever struck their fancy.[39]

India took up a central position on the psychological map of Victorian Britain as the biggest and richest colony of all, full of promised treasures. In 1851, Britain's conquest of India was far from finished. As recently as 1849, the East India Company had annexed the Punjab to its provinces and taken from its deceased ruler the Koh-i-noor, the large diamond that, more than any other display, came to embody the subcontinent, the 'Jewel in the Crown' of Queen Victoria's empire. Consequently, the Indian collection took up 30,000 square feet in the very heart of the Crystal Palace. In comparison, the second-largest display from a British colony, that of Canada, took up less than 15% of the area which India occupied.[40]

In 1851, the East India Company's future had been under discussion for some time. Therefore it was in its interest to present British dominions in a light that would justify its own existence and make it appear as a profitable resource in need of expert government but under control when in the East India Company's hands. In order to achieve this aim,

> the Company assembled an exhaustive display of raw materials that attested to the financial benefits of empire, a splendid array of artisanal manufactures that catered to contemporary fantasies of Oriental splendour, and exhibits of jewels and models that represented a domesticated India.[41]

While representing India as a vast mine of undeveloped resources in need of a civilising Western influence, though, the Exhibition also showed that metropolis and 'dependency' were in fact mutually dependent. A large portion of British machinery on display pertained to the cotton spinning process, which in 1851 still relied on imports of raw cotton from America, causing some anxiety about Britain's dependence. India was viewed as an alternative source of raw materials, grown inside the British Empire.

The Great Exhibition display of India offered room for a further set of contradictions. On the one hand, the manufacturing tools used in India looked primitive and poor in comparison to the steam-driven machinery supplied by Britain and other European countries. On the other hand, the artefacts, elaborate textiles, crystal vases, and jewellery produced with those simple tools outshone Britain's own in aesthetic value and craftsmanship. Since this conflicted with the agenda of showing India in an inferior, if valuable, position to Britain, some 'Exhibition-goers dismissed the ornate and fine products of India as evidence of Oriental savagery, backwardness, wastefulness' or 'consigned these goods alternatively to the realms of the past or the mythological'.[42] For instance, the *Illustrated London News* declared that Indian manufacture, 'except for show and luxury, has as yet experienced a very slight degree of development'.[43] An Anglocentric perspective thus influenced the gaze of visitors as much as it did the construction of exhibits themselves, and many displays tended to reaffirm rather than challenge popular stereotypes.[44]

Similar reactions were provoked by the Chinese section of the Great Exhibition, which consisted of large, painted porcelain vases, cabinets and other furniture, decorative figures, and paintings. One contemporary claimed that

> the curious workmanship [. . .] bears witness to the sort of instinctive learning which the Chinese have for the most difficult and delicate manual labour; but we need envy nothing that they have, unless it be the abundance of some natural productions, especially silk. Their porcelain has been known from time immemorial, and in everything else the Chinese are so stationary that they may be considered as the most ancient workmen on the earth. Among the articles which they displayed were some which were produced at a period nearly as remote as that of the deluge, and which, in truth, did not appear to be very dissimilar to those which they manufacture at the present day.[45]

Although the above commentator sees it as symptomatic of China, the Chinese collection at the Crystal Palace had not in fact been assembled 'by the Chinese, but by the East India Company' and thus reflected a British construction of China.[46] China, which European travellers only two centuries previously had admired as far advanced and more civilised than any state Europe had to offer, was popularly pictured as static and changeless in Victorian culture. Not surprisingly, this was what many contemporary commentators deduced from the Great Exhibition display.[47]

Richard Horne's and Charles Dickens's *Household Words* article 'The Great Exhibition and the Little One', which I shall examine in more detail further on, makes the same point more elaborately. The bulk of this article consists of a vitriolic comparison between Britain, the most advanced of nations, and China, the least advanced.[48] The article's criteria for measuring a civilisation's progress originate from George Porter's *The Progress of the Nation* from 1836, which, significantly, had gone into a fourth edition in 1851, the year when celebrations of progress were rife in Britain. Since most of these criteria take England as the benchmark of a progressive society, the article concludes, unsurprisingly, that England is the most progressive civilisation of all. Moreover, Horne's and Dickens's version of China is based on the Great Exhibition—already a biased, Western construction in itself—the Chinese Junk, a floating 'museum' moored in the Thames, and the Chinese exhibition that took place simultaneously in Hyde Park Place. The latter won considerable approval in the *Illustrated London News*, especially the human exhibit of a 'Chinese family' that formed its core:

> The group is one that has much to commend it—it is picturesque and peculiar, and presents an image in high relief of the native manners of a Chinese family. The conduct of the domestic [servant] blended the humble and the familiar in a significant manner; and there was an air of freedom and a sense of mutual obligation manifested in the whole party.[49]

Horne and Dickens, on the other hand, see China as the embodiment of despotism and ignorant pride. The Chinese are summarily and stereotypically ridiculed as stagnant, superstitious, pompous, ignorant, despotic, dirty, starved, pigtailed and parochial.[50] All they can produce are useless ornaments and 'ridiculous abortion[s]' such as the Chinese Junk.[51] The authors base this judgement of China as regressive largely on its porcelain production, which dominated the Chinese section of the Great Exhibition. In fact, however, Chinese manufacturers produced porcelain wares specifically for the British market, painting them to British taste, or exporting unpainted porcelain to Britain, where it was decorated in 'Chinese style'.[52] Hence, the very porcelain production which the authors see as symptomatic of China's supposed self-willed isolation and incapability to trade, proved that Chinese manufacturers were in fact perfectly able to cater for a particular demand in the international market. The predominance which porcelain manufacture took in the British concept of China finds ample proof in the circumstance that the material itself became known as china.[53] Ironically, Dickens and Horne then attempt to illustrate the contrast between the useless 'flowery Empire' and Britain's 'greatness' with the British 'silk-weaving and cotton-spinning' industry.[54] While these may well show Britain's achievements in *manufacturing*, the raw materials on which both supposedly arch-British manufactures depend originate from overseas, not least from China itself. This highlights once more the ambiguous question of dependence in Britain's relations with its (quasi-)dependencies.

In this way, both the Indian and the Chinese sections at the Great Exhibition, and the commentaries that they provoked, signified not the reality of those countries, but their representations in the collective Victorian imagination. Both displays 'exoticised' the respective countries, rendering them at once distant and mysterious in their fantastic wealth and elaborate artefacts, and accessible and consumable by bringing trophies from each to the heart of London. This process was mirrored in the elaborate system of classification that had been developed to label exhibits. Just as India was in need of an ordering Western influence, so its produce had to be ordered and accounted for. Hence, 'India's was the only collection other than the United Kingdom's that employed (or was subjected to) Playfair's system of categorisation'. Furthermore, 'the Catalogue also ordered India's raw materials through the use of Latin nomenclature [. . .] down to the last pea and lentil'.[55] Renaming native products, places, or people is to claim possession over them—it is thus a peculiarly imperial activity. The fact that the exhibits were relabelled not only in English but also in Latin further seemed to legitimise India as an object worthy of scientific investigation, metaphorically placing it onto the dissecting table.

The classification system thus acted out linguistically the same illusion that the Exhibition itself suggested on a visual level. Visitors could survey, investigate, and analyse at leisure, as the world seemed to lie at their feet. *Punch* makes this quality clear in an article describing Colonel Sibthorp's clandestine visit to the Crystal Palace:

> One day we catch him in Holland [. . .] the next in Turkey [. . .] the next in Greece [. . .] the next among the Queen of Spain's jewels [. . .] the next in America [. . .] and so he [. . .] will go on, from country to country, until he's gone all over the world of crystal [. . .].[56]

In some cases, displays could quite literally be consumed: visitors could taste tobacco, snuff, and chocolate drops in various sections.[57] In others, they were able not only to see but also to touch exhibits, as in the textile sections, or to smell them, as some perfumes were distributed around the building. The Great Exhibition variously appealed to all their senses, and thus intensified its compelling claim to authenticity. It is no wonder, perhaps, that visitors believed they had indeed experienced the whole world, and not just a highly selective representation of it.

JOURNAL AND EXHIBITION: GENERIC SIMILARITIES

Dickens's taste for public entertainments and shows of all kinds has been amply documented, yet he took a dislike to the Exhibition that was evident long before it even opened. In January 1851, *Household Words* published his article 'The Last Words of the Old Year', which reflected on England's shortcomings and demanded a 'great display of England's sins and negligences' to complement the impending 'great assemblage of the peaceful glories of the world'.[58] He rarely referred to it in his private correspondence except in tones of irritation and extended his summer residence at Broadstairs until October to avoid the hustle and bustle that it generated in London. His strongest sentiment committed to paper can be found in a letter to Count D'Orsay, from May 18, 1851: 'I can't bear the noise, and crowd, of London—where everybody is madder than usual due to the Exhibition [. . .] there is nothing—nothing at all—except the Exhibition'.[59] Paul Schlicke concludes that 'the sheer size of the Exhibition, it seems, offended him', and that he was doubtful about its actual entertainment value.[60]

The Exhibition was the one major event of 1851 that Dickens's subsequent novel *Bleak House* did not mention: 'If *Bleak House* was concerned with the Great Exhibition, it was to temper the mood of self-satisfaction that the Exhibition engendered; for otherwise it was allowed to pass unnoticed.'[61] Indeed, the very title of *Bleak House* stood in stark opposition to the Crystal Palace, 'that glittering show-place of the utilitarian values which [Dickens . . .] rejected.'[62] He was also doubtful about the actual use of the Exhibition to the working classes, and his initial involvement with the Central Working Classes Committee and its thwarted efforts must have had a sobering effect. Incidentally, Thomas Carlyle, whom Dickens warmly admired, declined to serve on the CWCC because he thought the working man's interest would not be attracted to this middle-class venture.[63] He described the Exhibition as 'a great ass. Enchanted ass,—for there is always a man imprisoned there withal, poor devil!'[64] He wrote that industrial improvements do not take place in an exhibition but in the minds of thinking workers in Lancashire[65], while 'this big Soapbubble, and all the gauderies spread out in it [are] beautiful to the fool [but] insignificant or even hateful to the wise'.[66]

Thus the Great Exhibition became one of the occasions in which *Household Words* adopted a stance that differed significantly from Dickens's own. The Exhibition was simply too large a public event to be omitted. From its first conception to its conclusion, the Exhibition provoked some dozen articles in *Household Words*, half of which appeared before the actual opening of the Crystal Palace. In fact, Dickens's journal published more material on the Exhibition than its rival *Chambers's Edinburgh Journal*, which excused itself from discussing it on the basis that it was such a ubiquitous topic almost everywhere else.[67] At the other end of the spectrum, the *Illustrated London News* featured plenty of illustrations and descriptions from the moment the construction of the Crystal Palace began, ran double numbers for the first two months of the Exhibition and supplements after that[68], and issued numbers in German and French for the benefit of foreign visitors.[69] *Punch*, meanwhile, cast regular and typically irreverent looks at the Exhibition from 1850 onwards.

Despite Dickens's personal distaste for the Exhibition, the two media actually shared many similarities in terms of content, values, intention, and format. Richard Altick suggests a close link between journals and exhibitions in general when he characterises his work on *The Shows of London* as a complement to his previous study of *The English Common Reader*:

'There, I dealt with what the English people paid to read; here, I am concerned with what Londoners paid to gaze at'.[70] An even closer link can be established between *Household Words* and the Great Exhibition of Industry in particular. Both professed to aim at the 'instruction and entertainment' of their audiences.[71] Both offered multifarious yet subjective views of the world, while claiming to present their respective subjects objectively. In fact, Dickens's agenda for *Household Words* could have been written for the Great Exhibition itself: both 'seek to bring [. . .] the knowledge of many social wonders' to their audience with the aim of rendering them 'ardently persevering in [them]selves, [. . .] tolerant of one another, [. . .] faithful in the progress of mankind, [. . .] thankful for the privilege of living in this summer-dawn of time'.[72] Their object was

> to teach the hardest workers at this whirling wheel of toil, that their lot is not necessarily a moody, brutal fact [. . .]; to bring the greater and the lesser in degree, together [. . .] and mutually dispose them to a better acquaintance and a kinder understanding.[73]

Both *Household Words* and Great Exhibition claimed an inherent internationalism, 'for nothing can be a source of real interest in [any nation upon earth], without concerning all the rest'.[74] Nevertheless, both tended to consider other countries from a strongly Anglocentric perspective.

Equally, both media had specific agendas in mind in their approach to representation and targeted audience, even though contradictions within each persisted. Both attempted to show the facts faithfully but in a more attractive light than their everyday settings normally allowed. Both claimed to be open to viewers/readers of all ages, material and social circumstances, and genders, and offered themselves at affordable prices to this aim, but they nevertheless addressed a rather more narrowly defined audience, comprised of the middle and upper classes.

Moreover, their format was malleable: both Exhibition and periodical offered a mass of pre-edited material from which the audience was expected to 'construct their own order' of reading / viewing contributions.[75] No two experiences were thus identical, as viewers / readers each assembled their own version. Margaret Beetham suggests that 'the concept of authorship becomes problematic in relation to the periodical, where typically even one number involves several writers, the editor, perhaps the proprietor, [. . .] artist or engraver and the printer'.[76] Similarly, the Great Exhibition was the product not only of the work of a multitude of artists, inventors, and labourers, but also mediated by the owners' selection of exhibits and their criteria for the choice[77], their and the Commissioners' manner of displaying, classifying and labelling them, the Commission's structuring of the exhibition area itself, and the conditions of the building.

Most importantly, both media were motivated not only by 'the desire for profit', but also 'the power to make one's meanings stick, the desire to educate'.[78] Beetham describes a journal as 'a complex process in which writers, editors, publishers and readers engaged in trying to understand themselves and their society; that is, they struggled to make their world meaningful'.[79] The same is true of the Great Exhibition, as is amply proven by the several accounts and explanations that it generated. Most of these interpretations attempt to view the Great Exhibition in the light of a single factor—for example, as proof of internationalism, or of British superiority over all other nations, or of the mutual friendship and harmony across class boundaries. Since both media were so markedly multifarious, however, any single, overarching explanation drawn from them will almost certainly conflict with some of the remaining material. For this reason, several of the ambiguities and contradictions that the Great Exhibition generated, also exist in the *Household Words* articles about the Great Exhibition (occasionally, as I will show, even within one single article), as well as between many pieces in general.

THE REPRESENTATION OF THE GREAT EXHIBITION IN *HOUSEHOLD WORDS*

Despite Dickens's dislike of the Exhibition, most *Household Words* reactions to the Exhibition are characterised by a tone of self-congratulatory complacency. *Household Words* celebrates the Great Exhibition as an opportunity for improving foreign impressions of Britain, and as a touchstone for British achievement and Britain's position in the world (naturally at the top of the global hierarchy). The only openly apprehensive notes appear in two articles published before the Exhibition even opened, one in Horne's 'The Wonders of 1851', which criticises the fraudulent competition for the best exhibition building design, and the other in Wills's 'The Invited Invasion', which warns of the traffic chaos that the expected foreign visitors may cause in London. Any *Household Words* articles published after the opening of the Exhibition on May 1, 1851, whole-heartedly celebrate the exhibition and mention only minor attendant problems such as cumbersome customs regulations.

Deborah Wynne rightly observes that Dickens solved the problem of how to represent an event that he did not personally approve of, by resorting 'to a strategy whereby *Household Words* discussed only the circumstances *surrounding* the event, rather than the event itself'.[80] Thus, *Household Words* published articles on the design of and future plans for the Exhibition building, the expected traffic chaos caused by visitors, the influx of foreign tourists, and the metropolitan police's competence to deal with it. Although *Household Words* also discussed a few exhibits, such as the model cottages for labourers and some general displays of machinery and manufactures, Wynne's claim is valid. Another of Dickens's strategies, according to Wynne, was to use humour in order 'gently to criticise the Exhibition without having openly to declare to readers his "horror of sights"'.[81] This is particularly evident in the later pieces by Dickens's 'young men', some of which I examine below:

> While contributors like Knight and Howitt attempted to impress *Household Words*' readers with details of the cheapness of the Crystal Palace and the superiority of British society, Sala and Morley treated the Exhibition as a joke, an irreverence which Dickens no doubt found more congenial to his own tastes.[82]

Thus far, I agree entirely with Wynne. However, she sees the main reason for Dickens's reluctance to publish about the Exhibition in his unease about

> the general sense of national superiority which the Exhibition had engendered in the British press [. . .] The social and political ideals which Dickens had in mind were in danger of being betrayed by the wave of nationalism which emanated from the Crystal Palace.[83]

This was certainly Dickens's attitude during events such as the Crimean War, and he repeatedly warned against the neglect of Britain's homespun 'savages' in favour of those abroad, while two poems published in November 1851 mention, as suitable objects of Britain's charitable 'missions', those classes 'pining to be taught at home'.[84] But it strikes me as an odd proposition in the context of the Great Exhibition, given that it follows a brief discussion of 'The Great Exhibition and the Little One', one of the most jingoistic pieces in all of *Household Words*, which Dickens wrote with Richard Horne. Wynne herself acknowledges that many of the earlier Exhibition pieces praise 'the superiority of British society'.[85] Although the later 'irreverent' articles use the Exhibition as an occasion for humour, they do not significantly challenge assumptions either about Englishness or about British national supremacy.[86] In contrast to Wynne, I argue that although *Household Words* focused more on the surrounding circumstances than the Exhibition itself, and although it did adopt a more facetious tone in later Exhibition pieces, it nevertheless maintained most assumptions about national character that the Exhibition's contrast between national and foreign products provoked. This is not to say that, elsewhere, the journal was not also critical either of Britain or of inflated national pride at times, and even of *aspects* of the Great Exhibition. Nevertheless, in the context of the Exhibition *Household Words* adopted the tone of national achievement and self-congratulation that pervaded the British press at large.

Household Words' construction of Englishness around the Great Exhibition takes place not only in terms of its increased 'articles about foreign countries', which 'formed a complex intertextuality around *Household Words*' representation of the Exhibition', but also in its attitude to class and gender.[87] While 'The Great Exhibition and the Little One' constructs a generic English voice, other articles break this all-inclusive voice down further, for instance to a particular gender or class, which often creates contradictions between the perspectives in different articles. In some pieces, *Household Words*' social ideals motivated its portrayal of the Great Exhibition as a celebration of the 'dignity of labour'.[88] In others, this does not sit easily with the reality of the Exhibition, as John Critchley Prince's poem 'A Voice from the Factory' will illustrate.[89]

Horne's and Dickens's article 'The Great Exhibition and the Little One' offers an interesting starting-point for a closer look at the materials for two reasons. To begin with, we have already seen that it constructs its idea of Englishness around the negative and supposedly diametrically opposed example of China, in much the same way as the Great Exhibition displays of China and India came to epitomise those countries and prove their backwardness in comparison to British superiority. Secondly, it performs a remarkable transition from internationalism to stridently nationalist rhetoric. In the space of a mere three paragraphs, it strips the voice of all humanity down to the point where England comes to represent the 'most human' of all nations. In a similar way, the Great Exhibition invited visitors from all social strata but organised its exhibits for the benefit of the consuming rather than manufacturing classes, as I showed earlier. Both media, while ostensibly addressing everybody, in fact construct an audience consisting of a dominant minority, and reduce other groups to a marginal position.

The article's introductory passage, in claiming to discuss the progress of mankind as a whole, uses the first-person plural pronoun to include the entire human race across the planet. However, at the beginning of the second paragraph it becomes clear that this generic 'we' excludes some sections of humanity:

> There may be an odd, barbarous, or eccentric nation, here and there, [. . .] who may see fit to exercise its free will, in the negative form of will-not, and who may seclude itself from the rest of the world, resolved not to move on with it.[90]

This 'perverse' use of 'free will' is condemned as regressive and antisocial. Such a judgement puts *ad absurdum* the suggestion that free will exists at all, if it wins approval only as long as it follows the principles prescribed by others. Later on in the article, China comes to occupy the place of this occasional 'odd, barbarous, or eccentric nation'. The initial 'we' next appears in a modified and reduced form:

> For the rest of earth's inhabitants, the shades, and steps, and gradations of the ascending scale will be various [. . .]; but, that we are moving in a right direction towards some superior condition of society [. . .] we humbly yet proudly [. . .] do fully recognise as a great fact.[91]

At this stage, it is not yet clear where, geographically, this 'we' is speaking from. In 1850s Britain, such a take on 'free will' naturally carries overtones of Empire with it, since the majority of the planet had, either voluntarily or forcefully, come under the command of British rule and trade.[92] The article makes the imperial dimension explicit in its second paragraph: 'Newly turned-up furrows of the earth are being sown with larger, nobler, and more healthy seed than the earth has ever yet received [This fact . . .] indicates the ultimate combination of all our noblest efforts'.[93] To paraphrase, the virgin colonial lands have become fertile only after being ploughed by Western interference and inseminated with Western ideas of civilisation and progress. All this is euphemised as 'free will' on the part of those 'new' nations, as if they had specifically invited colonial powers to 'turn them up', making the invasion appear as the altruistic 'noblest efforts' on somebody else's behalf.

By now the initially generic 'we' of mankind has been stripped down to a predominantly Western voice. The third paragraph narrows it down further to England by speaking out against the European revolutions of 1848–9. One of the signs of progress, the writers claim, is

> that the period of revolutionary excitement has [. . .] subsided into an industrial excitement. It looks as though England had said to the continental nations—"[. . .] Consider whether a good round of industrious work will not show us all whereabouts we are [. . .] the political rights of nations may be more easily and permanently attained by works of peace, by studious observation, and by steady persevering resolution, than by any number of *émeutes* [. . .]." [. . .] Such a speech from the mouth of sturdy Old England is very worthy of careful consideration, by many of those nations who have contributed to the present Exhibition of Industry.[94]

This passage suggests that 'industrial excitement', free trade, and capitalism are in fact 'works of peace' rather than the product of economic rivalry. England thus becomes the embodiment of peace, while Europe is associated with mutiny, rebellion and disorder (*émeute*) and attends the Exhibition in England in order to receive a lesson. Thus, by the end of three paragraphs, England has come to represent the most 'human' of humanity, and stands as an example to every other nation.

This short passage highlights the curious mixture of internationalism and nationalist rhetoric that surrounded the Great Exhibition. Within half a page, the initial idea of the 'peaceful progress of the world' and the entire 'human family' has been sent up as a sham and is replaced by rampant nationalism. The same two strands pervade a number of other *Household Words* articles about the Exhibition. For example, Richard Horne mockingly describes the Great Exhibition as the 'first trial of the respective strength of Nations', and the lack of British entries in the initial contest for the best exhibition building as 'our utter defeat'.[95]

A similar progression from internationalism to nationalism takes place in Charles Knight's 'Three May-Days in London'.[96] Knight first compares the magnificence of the Crystal Palace to Aladdin's Palace and the Pyramids, and then praises the Crystal Palace over the others because it does 'the greatest amount of good to the human race'.

> When history shall record that a Temple of Peace was erected in London [. . .] to which all the nations brought the trophies of their arts, it will forget that there were amongst us prophets of evil, who would desire to keep the great family of mankind in jealous isolation; and will remember only the grandeur of the spectacle, when every clime, without distinction of government or religion, sent its ambassadors of industry to the capital of the world, to teach and to learn, to give and to receive. [97]

Knight's choice of the word 'trophy' for some of the exhibits seems strikingly appropriate in the cases of the Koh-i-noor and the Indian and Chinese collections. Just as Horne and Dickens cast 'a good round of industrious work' as 'the works of peace', so does Knight transform the Exhibition of Industry into a 'Temple of Peace'.[98] Most importantly, he celebrates the equality and friendship among 'the great family of mankind' in the same sentence as casting London as 'the capital of the world', undermining the very inclusiveness he asserts. This reverberates both with Wills's earlier 'Invited Invasion', which ironically refers to 'this out-of-the-way corner of the earth, which is on terrestrial globes labelled "London", and with Horne's and Dickens's subsequent 'Little One', which describes the English as 'us outer barbarians', sarcastically adopting the perspective of China, which it attacks.[99] Both articles make their irony clear enough to indicate that London in fact is the centre of the earth, not its periphery. Again, we find the Empire at the heart of British self-perception: Dickens's and Horne's 'The Great Exhibition' and Knight's 'May Palace' both implicitly espouse it as a means of dissolving the 'jealous isolation' into which some 'odd, barbarous, or eccentric nation' has withdrawn, and thus as a humanitarian project.[100] The harmony between the 'great family of mankind' is thus not unconditional but heavily dependent on the British Empire.

From this benevolent embrace of all mankind, Knight swiftly moves on to discuss the 'rivalry' between various British and foreign products, and finds that several British exhibits 'contrast unfavourably' with other European nations.' [101] However, this apparent inferiority itself becomes a cause for admiration, as it is read to mean that Britain's virtue lies in its utilitarian emphasis on goods that are affordable and widely available, rather than in vainglorious debauchery:

> If Rome sends her costly mosaics for the halls of princes, Cornwall shows her serpentine and porphyry for the cheap adornment of our common

> English hearths. Belgium exhibits her richest laces [. . .] India brings her silk and golden shawls [. . .] But here are also the ribbons of Coventry, the shawls of Paisley, the calicoes of Manchester, the broadcloths of Leeds. These are for the comfort of the humblest in the land.[102]

In other words, while other nations pander to the luxurious taste of the rich, Britain's main concern is the comfort and support of the poor. This rhetorical move maps neatly onto Exhibition writers' construction of India as both primitive (in its manufacturing processes) and decadent (in its elaborate products), which I discussed earlier. According to Knight, British exhibitors are motivated not only by 'the love of fame' or 'the pride of country', but first and foremost by 'the determination to assert the dignity of labour; to [give . . .] throughout the habitable globe [. . .] the mechanic of the nineteenth century [. . .] a greater command of the comforts of life'. [103] Once more, British industry has been construed as a humanitarian, charitable project.

Class has thus taken centre stage in defining Englishness. For the remainder of this article, the concepts of class and nation appear bound up with each other, both crystallising Britain as superior to other nations. The power-loom is far more efficient than 'the nicest sempstress in Ind [sic]', whose livelihood it actively threatened: Britain demanded Indian raw cotton but raised high taxes on the export of finished textile products from India, in order to keep competition low for Britain's own cotton-weaving industry, while British goods 'were admitted duty free'.[104] In particular, Knight praises 'the steamboat, the railroad, and the printing machine—the three powers which are more and more lessening the inequalities of condition, of locality, of laws, amongst the great family of mankind' and have 'given new ideas of time and space to the civilised world'.[105] In case the imperialist gospel were still lost on his readers, Knight makes his point clearer yet:

> The assemblage of the Industry of all Nations, and the people of all nations, in the island whose ships bear the products of the earth to and from every port—whose arts, imitative at first, are now models of every form of labour—whose language and literature are spreading over vast regions, compared with which her area is but a speck on the globe—[. . .] appears to us a holy tribute to the Parent of Industry, and of all good.[106]

Again, it appears that this 'assemblage' of 'all nations' could only have happened because of Britain's widespread control over the globe. The 'Parent of Industry', it emerges, is God, and the products on display at the Crystal Palace (especially 'steamboat, railroad, and the printing machine') are in fact 'amongst the instruments—in companionship with pure science, with literature, with "divine philosophy"—by which God is accomplishing the destinies of the human race'.[107] To paraphrase: the Great Exhibition is both display and celebration of the works of God, who has appointed Britain as his direct agency to fulfil 'the destinies of the human race'.[108] To this end, God has made available to Britain three magic 'powers': the steamship, to reach all countries of 'the habitable globe' and maintain Britannia's rule of the waves, the railroad, to tap the interiors of those countries, and the printing press, to justify the imperial project and spread its values over 'vast regions'.[109] All ultimately aim at the greater comfort of the (British) labourer, as seen earlier.

Remarkably, Knight does not finish on this grand point but adds a further two paragraphs, which bring the discussion of Englishness and English concerns further into the arena of class:

> 'And what,' say some, 'is to be a benefit to the visitors of the Exhibition, who are neither artisans nor merchants—who are neither buyers nor sellers,—some of whom think, as Southey proclaimed, "that the nation which builds on manufactures sleeps upon gunpowder" [. . .].'[110]

The punctuation of the first phrase is significant: according to contemporary grammar at least, the relative clause ('who are neither . . . ') does not modify the preceding phrase ('visitors of the Exhibition') but is merely an additional attribute to it. If the relative clause were not preceded by a comma, the question would concern *only those* visitors who are not directly involved in the manufacturing process—in this case, the relative clause would further qualify the visitors. As it stands, the question seems to concern *all* visitors, and they are typically of the non-labouring classes. Perhaps I am overstretching the significance of one comma here, but even so the sentence is ambiguous at best. The Great Exhibition may well celebrate the 'dignity of labour', as Knight states, but those who go to see it do not belong to the labouring class. As I mentioned earlier, the Exhibition may have invited members of all social strata, but addressed predominantly those of the leisured, non-industrial classes.

To finish this point, Knight replies to the question about the benefit the leisured classes might derive from the Exhibition:

> We answer—'the enlargement of *your* minds, and of all minds [. . .]. These are the words of the heroes of this age. This is *their* May-day celebration. [. . .] In this goodly work there is hope beyond performance—hope of "Peace on earth, goodwill towards men."'[111]

Knight's use of the second person here suggests that he envisages the same, non-labouring classes who visit the Exhibition as the probable readership of his article in *Household Words*. In comparison, Knight refers to the 'heroes of this age' (the mechanics, artisans, and labourers who were his object earlier) in the third person ('*their*'), implying that they are not likely to read (or write) *Household Words*. In this context, Knight's final advocacy of 'goodwill among men' seems to put the British working classes on the same level as the non-British inhabitants of the 'earth', referring to both as the objects of the goodwill of their 'superiors', who visit the Exhibition and read *Household Words*. Once more, the initially universal 'voice' of 'the great family of mankind' has boiled down not just to a British perspective, but to the leisured classes in particular.

Not all *Household Words* articles are consistent in their surmises of likely Exhibition visitors. In 'The Invited Invasion', W.H. Wills expects that 'the bulk of visitors will be of the artisan and humbler classes', and advocates that arrangements for their accommodation be made.[112] William Howitt's 'A Pilgrimage to the Great Exhibition' suggests that class itself, or certainly the appearance of it, is circumstantial: after a gruelling night on a ramshackle boat, the narrator comments on his fellow-travellers that 'I had never seen so wretched, and even vulgar, a set of people'. At the end of the journey, however, 'a rapid metamorphosis took place [. . .] [the travellers] burnished themselves up into a most respectable, well-looking, and gentlemanly assembly [. . .] it was soon evident that we were in the midst of a very superior and intelligent class of people'.[113]

One of the most problematic Exhibition pieces in terms of class is John Critchley Prince's 'A Voice from the Factory'. Prince draws on first-hand experience: he was a reed-maker for weavers and spent much of his youth and adult life labouring in factories or looking for work. By the time he came to publish in Dickens's journal, he had made a name for himself as a working-class poet and attempted to eke out a living from writing alone. His poetry 'attracted much attention, partly by its own merits, and partly on account of the position of its author'.[114]

His poem begins in a familiar vein, celebrating the Great Exhibition as a harmonising assembly of all mankind:

> I hear men laud the coming Exhibition,
> I read its promise in the printed page,
> And thence I learn that its pacific mission
> Is to inform and dignify the age;
> It comes to congregate the alien nations;
> In new, but friendly bonds, old foes to bind;
> It comes to rouse to nobler emulations
> Man's skill of hand, man's energy of mind.[115]

The initial few lines indicate a certain detachment from the nation's excitement about the Great Exhibition, as the narrator experiences it not directly but both as mediated through 'men' and 'the printed page'.[116] The use of the first-person singular pronoun enhances the sense of his distance: whereas the articles I have previously discussed all resort to the unanimous 'we', whose exact position is only crystallised out by negation, the narrator in 'A Voice' asserts his individuality from the start.

The next stanza resorts to the more generic 'we' and a more grandiose rhetoric, but underneath the celebratory tone one can nevertheless detect some uneasiness about the 'snorting' fire-cars, the 'peaceable invasion', and the 'strange commotion' that will disturb 'the genial loveliness of May'.[117] Moreover, Prince is somewhat ambiguous about whether the Exhibition will fulfil its 'promise':

> And, in the grandeur of the great occasion, [we shall]
> See signs of brotherhood 'tween every land.[118]

This could be read either as an assertion that the Great Exhibition *will* create brotherhood among nations, or as a case of 'seeing things' rather too optimistically.

Subsequently, the narrator wishes that 'I might walk beneath that dome transcendent' and 'in its wondrous mazes'. This wish distinguishes him from his fellow workers, men with

> [. . .] vacant faces,
> Human in shape, in spirit dark and low;
> *They* do not care for Genius and its graces,
> Nor understand, nor do they seek to know.
> But I had read and pondered [. . .].[119]

The narrator insists on his difference from other labourers in the factory, who appear to be 'vacant', 'dark and low' by birth rather than by the mind-numbing work and poverty which they have to submit to. At least, these are to blame for the narrator's own exclusion from the Crystal Palace, as the next stanza shows:

> But what to me are these inspiring changes,
> That gorgeous show, that spectacle sublime?
> My labour, leagued with poverty, estranges
> Me from this mental marvel of our time.
> I cannot share the triumph and the pageant,
> I, a poor toiler at the whirling wheel,
> The slave, not servant, of a ponderous agent,
> With pounding steam-pulse, and with arms of steel.
>
> My ears are soothed by no melodious measures,
> No work of sculptor charms my longing gaze;
> No painter thrills me with exalted pleasures [. . .].

This is a bitter attack on the Exhibition, which intends to celebrate 'man's skill of hand' but excludes the very men to whom those skilled hands actually belong. The Crystal Palace, 'than Aladdin's palace more resplendent', appears like a pleasure park, appealing to all the senses and offering sophisticated delights for wealthy visitors. While other articles begin with a central 'we', from whom certain groups are excluded, this poem makes clear that it speaks from the periphery. [120]

However, the narrator does not end on this critical note, but expresses his gratitude for 'books and thoughts', which allow him to feel 'more reconciled to men and things'.[121] While, up to this point, he has expressed a sceptical or at least ambiguous attitude to the Great Exhibition, the pomp and 'commotion' surrounding it, the media's claims about it, and the visitors it is trying to attract, he now appears to 'reconcile' himself to the Exhibition in a wholesale sweep:

> I shall not see our Babel's summer wonder,
> Save in the proseman's page, the poet's song,
> But I shall hear it in the far-off thunder
> Of distant lands, applauding loud and long;
> Why should I murmur? I shall share with others
> The glorious fruits of that triumphant day:
> Hail to the time that makes all nations brothers!
> Hail to the advent of the coming May!

While the first stanza's approach to the 'printed page' was distant and measured, the press has now turned into a means of sharing the excitement: the narrator can only experience the 'far-off thunder' of applause through the accounts written by 'poets' for his benefit. The scepticism that the first two stanzas evoke about this potentially biased medium has apparently been allayed entirely. The narrator's keen perception of his own state of poverty and semi-slavery in the service of industry seems now appeased by 'books and thoughts', and 'Sundays', when 'impartial nature / Folds me within the shadow of her wings'. Similarly, the tentative doubts he seemed to have about the 'signs of brotherhood' that some optimistic souls might derive from the 'strange commotion', have given way to unquestioning acceptance that 'all nations' will indeed become 'brothers'.[122]

However, the positive factors that the Exhibition acquires in the last stanza all remain strangely hazy and immaterial, and the narrator's reconciliation to it appears hollow. For example, it is unclear *what* 'glorious fruits of that triumphant day' someone in the narrator's lowly position might reap. Neither does he allow any room for speculation about whether the other labourers spend *their* Sundays with books and thoughts, but implies that his is a singular case. Since he sees himself as the only factory worker capable of 'reverence for the lofty, good, and true', only he can feel 'estranged' from 'this mental marvel'; for the others, 'in spirit dark and low', their stupefying work seems quite appropriate.[123] What could have been a cutting condemnation of the laurels prematurely bestowed on the Great Exhibition subsides into a half-hearted attempt to resolve the several contradictions that became apparent even before the Exhibition opened.

In comparison, *Punch*'s 'The Exhibition of Industry—A Hint' pleads the case of 'the labourer pale' far more sharply and casts him as a typical example, not an exception. It accuses the complacent middle classes of ignorance and indifference to the plight of the working classes. In this poem, 'the gaunt weaver's face' is

Too often blurred with blood, blotted with tears,
With sin and sorrow writ, from rim to rim,
While they that ought to read [his face], with selfish fears
Avert their eyes from off the record grim.[124]

However concordant with Dickens's own views this accusation might have been, it would have upset its middle-class audience too much to be allowed in *Household Words*.[125] Hence Prince had to find a way to allay the initial sense of unfair exclusion and distance and to let the narrator, one of 'the hardest workers at this whirling wheel of toil', acknowledge that his 'lot is not necessarily a moody, brutal fact'.[126] One gets the impression that the narrator has suddenly remembered Dickens's policy of making *Household Words* readers 'tolerant of one another [. . .] faithful in the progress of mankind, [and . . .] thankful for the privilege of living in this summer-dawn of time'. [127] Even so, the u-turn comes too late in the poem to placate the prevalent sense of distance, unfair exclusion, and general disadvantage, which has determined most of the poem. The narrator's initial criticisms are too detailed and keen, and his later attempts at reconciliation too weak and indefinite, to alleviate the former entirely. Consequently, an atmosphere of anxiety prevails even at the end of Prince's poem.

Both Knight and Prince establish class as a central factor in *Household Words*' approach to the Great Exhibition and in its definition of Englishness itself. I do not mean to suggest that these writers see the entire population as a homogeneous social group, but that issues such as labourers' welfare, charity for the poor, better hygienic facilities for the lower social strata, and the 'dignity of labour' often come to be seen as particularly English concerns. Simultaneously, the labouring classes remain, in many articles, an *object* of charity and interest to benevolent Englishmen—they are rarely included in its implied audience. Hence, Henry Morley's piece discusses the model cottages for labourers from the point of view of a potential landlord rather than tenant[128], while the fictitious letter-writers in his 'What is not Clear about the Crystal Palace' are, respectively, a house-owner in the vicinity of the Crystal Palace, two merchants, and a spoilt young lady.[129]

Since the concern for the working classes and the poor is a peculiarly English characteristic, the very inferiority (and affordability) of British products often becomes a virtue, as we have already seen. This tendency is also present in Horne's discussion of entries into the competition for the design of the exhibition building, which sketchily portrays England as a hard-working, modest, straightforward, and masculine nation. After lamenting the lack of awards to British architects, Horne begins to mock those foreign (mostly French) architects whose designs consist of 'ornate and refined', 'extensive pleasure-grounds', and 'luxurious fancies'. The dainty structures proposed by the majority of entries are not to be touched by 'coarse and profane hands', hence 'enthusiasts in smoke-jacks, [. . .] humane chimney-sweeping apparatuses, [. . .] patent filters, portable kitchens, or electric telegraphs, dare [not] send their uncouth machinery and compounds; but only such things as are delicate of texture, rainbow-coloured, and exquisite to the smell'.[130] Horne's disapproval takes an interesting shape here: he represents these graceful designs both as effeminate and as exotic, likening one to 'a gigantic Oriental fan, made of the plumes of some fabulous peacock'.[131] Another is to consist exclusively 'of glass, such as we might find in an Arabian Nights' Tale'.[132]

Horne's disdain extends to the visitors that such a luxurious exhibition building might invite:

> Visitors (none of whom will be admitted except in full dress, and great numbers of whom will always appear in court dresses) perambulate about [. . .] to the sound of the seraphine and Moorish flutes.[133]

Those visitors will be 'lords and ladies and princes and princesses, of all nations', while the 'coarse and profane' common people are excluded from the Exhibition, just as the 'lumbering pieces of machinery' are. Horne adopts the same ironic tone as Knight did in his ostensible praise of the superior products of other countries, which are fit for 'the halls of princes'.[134] Like his attitude to the prospective building itself, Horne's image of the guests carries overtones of effeminacy and decadence.

Horne's aversion to fanciful palaces and highborn, delicate visitors is typical of the middle classes' changing attitude to the landed class of this period. The Exhibition marked the peak of a gradual shift in power from the aristocracy to the middle classes, but despite the cultural and economic ascendancy of the middle classes, their actual political power was still seriously limited even in the mid-nineteenth century. Therefore, they challenged the landed classes 'in moral and religious terms. [. . .] Their critique of the degeneracy and effeminacy of the aristocracy focused on its softness, sensuousness, indolence, luxuriousness, foppishness, and lack of a proper sense of purpose and direction.' The most common expression of the middle-classes' sense of moral superiority was, as we have already seen, the 'dignity of labour', ambiguous as the term 'labour' was at the time. The phrase thus actually indicated a change in status of the middle-classes in relation to the aristocracy, while the labouring classes still remained firmly at the bottom end of the social ladder.[135]

Accordingly, Horne characterises the proposed pleasure-gardens and glass domes as 'ante-industrial', and, implicitly, *anti*-industrial in their elimination of any traces of labour. Instead of these outlandish 'fancies', which are in direct conflict with the Western, masculine, 'horny-handed industry'[136] that the Exhibition is to put on show, Horne demands a building that represents the purpose of the Exhibition of industry as well as the exhibits themselves do. He does not deny that British architects deserve as much criticism as foreign ones, but they commit a different kind of mistake: while most foreign architects are exposed as fanciful airheads of lavish and expensive taste, who exclude anyone involved with industry, British architects are 'impracticable' because their designs are too expensive and are built to last. 'This latter mistake is very characteristic of our countrymen. They do not feel, nor comprehend, the art of knocking up a temporary structure; they are always for something that will endure'. One cannot help wondering whether this is not another case of a vice being transformed into a virtue. Their preference for sturdy, permanent buildings is certainly more in tune with the inherent British concern for the labouring classes that Knight affirmed, than the airy 'fancies' of the French competition entries. 'Our architects', Horne alleges, 'have been thinking too much of railway-stations, not of that sober, simple, and sufficient kind which the occasion requires, but [. . .] of that large, ornate, and redundant kind which is meant to be admired as much as used'. But this implies that at least they *can* be used. Furthermore, Horne is not entirely in favour of those 'plain, simple, practical' but 'not very attractive' competition entries, which look like 'a superior kind of barracks, hospitals, alms-houses, nursery grounds [and . . .] cucumber-frames'.[137]

Horne, then, voices a multitude of concerns in terms of gender, class, and nation about the Exhibition, some ten months before it opened.[138] His criticism evolves around the binaries of masculine and feminine, wage-earning and aristocratic, English and foreign (which includes anything from French to Oriental), simplicity and decadence, labour and leisure. His main fear seems to be that the Exhibition might turn into an exclusive event for a bunch of pampered aristocrats in court dresses, and demands that it be made instead a 'sober, simple, and sufficient', masculine sphere of machinery, technology, and labour.[139]

Horne's assertion of the Great Exhibition's 'masculinity' finds few counter-impulses in *Household Words*. All Exhibition writers are male, and most of them write from a masculine point of view. One rare exception occurs in Henry Morley's 'What is not Clear about the Crystal Palace', published July 19, 1851, which discusses the future of the Crystal Palace after the Exhibition has closed. Morley cites four fictitious letters from supposed readers of the magazine. Three of these letter writers are male businessmen, criticising the 'Monster Nuisance' for one reason or another—because it has lowered the value of their neighbouring property or allowed a rival manufacturer of 'quack' medicine to advertise their products.[140] A third, a sugar merchant, discourses authoritatively on the respective disadvantages and costs of a proposed scheme to turn the Crystal Palace into a winter garden.[141]

Morley's only 'letter' unequivocally in favour of the Exhibition is 'a short note from a young lady' who 'suggests a future for the Crystal Palace as a shopping mall'.[142] It is worth quoting at length:

> Dear, dear Mr. Conductor,—Mamma tells me that people are at a loss what to do with the Crystal Palace, if they do not take it down. Do please, dear, dear sir, put a word in for those lovely shawls, and those sweet muslin dresses. It is so tiresome having to stop in those nasty streets, where people smoke and push about [. . .]. I never enjoyed shop-windows till now, and I have looked at many. O the dear Exhibition, where you look at all the shops, and need not buy! but if you can persuade dear Pa to get you anything, there's always the address attached, and you know where to tell him to go. Dear Mr. Conductor, we shall never love shop windows in the dirty streets again. For the sake of the ladies, I appeal to you, sir, as a gentleman [. . .]; and please tell [the Commissioners] to send away the policemen who stand at the jewel cases, and keep crying—the parrots—'Move on, ladies; move on, if you please;' *les barbares*. Dear Mr. Conductor, please, dear, help me, and I will never use anything but *Household Words* for curl-paper, to the last moments of my existence.[143]

Wynne points out that although recent criticism has stressed 'the Great Exhibition's function in creating the birth of the consumer culture, the ideas proposed by Morley's "young lady" would have seemed comic [and absurd] to readers in 1851'.[144] Nevertheless, even as a joke this piece is compelling. We have already seen that the Great Exhibition struck an unsteady balance between manufacture and consumption of the articles it displayed. Morley resolves this conflict by adding another dimension: manufacturers are male, consumers are female. Men make money by producing, investing or trading commodities, and women spend it by buying the finished goods, providing they can 'persuade dear Pa' to part with his hard-earned money. Their seemingly boundless consumerism extends to the very pages of the periodical to which, presumably, dear Pa has subscribed for his family's edification. Thus, the tension between the leisurely, consuming gaze the Exhibition invites, and the benefits to industry that it was intended to generate, appears resolved by projecting the former onto women. Morley's young lady appropriates and welcomes Horne's horrified vision of the Exhibition as an event secluded from the coarse dirt and noise of 'horny-handed industry':

> While contemporary accounts of the Exhibition emphasised its ideological function as a site for the celebration of the 'masculine' values of

> laissez-faire capitalism and industrial expansion, the imaginary young lady persists in viewing the Crystal Palace as a feminised space offering refuge from the male-dominated, unregulated streets outside.[145]

Morley's projection has rendered Horne's sneering portrait of perambulating, effeminate visitors in court dresses, enjoying 'only such things as are delicate of texture, rainbow-coloured, and exquisite to the smell', more plausible by casting these visitors as women.[146]

Morley's 'What is not clear' is one of the articles which Wynne quotes as examples of the humour with which *Household Words* counteracted the publicity surrounding the Exhibition. Another is George Augustus Sala's 'The Foreign Invasion'.[147] Sala's title ties in with the popular contemporary discourse that figured the 'current of visitors' as an 'invited invasion' or a 'pilgrimage'.[148] Sala mocks those people who, when the Exhibition was announced, 'immediately set themselves to work to predict a series of horrors and misfortunes of every description [. . .] which were infallibly to result' from it. Their worst fears concern 'the nasty, dirty, greasy, wicked, plundering, devastating, murdering, frog-eating, atheistical foreigners!' Taking the 'invasion' literally, Sala then laughs at some contemporaries' fear that they would bring 'war, ruin, and desolation [. . .] Pestilence, of course; the plague, the yellow fever, the *vomito nero*, and the cholera morbus [. . .] Atheism, pantheism, deism, Mahommedanism, Buddhism, everywhere [. . .] Fire,

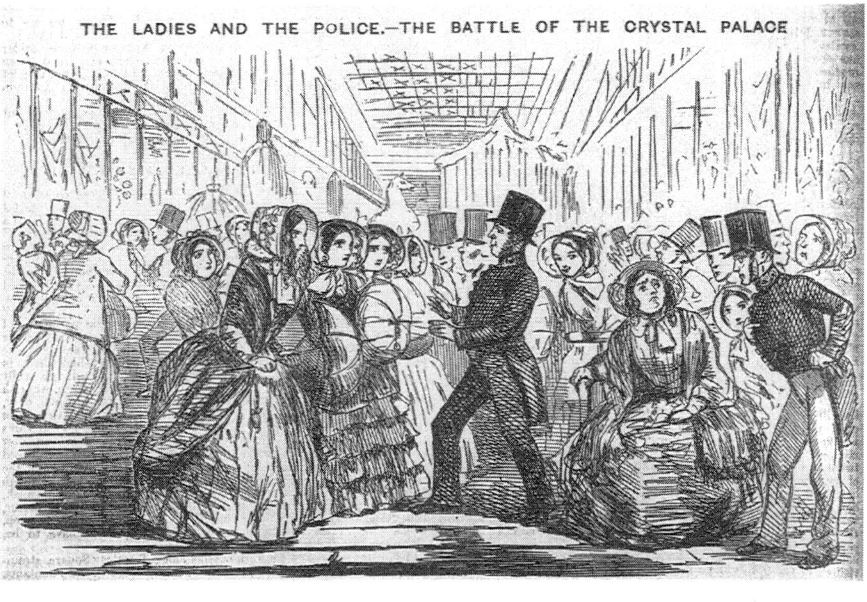

Figure 1.4 'The Ladies and the Police.—The Battle of the Crystal Palace', in *Punch*, 20 (January—June, 1851), 202.

famine, and slaughter; Popery, brass money, and wooden shoes!' [149] Some less extreme prejudices and expectations prevailed, too. The narrator admits that he has previously

> predicted Regent Street blocked up, and Pall Mall rendered impassable [. . .] a crop of fezzes in the streets [. . .] the confusion of tongues [. . .] The mercurial Gaul, with beard unkempt, and *chapeau á la Robespierre*. The German, meerschaumed, *kraut* perfumed, and thumb-ringed. [. . .] Also, churches for all nations and all creeds, from fire-worshippers to Obeahmen. [150]

Some of these fears, in fact, reverberate with former *Household Words* articles on the Exhibition. In particular, Horne voices his concern about the traffic chaos which is to be expected in both 'The Wonders of 1851' and 'The Invited Invasion', while the fear of the 'overthrow of the British Constitution' is assuaged humorously in Dickens and Wills's 'The Metropolitan Protectives'.[151]

Sala's narrator has to admit that the numbers of foreigners is far smaller than expected, and decides to go 'on a little voyage of discovery' through London and the Exhibition to find where they are[152]: 'Had I not *known* that they were here, and must be here, I should have been disheartened'. Finally, he recognises that 'there *are* immense numbers of foreigners in London', but that his failure to find them has another reason.[153] One might think at this stage that his criteria for classifying foreigners as a generic group are at fault, since they depend entirely on superficial factors: he spends most of his time looking for 'fezzes [. . .] the bernouse, the snowy camise, or the shaggy capote', and is disappointed at their small number. The most reliable characteristic of a foreigner seems to be their 'inevitable beard or moustache', which he mentions no less than eight times in four and a half pages, and perhaps 'the eccentric chapeau, or the enticing bonnet'. However, the 'real' reason for the relative invisibility of foreigners is that 'LONDON HAS SWALLOWED THEM ALL UP! This moloch of a city [. . .] holds them all in her capacious maw, and would hold twice as many'. Once this is established and 'I left off seeking them in the places I most expected to find them in, they started up by thousands in localities where I never had the least idea of seeing them', such as theatres, public dinners, markets, churches, the Derby, and seedy drinking-places.[154] It seems that they have adapted to, or been assimilated by, all institutions of metropolitan England.

The lack of fezzes and bernouses further indicates that visitors from the British colonies and the non-Western areas are scarce, highlighting again the bias on Europe and Northern America, which determined the Exhibition. The narrator meets Norwegians, French, Americans, Germans, and Belgians. Naturally, these are male except where he specifies otherwise: 'I lost my heart irrevocably to young (female) Germany'. While yet making fun of those Britons who have a constitutional dislike to "furriners" on principle', the narrator revels in the good understanding between these different nationalities: 'It does me good to see how the foreigners drink our beer and shake hands with us'.[155]

Sala's article concludes with a strong plea for continued understanding between the nations. Even steadfast xenophobes must concede that 'our foreign visitors have neither burnt our houses about our ears, nor endeavoured to overturn our government, nor run away with our daughters. They have behaved themselves peaceably and good-naturedly, and have borne with our little peculiarities amiably'. Therefore, he ventures that 'some little, some trifling good may arise' from the Exhibition and the increase in international tourism that it has engendered, and that the mutual prejudices of different nations may be allayed:

> Is it too wild a thought to hope that our children will not *quite* believe that the French necessarily eat frogs, and are all dancing-masters—that every Italian gentleman carries a stiletto in his bosom, and a bowl of poison in his left-hand pocket—that German babies are weaned on sauer-kraut—that revenge is the one inevitable passion with which all Spaniards are possessed—and that the unvarying fate of all Turkish ladies is to be sewn up in sacks, and cast into the Bosphorus? Is it really impossible that our grandchildren may discard those legends altogether? On the other hand [. . .] we shall [not] be called 'perfidious Albion' quite so frequently. [. . .] The editors of foreign newspaper will no longer declare that we live on raw beef-steaks [. . .]; that we are in the daily habit of selling our wives in Smithfield market; and that during the month of November three quarters of the population of London commit suicide. Altogether, I think that a little peace, and a little good-will, and a little brotherhood among nations will result from the foreign invasion [. . .].[156]

Although the tone of this excerpt is still light, the narrator's plea appears to be heartfelt. In this way, he certainly speaks out against 'the general sense of national superiority which the Exhibition had engendered', as Wynne puts forward, but he does so by celebrating the Exhibition as the means of bringing together the nations, not criticising it.[157]

However, although Sala's article appeals for understanding across national boundaries and differences, he does not question the concept of national characteristics and difference itself. Foreigners still stand out by their beards and apparel, their faith in their guide-books, and their mannerisms. Since they remain so clearly distinguishable from the English, they do not threaten the concept of Englishness and national character that is inherent in *Household Words* and other publications, and from which the 'wave of nationalism' emanated in the first place.[158] In this sense, Sala assuages the concern Horne had expressed about the 'confusion' to be expected from the mingling of the 'heterogeneous masses'.[159] Nations may become 'brothers', but only as long as their individual members are still clearly distinguishable from one another.

This chapter has argued that the Great Exhibition was not a realistic representation of the countries that appeared in the Crystal Palace, but an impression of how they looked on the 'psychological map' of the early Victorian Empire. This 'map' was not a static entity but continually contested and redefined; therefore, contemporary Exhibition writers often contradicted each other in their search for an overriding meaning of the 'heterogeneous mass' that the Exhibition put on show.[160] The representations of some countries, in particular the British dependencies, were heavily mediated, since British bodies such as the East India Company used the occasion to put across a specific agenda and promote their work. This agenda influenced the visitors' perception of the Exhibition, already pre-determined by the imperial discourse of their society. The Exhibition's concept of Englishness or 'self', moreover, centred not merely on all of England, but depended in particular on the British male middle-classes.

Frequently cited as one of the instances where his journal diverged from Dickens's own opinions, *Household Words* panders to and reproduces many of the contemporary attitudes surrounding the Exhibition. Far from opposing 'the wave of nationalism which emanated from the Crystal Palace', the journal actively participated in the celebration of Englishness and national identity.[161] Its writers filtered these concepts through the lenses not only of nationality but also of profession, class, and gender. As a result, *Household Words*' emergent 'English voice' excluded the majority of Victorian society, notably women and the labouring classes. Nevertheless, the latter played a crucial role in this construction of Englishness as the object of a supposedly inherent charity that defined the 'truly English' middle classes. In this process of tacit exclusion, both journal and Exhibition created their audiences as predominantly male, middle-class, and leisured. Their construction of a national identity vacillates between the opposing tendencies of an all-encompassing harmony between different nations and classes on the one hand, and a rampant rivalry between them on the other.

2 (Un-)Englishness and National Character in *Household Words*

> Why does that word 'un-English,' always act as a spell upon me, and why do I suffer it to settle any question? Twelve months ago, it was un-English to abstain from throttling our soldiers. Thirty years ago, it was un-English not to hang people up by scores every Monday. Sixty years ago, it was un-English to be sober after dinner. A hundred years ago, it was un-English not to love cock-fighting, prize-fighting, dog-fighting, bull-baiting, and other savageries. Why do I submit to the word as a clincher, without asking myself whether it has any meaning? I don't dispute that I do so, every day of my life; but I want to know why I do so? [1]
>
> Charles Dickens, 'Why?'

This short excerpt from Charles Dickens's 1856 article 'Why?' is one of the most pertinent inquiries into the nature of national identity in all of *Household Words*. In the first place, Dickens stresses both the arbitrary, fluid nature of what comprises 'Englishness' and its simultaneous, compulsive hold on its subjects—its power of interpellation, as Louis Althusser termed it.[2] Secondly, the choice of the term 'un-English' encapsulates the importance of contrast—of 'others'—in the formation of a national character: what is English is most easily expressed in terms of what is *not* English. As Catherine Hall states, it is the very 'assumptions about "others" which define the nature of Englishness itself.'[3] Finally, Dickens's question underlines strongly the point that national identity is equivalent to religion in its methods and functions. He implies codes of 'good' or 'bad' behaviour, values and 'moral conscience' (as Ernest Renan was to define the nation some thirty years later[4]) that resemble those rules of conduct that form the basis of most religious beliefs. Englishness, then, is not a static fact determined by geographical origin or parentage, but transitory and dynamic—it refers to instances of particular behaviour rather than to someone's nationality.[5] 'Un-English' is thus on a par with what modern colloquial English might term 'not the done thing'.

The question of Englishness, of nationhood and national character, is a core concern of *Household Words* and its conductor. Throughout his career his contemporaries saw Dickens as 'English to the backbone', and subsequent critics often ascribed the same attribute, though not always intended as a compliment.[6] The truth is, Malcolm Andrews states, that 'Dickens wrote very little that was not to do with England and the English. But he also wrote very little that specifically examined the state of England or the English character'.[7] The same is true of *Household Words,* whose very title suggests an inward, domestic perspective, but which is nonetheless riddled with contradictions. The journal rarely sets out to discuss national identity *per se*, but virtually every article is, to some extent, suffused with the values and ideas that pertain to Englishness. Those pieces that do consciously tackle the question of nationhood and English national character frequently contradict each other or even themselves, as the question of Englishness continues to be contested.

When *Household Words* began publication, the British Isles had only been a political entity for some fifty years since the foundation of the United Kingdom of Great Britain and Ireland[8], so the 'British nation' struggled to formulate a coherent sense of identity. Consequently, *Household Words'* distinction between England and Britain remains fuzzy and malleable throughout its nine years of publication. 'English' and 'British' are frequently used synonymously. Wales rarely receives recognition as an independent entity but is mostly subsumed in the collective 'England and Wales', while Scotland holds the status of a more separate country. But while 'English' is sometimes used to include Scotland too, the reverse never applies.[9] The idea of a core 'Englishness', contested and contradictory though it was, could expand and shrink fairly effortlessly to include or exclude the other British countries, as and when required. Ireland, finally, stood apart from the other three 'countries' in Victorian society as a whole and in the treatment it receives in *Household Words*. Although it was technically a part of the United Kingdom and sent MPs to Westminster, it also continued to exist as a colony.[10] While *Household Words*, with its heavily metropolitan perspective, is at times able to think of Scotland and Wales as part of the collective identity it constructs, the Irish always appear outside the loose unity that is perceived between the other three parts of the Kingdom.[11] Therefore I will return to discuss Ireland separately in the following chapter.

Despite the contradictions that inevitably pervade *Household Words'* use of these terms, the journal rarely doubts that an essential core of 'Englishness' does exist, a body of characteristics, values, and morals that seems to be shared by 'the English'. In order to define this national character, *Household Words* develops two key strategies. One is to look at England through the mirror of travel-writings and plays by continental writers, and to comment on the claims put forward by them. In most cases, *Household Words* writers dismiss them as absurd and unfair. The second strategy is to define Englishness in positive terms, i.e. to formulate what is English independently of another source and without the direct comparison to another nation (though most of these articles still implicitly use contrasting examples). In this case, the place of the contrasting nation is occasionally assigned to other groups that belong to the political construct England but are excluded from the emotive notion of 'Englishness'. This is not surprising, since Mary Poovey points out that the belief in national identity as a primary source of identity is 'generally characterized by a widespread perception that not everyone who lives in the country embodies its "national virtues".'[12] This chapter will show that such internal differentiations become inevitable when the 'foreign' contrast is missing.

But if certain groups who are born and bred in England can be 'un-English', while Scots and Welsh can occasionally be 'English', then Englishness must signify something beyond nationality or origin. My central claim in this chapter, then, is that the journal's sense of Englishness is not bound up with a political entity or nationality so much as with a code of behaviour, a set of morals. I follow Stuart Hall's claim that 'we should think [. . .] of identity as a "production", which is never complete, always in process, and always constituted within, not outside, representation'.[13] *Household Words*, then, was not merely an *expression* of English national identity as it perceived it at the time, but took an active part in *forming*, as well as formulating, that identity.

NATIONHOOD AND THE PERIODICAL PRESS

It is worth considering the particular 'generic' connections between nationhood, the periodical press, and English literature. As the introduction to this book showed, Benedict Anderson starts his study on nationhood by drawing a close affinity between the periodical press and the emergence of the nation as a primary order of identity, since both establish what Anderson calls an 'imagined community'. We have already had an insight of how this works in *Household Words* in both the creation of a unified 'voice' (as seen in some of the Exhibition articles) and in Dickens's 'Preliminary Word': after all, Dickens wanted the audience and producers of *Household Words* jointly to form a 'multitude moved by one sympathy'.[14] The underlying assumption is that although this community is imagined (in that its members will never physically meet each other), what connects its members is some shared values and beliefs, even though these are not defined. Six years later, however, Dickens's article 'Why?' concedes that there may be no factual, positive grounds for such a 'sympathy'—this time, between the members of a nation—beyond the feeling of togetherness (sym-pathy) itself. In other words, Dickens hints at the imagined nature of the national community, even while asserting its continued grip on its subjects: the community exists simply because its subjects imagine themselves as part of it, and the very act of imagination calls it into existence.

The imagined community of both the journal and the nation thus takes on a spiritual, semi-religious quality, and this is no coincidence. Terry

Eagleton suggests that nationalism stepped into the breach when religion gradually lost its appeal, and became the new dominant form of collective identity. He explains the power of religion in terms that apply equally to national ideology:

> Like all successful ideologies, it works much less by explicit concepts or formulated doctrines than by image, symbol, habit, ritual and mythology. It is affective and experiential, entwining itself with the deepest unconscious roots of the human subject; and any social ideology which is unable to engage with such deep-seated a-rational fears and needs [. . .] is unlikely to survive very long.[15]

Crucially, Eagleton raises this point in a discussion of the origin of English as a subject for study. He argues that English literature was introduced as an academic—and corrective—discipline for potentially subversive groups, such as the working classes, women, and colonial subjects, because it encapsulated national values and confirmed the existing order. *Household Words*, of course, held many of the same aims: it hoped to instruct, as well as entertain, its readers and educate them to tolerance, good will, imagination, gratitude, and acceptance of one's social position.[16] Indeed, the first ever professor of English literature was none other than *Household Words'* most prolific contributor, Henry Morley, who was appointed to King's College in 1857 and spent much of his subsequent career defining and anthologising the canon of English literature.[17]

It is possibly the room for interpretation that makes literature an ideal medium for expressing national values. Since collective identity is a continual process and site of contesting meanings[18], rather than a stable condition, any attempt to formulate and define it exactly must be incomplete, and 'there is always something "left over"'.[19] In fact, such marginal presences, exclusions, and blank spaces are an integral part of national identity itself. Nation and narration are closely linked, as Homi Bhabha has suggested in his eponymous work. Bhabha identifies two different but overlapping definitions of nation: one is a unified, organic, and continuous whole—the nation as a political, historical entity—the other is the discourse or 'narrative' in which this national identity is actually produced and contested:

> The linear equivalence of event and idea that historicism proposes, most commonly signifies a people, a nation, or a national culture as an empirical sociological category or a holistic cultural identity [. . .] [yet] the 'nation' as narrative strategy [. . .] produces a continual slippage of categories, like sexuality, class affiliation, territorial paranoia, or 'cultural difference' in the act of writing the nation.[20]

This chapter, then, sees *Household Words* as an attempt to 'write the nation'. *Household Words* engaged with Englishness over a period of nearly a decade, therefore we can expect to find plenty of 'leftovers' and slippage. A study of Englishness in *Household Words* is pertinent for a number of reasons. Firstly, the journal as a genre and *Household Words'* particular 'voice' re-enact its status as an imagined community in a similar way as the nation does. Secondly, the journal occasionally attempts to rationalise and define its view of the nation and national character as a unified, collective entity that has something in common despite its internal differences. Thirdly, its expressions of this identity inevitably create and reproduce slippages, exclusions and blank spaces.

Two *Household Words* articles merit particular consideration in this context. The first is Henry Morley's 'Views of the Country', which compares England to European countries and finds that England is superior to the continent and safe from revolution due to its love of liberty. The love of freedom was, of course, the defining feature of any attempt to formulate English identity, especially since the 1848 revolutions, which only confirmed Britain in the belief that continental nations were essentially atavistic and not yet ready for the mature, independent liberty that was its own trademark.[21] What makes Morley's assessment relevant here is that he sees this liberty as rooted specifically in the role of the British press:

> Perhaps there is no better guarantee of peace and process to this country than the freedom of the Press. Opinion is King of England, and Victoria is Queen. Every phase of opinion speaks through some book or journal [. . .] The freedom and the power of Opinion in England, have given an importance to the press which is attached to it, as a direct agent in producing social reforms, in no other European country.[22]

In casting the press as the main safeguard against revolution and tyranny, Morley reserves central importance to *Household Words*, amongst other journals, as a medium for Englishness. It is, indeed, possible to argue that the periodical genre itself is an embodiment of the love of freedom that mid-nineteenth-century Britain regarded as the most central English characteristic and monopoly: the heterogeneity of writers, editors, printers, and readers and their relative freedom (to choose and treat a subject, to edit and commission contributions, to introduce changes, to choose which contributions to read and in what order) allows for far more variety than any other media of the time.[23] Ironically, of course, Dickens tried to curb this multifariousness in *Household Words* more than any other editor in order to project a unified outlook and perspective, even though plenty of contradictions remained.[24]

Morley sees the only 'drawback' to the periodical's embodiment of freedom in the fact that not everybody has equal access to the printing press: 'the uneducated class amounts to a distressing number in this country' and needs to be educated in order to pick the right reading matter and thus participate in the political life of the nation.[25] Just how distressing a number of people were not part of the market that *Household Words* aimed at, is the subject of the second article I want to note here, namely Wilkie Collins's 'The Unknown Public'. Wandering around 'the second and third rate neighbourhoods' of London, Collins discovers that there is a huge readership for the so-called penny-dreadfuls.[26] This unknown public, he calculates, amounts to about three million people—a reading public

> unknown to the literary world; unknown, as disciples, to the whole body of professed critics; unknown, as customers, at the great libraries and the great publishing-houses; unknown, as an audience, to the distinguished English writers of our own time. A reading public of three millions which lies right out of the pale of literary civilisation is a phenomenon worth examining [. . .].[27]

Since this enormous reading public is 'unknown', it follows that the readers of *Household Words* must be 'known' and belong to a close-knit and recognised community—the exclusion thus furthers *Household Words'* own sense of unity and similarity. Although these 'unknown' readers are clearly a step up from the 'uneducated classes' of Morley, in that they can and do read, Collins does not for one moment assume that they are a part of 'literary civilisation'. Rather, the aim is to civilise these 'lost literary tribes':

> The future of English fiction may rest with this Unknown Public, which is now waiting to be taught the difference between a good book and a bad. It is probably a question of time only. The largest audience for periodical literature, in this age of periodicals, must obey the universal law of progress, and must, sooner or later, learn to discriminate.[28]

One could of course suspect a purely commercial motive here—after all, Collins suggests recruiting these readers for the market that *Household Words* caters for. But it is also clear, especially when read in conjunction with Morley's article, that Collins sees these supposedly unknown readers as benighted savages excluded from English political life. They need to be educated not merely to spend their money on *Household Words* and 'good' novels—e.g. by such 'distinguished English writers' as Dickens and Collins themselves—, but in order to form and express opinions. That this may also be done in the cheap penny magazines is not an option Collins considers. *Household Words* thus re-enacts the process by which such an imagined community is formed, and reinforces the 'national' dimension of this process by vocalising Englishness, nationality, and theories of national character. To be fully English is to read *Household Words* and equivalent journals.

CIVILISATIONAL AND BIOLOGICAL MODELS OF ENGLISHNESS

What, then, *is* Englishness? What different models existed at the time when *Household Words* was trying to formulate its sense of it? Catherine Hall identifies Englishness, crucially, not as a

> fixed identity but a series of contesting identities, a terrain of struggle as to what it means to be English. Different groups competed for the domination of this space and the political and cultural power which followed from such domination. Englishness is defined through the creation of an imagined community: who is 'one of us' [. . .] is quite as important in that definition as who is excluded.[29]

The same thought influences Lauren Goodlad's analysis of the 'Victorian national character', which argues that any perceived external contrast was usually a projection of internal ones: the Victorians 'obscured differences constituted by [mainly, but not exclusively] class with appeals to sameness evoked by national identity'.[30] Although the major events in the 1850s focused attention on Britain's empire (e.g. the Australian gold-rush or the Sepoy Rebellion) or the European context (e.g. Napoleon III's *coup d'état* or the Crimean War), and thus on areas other than Britain itself, the reactions and opinions that the external context brought were bound up with the current discourse on nationhood and Englishness, in particular English masculinity.[31] Thus, Catherine Hall sees the abolitionist position which held sway in the 1830s as symptomatic of a model of England that emphasised its role of teacher, liberator, and dispenser of justice throughout its empire, while the defence of Governor Eyre—whose fierce retributions after the Jamaican rebellion in 1865 had come under scrutiny—imagined an ideal of the Englishman as authoritative master over subject races as well as his wife, children, and staff.[32] The former view of Britain as a civilising, educating influence corresponds to what Peter Mandler calls the 'civilisational' perspective: the view that all races stem from one origin and have the potential to become equal, given the right tutelage.[33] The latter view, which defines Britain as a more authoritative disciplinarian, relied on a racial, biological model of mankind and frequently argued that different races constituted distinct species. Unsurprisingly, the Anglo-Saxon race was regarded as the most sophisticated of all.

Household Words' nine years of publication fell into the middle of the period when these two models of Englishness competed with each other. The journal started publication only four months after Thomas Carlyle had anonymously published his 'Occasional Discourse on the Negro Question', which argued 'in effect for a return to slavery'.[34] Dickens, in turn, admired Carlyle warmly for his social principles and stance on utilitarianism, and dedicated *Hard Times* to him a few years later.[35] The first year of *Household Words* also saw the first appearance of Robert Knox's *Races of Men*, a further milestone in the sharpening of racial discourse. On the other hand, the European context of the decade seemed to confirm a civilisational model of the progress of different peoples rather than a biologically determined one. Thus, the 1848 revolutions were seen as confirmation that nationalism—which in the first half of the century was 'associated with contemporary thought in Germany, France and Italy, but not with England'—was 'an atavism from which England had providentially escaped'.[36] In contrast to Europe, England was

> the directive centre of a multi-national kingdom and empire, precisely the form that advanced civilisations should take. If that kingdom and empire contained peoples not yet liberated from their uncivilised clannishness—Celts, Negroes, aborigines—it was the responsibility of the English to maintain their institutional hold on such peoples in order gradually to wean them from their childishness.[37]

Despite their differences in thought and argumentation, both views of what it meant to be English were formulated and contested in the same class—in Catherine Hall's terms, the white, male middle class.[38] Both views, moreover, left their mark on *Household Words*: pieces such as Dickens's 'The Noble Savage' or John Robertson's 'Coast Folk' negotiate biological and civilisational accounts of human progress, and neither comes up with a completely satisfying answer.[39]

'THE MIRROR HELD UP TO NATURE'

The existence of an Other, then, is a vital part of the concept of nation in particular, because 'even the largest [nation . . .] has finite, if elastic, boundaries, beyond which lie other nations. No nation imagines itself coterminous with mankind'.[40] In this spirit, *Household Words* published some dozen reviews of foreign plays, novels, and travel-guides that revealed popular European stereotypes about the English, and used them as a catalyst to express its own sense of Englishness.[41] This does not mean, however, that *Household Words* was unaware of its use of 'Others'—on the contrary, it often employs them self-consciously, as writers regularly comment on the motives, methods, and politics of constructing a national character in general. Before analysing the individual points that they take up, I shall examine the light in which *Household Words* approaches the question of national character itself.

Household Words reviews foreign guidebooks to England solely in order to disagree with them. Sidney Blanchard finds Max Schlesinger's *Wanderungen durch London* 'generally truthful, [and therefore] generally dull; and [it] would certainly be out of place' in a journal that aims as much at entertainment as at instruction.[42] Therefore Blanchard picks out only those snippets of Schlesinger's observations that make easy targets, such as the notoriously bad English weather and some people's excessive veneration for the royal family. Clearly, the aim is not to give a realistic overview of the impressions foreign visitors receive, but to establish what is, or rather is not, an English characteristic by bouncing it off foreign commentators. Henry Morley ridicules M. Méry's *Nuits Anglaises* for its initial claim that 'generally the people of a nation are very ignorant concerning the phenomena of their own land; they must turn to strangers to get the solution of them', because the stories in that volume are so far-fetched (though the title, 'English Nights', indicates that they are not to be taken at face-value).[43] Nevertheless, this is precisely how *Household Words* uses these works, with the difference that it defines English 'phenomena' by opposing whatever claims those 'strangers' put forward, rather than agreeing with them. Although *Household Words* repeatedly chafes at the idea of using foreign observers as a 'mirror held up to Nature—that is, English nature reflected by' other Europeans—, it does in fact conform to that practice.[44]

Rather than being the unconscious victim of their own delusions, some *Household Words* writers acknowledge the importance of an Other in the process of defining one's own nationality. This does not mean, however, that they hold the results they draw from such a contrast as any less valid—in the same way as one does not lose one's religious beliefs merely by becoming conscious *that* one believes them, or even *why* one believes them. An enlightening piece in this respect is Percy Fitzgerald's 'Bogie Albion', published in February 1859. Fitzgerald analyses the popular stereotypes England and France have about each other, and focuses in particular on 'a certain abstraction, known as Albion', by which he means the French prejudices against England.[45] This 'bogie' serves as an effigy that can be safely attacked in lieu of the real thing. Fitzgerald admits that 'there has existed a corresponding [. . .] pure French Bogie', even though that 'has gone long since' (p.265). The ultimate question is

> whether every nation, of whatsoever kind or quality, must not of necessity make to itself some sort of Bogie, which it may pillory and pelt with eggs, and other unpleasant matter? which thus becomes vent salve or easing pipe for the passions of the distilled rascality of our planet? (p.265)

Fitzgerald complains for the remainder of his article that the French are particularly stubborn in holding on to their bogie of England, but he has made it clear that every nation has the propensity, or even the need, to create a false image of its neighbours. More importantly, this bogie also serves the purpose of 'distilling' the population that has invented it into a unified 'it', a single entity rather than a polymorphous mass.

In everyday usage, too, the 'foreign' perspective helps to clarify what is 'national', hence a hypothetical '"intelligent foreigner", who goes about observing everything, [. . .] is always appealed to [. . .] whenever any question of national manners arises'.[46] The 'intelligent foreigner' embodies a neutral and purely rational perspective on national oddities, which observers from within the nation might not be aware of or react to too passionately. Only by stepping into the shoes of an outsider is it possible to assess the peculiarities of one's own country, because it is 'an excellent lesson to see ourselves as others see us', whether this be in terms of nationality or anything else.[47]

Dickens is one of those writers particularly outspoken about the politics at work in constructing a national character. His 'Insularities' starts out with the recognition that 'it is more or less the habit of every country [. . .] to exalt itself and its institutions above every other country, and be vainglorious'.[48] This is 'more or less commendable', but this 'boastfulness should not generate prejudice, conventionality, and a cherishing of unreasonable ways of acting and thinking'.[49] The English, in particular, have a 'prejudice against anything [. . .] that is new to the eye' and tend to sneer at it merely because it is not English.[50] Six weeks later, his article 'Why?' identifies that the essential problem is not *what* 'un-Englishness' means, but *whether* the term does mean anything at all. Yet neither Dickens nor *Household Words* as a whole answer his pertinent question, nor does he follow this thought through to its most radical conclusions. Instead, he speaks out in the next paragraph against '*really* non-English sentiments', for example the assumption that 'all Englishmen are drunkards', and wonders, 'why does my so-easily-frightened nationality not take offence at such things?' [51] While the existence of 'un-Englishness' may be open to doubt, that of an essential Englishness is not.

FOREIGNERS' PORTRAITS OF ENGLISHMEN

So what does it mean to be English, if indeed it does mean anything? Although *Household Words'* own stance on this is not without its contradictions, it inevitably finds that foreign writers have got it wrong. The journal mostly disagrees with the reviewed items—not surprisingly, since that is partly the purpose of reviewing them at all. But their genre makes a difference: if the reviewed item is a play or a work of fiction, *Household Words* writers mostly adopt a facetious tone and dismiss everything as farce. Most of the stereotypes they pick up on in plays refer to outward appearance and some behavioural quirks. Several of the reviewed items describe the English as melancholy, blasé, but very wealthy idlers who pass their time betting on anything and everything and drinking away their misery. Although *Household Words* pokes mild fun at this image, it does not object to the implicit assumption that the most essentially English citizens are wealthy and male—wherever that is not the case, this is explicitly emphasised.

In the case of 'the graver works' of travel literature, however, *Household Words* responds much more severely to the claims put forward.[52] Travel writers tend to speculate on 'mentality' and 'character' of the countries and peoples they visit, and *Household Words* repeatedly takes issue with the conclusions these draw, as well as with the observations on which these conclusions are based. Frequently, *Household Words* objects to a point made by a foreign commentator even though it may offer similar observations somewhere else. It also uses those foreign reviews to comment in turn on the countries they originate from.[53] An illustration of both of these tendencies is to be found in Sidney Blanchard's two 'Munchausen' articles. In the first, Blanchard discusses Edmond Texier's *Lettres sur l'Angleterre*, while the second focuses predominantly on a German newspaper article on England. The German article argues that British 'national peculiarities are all founded upon the fact that we are a nation of sailors', which explains, for example, the architectural discomfort of English houses and the general 'vulgarity of our pleasures'.[54] Blanchard finds this deduction absurd, yet three years later John Robertson's 'Coast Folk' articles, which I discuss in more detail below, propose that the greatness of the British Empire and the qualities of modern Britons rest exclusively upon their Scandinavian ancestry and thus upon a history of seafaring and hunting whales.[55] The only qualitative difference between the two claims seems to be that the former is made in order to justify undesirable aspects of English culture, while the latter seems to explain the magnitude and glory of the nation. Moreover, Blanchard then turns around and ridicules the German writer's conclusions themselves as a typical national trait—'a German must give a reason for everything'—and offers an explanation of the distinction between French and German 'describers of national characteristics':

> Both fall into not dissimilar errors, but from entirely different causes; the one because he does not see far enough, the other because he sees too far. The Frenchman judges by immediate impressions, which are sure to be wrong;—the German, in his anxiety to be right, reasons and deduces with such tortuous ingenuity, that the result, though delightful as a logical argument, is absurd as a matter of fact.[56]

Blanchard thus attacks the foreign writers' views about England by responding with generalisations as sweeping as those he sets out to criticise in the first place.

One accusation *Household Words* takes issue with is that of xenophobia, even though Dickens's 'Insularities' has made a similar claim in its observation that 'what is not English is [seen as] not natural'.[57] Texier in Blanchard's 'Munchausen Modernised' points out the 'antipathy of the English [. . .] to foreigners', especially the French, and describes the 'shocked' response his moustache provokes.[58] Blanchard ridicules this, even though several *Household Words* articles might be seen to prove Texier's point, in particular their continued preoccupation with the facial hair of continental men.[59] The German writer in Blanchard's subsequent 'More Modern Munchausens' reiterates Texier's points both about the English people's response to his beard and to their hostility 'to foreigners and foreign habits in the affairs of social life', even though they are 'open to innovation' if it helps them make money.[60] The German writer concludes that on the whole the English are backward, conservative, and primitive, and thus 'the very Chinaman of Europe', expressing one national stereotype through another. It is striking that Blanchard has no objections to using the metaphor of the Chinaman, clinging 'to institutions and habits thousands of years old' without any consideration of their use, but uses it a matter of course.[61] Yet Dickens's 'Proposals for a National Jestbook' implicitly makes the same criticism of the English reluctance to change: 'If the good old style were sufficient for our forefathers, it is sufficient for the present and future generations'.[62]

William Jerrold's 'An Old Portrait from The Hague', which summarises a Dutch book on the English from 1747, points out the English 'contempt for the rest of the world' right after deducing various 'English' qualities from 'the various races mixed up in his veins; 'He drinks like the Saxon; he loves hunting like the Danes; he cheats and plays false witness like the Normans, and he owes his love of bloody spectacles, and his fearlessness of death to the Romans'.[63] Jerrold hardly comments on any of the points taken from the book he reviews, and does not reveal whether he views them as 'ludicrous' or 'instructive'.[64]

An exception to the repeated reproach of xenophobia is the French writer Francis Wey's *Les Anglais Chez Eux*, which Dixon reviews in his 'Paris on London'. Dixon mostly approves of Wey, since he classes the French as the prejudiced nation and England as tolerant and cosmopolitan. In particular, Wey finds the English 'neither greedy of flattery from foreign visitors, nor over-sensitive to a little sharp criticism from the same', even though Dixon reacts quite snappily to some of the less agreeable points brought forward, and repeatedly reciprocates by poking fun at Wey's misspellings of English words.[65]

In several articles about England the British Empire takes a predominant position, and it provokes some of the strongest responses from *Household Words* writers: if the foreign commentator approves of the Empire, then they win *Household Words'* full praise; if they criticise the Empire, they receive a vitriolic review. Two articles ridicule the belief that every English gentleman has a Negro coachman[66], though this impression may be cemented further by characters such as Joseph Bagstock's 'native' in *Dombey and Son*, Julia Mills's return from India with a 'black man [. . .] and a copper-coloured woman' in *David Copperfield*, and black Sambo in *Vanity Fair.*[67] Otto von Wenckstern quotes without much comment what a German 'lady tourist' has to say on the subject of 'English Cookery'. The German writer wonders why English cooking is so 'antediluvian', especially as 'the inhabitants of this mighty isle are great and glorious in everything [else] they undertake'.[68] Since the article backs up the criticism of the low standard of 'Common Cookery' and people's scepticism of new ways of preparing food made in another *Household Words* article three weeks previously, von Wenckstern's lack of comment suggests tacit approval.[69]

More elaborate praise for the Empire is found in Wey's *Les Anglais Chez Eux*. Published in the last quarter of *Household Words'* lifespan, Dixon finds Wey's book a 'pleasant novelty' because, in contrast to several previous foreign works reviewed in *Household Words*, it admits that the French frequently underestimate England, due to their 'retired and domestic habits' and their 'maladroitness in colonising'.[70] The context in which Dixon uses the word 'colonising' here is ambiguous—the French word 'colonie' does not necessarily have an imperial connotation but may simply mean that the French are reluctant to settle elsewhere. Yet the very next sentence, which Dixon quotes with approval, refers explicitly to the British Empire:

> The statesmen of England are acquainted with the habitable globe, much as our police-agents are acquainted with the quarters of Paris. [. . .] Although endowed with a national sentiment amounting to superstition, [the English] have nevertheless chosen the whole world for their country.[71]

Recent theory suggests that there is in fact a causal link, rather than a contradiction, between running a global Empire and possessing 'national sentiment amounting to superstition', since it brings the colonisers into immediate contact with the 'un-English'.[72] The hub of this Empire strikes Wey as a 'commercial fairy-land', which expresses aptly 'the splendour, the preponderance, and the wealth of this nation, a monstrous polypus, whose suckers absorb the substance of every country'.[73] Not only is the image of England as a parasitical, wealth-sucking monstrosity on the one hand and a 'commercial fairy-land' on the other mildly ambiguous, but Wey also points out the great poverty to be found in the metropolis. Dixon lets these points pass without any comment, so it is not clear whether he endorses them or finds them so ludicrous as to require no further comment. I am inclined to assume the former, since both London's wealth and its immense poverty are topics that frequently recur throughout *Household Words'* publication history. An earlier article takes issue with another French writer, Alexandre Ledru-Rollin, a former revolutionary who fled to London in 1849 and in 1850 published *The Decline of England* (*La Décadence de l'Angleterre*). Similar to Wey/Dixon, Ledru-Rollin and Wills see England and the British Empire as more or less the same thing, although Wills disagrees with everything else in Ledru-Rollin's text. Indeed, most of the points on 'England' that Wills satirises actually relate to the Empire:

> I could hardly believe that a French gentleman residing, for a few months in the neighbourhood of Leicester Square, London, could possibly obtain a thorough knowledge either from study or personal observation,

> of the political, judicial, colonial, commercial, manufacturing, social, and educational systems and conditions of this empire [. . .].[74]

After counteracting Ledru-Rollin's criticism with a lengthy enumeration of Britain's national income, technological advances, and especially its possessions abroad, Wills comes to the main point to which he objects, namely Ledru-Rollin's claim that 'the fortune of maritime empires cannot be long, for they only reign by the oppression of the nations, and while they extend themselves abroad, they are undermining themselves within'.[75] In responding to this blasphemous prophecy, Wills's indignation reaches its most passionate tone:

> Upon my word, Mr. Rollin, this looks very likely [. . .] A hundred thousand Londoners can afford to enjoy themselves at Epsom Races [. . .] Throughout the country, there is just now more enjoyment and less grumbling than there has been for years [. . .] The plethora of prosperity increases, and will burst the sooner! We, eating, drinking, contented, trafficking, stupid, revolution-hating, spiritless, English people, "are undermining ourselves within".[76]

Nevertheless, within seven years of this article, Britain's control over its biggest overseas possession would be in serious danger in the Sepoy Rebellion, and for precisely the reasons that Ledru-Rollin predicted.

The epithet of the English as 'revolution-hating' is a point that *Household Words*, for once, agrees with.[77] Dickens's and Horne's 'Great Exhibition' highlights England's 'steady persevering resolution' and its 'industrious work' as a positive contrast and antidote to the 'revolutionary excitements' which 'the continental nations' are prone.[78] A similar point is addressed in Blanchard's 'Munchausen Modernised':

> M. Texier's grandest discovery is, perhaps, the light which throws upon [sic] the political character of the English people. The tractability and obedience of the lower classes (whom we are accustomed to consider rather alarmingly addicted to such bad habits as individual opinion, aspiring to legislation, and to be not the most manageable of mankind,) meets with the author's great admiration. 'The English people,' he informs us, 'is an infant, to whom you give formulas in the guise of sugar-plums. If they suffer too much and are tempted to throw off the yoke, you stop them in one word, "Have you not the right of petition?" and they say to themselves: "It is true!" Then they return to work, or to the tavern [. . .].'[79]

Texier surmises that this is what happened to the Chartist movement in April 1848. Blanchard considers this to be so absurd as to make comment almost unnecessary: 'Those who remember the events of the memorable tenth of April, will appreciate the accuracy of this description, not to mention the admirable knowledge of the locality exhibited by the historian'.[80] Yet although Blanchard disagrees with Texier's claim that the English have no spirit for revolution, he shares Texier's evaluation of this as a desirable state of affairs. Moreover, we have already seen that, three years earlier, Henry Morley's 'Views of the Country' made a similar claim, if in different terms: Morley sees the printing press as a forum for 'every phase of opinion', and the very spread and availability of opinions and differing viewpoints is a safeguard against revolution and dissent. The printing press is not merely the medium of 'opinion' but lays 'every day a mass of *fact* before all people capable of thought', providing 'education' for those who can read.[81] The mixture of 'opinion' and 'fact' exerts a potentially seductive influence on readers, and Morley thus reiterates the same argument that Texier proposes: the very freedom of speech silences any serious radical opposition.

The lack of revolutionary potential may also be seen as a more optimistic interpretation of the resistance to change that some reviewed foreign writers, as well as Dickens himself in 'Insularities' and 'The Toady Tree', diagnose in English culture. While in 'Munchausen Modernised', *Household Words'* attitude to this claim may be unclear, it recurs in several other articles throughout *Household Words.* In Dickens's 'Proposals for a National Jestbook', John Bull's demand for training up a larger English army is dismissed by a 'Person of Quality' as 'revolutionary' talk, which silences the argument at once.[82] Morley's 'Views of the Country', praising the freedom of the press and representational government as the reasons for Britain's immunity to revolutions, ironically pre-empts Ledru-Rollin's comparison of the English as 'an infant' to be pacified with sugar-plums: 'We are like children lavishly supplied with toys, who receive new gifts tranquilly enough'. Since there is (supposedly) no state censorship, 'the English people speak unreservedly their thoughts on public matters, and are open, though it be with honourable slowness, to all new convictions'.[83] Sala's 'Perfidious Patmos' and 'Music in Paving-Stones' both gently mock the continental refugees of the 1848 revolutions, some of whom are remarkably peaceable and therefore all the more worthy of praise: 'His beard [. . .] is decidedly the most revolutionary thing about him'.[84] It seems that once the direct contrast of a foreign writer's opinion (and the need to contradict it) is removed, *Household Words* more often than not agrees with Texier's claim that the English have no taste for revolution. In fact, this is one of the few actual characteristics that are consistently asserted as part of that elusive English character.[85]

The majority of reviewed texts and of the reviews themselves treat 'the English' as a homogeneous mass, and only occasionally distinguish groups of the population. A question one needs to ask is which group of the population comes to represent the norm of Englishness most. The fictional works with which *Household Words* takes issue feature mostly members of the aristocracy who idle their wealthy lives away and ultimately die of ennui. As mentioned before, *Household Words* writers find these works almost too absurd to comment. More enlightening are the 'graver works' of travel-writing, which hardly mention the aristocracy at all, but they do occasionally refer to the working classes, the poor, and to women. I have already discussed the supposed submissiveness of the lower classes who are easily silenced by reminding them of their freedom of speech, which Texier celebrates in Blanchard's 'Munchausen Modernised'. The German writer in 'More Modern Munchausens' talks in some detail about the misery of the poor in London who, although materially better off than their German counterparts, have greater aspirations due to the English obsession with gentility and 'pretensions to comfort', and therefore feel their privations more.[86] The claim to gentility and 'that curious phenomenon, an English gentleman' occupy other writers too: Morley cites a German writer who distinguishes between 'Gentlemen-at-heart, Gentlemen-in-manners, Gentlemen-born, [and] Perfect-gentlemen—which is the union of the three', although he is unable to define any of these beyond their unanimous use of white gloves[87], while Dixon's 'Paris on London' makes a similar point as Dickens's 'Toady-Tree', namely that 'legal equality [. . .] has no effect upon the national manners [and etiquette . . .] which mark the hierarchic degrees established between the different classes'.[88] In short, most foreign observers recognise that there is a class system in Britain but are often at a loss to define the characteristics of individual classes.

The concept of a gentleman underwent a significant change in this period. Catherine Hall argues that, as the middle classes slowly gained ascendancy over the aristocracy in the first half of the century, a gentleman 'was no longer predicated on having the wherewithal not to have to work but rather on the dignity of work itself.'[89] But we have already seen that 'work' was applied rather loosely to earning a living, including investors and factory-owners. Hence it is no surprise that *Household Words* gradually and tacitly eliminates the aristocracy and the labouring classes, so that the professional and entrepreneurial middle classes emerge as the standard specimen of an Englishman.[90] Although Blanchard, Morley, and Dixon mock the foreign texts they respectively review, they (and *Household Words* as a whole) rarely dispute this basic assumption. Dickens may passionately identify the labouring and lower middle classes as 'the life-blood of the nation', who have been bullied into being ashamed of their circumstances and aspiring to 'genteel' behaviour, instead of making 'the most of small resources, and the best of scanty means of enjoyment'.[91] Yet he does so from a superior point of view and in the third person—these classes are unlikely to read *Household Words*.

Finally, another sub-group that occasionally provokes comment in *Household Words*' 'Foreigners' Portraits' are women. One foreign writer finds them 'educated to within an inch of their lives' but otherwise quite tolerable, as he and some others comment on their beauty.[92] Significantly, one writer finds that women are one of the 'three *objects* [. . .] which, in this island, are remarkable for their marvellous beauty; the women, the trees, and the horses'.[93] Although Dixon may have intended this phrase as quiet mockery, this is nevertheless the position which women occupy in most of *Household Words'* articles on Englishness: they are either eliminated entirely, mentioned only in passing, or tacitly subsumed in the category of the 'Englishman'.[94]

INSULARITIES

Thus far, the image of the English that emerges from *Household Words'* debate of 'Foreigners' Portraits' is composed mostly of negatives: the normative English are *not* female, *not* aristocratic, *not* manual labourers, *not* obsequious, and *not* xenophobic. Where positive claims appear, these are often the result of *Household Words'* opposition to a point made to a claim by a foreign writer: since the English do not subscribe to despotism, they must be freedom-loving. The 'foreign' perspective thus generates a particular rhetoric and a set of characteristics that occasionally differ substantially from those that *Household Words* writers propose in other articles without a national contrast to draw upon, or without a foreign commentator against whose claims they need to defend their idea of Englishness. Consequently, *Household Words'* 'positive' definitions of essential English characteristics are fairly rare and far from comprehensive, addressing only a handful of issues. This may be a result of my selection criteria—any form of classification must remain somewhat arbitrary in a journal so deeply concerned with 'the hopes, the enterprises, triumphs, joys, and sorrows, of this country'.[95] The relative rarity of positive definitions also points to the 'philosophical poverty' that Anderson diagnoses in nationalist thought.[96] Since it is mainly a nation's beliefs about 'others' that form its own identity, not many pieces remain that deal with Englishness 'in a vacuum' and in general rather than specific terms.

From this selection, two phases emerge in which *Household Words* conceptualised its 'views of the country' more extensively than usual. The first lasted from August 1850 to November 1851 and features pieces on nationality and the state of the nation that are characterised by a tone of optimism and self-congratulation.[97] This is not surprising, as this period covers the wake of the 1848 European revolutions, which Britain had survived relatively peacefully and which therefore took a central place in *Household Words'* image of the nation, and the run-up to and duration of the Great Exhibition, when confidence in the nation ran high throughout the popular press. Moreover, *Household Words* was still finding its feet at this stage, and probably did not wish to alienate its audience by being overly critical. The second phase lasted from May 1855 until September 1856 and consists mostly of Dickens's writings on the subject of nationality and nation.[98] Dickens's five articles tend to be more sarcastic in tone and more critical than the early pieces, whereas Browne's 'Perfectly Contended', though mildly sardonic, expresses a fair degree of optimism and complacency.[99]

The early pieces celebrate British prosperity and success in its various industries and pursuits. Wills's 'Cheerful Arithmetic' compares the economic growth of Britain in 1812 and 1848, and finds that especially the 'middle and working classes' are much better off now. Wills sees the 'grumbling' of the 'well-to-do' as 'an Englishman's privilege' and as a sign that things are not so bad: 'It is only the very poor who gaze cheerfully into the future [. . .] for they have nothing to lose'.[100] Browne makes the same point: 'What a good world this must be, [. . .] when Londoners can find no worse tyranny to complain of than [. . .] foreign organ-boys'.[101] Morley's 'Views of the Country' mocks different theories for reform because he finds that Britain, although endowed with 'many faults, [is . . .], on the whole, magnanimous'.[102] Horne's 'A Time for All Things' discusses the achievements of different peoples and times and finds that modern Britain has done tolerably well in most areas, even though it is still outdone by some European states in 'the useful arts'.[103]

Although these pieces attempt to define English characteristics 'in a vacuum' and without the direct contrast of another nation or a foreign writer's view of England, most of them nevertheless rely on some form of contrasting Other in order to establish the values they hold as national. Most frequently, this 'Other' is expressed in terms of class. I have proposed earlier that Morley's 'Views of the Country', in celebrating the press as the safeguard of the freedom which forms the core of British identity, implicitly excludes the 'uneducated class' from the normative first-person voice that *Household Words* maintains throughout most of its publication history. Wilkie Collins's 'The Unknown Public' performs a similar exclusion of those who don't read at all, or who read mostly penny-dreadfuls—these are to be found mostly in the 'second and third rate neighbourhoods'.[104] Wills's 'Cheerful Arithmetic' distinguishes openly between the different classes, but claims that 'the poor have ceased to regard the rich, as a class, as their natural enemies'—in fact, 'it is the strength and safeguard of the English nation, that its [. . .] industry and commerce [. . .] effect a fusion of interests—a union of classes, and a dependence of each upon the others—which is true national power'.[105] But the only groups he allows a 'voice' in his article are tradesmen, mill-owners, and farmers—members of the professional, propertied classes, rather than the labourers these might employ. The speaker of Browne's 'Perfectly Contented' is a propertied, elderly gentleman who muses benevolently on the lowlife surrounding his London lodgings and 'the struggling industry they represent', since 'our street cries are notes of liberty'.[106] The article implies that 'we', *Household Words'* writers and readers, are not those uttering those street cries but those upper echelons that hear them. Finally, the two poems ' The Heart of

England' and 'Britain', published within a fortnight of each other and sandwiching James Hannay's celebration of 'English Songs', both wholeheartedly celebrate their chosen subject(s) as the epitome of liberty, courage, patience, constancy, purity, and innocence. Even the poems allude to a hierarchical class system and cast the lower strata in the role of objects, not subjects: Dora Greenwell's 'The Heart of England', for instance, sketches a tripartite structure and locates the poem's first-person plural narrator (the by now familiar 'we', which frequently seems to include the audience) somewhere between the 'Country's Chiefs' and the 'poor man'. This middle class reveals itself in the charitable appeal to 'our Country's Chiefs' to 'Look on [the poor man's] homely joys, his lowly griefs, /And feel what Peasants feel'.[107] Some classes are evidently 'more English' than others, and contrast thus remains an essential ingredient of Englishness and English culture even in those *Household Words* pieces that seem fairly straightforward. Both poems express some anxiety that Britain's imperial, missionary, and international endeavours might take place at the cost of the untaught poor in Britain itself, a sentiment that Dickens repeatedly stated throughout his career[108]:

> But never let her missions roam
> Unblest abroad, while age and youth
> Are pining to be taught at home.[109]

One curious assertion of Englishness is James Hannay's 'English Songs', in which Englishness seems to have nothing to do with the English population at all. Hannay himself was Scottish, but—like fellow Scot Thomas Carlyle and many other public figures of the period—seems to have fully identified with Englishness.[110] Hannay dismisses 'the songs circulated among the people' as 'inferior to the tone of the country's thought and the English mind', even though it is not at all clear who may be producing 'the country's thought' if not the people who live in it.[111] This seems all the more bizarre since Hannay praises Charles Dibdin, an eighteenth-century 'naval song writer' for giving 'us a body of songs, entirely national'.[112] Dibdin's 'homely, manly strain' is 'national' because this 'racy, salt, [. . .] hard', and 'rough music' expresses the 'trusting, sturdy courage, the jolly companionship, and the love of grog' of 'Jack'. Hannay's preference for naval songs perhaps not entirely surprising, since he had been in the navy himself for five years but struggled to submit to the monotonous work and control, which eventually led to his dismissal in 1845.[113] Yet Hannay explicitly prefers Dibdin's naval, hyper-masculine ideal to 'playful ditt[ies] [. . .] intended for the "ladies now on land"'.[114] While the actual 'people' are evidently not part of the country, it seems that Dibdin's romanticised sailors are—at least from the point of view of 'all sorts of idle brave lounging fellows about Pall Mall'.[115] Hannay's idea of Englishness does not have much to do with birth or residence either: he praises Scott, Byron, Shelley, and Burns, notwithstanding that two of these lived and died abroad in order to avoid censure by the British authorities, while the other two were Scottish and emphasised their Scottishness, rather than effacing it as Hannay did. Ironically, it is 'the exquisite melody of Shelley's "Lines to an Indian Air" in particular which 'remind[s] us, once more, that we are English'.[116] Hannay's sketch of Englishness thus remains a blurred, convoluted mass of sweaty, drunken masculinity and tough comradeship, although it is no less strongly asserted for its indistinctness or disconnectedness from any (national or naval) reality.

Apart from its eccentric attitude to Englishness, Hannay's article is interesting because it raises the question of genre. So far, none of the prose texts I have looked at in this chapter have been particularly convincing in asserting what it means to be English—the most compelling pieces are the ones that question it. The reason for this is that national values do not bear too much questioning but work on a predominantly 'affective and experiential' level.[117] Therefore they can be expressed more confidently in poetry, which appeals not to logical reasoning but to the emotions. This is certainly what Greenwell's 'Heart of England' and Meredith's 'Britain' attempt to do. Meredith celebrates his 'native land' in terms that cast it first and foremost as an Empire: Britain is the seat of honesty, faith and friendship, liberty and courage. Yet all of these effect chiefly 'that free-born men may free the slave'. Four out of five verses refer directly to Britain's relations with other countries and to its imperial destiny:

> She is not what she yet may be;
> And, therefore, till her work is done,
> I know she marches onward free,
> On to the setting of her sun.
> Great splendour will the world behold:
> The West will shine with wondrous light [. . .].[118]

Meredith also gives away that economic gains were an important part in the formation of Britain's Empire: 'Her may the distant sheening shore enrich'.[119] Yet Meredith's remaining points about Britain confine themselves to empty phrases and celebratory rhetoric without any definitive assertions about the country. Similarly, Dora Greenwell's 'Heart of England' does not offer any attributes of Englishness beyond imperialism: England's 'swift and generous' 'Freedom' is expressed in its 'widening sway' over 'distant lands', and the Empire is the result of 'the constant mind, /The patient courage, the enduring will [of the English . . .] to find /New paths—new homes to fill'. The 'sons of the Ocean Queen' are praised as 'the firm, unconquerable race', whose job it is 'the darkling nations to illume'.[120] Greenwell's and Meredith's poems both push the same buttons and buy into the same ideals. They seem to be more successful at rousing national pride than, for example, Hannay's 'English Songs', because their genre lends itself to an emotional rather than rational response and allows them to get away without any evidence or argumentation. Ironically, although one addresses 'England' and the other 'Britain', both poems could easily exchange titles without making any difference to their respective scope or meaning—the two terms are once again synonymous in this case.

It is precisely this vulnerability to interrogation of a 'so-easily-frightened nationality' which Dickens alludes to in the question of 'whether [the word "un-English"] has any meaning'.[121] While some positive assertions about the political state or maybe even the country England can be backed up by statistical or any other form of evidence, national identity remains a hazy emotion which, though perhaps strongly felt, is almost impossible to pin down. It is important that Dickens recognises the powerful influence that nationality has on him 'every day of my life; but I want to know why [. . .]?' [122] His five articles do not offer any answer to that, but as Dickens recognises the potential slipperiness of a debate about supposedly national traits, his articles are much more critical of England than most other *Household Words* pieces.[123]

For example, his 'Insularities' acknowledges that national feeling is often nothing more than simple bias and prejudice and a 'tendency to be firmly persuaded that what is not English is not natural'.[124] This, he claims, is particularly obvious in the public response to French pictures as 'all very well, but [. . .] "theatrical", as opposed to 'dramatic' (and English). Dickens presupposes that the difference between a dramatic and a theatrical picture is that a dramatic picture tells a story 'strikingly' but shows no 'apparent consciousness of a spectator', while in a 'theatrical picture' the characters 'are obtrusively conscious of a spectator, and are obviously dressed up, and doing [. . .] things with an eye to the spectator, and not for the sake of the story'. This could be significant not merely as an aesthetic preference, but also in its reference to nationality: foreign pictures make the spectator self-conscious; nationality is staged like a scene or play.[125] It is nationality itself that is 'not natural' but 'theatrical'. In order to verify this distinction, Dickens visits a French exhibition and finds that the only difference between 'dramatic' and 'theatrical' pictures is that 'the actions and gestures of the figures [in the latter] were not English', but display 'the vivacious manner natural to a greater or less degree to the whole great continent of Europe'. Since 'the manner of our little Island' is to preserve 'external formality and constraint' under all circumstances, English spectators perceive continental manners as 'overcharged and out of the truth'.[126] Ironically, 'external formality and constraint' thus come to be viewed as 'natural' behaviour. In order to counteract their insular isolation and prejudice, Dickens advocates that the English learn other living languages, travel abroad more, and widen their horizon.[127]

One claim that Dickens repeatedly views with scepticism is that England is the seat of liberty and meritocracy. Public opinion may hold 'that men are to be deferred to for their capacity for what they undertake, for their talents, and worth, and for nothing else', but most of the middle classes still look up and toady to the aristocracy.[128] Although Dickens asserts the 'quiet greatness and independence of the national character' in 'Insularities', he does so only to point out that the banal gossip about the royal family published in the Court Circular contradicts this independence.[129] Dickens's scepticism is in direct opposition to several other *Household Words* articles, as I have shown. In the same year as Dickens's 'Why?', Robertson's 'English Coast Folk', for example, claims that all other nations 'from Paris to Pekin [sic] [believe . . .] that it is right to have a master and obey his will', whereas the British descendents of the Scandinavians believe in 'individual independence'.[130] Moreover, Dickens distinguishes between professed public opinion and day-to-day reality, and refuses to take the former as the only measure of a nation, whereas writers like Hannay claim that Englishness has little to do with 'the people' or their actions. Even in a meritocracy, though, Dickens does not advocate removing social boundaries altogether, since 'many inequalities of condition and distinction there must always be'. The removal of the 'Toady Tree' would, in fact, make the 'great social staircase [. . .] safer and stronger', a prospect that wins Dickens's approval.[131]

ENGLISHNESS VS. BRITISHNESS

The issue of the difference between English and British still holds sway today, if popular culture is anything to go by. Whether it is the Olympic Games, the Queen's birthday, a football championship, or the Commonwealth Games, a multitude of flags is usually put on display by the British public. In England, the Union Jack and St. George's Cross are often flaunted indiscriminately and in roughly equal proportions, notwithstanding that some events emphasise the union between the different countries that make up the United Kingdom (e.g. the Olympic Games), while others force them to compete against each other (e.g. the European Football Championship). Since pop-singer Geri Haliwell sported the Union Jack as a dress at the 1997 Brit Awards, both it and the St George's Cross have become fashion statements in their own right. *Household Words'* pages are likewise populated with national symbols. John Bull, Britannia, and the British Lion make frequent appearances, and there is, apparently, no doubt what they represent in each case.[132] However, the matter is more complicated than it seems at first glance. An article entitled 'Britannia's Figures' cites statistics of England, Wales, Australia, and New Zealand, but not Scotland, while it splits emigration figures into emigrants from England, Scotland, and Ireland, but not Wales.[133] Another on 'English Coast Folk' focuses mostly on Scotland, notwithstanding that a previous article by the same author has already dealt with 'Scotch Coast Folk', and classes the coast folk of both Scotland and England as a superior race who have gained Britain its place in the world.[134] In this case, 'English' has come to include the other countries of Great Britain. This section, then, will focus on how the metropolitan *Household Words* treats 'the other' British countries and where it locates the conceptual boundary between England and Britain.

There are relatively few pieces in *Household Words* that discuss British rather than English concerns.[135] Those that do refer to Britain in the title are mostly about British colonies or British exiles rather than Britain itself. Meredith's 'Britain' is one rare exception but, as we have seen, it is nevertheless suffused by imperial rhetoric and imagery. Raphael Samuel finds that the term 'British' generally tends to be bound up with the Empire, whereas 'English' is associated with home, landscape, beauty, and literature, and this is largely borne out by *Household Words'* use of the two terms.[136] Like many other critics, Linda Colley shows that in the eighteenth and early nineteenth centuries, Britishness emerged in contrast to continental Europe and the non-European 'Others' that the Empire came into contact with.[137] According to Colley, it would be a mistake to presume that 'Britishness' means the formation of a homogeneous population, but rather that Britain—and its Empire—'allowed its diverse inhabitants to focus on what they had in common, rather than on what divided them'.[138] Therefore British identity formed not as a political construct that aimed to replace local identities, but as an additional identity:

> In practice, men and women often had double, triple, or even quadruple loyalties [. . .] It was quite possible for an individual to see himself as being, at one and the same time, a citizen of Edinburgh, a Lowlander, a Scot, and a Briton.[139]

Yet England had been 'demographically, economically and politically the dominant partner in "Great Britain" since the eighteenth century. Therefore, the separate identities of the 'peripheral' British countries, i.e. Ireland, Scotland, and Wales, tended to define themselves in contrast to the hegemonic power of England; the example of the dominant 'other' helped to bring out the distinctions of the other British nations, since 'smaller nations gain strength from defensive distinctiveness.' [140] England, on the other hand, rarely defined itself against the 'inferior' peripheries but against Europe or Britain's imperial possessions, and the distinctions between England and Britain—in contrast to Scotland and Britain—tended to fuse as a consequence.[141] The values attached to Britishness, such as they were, typically stemmed from Englishness and not the peripheral British countries. As an ethnicity[142], Englishness had the capacity of expanding to envelop the whole of the British Isles, as Catherine Hall convincingly argues:

> Englishness marginalizes other identities, those from the peripheries, the Welsh, the Scottish and the Irish. In constructing what it meant to be English, a further claim was constantly being made—that Englishness was British, whereas those on the margins could never claim the right to speak for the whole.[143]

Thus, if a writer uses the term 'English' it is rarely clear where they perceive the boundaries of the term—we have already seen examples of Scotsmen who, possibly in order to reach a broader audience or circle of influence, defined themselves and their values as 'English', in its inclusive sense.[144] In contrast to Colley's Lowland Scot, most *Household Words* articles speak from a London perspective and thus from the epicentre of power of England, Great Britain, and the Empire. From such an angle, these different categories often appear less pronounced and are more likely to merge, and metropolitan commentators often 'take their identity for granted'.[145]

Raphael Samuel accounts for current historians' preoccupation with Britishness rather differently than Colley: 'Instead of being a secure, genetic identity, [Britishness] can be seen as something culturally and historically conditioned, always in the making, never made', and continually contested.[146] Although this is, arguably, the case for all national identities, Samuel sees added reason for this inference in the relative youth of the British state and the prolonged, at times violent, strife between its member nations. Samuel argues that a concern with British history 'makes "Englishness" problematic and invites us to see it as one amongst a number of competing ethnicities'.[147] Where Colley stresses unity and similarity, Samuel's emphasis rests on competition and difference. In *Household Words*, this becomes particularly relevant in John Robertson's 'coast folk' articles, as we shall shortly see.

In all of *Household Words* there are only two articles directly about Wales. One is a short 'chip' on 'A Welsh Wedding', sketching traditional wedding customs. Much of the wedding ceremony in rural Wales, according to this article, revolves around money, which the writer attributes to 'the poverty of the Welsh peasantry, and their simple habits'. The writer also finds that Welsh singing is 'generally rather dismal'.[148] The other *Household Words* piece is a short story of a traveller who is forced to spend a wet Sunday in a small Welsh village and is overcome by boredom. His landlady tells him the story of 'Miss Davies', who watched her lover drown in the sea and devoted her life and wealth to charitable projects to save the families of sailors lost at sea. The romance itself is irrelevant here, but the framework for it is revealing. The disgruntled narrator jokes about Welsh rabbit, the polysyllabic Welsh language, and about 'two Jenny Joneses, who could not speak one word of English'.[149] He finds no books worth mentioning and is finally so bored and 'out of temper' with the village that he 'didn't think [its] people much worth saving'.[150] Both articles sketch Wales as a quaint, backward, and miserable place cut off from the hub of civilisation. Everywhere else, *Household Words* seems to include Wales in 'England'. Thus, Wilkie Collins asserts that 'The Great (Forgotten) Invasion' of the British Isles by the French in 1797 'took place in England', even though he specifies clearly that the French ships landed in Wales.[151]

Household Words' treatment of Scotland differs slightly from that of Wales. For one, there is more coverage—at least five articles devote themselves entirely to Scotland. One of these is a review of a German play about a Scotsman, another 'chip' advocates the emigration of Highlands people.[152] Two more articles deal with different aspects of Scotland's history from the sixteenth and seventeenth centuries.[153] The most intriguing of all are Robertson's pieces on the population of Scotland's east coast. Strikingly, most of these articles either focus on Scotland's past or portray aspects of contemporary Scottish life as rustic and outdated.

While Wales appears mostly as a curious appendage to England, *Household Words* treats Scotland as a separate—if not overly important—entity in its own right. Eliza Lynn's 'National Contrasts' outlines the alleged eccentricities of a number of nations, only to conclude with a biting satire of England. Rhetorically, this article moves from the most distant perceived country, China, through India, some European countries such as Andorra and Spain, and then, 'nearer home', to France, Scotland, and Ireland before turning to England. Scotland and Ireland clearly represent separate 'nations' here. Both are completely riddled with superstitions. A similar claim is put forth in Lynn's earlier article on 'The Witches of Scotland', which narrates incidents of witch-trials from Scotland's past and condemns them as superstitious, barbaric, and so bloodthirsty that they 'will leave a stain on [Scotland's] history, so long as that history shall endure'.[154] Lynn's treatment of 'The Witches of England' is not much different, but it only takes up four pages rather than seven. Lynn cites the example of a girl who refuses to save her life by falsely claiming to be pregnant:

> The proud disdainful answer of that ignorant English girl, who refused to buy her life by her dishonour, may be classed among those unnoted heroisms of life which are equal in grandeur, if not in importance, to the most famous anecdotes of history.[155]

The emphasis that this was an 'English girl' reverberates with ideas of English character—honesty and independence, after all, rank high in the contemporary view of English virtues. But modern England's sophisticated civilisation is demolished somewhat two pages later by Lynn's condemnation of modern-day beliefs in 'spirit-rappers', 'diabolical possession, and distinct Satanic agency': 'With such instances against us, we have little cause of self-congratulation on the score of national exemption from superstition'.[156] Nevertheless, in Lynn's articles on witchcraft England seems to get off more lightly than Scotland for the same offences. While she pre-empts that 'witchcraft in England was very much the same thing as witchcraft everywhere else' and thus generalises the context, in the case of Scotland Lynn offers plenty of transcriptions of Scottish dialect, which she then translates, stressing the particular reference to Scotland.[157]

Morley's 'The Thistle in Bud' reviews a book by Robert Chambers—the younger of the two brothers who edited the journal of the same name—on *The Domestic Annals of Scotland from the Reformation to the Revolution*. Morley finds that during the sixteeth and seventeenth centuries, Scotland, a 'society full of strange features of barbarity and violence', underwent over a century of religious struggles, which left the country primitive and destitute: 'They had incompetent universities, no bank, no newspaper, no permanent stage-coach communication, no system of police [. . .] Judges were partial, witches were burnt; [. . .] monopolies were the great rule of trade; intolerance was universal'. Once the religious strife was settled, according to Chambers, a few years sufficed to introduce a national bank and the first newspaper, while 'other troubles [were . . .] removed by union with England', such as commerce, manufacture, education, the press, and literature.[158] On all these counts, *Household Words* considers England as exemplary.

Most of Morley's article is taken up by highlighting various shortcomings of reformation, as these 'romantic pictures of Scottish life, [. . .] startle an Englishman familiar with the social state of his own nation during the contemporary period, by their dark shadows'.[159] Morley also states that Scotland was first mentioned in a London newspaper in the mid-seventeenth century, 'though the whole English nation was solicitous to know what passed weekly in Germany, Poland, and other parts of Europe'.[160] The implication is that it was not considered very important—and, judging by the total of Scotland-related articles in *Household Words*, still is not at the time Morley is writing.[161] Oddly enough, the article hardly mentions religion at all. Instead, it creates the impression that Scotland was a regressive, xenophobic, and barbaric country and a 'low civilisation' until the union with England propelled it towards modernity.[162] By contrast, England emerges as enlightened and civilised.

The majority of *Household Words* coverage of Scotland is directed towards the past.[163] Those articles that focus on contemporary Scotland are brief and matter-of-fact. One of these advocates emigration for the population of the Scottish Highlands, as 'these people are the very men and women needed [. . .] in our Australian colonies'.[164] They have a

> strong predilection and complete fitness for a pastoral life [. . .] Gold diggings would scarcely tempt them from the charge of cattle; they are strongly attached to their homes and families, are not people of gregarious habits otherwise, and know little or nothing of English.[165]

In other words, these particular Scots are remarkable for their self-reliance, simplicity, and seclusion from mainstream British culture—ironically, it is this very seclusion that makes them good colonials. This sketch characterises these Scots in a similar manner as the earlier articles, although their supposed regressiveness now, in the context of the British colonial project, wins the approval of the author, whereas other articles criticised the same points. This confirms Gikandi's claim that a shared British identity 'depended on imperial possession'.[166] In Chambers's terms,

'Scotsmen, frugally reared, [. . .] go forth into every realm to take leading positions.'[167]

Incidentally, the Chambers brothers offer an illuminating example of a Scottish negotiation of their national identity. While most other Scotsmen mentioned in this chapter simply obliterated their Scottish background and identified whole-heartedly with 'English' values, the Chambers brothers emphasised their Scottishness while staking their claim in Britain as a whole. For the first twenty-two years, their journal's title was *Chambers's Edinburgh Journal*, changing only in 1854 to the more general *Chambers's Journal of Popular Literature, Science, and Arts*. Every issue of *Chambers's Edinburgh Journal* announced that it was 'conducted by William Chambers, author of "The Book of Scotland", "Gazetteer of Scotland", &c., and Robert Chambers, author of "Traditions of Edinburgh", "History of the Scottish Rebellions", "Scottish Biographical Dictionary," &c.' But the editor's initial address desired an audience drawn from all 'the people of Great Britain and Ireland' and claimed to cater for '*every man in the British dominions*'. Similarly, it promised the boys among its readers stories of 'long and painful journeys in Asia and Africe [. . .] knowledge regarding the produce and peculiarities of unknown countries', and of 'naked savage men'.[168] Even while they asserted their Scottish background, they took pride in the British Empire and claimed a part in it, in the same terms as their English contemporaries did. As such, they were prime examples of Colley's claim that people in the peripheries could have 'double, triple, or even quadruple loyalties'.[169]

A final, intriguing example of Scotland asserting its claim in the British Empire is found in John Robertson's 'Coast Folk' articles. Robertson mirrors Chambers's assertion that the Scottish take their share in Empire-building, but he finds different explanations for Scottish characteristics and discusses the Scottish coast folk in terms of race rather than nationality. Robertson's aim is to outline the 'ethnological characteristics' of coast people, since 'the classifications of men according to nations and races, in which men of science have studied mankind, might be advantageously increased by dividing and observing them under the divisions of country folk [. . .] and town folk and coast folk'.[170] Although 'all classifications are just turns and shakes of the kaleidoscope' and 'the European, Ethiopian, Mongolian, and American, are but different varieties of one species', there are 'great moral [. . .] anatomical and physiological' differences between the races.[171] According to Robertson, the explanation for the superior qualities of the Scottish coast folk lies in their Scandinavian origins. In order to delineate their characteristics, Robertson—himself a Scotsman—presents a fairly random selection of anecdotes about the people amongst whom he grew up. He narrates incidents of salmon-fishing, seal-hunting, and various social occasions, all of which present the population of the Scottish east coast as self-sufficient, stern, honourable, independent, and proud.

Only once does Robertson attempt to distinguish between Scotland and England in the common usage rather than in racial terms, and to define their national characters:

> Were I asked to describe the intellectual condition of the Scotch by a phrase, I should say they are the nation who ask what stands to reason. [The Englishman . . .] has an eye to business; [the Frenchman] has appearance, decoration, glory in his mind [. . .] Reason, business, glory, resume three nations in three words.[172]

This passage takes up only half a page in the article on 'Scotch Coast Folk', and does not move beyond some broad and emblematic generalisations. For the rest of his series, Robertson draws the main categories in terms of race, as he makes much of the fact that 'the folks of the eastern and northern coasts of Scotland are just Dutch and Scandinavian colonies'.[173]

Although Robertson anchors his description of the coast folk of Scotland in their particular racial origin, it is striking that most of their characteristics are also central to the English self-image and ideal of the time. The coast folk of Scotland stand out through their simplicity, chastity, and pride. 'The fishers of the Scotch East Coast have never been degraded by feudal institutions. [. . .] there was no trace in their manners of pauperism, prostitution, or profligacy'.[174] They are remarkable for their health and spirits, their 'stern austerity', rigid morality, and hard work. They value 'liberty of speech', fair distribution of power, 'honest trade', independence, and courage, and despise 'feudal hierarchy', 'the insolence of rank', and 'vanity'.[175] In some ways, these fishermen turn out to be *über*-English.

Robertson remains somewhat noncommittal on the question whether these characteristics stem from social conditioning or genetic, racial inheritance. Races are 'modified by locality' as to their physical appearance and body shape, although 'it would be wrong to look for the signs of race in the effects of climate' on 'the colour of the skin'.[176] On the one hand, the success of the Scandinavian race 'all comes from the whale-fishing' and from morals, and thus from culture. On the other hand, 'the hereditary independence of race must be counted for something in making up the strength of the heroism of which Scotland was the scene'. Hereditary, too, are their 'knowledge of ship and boat-building' and their 'code of manners', and their racial qualities persist even though 'they may not now be addicted to seafaring pursuits'. Robertson seems undecided between the two models of human development, the civilisational and the biological, although his tendency is to veer towards the biological explanation.[177]

The racial dimension of these articles reveal a marked shift when seen in comparison to an article Robertson published in *Blackwood's Edinburgh Magazine* fourteen years earlier. In 'Notes on the Fishers of the Scotch East Coast', he offers similar observations to those he makes in *Household Words*, but he focuses exclusively on habits, appearance, and social customs, and shows no interest in racial origins beyond the fact that the fishers are 'perhaps, partly of a foreign stock', and seem 'more like the French of the same class, than any persons we have born in England or Ireland'.[178] In *Household Words*, his attention turns to the Scandinavian blood and heritage that, supposedly, marks the coast population of Britain. He places these, as part of 'the Northern races'[179], in a global context and thus claims a central share for Scottish coast folk in the success of the British Empire, proving Gikandi's point that 'empire was the cultural and political entity that sustained the core of a common British identity against the pressures of nationalism on the fringe'.[180] This change of emphasis pays tribute to the sharpening racial discourse that dominated the 1850s, as we have already seen.

According to Robertson, the Scottish descendants of the 'Scandinavian' race stand in marked contrast to the Celtic and Saxon populations, with whom they compete for the right of origin in Britain:

> The descendant of the Scandinavian [. . .] denied with indignation the pretension of the Celt, that his ancestors were the less ancient inhabitants of Scotland. He said, compare our numbers, and that will show you that we were here first, and have had the longest time to multiply in the land [. . .] The Scandinavians, Northmen, or Normans have been for a thousand years the masters of Gauls and Saxons.[181]

In another section, Robertson hints that a more sinister contest may have caused their relative numbers, as 'the expatriated Celts [. . .] have been cleared away to make room' for cattle.[182] Through race, Robertson tries to move the Scottish from the periphery to a position of central importance in Britain. But the 'race' he discusses is not confined merely to the Scottish successors of Scandinavians but to a wider group, the 'true Normans', who can be found 'on the shores of the Arctic and Atlantic oceans from Iceland to the Bay of Biscay'. These are distinct from the 'Frenchified Normans of the French Duke of Normandy', who, 'expressing northern ideas in Roman words, came over to England, and calling themselves conquerors, [. . .] have ever since given themselves the airs of masters among the inhabitants of the British islands'. The 'northern ideas' which guided them, presumably, centred on conquest and colonialism. Yet, while a thousand years or so have not erased the difference between Celts, Saxons, and Scandinavians in Britain, it seems that a mere 'hundred years' of ruling 'over the north of France' were enough to render the Scandinavian colony there 'Frenchified' and thus 'untrue', having forgotten all about the seafaring arts' which are the trademark of the 'true' Normans.[183]

As evidence of the racial 'superiority of the sea-kings', Robertson enlists the fact that 'their descendants are located as masters, in America, India, China, and Australia'. He celebrates the 'oceanic supremacy of the united kingdoms' and claims that the British 'sovereignty of the seas can be traced to the Scandinavian colonies established upon the coasts of Great Britain and Ireland'.[184] However, this does not mean that Robertson approves of imperialism—or rather, he does not regard the British dominions as an empire: he calls Charlemagne 'that what is politely called a conqueror, and unpolitely a brigand', and resents the fact that 'conquerors or brigands [. . .] have lorded it over the populations of the continents of Europe and Asia, [terrifying . . .] into slavery the generations and races of men inhabiting the vast regions which stretch from the deserts of Siberia to the Straits of Malacca'.[185] Robertson regards most European countries and a few non-European ones as guilty of such atrocities, 'from Timor, Alexander, and the Caesars, down to the Osmanli, the Hapsburgs, the Romanoffs, and the Bonapartes', 'from Paris to Pekin [sic]'. In these cases, the rule over an empire is a sign of tyranny and despotism. The British Empire differs from these because the British descendants of the Scandinavians distinguish themselves 'from the Asiatic, Greek, and Roman nations' through their love of 'individual independence' and refusal to be ruled by anyone else.[186] This love of freedom made the Scandinavians 'the sea-kings of their time, and Britannia is their daughter'.[187] Robertson thus reiterates the sentiment expressed in 'Rule Britannia'—in order not to be slaves, Britons must rule over others. In Robertson's version, the Scots do not only participate in the British Empire but are vital in defending Britain itself from invasion: 'When their fierce puritanism was rebuked by the milder liberalism of the nineteenth century, they answered, "You will never in any other way keep up a breed of men to fight the French."'[188]

In conclusion, Robertson develops a master narrative of racial superiority in order to explain and justify Britain's multicultural history of conquests and occupation as well as its contemporary involvement in colonialism. He uses the Empire to claim a place of central importance for the Scots in the United Kingdom, who are generally seen in a more peripheral position, especially from a metropolitan point of view such as *Household Words* represents. To manifest his stake, Robertson finds a racial explanation for the Scottish centrality that he advocates, and asserts that the Scottish coastal population is intrinsically not only the hardiest but also the oldest and most authentic community in Britain and therefore the rightful 'owners' of it.[189] His argument has moved from a strong emphasis on the equality of all races of men in his first article, to one on the superiority of the British in the last. Despite—or perhaps because of—Robertson's assertiveness, plenty of contradictions and slippage occur in his argument. The distinction between 'Frenchified Normans' and 'true Normans' is rather arbitrary, given the respective time-scale which sufficed to falsify the former and preserve the purity of the latter, and the factors which Robertson counts as racial are fairly random—the shape of the face counts, but the colour of the skin does not; the supremacy of the race is produced by a seafaring culture, yet it persists even though the population is no longer a seafaring one.

Yet Robertson adds a novel perspective to *Household Words'* stance on British- and Englishness. His assertion that 'the classifications of men according to nations and races [. . .] are just turns and shakes of the kaleidoscope' suggests that such categories are in fact arbitrary and subjective. Moreover, even though he attempts to assert a Scottish identity in contrast to an English one, he only does so in the article on 'Scotch Coast Folk'—yet later on, the Scottish are subsumed under the 'English Coast Folk', which his final article discusses. This proves Colley's point that to those in powerful positions, whether they be English, Scottish, Irish or Welsh, '"England" [. . .] meant much more than just one part of the island they inhabited. The term became for them [. . .] a synonym for Great Britain as a whole and very often for its empire as well'.[190] While 'Scottish', as a marked term, referred exclusively to the inhabitants of Scotland, 'English', as the unmarked term, could refer to both England alone and to Great Britain as a whole.

This chapter has shown that *Household Words'* attitude to Englishness and its implications is very complex and often contradictory. Many *Household Words* writers reveal their awareness of the politics, mechanics, and objectives involved in forming such a national identity, which does not, however, mean that the existence of the identity itself is doubt.

A specific English national identity is formulated most smoothly in contrast to various Others. Typically, *Household Words* compares England to other European nations or takes issue with continental writers on England. Foreign writers, it seems, cannot help but misinterpret English characteristics (at any rate, if they do give a 'truthful' account of England, this is branded as 'dull' and not worth commenting on).[191] Through the contrast with 'Foreigners' Portraits' the English emerge, in *Household Words*, as freedom-loving, independent, and hard-working urban, metropolitan, middle-class males, even though many of the characteristics which *Household Words* asserts against foreign writers are questioned somewhere else in the journal. Where a national point of comparison is lacking, this role is frequently assigned to other forms of distinction, such as class. For the most part, the professional, male, urban middle classes emerge as the 'typical Englishman' and the 'we' of *Household Words'* voice.

Finally, plenty of slippage occurs between England, the United Kingdom, and Britain, and the hazy distinctions between the different 'countries' that make up these respective entities. For the most part, *Household Words* writers use 'English' and 'British' interchangeably, although the other countries' scope is much more clearly delineated. *Household Words* demonstrates that the composite parts' political interest is at stake in formulating the identity and origin of the multicultural United Kingdom. Writers whose bias is English often make out Scotland and Wales to be a regressive, barbaric hinterland left behind the mainstream civilised English culture, while a Scottish writer like Robertson sets out to prove the central significance of Scotland in the success of the British Empire and nation. Both English and

British identity and their scopes of influence thus remain a hotly contested battlefield throughout *Household Words'* nine years of publication.

What does emerge clearly, however, is the firm hold that the idea of an essential Englishness has in the journal, even though it never satisfactorily defines what this Englishness consists of. Even 'un-Englishness', which—since contrast is such an inbuilt part of national identity—should be easier to define, remains elusive throughout. Significantly, it is the conductor of the journal himself who voices the most radical criticism of fairly basic ingredients of 'Englishness'. Dickens makes clear that national feeling has little to do with an external, shared 'reality' beyond the emotional appeal of an 'imagined community'. He also shows that recognising this fact does not necessarily lessen the influence that national feeling exerts. Dickens hit the nail on the head when he described it as 'a clincher' that has the power to 'settle any question', notwithstanding his inability to explain why this might be the case.[192]

3 *Household Words'* Treatment of Ireland

> Every 17 March brings to a head the inability of the English middle classes to deal with the Irish problem, in the sense that Ireland is a problem because it exists.[1]
>
> Pete McCarthy, *McCarthy's Bar*

THE IRISH DIFFICULTY

The 'Irish difficulty' is one of the most elusive tropes in all of *Household Words*. Several *Household Words* articles on Ireland point out individual troubles and offer a variety of solutions to these, and virtually all articles take it for granted that there *is* an underlying problem with Ireland. Yet none of them define what this root problem actually consists of. In other words, *Household Words* writers name several factors (famine, encumbered estates, Catholicism), but see these as symptoms rather than as the original problem. Thus, the journal's first article on Ireland, 'The "Irish Difficulty" Solved by Con McNale', proposes a solution, but no analysis of the problem.[2] In the first place, the 'Irish difficulty' seems to be that Ireland exists, as Pete McCarthy puts it, and that Britain, by first claiming it as a colony and then making it part of the United Kingdom, has taken responsibility for it. Yet Britain's right to rule over Ireland is never once questioned in *Household Words*.

This chapter looks at a selection of articles that explicitly deal with Ireland, the Irish, and individual Irish affairs, casting it either as a 'case' demanding British intervention or as a morsel of amusement. It is in the nature of my selection criteria that Ireland is turned into an 'Other', an object for 'English' writers and readers to describe, study, and (eventually) 'solve'. Edward Said's four stages of imperialism—describing, teaching, settling, ruling—therefore apply neatly to the relationship between Great Britain and Ireland.[3] But it is important to bear in mind that other articles may summarily deal with Ireland as subsumed under the United Kingdom, of which it had technically been a full member since the Union in 1800. Thus, 'British Phenomena' includes an anecdote about an Irishman living in Manchester, and 'Britannia's Figures' and 'Cheerful Arithmetic' both cite some statistical facts about Ireland as well as England and Scotland.

At first glance, this appears to be a contradiction to my previous chapter's claim that the Irish always appear outside the collective national identity that *Household Words* constructs, while the Welsh and Scottish occasionally merge with it. But 'Ireland' and 'the Irish' are two radically distinct concerns and provoke contradictory reactions, much more so than either England and the English (both personified in John Bull) or any of the subjects in other British colonies do. 'Ireland' is treated mostly as a physical resource, a collection of agricultural and mineral material, in much the same way as India or Australia are portrayed. As such, *Household Words* is eager to claim the country as an integral part of the United Kingdom. 'The Irish', however, are a different matter. Whereas it was possible to imagine Australia as empty and to dismiss India's population, although undeniably existent, as visibly 'Other', pagan, savage, and in need of British influence, the Irish people and their culture and religion were all uncomfortably close to Britain's own. Furthermore, the Irish had a voice that is far less easily ignored than that of other, non-European colonial subjects—most Irish people in the mid-nineteenth century were native speakers of English, and those who spoke Irish at all (up to a third of the population) were predominantly bilingual.[4] Thus, they had the potential to talk back and resist the easy dehumanisation that the populations of other British colonies underwent in imperial discourse.

Neither did the sharpening discourse of race help to distinguish between Irish and English—on the contrary, it often tended to emphasise their similarities rather than their differences. Although Robert Knox's *The Races of Men* set out to prove that racial marks between white races were as distinct from each other as between those marked by colour difference, and although a host of physiognomists analysed the facial angle and shape in order to distinguish the racial idiosyncrasies of the 'Celt', the most popular and widely accepted signifier of race during the period remained skin colour, which inevitably failed to distinguish 'Celts' from 'Anglo-Saxons'.[5] The racial explanation did inspire plenty of followers, as an article from *The Times* of October 7, 1852, indicated: 'In [the] remarks which our position impels us to make on Irish shortcomings and Irish excesses a spirit of charity often induces us to refer to the race of the people who thus painfully obtrude themselves on our attention.' Treachery, laziness, violence, xenophobia, and general degradation are all found to be racial attributes of the pure Celt. By contrast, 'the Englishman is a born cosmopolite, and to that mixed composition [of his blood] he owes the universality of his moral affinities and mental powers [. . .] no people are so free as we are from the follies of nationality.'[6] Ironically, genetic purity spells 'degradation' and unfitness for survival here, while tolerance and morality are the result of mixed blood—whereas Knox had argued that 'miscegenation as a means of making a "new" composite race was genetically doomed'.[7] Although the racial category of the 'Celt' repeatedly surfaced throughout the period and fired up the public imagination, its boundaries and characteristics were never clear-cut, and its scientific basis remained heavily defective, to say the least. The Irish were therefore not a distinct and visible category but 'wild cards which can take on value and suit to aid the player in a game of identities', as Cora Kaplan puts it: 'Ireland and the Irish often have radically contingent functions in which definitions and distinctions of class and gender, as well as religion and race play a part.'[8]

Ireland is thus potentially the most volatile of the categories in *Household Words'* model of the world, occupying the alternating positions of a full member of the United Kingdom and 'sister isle'[9], a European neighbour, and a subject colony. I propose that the ambiguity in *Household Words* in particular stems from the fact that the journal views Ire*land* as a colony of the British Empire, but *the Irish* actively resist colonisation and reject the subject status that is imposed on the natives of other colonies. Throughout, *Household Words* is far more eager to appropriate Ireland than the Irish. On the one hand, it attempts to 'create boundaries around the Irish' and stress their (physical, linguistic, religious, social, intellectual) difference, on the other it strives to belittle this difference, assimilate them to the English, and 'deprive them of their Irishness'.[10] The tension between these two contradictory strategies is never quite resolved. Thus, for instance, Murray's 'Roving Englishman' praises 'the Lakes of Killarney in Ireland' and maintains that a traveller 'really will find nothing so lovely the whole world over'.[11] Yet he finds the Irish themselves violent and obstinate: even though they can be very loyal to their master, their 'consummate impudence' makes them unfit as servants to a travelling Englishman.[12] Clearly, the Irish are too inconveniently outspoken to make into subjects easily.

Another reason for the suspicion against the Irish was their sheer number. The census of 1801 showed that 54% of the United Kingdom's population were English and 33% Irish, while Scotland and Wales combined came only to 13%. The Potato Famine of the 1840s changed the balance dramatically, and by 1871 England accounted for 68.7%, Scotland and Wales jointly made up 14.6%, but Ireland only 16.7%, the only population to decrease in proportion. Yet together with this shift in relative numbers came the wide-spread emigration of Irish labourers to Britain—in some industrial towns (such as Liverpool or Glasgow) as much as 20% of the population were Irish-born—, which resulted in a 'direct threat to both wage levels and job security' that in turn triggered many of the anti-Irish riots in the early 1850s.[13] In her article on James Phillips Kay and the Manchester Irish, Mary Poovey provides a sharp and insightful analysis of the rhetorical attempt both to disown any connection between Ireland and England (so that England would not be responsible for Irish poor relief) and to keep Ireland 'sufficiently accessible to the needs of English manufacturers to provide cheap labor [. . .] and noncompetitive markets' in times of need.[14] Hence the Irish and English were alternately cast as completely different and as similar.

Catherine Hall points to the 'mission to imperialise others' and thus the Empire as a means of unifying the British and Irish peoples and resolving the conflict between them.[15] Whereas Englishmen and the subjects of their non-European colonies offered two apparently stable categories, 'self' and 'other', marked by observable physical difference, the Irish—even more so than the Scottish and Welsh—occupied a shifting position between the two binary opposites. John Barrell's tripartite model of 'this, that, and the other' helps to dissolve the discursive difficulty that the traditional opposition of self and other poses:

> The terms self and other can be thought of as superseded by 'this' and 'that', in a narrative which now says, there is this here, and it is different from that there, but the difference between them, though in its own way important, is as nothing compared with the difference between the two of them considered together, and that third thing, way over there, which is truly other to them both.[16]

The addition of the third, middle term makes it possible to acknowledge the difference between two groups while simultaneously representing it 'as almost trivial, when compared with the civilisation they both share, but which is emphatically not shared by whatever [other . . .] is in season at the time'.[17] Although Barrell develops this concept to account for the perception of class difference amongst British imperialists, it is equally valid for *Household Words*', and much of Victorian Britain's, attitude to Ireland. Leon Litvack states that, in the 1850s, 'the Irish [. . .] represented, in the words of Bhabha, a "social reality which is at once an 'other' and yet entirely knowable and visible".[18] Litvack examines in particular the double standard that the *Illustrated London News* adopted in its treatment of Irish contributions to the Great Exhibition of 1851: whenever the *ILN* approved of Irish productions, it classified them as British, but it categorised 'them as peculiarly Irish in areas [. . .] where Ireland could never hope to compete on an equal basis', such as agriculture.[19] In the same way, *Household Words* changes its tack on Ireland. As long as the journal looks at Ireland as a subject or 'problem' in its own right, it focuses on the difficulties that Ireland poses, and stresses the difference between the English and Irish people, yet this difference is frequently belittled or ignored entirely in the context of the British Empire. Thus, some authors stress that although popular prejudice depicts the Irish as lazy and good-for-nothing, they thrive just as well in 'all our colonies' and 'get to prosper and to grumble quite as readily as Anglo-Saxons'.[20] If Ireland itself turns up something good for once, *Household Words* frequently ascribes the credit to English influence. It is therefore not surprising that the articles that specifically focus on Ireland should regularly criticise it.

In the course of its nine years, *Household Words* published contributions from at least fourteen Irish authors, some of whom, such as Percy Fitzgerald, were hugely prolific.[21] Yet most articles *about* Ireland came from the pens of English authors, Harriet Martineau most prominent amongst them. Of the sixteen or so authors who published material on Ireland, only four were Irish, and two of these only contributed one piece each. Regardless of the author's country of origin, almost every single *Household Words* piece on Ireland adopted an outsider's perspective and clearly had an English audience in mind. A striking example of this is the work of William Allingham, a poet of rising fame who contributed four prose pieces as well as several poems to *Household Words.* Allingham's family had lived in Ireland since the reign of Elizabeth I, at least 200 years before Allingham was born; yet he identified himself as English rather than Irish, travelled to London on an annual basis, and finally resettled in Lymington.[22] Kevin Whelan explains this apparent contradiction:

> Consider the narrative options open to Irish writers in the post-Union period, operating under the disabling weight of British perceptions. Their self-imposed function became the representation of Irish life for the education and elucidation of an invincibly ignorant and incredulous British audience [. . .] The auto-exotic or auto-ethnographic imperative created an unstable tone—at once moralizing, apologetic, defensive and didactic [. . .] The technical problems of writing Ireland while reading England could be insurmountable.[23]

Writers like Allingham, in addition to their personal affinities, could only write in the language of British imperialism and, rather than setting out on the apparently hopeless project of 'writing back' to the British hegemony, must have found it easier simply to identify with it. Thus, Allingham consistently writes about Ireland from a knowledgeable outsider's perspective (adopting, in fact, the point of view of the 'intelligent foreigner' in Ireland, which the previous chapter has briefly touched upon).[24]

HARRIET MARTINEAU'S CONTRIBUTIONS ON IRELAND

Harriet Martineau's articles on Ireland are exemplary of much of *Household Words*' material on Ireland and unite many of the contradictions that riddle the journal's attitude. In 1852, a year of particularly pronounced anti-Irish disturbances in England[25], Martineau spent several months in Ireland as correspondent for the *Daily News*, in which she published some twenty-seven 'Letters from Ireland'. In his introduction to the edited *Letters from Ireland*, Glenn Hooper points out that Martineau's *Letters* see 'the country less in terms of its human complexity, than as a laboratory which requires only sociological analysis.' [26] This analysis can frequently seem 'cold and unfeeling', as Martineau tried to distance herself from the painful human reality and restrained any emotional response as far as possible: 'As an individual, Martineau responds to the emotion; as an improving economist [. . .], she displays impatience with these wilfully childish people who cling to outmoded associations and practices.'[27]

A similar tension emerges in Martineau's five articles on Ireland that appeared in *Household Words* between September and November 1852. They are a condensed, simplified, and more playful version of her *Daily News* contributions, attempting a sympathetic and lighter tone and leaving out much of the statistical and factual evidence that the *Letters* contain. In *Household Words*, Martineau discusses the geological history and potential uses of peat, a coach manufacture in Dublin, a slate quarry on a West coast island, a workhouse, and an eyewitness's account of the Famine. The first three articles, in other words, address the resources of the land and point to areas in which Irish industry might be (or, in the case of the coach manufacture, already has been) 'developed' and rendered profitable, while the latter two focus predominantly on the Irish people and their recent misfortunes.

Martineau's view of the country itself, its resources and potential, is cautiously hopeful. Although the current state of the peat industry 'is not encouraging', the project has 'everybody's good will meanwhile', so that it may lead to 'the employment of plenty of Irish labour, and the creation of plenty of Irish wealth'.[28] The slate quarry on the western Irish island Valentia is a promising if singular instance and may yet become 'a school of social progress to the whole West of Ireland, where such a school is sorely needed'.[29] The coach manufacture in Dublin stands, again, as a shining if isolated example of Irish entrepreneurship and craft.

The reason why Martineau's optimism is restrained lies not in Ireland's resources but in the people who develop them. The Irish Peat Company only employs fifteen men who 'look as if they did not know what hearty work was'[30], while the coach manufacture is nearly brought to its knees by the bigotry, stupidity, and obstinacy of its ungrateful employees who repeatedly turn violent and mutinous. Valentia's slate-labourers, on the other hand, work 'steadily and gravely', but they are seen as exceptional, since 'the slate-quarrymen of our [British] islands are, for the most part, a primitive, and even semi-barbarous set of people'.[31] Throughout the article Martineau stresses how exceptional these Irish workers are: they work hard, and 'if spoken to, they answer calmly, and with an air of independence—without vociferation, cant, flattery, or any kind of passion. *Yet* these people are all Irish'.[32]

As her surprise in this passage indicates, Martineau's view of the Irish and their recent misfortunes is ambivalent. For example, she describes the workhouse inmates as helpless, innocent victims of the Famine, 'a calamity which has swept over the length and breadth of their country'.[33] On the other hand, she implies that 'working for wages was never the rule among the poorer classes', and poverty is seen as 'less of a fault and disgrace than it is usually esteemed'.[34] Thus, beggars refuse to enter the workhouse because they are 'accustomed to whiskey, tobacco, gossip, and idleness' and don't want to give these pleasures up. Some inmates are 'incorrigibly idle', even deliberately infecting themselves with diseases since they 'would suffer a good deal to avoid work, or to obtain the superior diet necessary' for recovery.[35] In a similar rhetoric move, 'The Famine Time' starts off with the description of a beggar who 'always came back, refusing to work, and preferring [. . .] to beg' and a girl who 'got into a passion, and showed it, as Irish people do when they get angry'.[36] These instances of incurable laziness and lack of self-control, both of which Martineau repeatedly notes with disapproval, qualify the otherwise heart-rending and sympathetic account of the Famine that follows. The tension between compassion and disgust, between viewing the Famine as arbitrary misfortune and as self-inflicted, is never resolved in Martineau's articles. Frequently, when sympathy is about to take over, for example at the meagre and monotonous diet of the workhouse occupants, she reminds herself and her readers that 'sentiment on the subject would be quite misplaced', since the current state of affairs is better than the previous.[37]

To prevent another famine, Martineau advocates workhouses, intermarriage with 'English girls, or girls who have received English training in household ways'[38], emigration to British colonies, and other wholesome innovations brought from England since the Act of Union. Emigration in particular is a useful way of siphoning off the excess population, since 'there is nothing to stay for here [. . .] and in Australia they are so pressingly wanted—both to spread comfort through existing homes, and to make new homes'.[39] Martineau pictures emigration mechanically and as the natural consequence of surviving the Famine. Thus, she disapproves of the workhouse inmates doing crochet-work, since

> that sort of work is a good maintenance for a woman in Ireland now [but . . .] it is to be supposed that the greater number of these girls will emigrate. Their art will not be of much use to them in an American wood, or on an Australian sheep-walk. I hope they are taught cooking, and washing, and plain-sewing, too.[40]

Evidently, sentiment would be 'misplaced' on this subject, too; emigration emerges as the golden solution to Ireland's problems. In her *Letters*, she states that 'we do not share this regret [of emigration as "an unmitigated misfortune"], though we can easily understand and cordially respect it. The clearance of the land by a method which secures the maintenance of the inhabitants seems to us a very great good', especially since it leaves the land free for British development and investment.[41] Harriet Martineau's articles on Ireland, then, are characterised by the same ambiguities and contradictions that are to be found in *Household Words*' treatment of Ireland at large, as the next section will show.

SOME IRISH DIFFICULTIES AND SOLUTIONS

Harriet Martineau's articles are further exemplary of *Household Words'* stance in that they treat Ireland as a problem that demands some form of English intervention. Although no single problem named in *Household Words* qualifies as *the* 'Irish difficulty', a number of individual problems are addressed in the journal's coverage of Ireland and Irish affairs.

Predictably, the Famine takes priority amongst these, since it killed nearly a million victims and forced as many again to emigrate, reducing Ireland's population by over twenty per cent in the years preceding *Household Words*.[42] Out of approximately thirty-three articles that *Household Words* published on Ireland, twenty-six appeared in the years 1850–1853, in the direct aftermath of the Famine, and most of these discuss explanations and possible remedies for poverty and famine in Ireland. To what extent Ireland is associated with squalor, poverty, and dirt, is shown by the fact that T.M. Thomas entitles his article on a sordid London district 'A Suburban Connemara' and describes its 'picturesque' poverty, the 'genuine Irish apathy' of its inhabitants, who live without 'communication to the civilised world'. To emphasise the 'Irish misery' that hangs about the place, Thomas asserts that it is 'a perfect reproduction of one of the worst towns in Ireland' and finds the experience in London 'as good as being there'.[43]

The causes *Household Words* writers ascribe to the Famine are manifold. One article, incredibly, attributes it to the dainty palate of the Irish poor: 'Starving men refused to eat Indian meal [. . .] In Ireland no one will eat bullock's liver [even] when men and women were dying under the hedges of bare hunger [. . .] It is a social disgrace to eat rye-bread.'[44] Other articles facetiously suggest that the Irish refuse to eat anything but potatoes, for which crop they have an insatiable appetite. Many articles, although sympathetic to the victims of the Famine, nevertheless imply that it was somehow due to a collective character flaw in the Irish themselves. For example, the narrator of 'The "Irish difficulty"' initially criticises the common stereotypes of the Irish and asserts that Con McNale, *although* neither alcoholic, aggressive, crude, nor blundering, is nevertheless 'a fine specimen of the finest *pisantry* in the world'.[45] But after Con has told his story of success (which he achieves by hard work, some luck, and an indulgent landlord) and suggests that other Irishmen should be encouraged to follow his example, the narrator replies, 'But all are not so persevering, so knowing, and so fond of work as you'. 'The force of my suggestion' shuts Con up.[46] He is, in other words, an exception after all.

The majority of *Household Words* writers, however, blame the Famine on Ireland's complex hierarchy of landownership, which the Encumbered Estates Act of 1849 intended to solve by accelerating the sale and redevelopment of bankrupt estates. A class of large-scale landowners let out their land to middlemen, who let it in smaller parcels to farmers, who in turn let some of it to their labourers and other tenants to grow their own food. The latter's direct dependency on their small piece of land, as well as the ever-increasing rents towards the lower end of the hierarchy, meant that small tenants and labourers had little to defend themselves against the Famine when the potato crop failed in 1845, even though most agriculture in larger farms was commercialised rather than hand to mouth.[47] If they failed to pay their rent, the farmers evicted them, often by brutal force.

Most *Household Words* writers are sympathetic to the tenants, who have no way of acquiring land or property through their labour, and argue that poverty and recklessness reign in Ireland 'because a labouring Irishman, in Ireland, can, by no labour, human or superhuman, living in Ireland, raise himself in the social scale'.[48] In comparison, *The Times* is sympathetic too, but also points out at regular intervals that the Irish themselves are not without blame and tend to violence and aggression against their landlords.[49] To amend this state of affairs, these writers propose changing Ireland into a meritocracy under the patronage of British capital and British management.[50] William Howitt imagines that the solution to Ireland's problems lies in persuading wealthy Englishmen to buy up estates in Ireland, and directs his article at them:

> Wherever Englishmen have purchased, they are satisfied with their bargains—and they find the people delighted to work for them [. . .] The people say, 'We like you Englishmen, because we can rely on you—and we like your money.' [. . .] Labourers here are plentiful, cheap, and good. I would not have a single Englishman employed here, except as a farmer. Let us have some good, substantial, intelligent farmers, as models and examples; but let us employ—as builders, carpenters, artisans, labourers—none but Irish. That will spread universal satisfaction.[51]

Like Fitzgerald, Howitt can only perceive the Irish in a subject position, although his judgement of their suitability as employees is far more sanguine than the former's. However, his model of English influence does not look quite so delightful if one considers that the great social divide in Irish society during and after the Famine was not between landowners and those who rented their land, but between farmers who controlled (though not necessarily owned) more than 20 acres and those who held less or no land at all.[52] In effect, Howitt demotes the Irish population to the status of dependent labourers and imagines a select elite of Englishmen in possession and control of Ireland. This corresponds exactly to the 'sovereign remedy' which contemporary British politicians envisaged as the solution to Irish agrarian unrest and agitation, namely 'the "reduction" of cottiers and smallholders to the status of wage labourers'.[53] For instance, *The Times* suggested that there was something inherently 'immoral' in a family's reliance on their own potato patch, as most of the year, 'except so much as may be requisite to raising the crop, is passed in almost complete idleness

[. . .] A population dependent on such a means of support must be thriftless, reckless, idle, and therefore immoral.' In contrast, the cultivation of wheat and other grains demanded the maintenance of a larger field, steady exertion, and a high level of co-operation of waged labourers, all of which encouraged 'physical and mental' wellbeing.[54] In this light, Howitt's assurance that the satisfaction would be 'universal' looks a little sanguine.

Howitt's fictitious English landowner, at any rate, is fully satisfied with his new estate, since

> he has discovered a new pleasure in life—that of planting a new colony. [. . .] He has all the freshness of adventure and enterprise of a far-off land, and yet he is in the United Kingdom of Great Britain and Ireland.[55]

This vision of Ireland as a colony in Great Britain's back-yard, a giant theme park within one day's travel from London, is typical of the attitude of many other *Household Words* writers—and contemporary thought—on the subject.[56] Browne's 'Con McNale' prospers under the patronage of his new Scottish landlord; Anna Sophia Grey describes the exemplary condition of a Mayo estate run as an experiment by some Scottish gentlemen; Percival Leigh suggests that wealthy (British) entrepreneurs might benefit from investing in large-scale peat mining and thus make Ireland 'respectable', 'ornamental', and 'useful'; and the slate quarry which Harriet Martineau visits is run by a Welshman and the living conditions of its Irish labourers improved by their intermarriage with English (or English-trained) girls.[57] Only the British—and especially English—influence can ensure that 'a new race, and new blood, will supersede the old half-caste, wrong-headed, and "encumbered" generation'.[58]

This process can be accelerated by helping impoverished Irishmen emigrate, which, according to *Household Words*, is as useful a solution to Irish difficulties as to English ones. Emigration comes up in virtually every *Household Words* article on Ireland, since it was such an intrinsic part of Irish reality during and after the Famine. Harriet Martineau is not alone in regarding large-scale emigration as the logical solution to Ireland's predicaments. Similarly, part of William Howitt's plan of colonising Ireland foresees that waged labourers use their saved earnings to emigrate to America, making room for 'active, intelligent Englishmen to settle [in Ireland], instead of going all the way to Western America, Canada, or to Australia.'[59] Emigration here turns into a game of musical chairs in which the English come out as the winners. It is quite illogical that the journal advocates emigration so strongly even after the Famine has already reduced Ireland's inhabitants by nearly a quarter (over-population should hardly be a problem), and that the same people who are, by implication, so much trouble while residing in Ireland, should suddenly become useful contributors to society in the colonies. This irrational solution, however, is tempting because it appears to resolve not only the economic difficulties in Ireland, but would also settle the discursive ambiguities. By emigrating, the Irish make a transition from being the absolute 'Other' within the framework of the British Isles, to becoming 'as good as English' in the context of the non-European colonies and their native populations.

Household Words' suggestions to end the Famine are, as Hoppen suggests, fairly typical of its time. Far more radical are the articles that regard the Famine not so much as the problem but as a God-sent *solution* to the 'Irish difficulty'. Howitt finds that the Famine has proven quite useful, since it 'annihilated, with mortal life, inborn prejudices more powerful than life or death itself', 'undeceived' the Irish population, and paved the way for a 'great, real, and progressive' future under the auspices of English investment and control.[60] The Famine thus becomes the deserved punishment of Irishmen's stubborn resistance to British rule, an act of divine retribution straight from the Old Testament. Mitchell's article on 'An Encumbered Estate' makes the same point in passing, although a lot less radically: 'The property became more and more steeped in pauperism and disorder, until at length it was cleared out by the famine and emigration.'[61] Indeed, the Famine actually conducted much of the 'social engineering' that the government hoped to implement in Ireland.[62]

One of those 'prejudices' to be eradicated is Catholicism, though this is less pronounced in *Household Words* than in other media of the time.[63] *The Times* claimed to have taken a fairly moderate view so far: 'While admitting that the state of [Ireland] is as little satisfactory in point of religion as in every other respect, [we want to] adjourn to a calmer time and a more opportune season the remedies which her case may require.' It gives the blame for the need to address this evil to 'the pope and his advisors', who have forced the issue prematurely.[64] After this, *The Times* consistently blames Catholicism for much of Ireland's miseries: 'It is impossible for the liveliest imagination [. . .] to keep pace with the Protean varieties of the Irish mind [. . .] the effect of all the operations of Irish priests and landlords is to cover their unhappy country with fresh disgrace.'[65] The Catholic Church and its officials are no better than 'grievance-mongers' throughout, seducing and misleading the hapless Irish population.[66] In comparison, *Household Words'* stance is relatively moderate. Charles Dickens's allegory 'A Crisis in the Affairs of Mr John Bull' personifies Ireland as John Bull's 'grovelling' sister, a lady 'in a horrible condition of mind and body [who] presented a most lamentable spectacle of disease, dirt, rags, superstition, and degradation'. This is because Catholics, represented as 'the Bulls of R.',

> are, by nature, an insolent, audacious, oppressive, intolerable race [and] the enemies of [. . .] the whole human race. [. . .] Wherever they go, they perpetuate misery, oppression, darkness, and ignorance. [Catholicism has] had far too much to do with [Ireland's] present state. There

> have been many other causes at work to destroy the strength of her constitution, but [Catholicism has] been at the bottom of it.[67]

Dickens imagines Catholicism not as an inherent part of Ireland but a parasitic external influence that Ireland foolishly invited in, and which has now irreparably taken hold of it. 'Squalor and ignorance' are the 'inevitable' consequences of adopting Catholicism.[68] Dickens does not explain exactly what is so bad about Catholicism or why it should lead to so much misery. Neither does he pay any attention to the fact that the most recent organised form of Irish opposition to British rule, the 'Young Ireland' movement, was a joint effort of both Catholic and Protestant Irishmen who aimed to transcend denominational differences.[69] Dickens's article is an extreme example (partly due to the farcical tone his fable adopts), but he is not entirely alone with this sentiment. Lady Grey's letter on 'Ballinglen' also states that

> the greatest difficulty in dealing with the Irish, is their religion; [but . . .] I am confident that there is much to be done with poor Paddy [. . .] schools and Scripture readers are, thank God, [. . .] bringing the greatest blessings of all—the Bible—within reach of these neglected creatures.[70]

Grey writes about 'poor Paddy' in much the same patronising tone as other *Household Words* contributors write about the benighted savages in exotic locations, as poor heathens who are in need of enlightenment by British missionaries. Both Dickens and Grey imply that Catholicism has nothing whatsoever in common with Christianity or the Bible, even though the actual differences in doctrine between the two denominations are relatively small. Harriet Martineau's article 'Peatal Aggression' puns, obviously enough, on the 'papal aggression' which was often seen as the root of all evil, notwithstanding that most aggression during this period *targeted* Catholics rather than emanating from them.[71] She also makes occasional reference to Catholicism as superstitious, but treats it more as an ineradicable fact that had best be treated with tolerance: 'Here may be seen the pleasant sight of Catholic and Protestant children sitting side by side, without any thought of quarrelling on theological subjects'.[72]

A more sympathetic view of Catholicism emerges in William Allingham's articles. 'The Irish Stationers', for example, describes a Catholic pilgrimage to a holy island in Lough Derg, County Donegal.[73] Although Allingham describes the experience from a 'heretic' perspective and initially jokes about his fellow pilgrims' superstitious beliefs, he nevertheless shows great approval of the concluding sermon:

> The Prior [. . .] addressed his audience in the most familiar conversational tone, and even translated the language of Scripture into the humblest and most modern vernacular. Yet, doubtless, this is the right

> way to preach to the understanding and hearts of the uneducated, and the Prior spoke like a man who took an interest in what he was talking about; while his language, though unadorned, was always correct and forcible; and his illustrations—in the course of which he introduced Tenant Right, Napoleon crossing the Alps, the Marquis of Anglesea, and the Pork Trade—were very much to the purpose. The congregation, on the whole, were earnestly attentive.[74]

Household Words thus at least allows for different perspectives to be shown, even though its overriding judgement tends towards seeing Catholicism as a superstitious nuisance.

Even without going into any more of the various Irish difficulties, the comparison between the different problems and solutions offered in *Household Words* suggests once again that the overriding trouble with Ireland is, after all, the Irish themselves. In the following, I will consider how *Household Words* characterises the Irish people as a whole.

IRISH PECULIARITIES

As with the English national character, *Household Words* never doubts for a moment that there is an essential, collective Irishness. However, in contrast to the relative hesitancy it showed in defining Englishness, the journal offers plenty of judgements on what the Irish are 'really' like.

Household Words writers are well aware of the long-standing culture of stereotyping the Irish. Yet, curiously, most of the writers who show their awareness of the artificiality of these stereotypes nevertheless end up confirming them to some degree. Browne's 'The "Irish Difficulty"' begins with the remark that 'Con McNale would have been summarily repudiated as an Irishman by our favourite farce-writers and slashing novelists', since he 'neither drank, fought, nor swore', but the article then suggests that Con is exceptional.[75] Henry Morley sets out to dismantle the image of the Irish as 'hot-blooded Celts', but then confirms that 'the fervid character of the Irish makes them as apt for hope as for despair'.[76] Mrs Hoare, an Irish writer from Cork, launches into her first article for *Household Words*, 'An Irish Peculiarity', by stating that national stereotypes 'are never patented without some foundation in truth', but that they transmute into 'glaring caricatures'. Thus, the typecast Irishman is 'always either immersed in love or drink and often a victim of both of these exciting predicaments:—telling humorous lies, making unheard-of blunders, winning money by his tricking cleverness, and losing it by his unaccountable folly; leading a good-humoured, reckless, rollicking life', and so on.[77] Such a beginning raises the expectation that the following anecdote will disprove these stereotypes, but not so. Hoare instead employs an Elizabethan division of the Irish into 'the Irish, the wild Irish, and the extreme wild Irish':

> The "Irish" of the present day are [. . .] pretty much like other well-bred members of the civilised world [But . . .] the lower orders—the "wild Irish" of the towns, and the "extreme wild Irish" of the bogs and mountains,—present some striking and picturesque peculiarities to justify the conventional Irishman of the old novel [. . .] Very deplorable, indeed, must be the state of an Irishman [. . .] when he can neither smile nor quarrel [. . .] He loves fun; but fighting is his pride and his glory. For fighting he forswears name and wealth.[78]

Thus we are back in the territory of the ethnographer's 'timeless present tense', which Mary Louise Pratt has diagnosed so perceptively.[79] The subsequent anecdote tells of a court case about a brawl. The defendant, who should try to prove his innocence, ends up bragging about his prowess in the fight, while the witness, who should 'prove that the [defendant] had used unnecessary violence', claims that the defendant was unable to knock him down, since neither would 'establish such proofs at the expense of their respective reputations'.[80] In a movement that mimics the role-reversal of the two brawling Irishmen, the article thus ends up reconfirming the same stereotypes it set out, apparently, to dismantle. Hoare clearly imagines the 'Irish' as equivalent to the middle stratum of Barrell's model—different from England, but on the same par (along with Europe, the remainder of 'the civilised world')—and the 'wild' and 'extreme wild' Irish as the Other, beyond the reach of civilising influence: 'It is no wild speculation to anticipate the probability, that fifty years hence there may be little apparent difference between an average native of England, Ireland (always excepting the "extreme wild Irishman") and Scotland.' [81] Yet for most of the article, Mrs Hoare refers to these 'extreme wild Irish' simply as 'Irishmen' without any further qualifications. Thus 'the Irish' as a collective group are still defined by what she initially perceives as 'extreme' and exceptional cases, which seem to justify the popular English stereotype about them.

Despite Mrs Hoare's concession that *some* Irish people are almost as civilised as the English, *Household Words* writers concur that the Irish as a whole are predominantly different, at least as long as they are viewed by themselves, rather than in conjunction with another subject people. This difference emerges in a number of ways besides the outright description of an Irish mentality. In describing some desperate assassins, Howitt makes much of the 'Celtic physiognomy [. . .]—the small and somewhat upturned nose; the black tint of skin; the eye now looking grey, now black; the freckled cheek, and sandy hair'.[82] Grey speaks of the 'usual Irish stature' as though it were perfectly obvious what she means by it.[83] Physical difference also extends to the ragged clothes and refusal to wear shoes, which Martineau and Sala comment upon.[84] Moreover, the speech of Irish characters is frequently transcribed as heavily accented. Even words that actually sound identical are spelled differently to mark the perceived contrast further. Thus, Con McNale's 'great' becomes 'grate', 'old' becomes 'ould', 'fuel' becomes 'fewel', and so on.[85] Occasionally, a writer explicitly points to the fact that they 'translate' the Irish dialect into English, since 'their brogue would have been unintelligible to English ears'.[86]

Most of *Household Words'* debate about the Irish character focuses, like Mrs Hoare, on the 'lower orders', and some characteristics seem to be uncontested.[87] *Household Words* finds that the Irish are merry, instinctively tactful[88], intelligent[89], generous[90], and loyal to their families and, occasionally, landlords[91]. On the negative side, they are given to violence[92], drink[93], superstition and prejudice[94], laziness[95], and dirtiness[96]. Many of the positive attributes have the potential to veer into negatives or are expressed in negative terms. For example, Henry Morley proves that the Irish are not inherently perverse, but rather rendered so by circumstances. Their 'success' in the colonies, however, only makes them 'grumble' as much as their English counterparts.[97] Other articles find that the Irish are clever, but they use their cleverness to tell lies and make excuses to get out of work or payment, or they become lippy (either amusingly or insolently so).[98] Anna Grey expresses her surprise at how clean the children of poor peasants are.[99] Allingham mentions the rebellious potential of the 'freedom of speech' that Irish street ballads express.[100] Crowe attributes questionable value to 'Irish earnestness', since it appears in the context of a relentless and bitter lawsuit which leads to the ruin and death of both parties. George Sala experiences 'agreeable disappointment' at finding Dublin and its inhabitants clean, wealthy, sober, and peaceful.[101] Martineau, as mentioned above, expresses her surprise that the slate-quarrymen she encounters work hard, behave impeccably, and cannot even 'properly be called ragged'.[102] Morley, Grey, and Howitt all share Martineau's astonishment at the fact that the Irish are willing to work for fair pay.[103]

By contrast, *Household Words* writers are never surprised by negative qualities in the Irish. George Sala's two articles about Dublin serve as a poignant illustration. The first describes the magnificence of Dublin and its unexpected *lack* of alcoholism, street crime, dirt, and xenophobia, all of which lead the narrator to wonder whether the expatriate Irish population in England is 'more Irish than Ireland?'—rather than whether the English idea of what 'Irish' means is perhaps mistaken.[104] After enthusing about the beauty of Dublin for the first two pages of the first article, he suddenly changes tone:

> There, gentlemen and brigadiers of Ireland! have I put enough *couleur de rose* on my palette? Is the picture sufficiently gaily tinted for you? [. . .] The more so, because I honestly aver that all I have stated of the splendour of the *first* aspect of Dublin is strictly unexaggerated and correct. The first! alas, the first! [. . .] but the second buys—experience, disillusion. [. . .] Remove my lady's false hair and paint; take out her false teeth; tear out her false eyes.[105]

He continues in this tone for two substantial paragraphs, only to conduct another U-turn: 'Mind! I don't say that all this is the case with Dublin—that there must needs be dirt and wretchedness behind the [. . .] splendour'. However, despite the denial, and although the rest of the article continues to describe the beauty, taste, and wealth of Dublin, the impression has now been raised that this is merely a façade. Little surprise, then, that the next article triumphantly proclaims: 'I have found them! The rags, the bones, the sawdust and the dirt, which I was at first unable [. . .] to discover'. Sala revels in the 'semi-continental picturesqueness, shabbiness [. . .] over-population, and frowsiness' and 'would strongly advise all travellers in Ireland, all painters of still life and *genre* subjects' to view the district where he has found these.[106] Sala's gleeful voyeurism is unusual for *Household Words* only in degree—many other articles find the misery and filth of the Irish population 'picturesque', too. Incidentally, Sala only describes the squalor of a single district, the Coombe, throughout, but this one area serves to erase the good first impression that Dublin has made, and Sala applies most of his inferences to the Irish in general. He concludes by admitting his 'inability to discover [. . .] why [the inhabitants of the Coombe] should appear to hold soap and water in such apparent detestation [. . .] and why they should not live a little less than pigs, and a little more like humans.'[107]

The implication that the Irish prefer to live like pigs is widespread. The manager of Howitt's imagined English colony admits that the neatness of their new accommodation

> would be very troublesome to the inhabitants for a good while. They would miss the nice holes in mud floors, where geese could paddle and pigs wallow, and they would miss still more the refuse pit at the front door [. . .] but he meant to accustom them to somewhat more civilised habits.[108]

Martineau asserts that the poor 'all shrank from the necessity of being washed on entering the [workhouse . . .] The inmates said—and say to this hour—that the washing is like stripping them of a skin, or a suit of clothes; the feel of the air directly meeting their skins so new and strange!' [109] Only 'English training in household ways' can improve this reckless predilection for dirt.[110]

More concerning to *Household Words* is the Irish hatred of England and their potential for revolution. Two articles mention the 1798 rebellion[111], several more the Irish suspicion against all things English. Thus, the labourers in a Dublin coach manufacture refuse to touch parts that were made in England and rebel against the employment of an English coach painter[112], and the villagers in 'Little Mary' become dependent on the benevolent heroine and 'at last [left] off abusing her "fine English ways"'.[113] Allingham is singular amongst *Household Words* writers in proposing that the Irish people are not merely rebellious out of principle and habit, but are consciously and intellectually involved in current affairs:

> Two butchers and a pensioner are talking politics, with a select audience, and showing a very intimate acquaintance with the news of the day (distinctly coloured, though, by the medium through which it has come), as well as no mean amount of general information and intelligence.[114]

William Allingham's 'Irish ballads', however, strikes a more ambiguous tone. First, he assures his readers that the market-criers' talk of shooting government agents 'is mere fun; but we must confess, too, that it is freedom of speech', a quality so essential to Englishness.[115] Later on, Allingham takes a less favourable view of the ordinary Irish people's political involvement:

> In Ireland, the mass of the people recognise but two great parties, the one, composed of Catholics, patriots, would-be rebels—these being interchangeable ideas; the other, of Protestants, Orangemen, wrongful holders of estates, and oppressors in general—these also being interchangeable ideas [. . .] It is true, there are Protestants who rank on the popular side [. . .] and the Young Irelanders exerted themselves to build an Irish party, on other than the old ground of priestly Catholicism; but herein lay one cause of their failure. THE PEOPLE, IN THE CONFUSED BRAINS OF ITS MANY HEADS, COULD NOT, WOULD NOT, AND WILL NOT UNDERSTAND MORE THAN TWO PARTIES.[116]

But despite this negative judgement of the political involvement of the Irish people, at least *Household Words* admits in places that the Irish are entitled to a political opinion and that they are discussing politics at all levels—something that is very rarely acknowledged in the case of Britain's non-European colonies, where only one or two high native dignitaries are allowed to speak about the subject at all, and then only to advise that the British rule should be stricter and more ruthless. No matter how much it may sneer at the ignorance and simple-mindedness of the Irish, *Household Words* does not entirely deny them a voice.

The picture that emerges from this brief sketch of *Household Words'* treatment of Ireland implies that the trouble with Ireland is the Irish people themselves. The physical qualities of Ireland receive much praise, and its resources in peat, pasture, game, agriculture and even industry excite *Household Words* writers' full approval. However, the people who live there are far more volatile and prevent England from exploiting these resources to their best potential. At best, the Irish are currently a 'poor ignorant helpless race', 'unfortunate and neglected', but show plenty of promise and are worthy of British intervention and patronage.[117] At worst, they are idle, deceitful, and given to drinking, swearing, mindless violence, and rebellion for rebellion's sake.[118]

Percival Leigh aptly expresses the 'Irish difficulty' as seen by *Household Words* in the conclusion of his second article on peat:

> If, therefore, by the kind permission of the various Irish agitators, political and theological, the Irish people could be enabled to devote their attention and energies to wholesome labour [. . .] they would go far towards realising those blessings which the hierarchy they are squabbling about has so long been invoking to such little purpose; and Ireland might be in the way of becoming a decent 'flower of the earth,' and a respectable 'gem of the sea;' instead of being [. . .] but indifferently ornamental, and inconsiderably useful either to the one or the other.[119]

England, of course, holds the monopoly on 'wholesome labour', as we have seen—ten weeks prior to Leigh's article, Charles Dickens and Richard Horne suggested the same antidote to those European nations plagued by rebellion.[120] Although *Household Words* is not always entirely clear what exactly is to be done about it, it leaves no doubt that Ireland's only hope of becoming 'decent', 'respectable', 'ornamental', and 'useful'—in other words, of becoming English—lies in the intervention and benevolent patronage of the British. Only then can the Irish develop into 'well-bred, well-educated members of the civilised world'.[121]

4 'Continental ways and means'
Europe in *Household Words*

THE AGE OF EQUIPOISE?

The decade in which *Household Words* appeared has famously been termed the 'Age of Equipoise' by William Burns in his book of the same title. Although subsequent criticism has re-appropriated and (mis)understood the term as a synonym of peace and stability, Burns used this phrase to indicate a precarious and fragile balance of several conflicting factors. Nowhere are the underlying tensions of the period more evident than in Britain's relationship with the European continent and its alternating self-definition as European and as insular. This chapter aims not to find out how *Household Words* depicts individual European countries—the mass of available material for such a project would justify making it the focus of a book in its own right, and there are a number of studies on Dickens and France or Italy already.[1] Instead, it attempts to determine how *Household Words* envisages such a thing as 'continentalness', a common ground that these individual countries share, or—if not—what structures this heterogeneous collection of countries falls into.

It also examines how *Household Words* reacted to contemporary affairs that affected Britain's relationship with Europe. A weekly journal that had to be prepared three weeks in advance could not provide news coverage of events as they unfolded. Moreover, *Household Words* did not intend to report so much as to instruct and entertain, and both these aims required a deeper curiosity than a mere skimming of current events—and more than skimming would scarcely have been possible in a weekly miscellany of twenty-four pages. Rather, it complemented the daily press and commented on the larger developments from a somewhat detached point of view. This chapter will show that its stance was often remarkably even-handed and 'pro-European', compared to the drift of the daily newspapers.

At the centre of my selection is Grenville Murray's series 'The Roving Englishman', which appeared in fifty-nine instalments from November 1851 until March 1856[2] and covers, geographically, Germany, France, Greece, and Turkey. Because of its relative range of material, its particular time of publication, and its idiosyncratic narrator, the 'Roving Englishman' series offers a rich source of material for examining where the boundaries of the European continent lie in the mid-Victorian imagination, and how the itinerant Englishman himself relates to the cultures he encounters.

BRITAIN AND EUROPE IN THE MID-NINETEENTH CENTURY

Martin Hewitt's reprise of Burns's *Age of Equipoise* states that 'tension is fundamental to [Burns's] equipoise. [. . .] Far from being "a lull, a centre of indifference", as Kitson Clark put it in 1962, it was a period of conflict and contestation on an almost unprecedented scale.'[3] Burns's examples of this contestation are mostly taken from domestic affairs, but it is no less evident on an international level, as this chapter will show.

One reason for recent writers' interpretation of 'equipoise' as 'stability' is that, on the face of it, Britain was in a relative state of peace in the 1850s. Both its armed conflicts in the period—the Crimean War and the Indian Rebellion—took place thousands of miles away, and the European continent seemed comparatively stable after the 1848 revolutions had subsided, although the memory of it lingered. 1848 was also significant because it reinforced the sense of Europe over and beyond its constituent countries. Hobsbawm writes that the 1848 revolutions were 'the first and last European revolution in the (almost) literal sense'.[4] The impression that this was a unanimous event across Europe is neatly captured in Sala's articles 'Perfidious Patmos' and 'Music in Paving Stones', which describe the motley assemblage of European refugees that have moved to London—German baritones, Greek merchants, Italian valets, and French contraltos.[5] Sala does not distinguish between the political situations in the countries they fled from or their reasons for coming to England; throughout, he treats them as a colourful but homogeneous mass.

Not only did 1848 strengthen the British concept of Europe as a single body, however; it also stressed the separation of 'insular' Britain from 'the continent' and caused Britons to feel 'more distinct from foreigners than at any time in their history', since the revolution, violent and far-reaching elsewhere, 'passed almost without a shudder' in Britain.[6] This allowed Britain to play the role of observer in the revolutions, viewing events from a distant—and higher—plateau.[7] The Victorians did not attribute their escape from revolution to any racial or 'natural' supremacy, even though it might have been expressed in those terms, but to the liberty supposedly inherent in British politics, its freedom of speech, and *laissez-faire* approach to economics.[8] In theory, it was thus possible for all civilisations to attain to this higher state of being. Until that day, though, all Britain could do was to give its European neighbours a helping hand and patiently wait for them to catch up.

This was the state of Britain when it entered the supposedly stable and confident 'age of equipoise'. But a brief look at the newspapers of the period, in particular *The Times*, suffices to show that Britain was actually in a very nervous state for most of the decade, always expecting an imminent war.[9] I have already mentioned the fears of revolution and invasion that the Great Exhibition, following so closely after the 1848 revolutions, invited. These fears proved wrong, of course, but only a few weeks after the Exhibition closed without any violent incident, Britain found new cause for alarm: on December 2, 1851, the elected French president Louis Napoleon seized complete power in a *coup d'état* and made himself emperor, raising new spectres of revolution and invasion, which continued to haunt the British press for over a year.

This balance only changed when, in 1853, tensions mounted towards Russia in the run-up to the Crimean War. While in the aftermath of the French *coup d'état*, *The Times* had been full of praise for the Russian emperor Nicholas, who single-handedly ensured the peace of Northern Europe against French aggression, it now reported that the czar had secret designs on Turkey and, simultaneously, that France and England had all along thought exactly alike—in other words, the roles of ally and enemy were reversed. Compared to the tone of the previous three years, with their emphases on the despotism and warmongering of France, its tyranny and oppression, this represents an extraordinary u-turn.

After the Crimean War, a slight lull occurred in Britain's relationship with the continent, since the emerging Indian Revolt took over public attention for some time. However, it was not long before British suspicions against France arose afresh. Since all available British troops had been dispatched to the Indian subcontinent in order to suppress and avenge the Rebellion, Britain suddenly felt vulnerable and exposed to its envious European neighbours.[10] By 1859, the happy friendship between France and Britain had already found an end, as

> France's naval building programme, coupled with Napoleon III's victories over the Austrians in Italy [. . .] revived in Britain the image of a dominant Imperial France; while in Paris it was discovered that it was in London that the revolutionary conspirator Orsini had hatched a plot, nearly successful, to blow up the Emperor on the way to the Opera.[11]

The tension was further exacerbated by two French publications in 1859: one was a 'Map of Europe in 1860', which proposed to redistribute the continent between its nations (though Britain's territory remained unchanged), the other a book that imagined what Napoleon Bonaparte would have done, had he won the battle of Waterloo—namely, to conquer England in 1817.[12] Britain's growing fears seemed confirmed when France and Russia, the two powers who had alternately aroused Britain's fears and suspicions during the decade, entered an alliance with each other in April 1859. This promptly led *The Times* to suspect that an all-out European war was inevitable, since between them France and Russia threatened 'not only Italy, but the East and the Rhine'.[13] Britain suddenly found itself alone, insular and isolated indeed.

From this quick survey, two different models of collective European characteristics are evident that continue and alternate throughout the decade—or rather, a distinction between 'the continent' and 'Europe' can be made. The first sees France, Russia, Austria, and Prussia as the 'Four Powers', and England as aloof from (and superior to) these. The fundamental characteristic that these powers share, according to this model, are 'despotism', highly repressive institutions, and a heightened military presence that borders on the absurd. This is the model that Bernard Porter sees summed up perfectly in Charles Lever's phrase 'Bureau and Barrack'[14], and which reigns during the various conflicts with France—roughly, between the European revolutions and early 1853, then again from early 1858. This model I shall call the 'continent', from which Britain sees itself as distinct. The alternative model—which prevails during the middle of the decade, when Britain and France were allies in the Crimean War—sees the 'four powers of Europe' as Britain, France, Prussia, and Austria, all pitted against Russia, the aggressor from outside. In this second version, 'Europe' stands for enlightenment, civilisation, and liberty, and Britain is not only included but central to it. Whereas the 'continental' model stresses Britain's difference and superiority, the 'European' model is inclusive and sees Britain as symptomatic of all that is best in Europe. Although their prevalence and meaning varied during the decade, there was nevertheless a continuing sense that a core of European / continental power and identity existed.

Of course, there were also numerous non-political influences on Britain's attitude to Europe in the 1850s.[15] One was the growing railway network over Western Europe, in particularly France and Germany—thus, in 1851, Charles Dickens recorded his amazement at a journey from London to Paris that took only eleven hours.[16] A writer in *Chambers's Edinburgh Journal* took great pride in the civilising influence of the railway, which is 'essentially English': 'England may be said to have sent out a missionary of improvement, whom nothing can withstand. The continent, with all its stupid despotisms, must improve, and become enlightened in spite of itself.'[17] Another, more important element was the spreading of the electric telegraph, which made it possible, for the first time, to transmit news from one country to the next in a matter of moments.[18] The first telegraph cable across the English Channel was laid in 1851, and over the following decade several European countries were connected to this network, from Sweden to Italy, famously resulting in the first 'electronic' war coverage from the Crimea.[19]

Both political and technical criteria cast France, Prussia, and Austria as the key players in Europe. Places such as Scandinavia, Spain, and even Italy remained the 'outposts of Europe', in *Chambers's* phrase, although they received attention in their own right.[20] 'The Roving Englishman' in

Household Words saw Constantinople, Malta, Gibraltar, and Cairo as the last boundaries of European influence, beyond which a traveller would be left to their own devices.[21] Mary-Louise Pratt, in her examination of European travel narratives about non-European parts of the world, states that the eighteenth- and nineteenth-century concept of 'European' excludes 'many regions of the geographical entity known as Europe' and usually refers to 'a network of literate Northern Europeans'.[22]

Naturally, Europe was not *always* viewed as a single unity—on the contrary, the overriding discourse in *Household Words* concerns individual countries and their idiosyncrasies. Neither did judgements on individual countries always agree. For most mid-Victorians, 'continental' was almost always synonymous with 'French', as the 'grand tour' that wealthy young Britons undertook to complete their education rarely went beyond France or, at best, Rome. France was Britain's direct comparator and erstwhile rival[23]; it attracted the greatest share of British diplomacy and of its trade in Europe and determined much of Britain's foreign policy[24]; French imperialism offered a counter-example to the British Empire and determined the British definition of the term at this time.[25] Not surprisingly, France also received by far the most coverage of any country in *Household Words*, with approximately 120 articles. In other words, 'continentalness' and 'Europeanness' clearly existed in degrees. In addition to the particular circumstances of the time, I propose that *Household Words* judges Europe along a line that runs, geographically, from northwest to southeast. France and some German states are more or less equivalent to Britain, if a little bit behind, and have some features that Britain would do well to emulate, such as the meritocracy of the French military or the German education system.[26] To the south, Italy and Spain are sloppy and romantic.[27] Greece, further east, is sloppy but no longer romantic, sporting a population that consists, all and sundry, of liars, traitors, and cheats. Greece and its neighbour Turkey, in actual fact, represent the very boundary of Europe; both are frequently termed 'Oriental' and almost indistinguishable.[28] Equally, the boundaries are vague in Eastern Europe, especially at the time of the Crimean war.

Yet, overwhelming as the discourse may be that focuses exclusively on individual countries, a second, alternative discourse of Europe as a single entity is in existence, even though the individual characteristics and even geographical coordinates attributed to that entity may vary from article to article.

EUROPEAN CONTRASTS

Compared to some of the articles in *The Times*, *Household Words'* general stance on Europe, and France in particular, appears positively cosmopolitan, and so does Dickens's own in his private life and travels. In Dickens's fiction of the period the continent repeatedly served as a refuge, if only a temporary one—Carker flees across the Channel with Edith Dombey, David Copperfield recovers from Dora's death in Switzerland, and Little Dorrit's family attempt to escape their prison past on a grand tour through France and Italy. In *Bleak House*, the continent does not feature as an actual location, but merely as a marker of importance in the repeated reverential reference to Professor Dingo's 'European reputation'—clearly, Europe matters.[29] The only markedly negative response is to be found in *A Tale of Two* Cities, although Dickens places the plot firmly in the historical past of the French Revolution and never sees 1789 France as symptomatic of 'the continent' in general. Tore Rem proposes that 'Dickens had both a critical attitude towards his own people regarding national identity and—for an Englishman at the time—a rather unusual openness to what Europe represented.'[30] Dickens's son Henry Fielding Dickens qualified this in the claim that Dickens 'had a very strong love for his country, though he himself used to say, laughingly, that his sympathies were so much with the French that he ought to have been born a Frenchman.'[31] His travels in the 1850s certainly seemed to confirm this judgement: in 1850 Dickens spent a week and in 1852 a fortnight in France; in 1853 he lived in France, Switzerland, and Italy for six continuous months; 1854 saw him in France for another three months, and between November 1855 and September 1856 he spent eight months in France, coming back to England only for a fortnight before Christmas and a spell of six weeks from April to June.[32] In his private letters, moreover, Dickens didn't mention Louis Napoleon or the *coup d'état* at all, and the Crimean War only came up when he expressed his annoyance that it diverted public attention away from more pressing social issues at home.

All in all, then, Dickens was comparatively tolerant of and receptive towards Europe and seems to have seen England as part of it—where he distinguishes England from it, it is often to point out England's shortcomings, as in 'Insularities'. Although Dickens is not synonymous with *Household Words*, this gives some clue as to the attitude that the journal would take. And indeed, given the political upheavals of the period, *Household Words'* coverage of Europe is remarkably apolitical. Only one article focused on the French *coup d'état* of 1851, and that concentrated mainly on personal observation of the events from a traveller's perspective; its judgements are restrained throughout. Although *Household Words* published plenty of material on the Crimean War, it either tended to describe the cultures and people in the Crimea without passing much political judgement, or it criticised the British government (rather than foreign ones) for its handling of military matters, and that usually in the form of a parable.[33] Compared to its coverage of Ireland or India and its views on the causes and solutions of Britain's difficulties with these, *Household Words* exercised a comparative reticence with regard to Europe.

From this follows an obvious point, but one nonetheless worth making—namely, that *Household Words* contemplates Europe and its countries from the perspective of a traveller and potential tourist, rather than that of a colonial settler and 'developer'. Writers on Europe focus on hotels, transport options, passport procedures, prices of fare and board, and the hospitality of the locals, rather than—as is the case with the colonies—on agricultural potential, mineral resources, and the tractability of the people. Regardless of the individual judgements the journal offers on European countries, the fact that Britain has no direct territorial claim in Europe remains evident throughout.

The Europe *Household Words* envisages is one of travel, tourism, and polite, social intercourse. One might perhaps expect this increased mutual contact to make Britain's view of Europe more complex and diversified, yet the exchange of travellers—in both directions—also cements the impression of Europe as a generic whole. To begin with, *Household Words* suggests that continental men share a visible characteristic: the most common mark of continentalness is male facial hair. The French writer Edmond Texier, in Sidney Blanchard's unfavourable review, finds that many English people perceive his moustache as 'shocking' (and, presumably, 'un-English').[34] The European expatriates in Sala's London form a pleasant mixture of beards, extravagant clothing, and foreign smells—one article mentions beards and moustaches no less than eight times in four pages.[35] William Duthie mentions a French nobleman who is so vain that he dyes his moustache.[36] On arrival after his speedy train journey, Dickens's first impression of France is a mass of, amongst other things, 'uniforms, beards, moustaches'.[37] Like Texier, he finds that the insular British attitude to facial hair is one of uncompromising intolerance, whereas 'in almost all the other countries of Europe, more or less of moustache and beard was habitually worn'—perhaps Dickens's own beard testified to his cosmopolitan outlook.[38] In other words, 'beard and moustache betray [the wearer's] foreign origin'—at least until returning soldiers from the Crimean War brought beards into fashion in the middle of the decade.[39]

Two articles in particular provide important clues to the respective value of Europe in *Household Words'* view of the world, Wilkie Collins' 'My Black Mirror', from September 1856, and Eliza Lynn Linton's 'National Contrasts' from October 1858. Collins's narrator reminisces, with the help of a magical mirror, on various continental holiday destinations that he has visited in the past.[40] He muses about his travels 'in civilised countries' such as Austrian Italy, German-Switzerland, and Switzerland Proper, only to find shortcomings in all of them. These range from the narrator's own prejudices (e.g. the 'suspicion of a stiletto' under men's cloaks in Austrian Italy[41]), geological or practical obstacles (e.g. the dangerous mountain-paths and obstinate mules of Switzerland), local mentality (e.g. a German-Swiss waiter's failure to 'genially amuse and gently tickle my [. . .] self-esteem'[42]), or fleas, to the surveillance state and passport controls in 'a despotic country' such as Austria. In spite of all these differences, however, the individual regions are nevertheless subsumed under an overriding sense of unanimity and sameness. They are still, all and sundry, 'civilised countries' running the same race as Britain, even though they are lagging behind, while places like the colonies are not deemed worthy to compete on this high level.[43] Questioned by Austrian authorities, the narrator adds his own internal monologues: 'Second, What is my nation? (British, and glad to cast it in the teeth of continental tyrants.)' A single, local feature—here, the bureaucratic demands of the Austro-Hungarian Empire—is attributed to the entire continent, since it confirms one of the two key characteristics that the mid-Victorians identified in their European neighbours: 'For the "free-born Briton," "Bureau and Barrack" just about summed it up.'[44] In the end, the narrator decides to go yachting around the British coast as the ideal combination of adventure and creature comforts, avoiding all 'anxieties about strange beds', 'strange cooks', and the dangers of trespassing borders and boundaries.[45] The idea of a 'black mirror' is a significant clue to the piece's attitude to the continent: it is an imperfect but comparable version of Britain itself.

Eliza Lynn Linton's 'National Contrasts' hints at an underlying structure of the world, moving from the most remote edges of humanity—such as China or India—closer to home, moving from the edge of the 'concentric circles' to its centre. Importantly, she reminds her readers: 'See what contrasts we have even in Europe itself, where one would most look for likeness.'[46] John Barrell's 'this, that, and the Other' springs to mind once again: compared to completely 'alien', non-Europeans nations such as China or India, Europe is very similar to England, yet a closer look reveals contrasts that in turn allow England to emerge as a unified nation with a stable set of characteristics. As the article draws ever narrower circles around England, Europe moves from the centre ('we [. . .] in Europe') of the rhetorical model towards the periphery, where contrast is everything.

Recent criticism has made an important distinction between 'difference' and 'diversity'.[47] 'Difference' implies a vertical hierarchy of value—the more something deviates from the norm, the less it is perceived to be worth. 'Diversity', on the other hand, acknowledges that difference may exist on the same, horizontal plane of value—two things may be different from each other, yet be of comparable worth. In the terms of this framework, Lynn's article establishes a continuum of difference, stretching from China to England. Europe represents a turn-off from this otherwise relatively straight vertical line: European countries are distinct (and diverse), but exist on the same level of worth as England. It adds multiplicity to an otherwise fairly linear hierarchy of the world. The same could be said of Ireland, as I discussed in my last chapter. But whereas Ireland complicates matters because its position on the linear continuum itself is unclear—it fluctuates between 'same' (as a part of the United Kingdom) and 'different' (as a colony)—, Europe adds a new term to the model and renders the linear scale of difference insufficient. In *Household Words'* view, European countries are diverse, but comparable to Britain; they exist on a similar level of worth and 'civilisation'—the overriding impression, in a global context, is 'likeness', not 'contrast'. Whenever the journal mentions 'foreigners', these invariably turn out to be Europeans (regardless of the writer's initial expectations of more exotic visitors[48]). For example, Dickens defines 'insularities' by comparing British attitudes to those of the adjacent 'continent of Europe' as a whole. As Bernard Porter phrases it, 'Nowhere in the world was more important than Europe: Europe *was* the world. The rest was periphery.'[49] Ridicule them as it might, Britain could not but recognise European countries as partners—or rivals—of similar might and weight. Europe offered an arena for Britain to compete in and play opponents in the same class; non-European countries formed, as it were, the instruments with which the contest was fought.

Of course, Lynn's version of Europe is by no means exhaustive—the only countries she mentions 'nearer home' are Andorra, Spain, France, Scotland, and Ireland.[50] In the final paragraph of her article (which at times veers into satire), Lynn turns the argument on its head, as indicated in a previous chapter: 'Fancy all these things [such as the injustices of the social system, the trade in adulterated goods], [. . .] and then say whether Chinaman or Hindu submits to more absurdities than the Englishman of the nineteenth century does.'[51] But the joke depends on the reader's general assumption that Chinaman and Hindu are as far removed from the Englishman as it is possible to be. Whether or not one reads the characterisation of the different nations as serious or satire, Lynn's article suggests the simultaneous existence of a sense of Europe as a single entity, and of a continuum of difference within that entity, possibly according to distance from 'home', i.e. Britain.

THE ROVING ENGLISHMAN

The wealth of material and the geographical areas covered makes Murray's 'Roving Englishman' series particularly pertinent in a consideration of *Household Words*' stance on Europe, especially as its changing focus mimics that of Britain at large in this period. Murray's narrative begins, in November 1851, in Germany and Austria, then moves—by March 1853—briefly to France and Italy, all interspersed with some general advice and opinion on travelling, dining, choosing servants, buying horses, and the British diplomatic service. From July 1853 until January 1855, the series turns its attention to Greece and Turkey (in approximately 22 instalments), the Northwestern corner of the Ottoman Empire.[52] After that, there is a detour of three instalments to the locations of the Crimean war, before the series turns to Bulgaria, along the Danube, then to Belgium and London (with three articles, two more about the Danube and one on Messina, added as an afterthought). In particular, the articles that focus on Greece and Turkey raise the question of where Europe actually ends and 'the Orient' begins. It is precisely the hybridity of Western and Eastern elements in this location that excites much comment, which sits side by side with simultaneous sweeping generalisations about the character and disposition of 'all Orientals'. Finally, the central focus and unifying factor of the series is rarely the places that the narrator visits, but the narrator, the self-styled 'roving Englishman', himself. Before turning to the series' judgements and observations on the places it discusses, I will therefore consider Murray's narrator as a traveller and travel-writer *per se*.

The title of the series itself is enlightening in this context. The first two instalments started off as 'A Roving Englishman', but from the third onwards the indefinite article changed to the definite 'the'. This alteration indicates a shift of emphasis from an individual traveller to 'the Englishman abroad' as a type. Fundamentally, the series is not so much about Europe by itself, but about the relation between Britain and Europe, as exemplified by one archetypal Englishman.

Eustace Clare Grenville Murray wrote his sketches largely from personal experience. Born in 1824 as the illegitimate son of a nobleman, he worked in the diplomatic corps from 1851 onwards, serving 'successively in Vienna, Hanover, Constantinople, Mytilene, and Odessa, in a career marked by bitter friction with officials under whom he served.'[53] After he left the diplomatic service in 1868, he returned to England but shortly afterwards fled to France while on bail from a lawsuit for libel. For a diplomat, he seems to have been rather indiscreet at times, and this belligerence is traceable in his narrator, too. Murray never went back to England, working as a journalist and foreign correspondent for various British publications until his death in 1881.

Although 'The Roving Englishman' is based to some extent on Murray's own biography, he develops a fictional persona in the series—the first instalment suggests that his name is 'Smith'[54], a later one claims that he is an 'old gentleman in a dressing-gown and slippers', although his opinions and narrative style usually belie this claim.[55] What his business is in travelling or residing in the countries he visits, he never openly states, yet one may infer that he acts as a diplomat for the British government. It is apt that the narrator should be a representative of Britain professionally as well as rhetorically—the lack of information about himself and his conventional name indicate that he is more a type than a person, offering a counterpart 'Briton' to the typecast Greek, German, Turk, and Frenchman whom he consciously sketches not as individuals but as specimens exemplary of the entire country.[56] The implication is that his opinions and judgements—and there is no shortage of either—are as typically English as the roving Englishman himself.

However, some of his views are clearly subjective and influenced by a particular, predictably wealthy background.[57] For example, 'His Hints to Travellers' recommends certain nationalities as servants (a subject on which he elaborates five instalments later in 'Travelling Servants') and contains a range of random advice on luggage, bribes, means of transport, food, and how to travel cheaply and comfortably. This indicates that Smith is (and expects his readers to be) quite well off, if not exactly rich: economy is advisable, as long as it does not conflict with comfort.

One of the most persistent features of Smith's worldview is a degree of chauvinism. He offers some advice to travelling women (or rather, to men travelling in the company of women), from choosing sensible clothes ('tight lacing has spoiled many a pleasant tour') to avoiding the *table d'hôte* and the vulgar company it attracts. Here, as elsewhere, Smith adopts a fairly patronising tone: 'Ladies who are not in time to start by the train they have fixed upon, should be threatened with the penalties of the second class, and [. . .] actually be once shown into it just to frighten them'.[58] Therefore they 'had better stay at home as much as possible', if they cannot afford to travel first class (or perhaps altogether).[59] In an instalment on equestrianism, Smith claims that horses suffer torments 'in the hands of ladies, boys, and other utterly misguided people'.[60] Women, where they feature at all, tend to be an encumbrance and a distraction from the manly business of travelling; at best, they offer sanctuary as hostesses. Thus, the narrator expresses his admiration of the landlady of an Austrian inn who anticipates and satisfies his every need and 'is quite a mother to me'. However, the landlady's bill mars that impression of domestic bliss, and Smith resorts to sarcasm: 'What cares she for [her guests...] except as materials of trade? She is true to the nature of her sex, in working these materials energetically.'[61] The confirmation that she is hospitable for a living, not out of generosity and altruism, taints the über-feminine landlady—but then, that initially un-feminine mercantility itself becomes a telltale mark for the entire sex.[62] Much better the ladies in an all-female convent on Lesbos, who freely ply Smith and his companions with rakee, coffee, sweetmeats, and tobacco. So far from Britain and its notions of gentility, Smith drops any pretences of delicacy and appraises the convent's inmates outright: 'as those in our room were rather elderly, we asked to see some more of the sisterhood.'[63] Although he occasionally criticises the Greeks and Turks for keeping their women as 'beautiful dolls, without mind, or heart'[64], he in fact views them in the same way as dehumanised objects for aesthetic contemplation, whether negatively—Greek women's figures 'are the same size all the way down, with no more symmetry than sacks of wheat'[65]—or positively: 'The next time our friends in Australia want a few ship-loads of wives, I think they might do many less sensible things than send to Mytilene.'[66] At best, women are hospitable (without mercenary motives), beautiful, and quiet; at worst, they are greedy, stupid, man-eating tyrants.

Some curious contradictions emerge in the narrator's attitude to travel in general. For one, Smith has very distinct ideas on how much time a traveller should take to get accustomed to a country: 'As a rule, a young man travelling to complete his education should pass at least three months in each of the great countries of Europe, or he is likely to carry away a very incorrect idea of each.'[67] On the other hand, 'Englishmen long established in any foreign country are generally full of prejudices against it'.[68] This suggests that diplomats like Smith himself are in an ideal position to get to know a place best without diluting their judgement with prejudice born from long residence. Smith advises travellers to make their way into society of the place they are visiting, but to be careful what they say, since their 'very valet is almost certain to be a spy'. For this reason, the best company they can choose are 'the gentlemen of [their] own embassy' (diplomats again), even though this seems to defy the point of travelling in the first place, and he has earlier advised travellers to 'seclude yourself altogether from the society of your countrymen' in order to learn the local language.[69]

Once on the road, Smith advises British travellers to be polite, since 'foreigners do not all of them think England is the finest country in the world', and to 'make [themselves] as little remarkable in any way as possible' in order to avoid gold-diggers.[70] Yet he also tells them to lodge only in the best hotel in any place, or if this be unsatisfactory, to ride up to the 'first man in the village' and 'ask [outright] for entertainment for himself and suite'.[71] If anything were unsatisfactory, they should raise an immediate complaint in no uncertain terms. Smith repeatedly criticises (Northern) Europeans' condescension and arrogance when they're abroad, yet patronises and belittles most people he comes across. For example, while staying with a winegrower in Greece, he graciously gives 'our host some hints about his trade of wine-making, which I picked up long ago in Spain'.[72] In discussing hunting in Greece, he condescendingly expresses his approval of a huntsman who 'understands his business pretty well for a Greek'.[73] All in all, Smith emerges as an opinionated and cantankerous traveller, in spite of his repeated advice to behave in a good-natured, amiable, and unobtrusive way.

The question remains what his aims are in writing down and narrating his experiences, and how he goes about it, given that English travel-writers are so ubiquitous in his period that, on the European continent, 'it is generally thought that an Englishman travelling, is making notes for a book, to be published when he gets home'.[74] Smith announces his intentions most clearly about halfway through the series:

> I do not know whether such little sketches of far away life and manners as I paint so poorly may please you; but at any rate they are fresh from nature, and I hope no word ever creeps into them to make any man the worse. If, therefore, in passing an idle half hour with the Roving Englishman, you should acquire a better knowledge of other nations than you had before, it will not be time misspent; for I honestly believe that most of the wars and ill feeling between nations arise from not knowing each other better.[75]

Remarkably, this statement concludes an instalment of almost undiluted criticism of the Greeks—or at least of one of the two 'types' of Greeks—as cowardly, lazy, dishonourable rogues[76], so it is questionable how well suited to remove ill feeling it may be. The contrast between declared intention and tone of this piece is so extreme, in fact, that one might almost suspect irony. Similarly, the narrator frequently criticises a particular thought pattern or habit and then does precisely that of which he disapproves. For example, he criticises the voyeurism of some bystanders who watch an epileptic suffer a fit: 'half-scared and half-amused [. . .] at his contortions [. . .], they stood so obstinately near to see what was going on, that the whole apartment was one living mass.'[77] These people are, however, the epileptic's relations, whereas Smith does not explain what his own business on the scene is. Earlier in the same instalment, he had 'sprung out of bed' to watch a village fire, 'anxious to visit a scene so fearfully interesting.'[78] On neither occasion is the narrator directly affected by or involved in the goings-on; he merely satisfies his curiosity and condescendingly professes 'quite an admiration' for a 'Greek despot' who saves a woman from a burning building.[79] The most poignant example of his tendency to disavow his own actions comes towards the end of the series, when Smith paradoxically moralises, 'We certainly have no right to judge other countries by our own peculiar standard of right and wrong; but there must surely be something radically rotten in all this'.[80]

Finally, Smith states in his last instalment that travelling makes observers 'discern that the most ordinary person is invested with some noticeable characteristic'.[81] One might expect travel writing to reflect this individuality, yet Smith's narrative does quite the opposite: it makes sweeping generalisations, portrays people not as individuals but as 'types'[82], and finds enough evidence in a handful of Greeks or Turks to conclude on 'all Orientals'.[83] This suggests that Smith is aware of the simplifications he makes—yet he seems to believe that he makes them in order so that his English readers may have a better knowledge of other cultures and peoples.[84]. He is also aware that he may be seen as prejudiced: 'Russian despotism is diabolical. [. . .] This is not a mere figure of speech; it is not an ungenerous and illiberal sneer at Russia, because we are at war with her; it is merely a plain, indisputable fact.'[85] All in all, then, Murray's narrator emerges as a shrewd rhetorician who boosts his own profile as an expert on the countries he visits and the judgements he offers, even though he does not always follow his own advice, and who pre-empts any potential accusations of bias.

Inderpal Grewal's book *Home and Harem* starts off on the premise that travel narratives (in colonial and 'exotic' territory) usually show 'a disdain for "natives"'.[86] This is certainly the case in such purely colonial narratives as John Lang's 'Wanderings in India' (see chapter 5). Murray's series shows some ambiguity in these criteria, though. The narrator rarely has a good word for the native cultures that he encounters, but frequently he compares them, at their worst, to Britain, which is found to be equally bad. For example, after a lengthy criticism of the 'short-sighted cunning', 'ungenerous enmity and ignorant perseverance' of the Turkish aristocracy, Smith concludes that

> we must not think that Britain is the only land which has such precious work with little great men. Huffi Pacha and Scruffi Effendi are to the full as wicked and wrong-headed as our own white-gloved cousinocracy.[87]

In other points of criticism (unrelated to class), too, does Smith relate the worst behaviour he can find in his host country to Britain—for example, the Turkish love of gossiping and scandal is as extreme as that 'amongst the western nation of which I am a native'[88], and in some points—such as burying the dead[89]—Turkey is actually more civilised than England.

Grewal identifies the 'need to merge with the "native" culture and not be seen as a visitor' as another characteristic of imperial travel-narratives.[90] Perhaps it is a consequence of the fact that Murray's narrative is set in non-imperial, European areas that Smith prefers to stand out. Since such a fundamental visual difference was perceived between Englishman and, say, native Indians, the boundaries could only be blurred momentarily and deliberately. In a European context, on the other hand, the difference is slippery enough to disappear altogether at times, therefore Smith usually insists on maintaining his distance. He advises travellers to be unobtrusive and to learn the language of a country they visit, but he nevertheless prefers observing proceedings from afar to getting involved in them directly, not from shyness but from superiority. The conflicting attitudes in Smith's narrative stem from the fact that he cannot quite decide whether the areas he writes about are European or not. Thus, the narrator certainly has the propensity to look out passively and to appropriate discursively what he sees in the ways he sees fit, but time and again he has to remind himself and his readers that 'your true-bred Briton, [who...] is not a linguist, [. . .] gets hot and excited, [. . .] blusters, bullies'—in other words, a stereotypical imperialist—must mind his manners in Europe: 'A guest among strangers—this is his position, and he should never forget it.'[91]

REVOLUTION, EXHIBITION, AND COUP D'ÉTAT: 1850 TO 1853

Since the decade is so clearly divided into distinct periods with regard to Britain's relationship with Europe, I will look at the remaining key issues in chronological order, in order to assess how *Household Words* compares to the pattern set by *The Times* and other media of the period. The first of these periods comprises the years between the European revolutions and the beginning of the Crimean War, including the Great Exhibition and Louis Napoleon's seizure of power.

As indicated previously, Britain was in a permanent state of worry and nervousness during these years. While the technical advances such as railway and telegraph promoted cohesion and unity across national boundaries, the political events in Europe and Britain's reaction to them suggested a temporary lull rather than a proper peace. For instance, *Bentley's Miscellany* seemed to be equally worried about Russia and France at the beginning of this period. Russia's ambition, it surmised, was to become a new superpower to replace the old hegemonies of England and France. It outnumbered the rest of European nations in both population and territory and was completely different from Europe in 'the originality of ideas and manners, and [. . .] the singularity of [its...]social and political life'.[92] Although it described incredulously the near-divine level of worship of the czar, the censorship, and Russia's general harshness to other nations, the magazine also could not suppress a faint tone of admiration: 'The Russian nation being thus richly endowed with the valuable gifts of penetration, of sociability, and of courage, which she inherits from the Slave blood, has a wide field open to her.'[93] The same grudging admiration occasionally surfaced in *The Times* during this period. With regard to France, *Bentley's Miscellany*, abandoned its initial vow not to meddle in politics and worried about the newly elected president Louis Napoleon III:

> One of the most striking and unexpected [results of 1848] has assuredly been the re-installation of the name of Bonaparte at the head of the government. The circumstance naturally [. . .] leads to the assumption that what is styled his system of government may, in all probability, be revived. In which case the French will not have to be lauded and congratulated on their progress towards freedom.[94]

It outlined in detail Napoleon Bonaparte's reign and implicitly suggested that 'his system of government' could soon be ascending again, and with it his aggressive attitude to Britain.

In contrast to these highly political appraisals of current affairs, *Household Words* began the period with some general comparisons of the state of the press, education, and social reform in Britain and Europe. In these articles, Britain usually stands out as separate from its European neighbours, but not always as superior. Henry Morley's 'Views of the Country' celebrates the British press as the single guarantor that ensures that liberty and social reform will continue to improve in England, which is to be rivalled by 'no other European country'. On the other hand, Morley accedes that England is behind most of Europe in its retention of the feudal system of landownership, a drawback it shares only with 'Russia and some of the worst governed portions of the Austrian Empire'.[95] W.H. Wills finds that, in the realm of education, 'England stands the lowest in the scale of [. . .] civilisation', since 'with us, education is a commodity to be trafficked in; abroad, it is a duty'. 'Abroad', in this case, is 'the whole of Northern

Europe—including Scotland—and France and Belgium'.[96] When Dickens and Morley make the same point eight months later, they use Germany as a positive counter-example, as well as Scandinavia and France: 'Your true ignorant children are to be found—out of England—only in Spain, Portugal, and South Italy, or among Turks and Russians.'[97] Between them, these two articles define 'civilised' Europe as Northern. The exception of England, naturally, only applies to individual areas and is ironic—criticism stands out because England is *typically* at the head of civilisation. The condemnation of English education is also not set in stone—two years later, Charles Lever criticises education especially in France and Germany, compared to an English education.[98] The division of Europe into Northern and Southern characteristics is a popular one: Lynn's 'The Workmen of Europe' makes a clear distinction between south-east and north-west Europe[99], and Murray's 'Roving Englishman' finds that 'southern nations are less given to excess than northern ones' in matters of food and drink.[100]

We have already seen that *Household Words'* treatment of the Great Exhibition as a union of nations was tentative at best. Articles that started off by celebrating universal harmony usually ended up singling Britain out as the most advanced of all countries, standing in the 'honourable relation of teachers to other nations'.[101] *Household Words* tried to dispel fears of revolution and invasion, and advocated a welcoming and friendly attitude to foreign visitors, but these visitors never ceased to be foreign and distinct.[102]

During the Exhibition summer of 1851, both *The Times* and the *Illustrated London News* criticised the continental nations bitterly, and particularly France, for refusing the 'uncongenial friendship of free England' in favour of tyranny and despotism.[103] For all their declared love of liberty and independence, the 'three great nations of Continental Europe' were still unfit for a properly liberal government. France, for example, 'is, after all, but a semi-barbarous nation, splendid, no doubt, but rotten and unsafe; having all to learn and much to endure before it can really be fitted for the enjoyment of equable and rational liberty.'[104] Louis Napoleon's *coup d'état* in December of that year only confirmed these publications' worst fears and threw the British press into confusion and sinister prophecies. One letter-writer to *The Times*, Lord Mount-Edgcombe, claimed to have accurate and specific information that France was planning to invade Britain in the imminent future, since Louis Napoleon needed to win popular support for his reign—and what could be better suited to win the French than the promise of 'humbling "*les fiers Anglais*"'?[105] The *Illustrated London News*, which frequently lectured the public to keep up its morale in the midst of reporting crises, proposed that Britain look forward instead of criticising the done deed retrospectively, since the urgent question in hand was Britain's future relation with France. It predicted three possibilities: France would either try to conquer central Europe and start an all-out European war, or join forces with the other 'military and absolutist states' of Europe and attack Britain—conceivably, though, Louis Napoleon might actually turn out to be 'a statesman as well as a soldier' and desire to give his country genuine freedom through an alliance with Britain, which held the monopoly on liberty.[106] By 1852, *The Times* conceded that 'Europe has not been torn piecemeal by invasion and defeat', and that France's revolution had not managed to overturn the 'present European Union'.[107] But it continued to worry about the balance of power in Europe, and saw France as the main source of trouble until halfway through 1853. Even then, when the Russian czar emerged as the new aggressor and France was discovered to have been thinking along the same lines as Britain after all, *The Times* found that Queen Victoria was the only just, and therefore stable, monarch in Europe, while all of 'continental Europe' held a 'frail tenure of power', demonstrating the advantages of a constitutional government over a 'despotic' one.[108]

By comparison, *Household Words*, which was not usually afraid to express an opinion, remained remarkably quiet on the subject of the French *coup d'état*. It published only one article, written by George Augustus Sala, as soon after the event as *Household Words'* publication process allowed. However, Sala had little to say on the political motivation behind the events he witnessed—his account is first and foremost a description of events from a foreign traveller's perspective. Although Sala sharply condemns the brutal violence he witnessed and the apparent lack of concern of the French, his notoriously flippant style also shines through.[109] Only six weeks later, Charles Lever asserted in *Household Words* that 'there are many valid reasons for at least an occasional residence' on the continent.[110] Compared to the state of alarm that other publications were in, Lever's reasons against living on the continent—the bad foreign education and the surprising cost of living in comfort—seemed negligible.

Lever, the Anglo-Irish novelist and later a regular contributor to *All the Year Round*, had coined the phrase 'Bureau and Barrack', which Bernard Porter sees as symptomatic of the mid-Victorian attitude to the European mainland. His one article in *Household Words*, 'Continental Ways and Means', is an enlightening example of the confusion and contradiction that often crept into contemporary views of Europe. On the one hand, Lever mocks 'the unqualified opinion of every Englishman [. . .] that the whole Continent is miserably poor [. . .] from Norway to Naples', and thus ridicules the overriding generalisations on which the concept of a unified 'Continent' rests. On the other, Lever swerves between the macroscopic (continental) and microscopic (local) perspectives without much warning or, indeed, distinction. For example, he opines that the climate of Europe is not much better than in Britain, that 'continental summers are almost unexceptionally good', whereas the winters in Paris, Brussels, Germany, or that quarter of Pisa which runs along the Arno, all differ from each other (thus, 'Italy has a dozen climates'). Both the sweeping simplification, which regards the entire continent as one, and the highly localised distinctions between individual towns all within a 100-mile radius of each other (such as Milan, Pisa, Florence, and Spezzia), evoke the impression that the European continent is a mass of largely interchangeable and randomly assembled parts. At the same time, this mass is clearly restricted to the European continent, and non-European countries do not enter into the equation. Thus, Lever uses the words 'continental', 'foreign', and 'abroad' synonymously throughout his article.[111] If Europe is 'foreign', the world outside Europe is nothing short of alien.

Not only does 'the Continent' have 'few advantages on the score of climate', but Lever also finds that the necessities of life—such as houses, servants, wine, and education—are no cheaper on the continent than in Britain, or 'if these be cheaper, they are inferior also'.[112] But Europe holds one enormous advantage over Britain: the 'great charm of the Continent' for English travellers lies in the freedom and ease of social intercourse in continental society, based on merit, not titles or money: 'The claim of being a gentleman suffices for admission and acceptance everywhere [. . .] the whole tone of society abroad is more natural and more free', and characterised by 'social equality'. This seems to be the only redeeming feature of the continent, but Lever accords it a great deal of importance:

> It will perhaps be said, that in this kind of intercourse we lose much of our nationality, and that our distinctly English features of character usually wear away. If by such are meant, our native coldness and distance—our distrust of everybody we do not know intimately—our overweening belief in the superiority of England in all things,—then, so much the better.[113]

Lever's article illustrates the use of 'the continent' as a stable term of reference and the staple comparator of Englishness throughout *Household Words*, even though the exact characteristics that allegedly constitute 'continentalness' are still contested. More remarkably, *Household Words* published his piece at a time when the rest of the British press was denouncing the despotism and tyranny of the very places that Lever recommended for the residence of English expatriates.

Around this time, Murray's 'Roving Englishman' began to appear in irregular intervals. The first few instalments are mostly set in Germany and Austria, places which the narrator initially appreciates for the pastoral harmony he finds amongst the local peasants, their rustic simplicity, and their 'old-world manners and old-world people'.[114] However, he also finds the German peoples uncultured, grave, vain, and obsessed with 'their own dignity and importance' in the most absurd circumstances.[115] Germans take more pleasure in their colourful hunting dress than in the actual sport and show no sense of propriety in their personal newspaper advertisements. At the same time, they absolutely cannot see when they are making fools of themselves with their inflated sense of pomp and circumstance. For example, the narrator attends a parade for a German petty-noble's court and describes in detail the cannons, uniforms, carriages, and maids of honour, only to conclude that 'the fussy pageant [impressed...] every one but a roving Englishman like me, with a grand idea of the splendour of his Effulgency's court.'[116] In other words, it takes an Englishman to penetrate show and pretence and see to the bottom of things. In Mary Louise Pratt's terminology, Smith is the 'seeing-man'—'he whose imperial eyes passively look out and possess', who keeps his distance from proceedings around him and recognises their true nature and meaning, which is hidden from everybody else present.[117] Other early instalments criticise endlessly the cumbersome passport and customs operations on the continent, especially in France—in one instance, Smith arrogantly refuses to cooperate with these regulations before breakfast and finds himself under arrest.[118]

Although these pieces seem highly localised, they also reveal a sense of common 'continentalness'. Smith occasionally uses 'German' and 'Austrian' as synonymous[119], and sees both these and France as symptomatic of 'continental peoples' at large. Thus, 'the English generally are [. . .] deficient in [. . .] the art of being happy. [. . .] It is not that we have not as keen an appetite for enjoyment as Continental people, but we do not know how to gratify it.'[120] In particular, this judgement applies to the lower orders, who are 'enthusiastic', simple, and given to music and enjoyment.[121] Continental aristocracy, on the other hand, is 'base and mean', 'low', and 'utterly worthless as a class' (although Smith's judgement of British noblemen in the diplomatic service is only marginally kinder).[122]

Varied and contradictory as some of these judgements may be—both the roving Englishman's own, and those of *Household Words* at large—one can nevertheless see a common tendency. In the early years of this decade, *Household Words* obviously subscribes to 'continentalness'—in other words, it assumes that the 'great powers of Europe', in particular France, Prussia and Austria, share many characteristics, and that Britain is distinct and separate from them. The staple condemnations of continental bureaucracy, the violence of the French *coup d'état*, and the general backwardness of the European continent, which are so widespread in other media, appear in *Household Words* too[123], but to a much lesser degree than in other British publications of the time. Simultaneously, *Household Words* is prepared to praise some continental institutions over British ones, and is generally more interested in the everyday life of the people rather than political and national affairs at large. Where other journals give a positive opinion on the continent, it tends to be backhanded. Thus, an article in *Chambers's Edinburgh Journal* first celebrates the railway as an 'essentially English' invention—under its influence, 'the continent, with all its stupid despotisms, must improve, and become enlightened in spite of itself.'[124] However, the article subsequently admits that continental railways are actually safer, more reliable, more comfortable, and cheaper than British ones:

> The continental railways are evidently more under control than those of the United Kingdom. Government interference abroad is, therefore,

> not altogether a wrong. Annoying as it may sometimes be, and bad as it avowedly is in principle, there is in it the spirit of protection against private oppression. And perhaps the English may by and by discover that jobbing-companies, with stupendous capital and a monopoly of conveyance, are capable of doing as tyrannical things as any continental autocrat![125]

Although *Household Words* is not exactly radical in its stance on Europe in this period, it is nonetheless more guarded in its condemnations and often describes certain European aspects not with a view to highlight Britain's advantages but its shortcomings, and improve it by comparison.

THE CRIMEAN CRISIS: 1853—1857

We move now into the middle of the decade, which covers the run-up to, duration, and aftermath of the Crimean War. As indicated above, 1853 marked the turning point for Britain's attitude to France and Russia in particular. Whereas in May 1852 *The Times* had praised the Russian emperor's great diplomatic skill in ensuring a large-scale European alliance against France's aggressions[126], the roles were suddenly reversed in 1853, when it turned out that Russia had designs on Greece and Turkey, whereas France was now discovered to share Britain's thinking entirely[127]: 'France has become the defender, as Russia the assailant, of the European equilibrium. The two Powers have, in fact, exchanged places, characters, and views.'[128] Simultaneously, Britain's attention turned towards the south-eastern edges of Europe. Initially, *The Times* could not quite decide on who the good and bad parties in the Crimea were—in summer 1853, it ran a series of articles on 'Christians in Turkey', which found that the Christian peoples (Greeks, Armenians, Serbs, and Wallachians) in the Ottoman empire were far superior to their Muslim oppressors and deserved liberation, but that this would happen anyway due to natural selection:

> The Mahomedans of Asia are morally superior to those of Europe. They are more themselves; they are stronger, because their state is in harmony with their nature. The reformed Turk aping Europe is an affectation [. . .] Indeed, a blight seems to have fallen on the race in Europe,—the population decays, the form degenerates, the mind becomes enfeebled. It would seem as if something more than chance had fixed the divisions of the globe [. . .] The Asiatic Mussulman [. . .] is a barbarian; he knows it, and wishes to be nothing else.[129]

Nine months on, however, the Greeks, incited by Russia, had staged an insurrection against their Turkish rulers, and Britain's sympathies changed again. It saw its moral duty in supporting Turkey and realised that the

Greeks were unlike 'other nations of Europe, who seek change by allaying themselves with the principles of democratic revolution'—hence, their Europeanness was denied, and they became 'Oriental Christians'.[130] *Chambers's Edinburgh Journal* made the same point in two articles on the 'Peoples and Prospects of Eastern Europe':

> No Eastern people can comprehend our idea of a state, it is too complicated for them [. . .] All [the Greeks'] notions are Oriental. Now, the Oriental idea of a state is the authority of one man, controlled more or less by public opinion. Few of what are called Asiatic despotisms are strictly autocratic.[131]

Two years previously, the media had accused the rest of Europe of adhering to the same 'Oriental' definition of a state, and especially France. Even though it stopped supporting the Greeks, Britain was interested not so much in the Turks, whom it still regarded with some ambiguity and suspicion, but in the resources of the land: 'We go to war for Turkey, not the Turks [... for] fertile plains, navigable rivers, spacious harbours, and important passes.'[132] In other words, Britain wanted to protect both the commercial potential of Turkey itself and the trade routes through Turkey to the Middle and Far East. In this sense, as Bernard Porter points out, the Crimean War was not a European war at all.[133]

Nevertheless, it obviously had repercussions on Britain's relationship with the rest of Europe. For one, it forced Britain to define what was European and what was not. After denouncing the continental nations as absolutist and militaristic tyrannies, *The Times* now found that to be 'European' meant, after all, to desire democratic and peaceful change and liberty. The *Illustrated London News*, at the beginning of its extensive coverage of the war, delivered a pep talk to Britain, scolding any doubters and claiming that 'the whole civilised world' recognised France and Britain's intervention in the Crimea as disinterested and just, and prayed for their success. 'All Europe knows that [the Czar] is the Disturber and the Anarchist, while he pretends to be the Conservator.'[134]

It is plain from these excerpts that the main division in this period is not between Britain and 'the continent', but between 'Europe' (in particular Britain, France, and to some extent Prussia and Austria) and 'the Orient', West and East. Britain had now joined Europe and even become the embodiment of European values such as liberty (which it had claimed exclusively for itself only two or three years earlier). Differences closer to home were, for the time being, glossed over or forgotten.[135] Indeed, the 'holy alliance' between France and Britain was celebrated in the highest terms as a model for the less fortunate European states to follow:

> The war, if it shows to some extent the Civilisation, shows to an extent still greater the Barbarism, of the European system. Whatever may be

> the individual character of its separate States, Europe collectively is not civilised. [. . .] France and England alone vindicated the title of Europe to rank as an aggregation of civilised communities, by standing forward with noble disinterestedness in the cause of right.[136]

This excerpt criticises the lack of trans-national cohesion and cooperation in Europe and implicitly desires a more pan-European, collective influence and thinking. Remarkably, this period also saw schemes published on the construction of a submarine Channel tunnel between France and England, some 135 years before the scheme was finally put into action[137]:

> The tunnel [. . .] would bind upon the most solid foundation with Great Britain, which is at present isolated from the rest of Europe. It would unite the two peoples in the most intimate and familiar relations—peoples who are to-day placed at the very head of civilization, and who, according to the current events, seem, by the community of their sentiments, and their interests, to form but one great nation.[138]

Such jubilant approval would have been difficult to imagine at the beginning of the decade, when even the prospect of European visitors to the Exhibition filled the media with panic. By 1854, the fear of French invasion was still remembered, but was sufficiently distant for *Chambers's Edinburgh Journal* to refer to it as a joke when it named an article 'Alarm of a French Invasion' that was actually about the migration of termites and other insects.[139] Meanwhile, the *Illustrated London News* agreed with *The Times* that 'England and France do not arrogate themselves too much in claiming to be at the head of civilisation [. . .] If other States of Europe compete with them, they compete at a respectful distance.'[140]

In *Household Words*, the change in tone from the preceding years was less pronounced than in other publications, partly because it had never been quite as scathing on Europe in the first place. For the most part, it kept up its sense of friendly distance—thus, the idea of Wilkie Collins' 'Black Mirror' was an apt emblem of *Household Words'* attitude in this period. Some slight shift may be detected between Sala's two articles on European exiles in London, seventeen months apart. Whereas 'Perfidious Patmos', in March 1853, had taken a more judgemental tone in praising England's liberty and condemning the unjust attribute 'perfidious Albion', 'Music in Paving Stones' (August 1854) was more descriptive and humorous. Eliza Lynn's 'Workmen of Europe', a review of Pierre-Guillaume-Frédéric Le Play's 1855 monograph *Les Ouvriers Européens*, moves, more or less, from East to West and summarises Le Play's judgement of the workers he found, in order to criticise it. While Le Play—on the basis of some twenty years' travel—favours the primitive and migrant, polygamous and patriarchal peoples of Russia and Eastern Europe, Lynn disagrees with him at every turn, since 'the writer's desire is to uphold all such of the working classes as live under the immediate government and in the power of their masters, and to decry those who are free and independent.'[141] And of course, these years also saw the series of articles by Dickens—such as 'Insularities', 'Proposals for a National Jest-Book', and 'Why?'—that questioned various British institutions and characteristics and often used the continent as a positive counter-example, as discussed in chapter 2.

While *Household Words* continued, for the most part, in the vein of its earlier numbers, some articles did occasionally set a new tone. Edmund Dixon's 'Wheel within Wheel', for instance, relates a dialogue between some French and British traders, which focuses on various obstacles in their trade and its influence on 'European civilisation'.[142] The French trader, the narrator asserts, is polite, 'an affectionate father and a faithful husband', and 'did not make insulting speeches about English perfidy and the English accent. In short, he was not the ill-behaved rogue which certain tourists have painted him.' The conversation between the traders traces the various mutual repercussions of sugar and wheat production. They conclude that

> France and England are not independent of each other, but have mutual requirements which must be mutually supplied. We are no more than distinct parts of one great machine, which is meant to act in harmony and union, wheel within wheel.[143]

This points to a higher degree of harmony, cooperation, and indeed similarity between Britain and France than *Household Words* had previously indicated, even though it does not go to the euphoric extremes that *The Times* occasionally lunged into.

1853 also saw the shift of focus in 'The Roving Englishman', who now—in unison with the whole country—turned his attention from Central Europe to the Ottoman Empire and stayed, variously, in occupied Greece and Turkey. In the earlier instalments 'Smith' found plenty of differences between individual nations—such as the Germans' love of pomp and of music, their lack of dress sense and personal hygiene; the French population's discord and revolutionary potential, their flamboyance and capacity for cheating and lying; the Italians' buffoonery and theatrical gesticulation, their liveliness and excitability; the Irish unruliness, and so on. Yet there is something that all these continental nations have in common. Smith rarely hazards a guess what this 'something' may be, but he nevertheless relies on it to justify the distinction between 'continental' and 'Oriental' when the series turns to Greece and Turkey. Here, he rarely distinguishes between individual (western) European nationalities but typically summarises them as 'Franks' or 'Europeans'.

The dichotomy that Smith develops from the contrast of East and West is a fairly standard one.[144] The Orient has remained the same for over a thousand years, while Europe has changed and progressed.[145] Europe—in particular Britain—is driven by steam power, railways, education, and administration, whereas the Orient is 'strange and unreal' and generally reminiscent of an 'Arabian Nights' Entertainment'.[146] Orientals are 'fond of intrigue'[147], easily blinded and led by appearances[148], and incurably lazy and disorganised.[149] Europeans in exile, on the other hand, have the tendency to be arrogant and condescending towards the 'natives'[150], usually think it below them to learn the local language, and meddle too much in the politics of other countries, exploiting their influence.[151]

But Smith repeatedly finds that the area on which he bases his insights on 'all Orientals' is not pure after all, but a hybrid of European and Oriental aspects. 'His Hints to Travellers', published some eight months before the series turns to Turkey and Greece, identifies Constantinople as one of the outposts of European trade and influence.[152] Steven Sowards states that Eastern Europe and the Balkan have often been termed the 'Zwischenländer', the 'lands between'.[153] In other words, the area poses a grey zone between Europe 'proper' and Asia, and incorporates elements of both. It is precisely the meeting of these in Turkey and Greece that causes the roving Englishman so much difficulty and distaste. This is particularly evident in Constantinople, where Smith takes up his residence in Turkey. Even today, modern Constantinople—Istanbul—markets itself as the place 'where the continents meet'[154], and Smith experiences it in the same way, although he derives some discomfort from this mixture of elements. He repeatedly finds that Turks would be much better off without meddling with European fashions: Turks can 'give good dinners, when they do not attempt to serve them in the European style'[155]; they look good in 'the manly beard and long moustache of the Oriental', but 'European costume [. . .] sits on [them] ungracefully', even on the Sultan himself.[156] European clothes are worn not for their convenience or appearance, however, but because they serve as a sign of 'superiority' and power.[157] In Constantinople, the narrator encounters some 'semi-civilised natives who have been half-educated somewhere in Europe'.[158] All in all, his attitude to Turkey is as mixed as he finds the place itself, occasionally even diverging on the same point. On the one hand, he admires the cleanliness, gentleness and love of peace he finds amongst its inhabitants.[159] On the other, he condemns their love of fleas and dirt[160], their laziness[161], and their scrawny physique.[162] Yet these contradictions do not stop Smith from taking every observation he makes as symptomatic of the entire race. Indeed, in a later piece entitled 'Turkish Contrasts', Murray sees contradictoriness as a defining characteristic of Turks: 'Turks are both clean and dirty', dabbling with water yet eating with their fingers; they are 'compassionate' in general yet 'cruel' to Christians and to their slaves; their women are admired yet imprisoned behind the veil; Turks are brave yet never engage in a duel or in suicide, and so on.[163] Some of these statements—for instance on the treatment of women and on alleged polygamy—stand in stark contrast to William B. Jerrold's earlier *Household Words* article 'The Turk at Home'. Both articles, in spite of Turkey's 'despotic' rule, find it both a meritocracy and democracy—in the sense that pride on the grounds of ancestry is despised, and 'any office is open [. . .] to any man'.[164] Both articles conclude that 'the Turks are a great deal better than the institutions under which they have hitherto lived.'[165] Murray even allows a Turkish gentleman the final word: on being asked 'whether Mohamedanism was in itself opposed to what the Western Franks [. . .] call progress?', the gentleman replies that Turks had been 'for some centuries perhaps the most learned and enlightened people in the world':

> Since, also, the Christians are often avaricious, selfish, intemperate, and unjust—qualities which, I am informed, are much condemned by your sacred writings—do you not think it possible that a Mohammedan of our age might take example from them, and break through those precepts of the Koran which have been misinterpreted to counsel us an eternity of ignorance?[166]

Remarkably, Murray does not on this occasion claim the credit of such progress for Britain, as other writers did.[167]

The ambiguity in Murray's attitude to Turkey mirrors that of the British press as a whole throughout the Crimean crisis, during which the country excited new interest.[168] At the beginning of his residence there, Smith is therefore at pains to explain and redeem Turkey as full of promise. He does this by pointing out that Turkey may be underdeveloped but has the potential to become 'powerful [and] civilised'[169], although the Turks themselves, whose only interest lies in 'pipes and peace'[170], will need the help of European nations to achieve this high aim. Smith emphasises that Turkey is rich in resources but needs 'railways, engineers, schoolmasters, accountants, artisans, machinery for her mines and agriculture', and England, which has all these as well as 'millions of unemployed capital', is just the nation to spring to Turkey's aid. In fact, Smith considers it 'the right' of those nations 'who help [the Turks] to maintain a position they could not maintain alone [. . .] to hint a friendly counsel to them without being considered either meddling or offensive.' In particular, England should make Turkey stop all discrimination against Christians, administer justice, and abolish corruption. This would turn Turkey not into a 'formidable rival to our commerce', as some fear, but into an economic ally that allows Englishmen to 'make their own fame and fortunes'. If England had a free hand with Turkey, Smith implies, Russia's 'marauding attempt' on Turkey would be doomed, and 'Admiral Slade and Omar Pasha would drive them from sea and land single-handed.'[171] In other words, Smith can incorporate Turkey into his concept of Europe by imagining as a semi-dependency of Britain, by now a familiar trope.[172]

Over the next one and a half years of his residence in Turkey, however, Smith appears to lose interest or faith in this project. Indeed, he warns that Europeans—and Britons in particular—should not exploit their considerable influence and weight in Turkey[173], and that they should occasionally be prepared to take rather than give advice:

> Let us not be too proud to learn. We have so often stood in the honourable relation of teachers to other nations that we can afford now and then to turn pupils with a better grace [even if...] the lesson comes from a place whence we are not generally in the habit of receiving lessons [. . .].[174]

These moments of understanding and respect are rare, however, and for the most part, Smith reverts to the facetious stereotyping of 'Orientals', however contradictory, that pervaded the culture at large.

It is not surprising that most references to Europe in the inclusive sense (rather than Britons and 'continentals') should occur in contrast with supposedly non-European cultures. But 'The Roving Englishman' also has a sense of Europe in its own right, without any contrast, as growing closer together. Most symptomatic of the new age of travel and tourism is the instalment 'From Kraiova to London', in which the narrator expresses his surprise that the shooting-grounds on 'the banks of the Danube should have been so neglected by English sportsmen', since they are 'but ten days' delightful journey from England'.[175] The ease with which Murray's narrator assumes that tourists will be happy to cross the length of the European continent in order to shoot birds, and that he sees the distance of over a thousand miles simply as an added bonus, speaks volumes about (wealthy) Britain's emerging view of Europe as effectively just round the corner.

Towards the end of the Crimean crisis, *Household Words* turned its attention once more to European countries as holiday destinations and places for residence—for example, in Sala's short series on 'The Great Hotel Question' or Wilkie Collins' 'Laid up in Two Lodgings'[176]—and focused once again on the diversity rather than similarity in European cultures, for example in William Duthie's 'Sundays Abroad' series.[177] As before, Britain did not always come out as the winner of any comparison—in addition to the 'insularities' that Dickens identified, Britain's slovenliness with regard to learning foreign languages and the flaws in the British army's promotion system came under attack.[178] The latter point of criticism is particularly interesting, given Britain's earlier disgust at the inflated military presence of the continental states. Dickens, for instance, deplored that the English were 'quite untrained in the power of associating to defend themselves, their children, their women, and their native land' and had allowed 'the old British spirit and British hand' to go to waste, while the French were able to mobilise large armies quickly.[179]

THE AFTERMATH OF THE CRIMEAN WAR AND THE INDIAN CRISIS: 1857–1859

In summer 1857, the unfolding news from the Indian Rebellion took over British public interest and distracted it, for a little while, from the question of Europe, which was at any rate left in a lull after the Crimean War. But it was not long before the two issues became connected. As early as July 1857, a mere week after *The Times* revealed the full extent of the Indian Rebellion, the *Illustrated London News* suspected Russia of inciting the Indians against British rule, just as it had stirred up the Greeks four years earlier. This was all the more likely since 'Asiatics know but two European Powers. They do not believe in the separate identity of the French, and they never heard of the Germans; and in their minds Europe is divided between the English and the Russians.'[180] Initially, it still cast the Rebellion as a war between European civilisation and Asian barbarism[181], but as the crisis continued, it found that, 'as regards other nations, England stands [. . .] alone in the world, not only without sympathy, but with a scarcely concealed gladness that a blow has been struck at her power.'[182] Of course, the 'isolation in which she stands in Europe' was only due to Britain's 'success and greatness', but unfortunately 'it must be remembered that among the Continental nations the standard and the measure of power is a military one', and all of Britain's military strength was currently engaged in India.[183] In other words, Britain suddenly felt naked and vulnerable, no longer part of 'Europe' but confronting the 'Continental nations' by itself. The 'holy alliance' between France and Britain, which the *Illustrated London News* had hailed only two years before, seemed well and truly dead, and new discord was under way.

The Times slowly came round to the same view. In September 1857, it was still assuring its readers that England and France were friends and competed with each other only in commerce and manufacture.[184] Two months later, it recorded stiffly that 'some French journals have started the cry of English cruelty and barbarity in India.'[185] The article then set out to disprove these accusations and claimed that the liberty of the British press ensured that 'if we do anything wrong the whole world knows it'. It concluded by intimating that the French, of all people, should not accuse others of cruelty and misrule, given their revolutionary past.[186] In 1858 *The Times* repeatedly asserted that the restraint of the French press, whether due to false politeness or government censure, stood in a negative contrast to the freedom of the British press.[187] By 1859, *The Times* accused France of war-mongering and conspiring against the European peace and cast Britain as the observer and peacekeeper of Europe[188], although Britain was unable to prevent a new alliance between Russia and France.[189] At the close of the decade, Britain appeared to be in a worse position than it had been able to imagine at the beginning, as its two alternating enemies seemed to close ranks.

Once again, the renewed suspicion against the continent in general and France in particular left only faint traces on *Household Words*, and its coverage of Europe during these years is unspectacular and mostly apolitical. Lynn Linton's 'National Contrasts' does not make any political comment on France, merely touching upon the superstitions rife amongst the French, 'as may be almost seen daily by the Times reports.'[190] Edmund Dixon's 'Literary Small Change' culture focuses mostly on the economic and topical changes in cheap French journals, rather than reviling the censure of the continental press, as was customary. If anything, Dixon hints at a more cosmopolitan outlook in the French press: 'Our neighbours are fond of titles which imply a vast scope of action and a wide-spread reputation. Nothing is more common than a Café de l'Europe, a literary Monde, and an Hôtel de l'Univers.'[191] Incidentally, Dixon mentions that 'the submarine tunnel between England and France' is still discussed in neighbouring France; *The Times*, meanwhile, had dismissed it as an inspired but crazy scheme.[192]

Negative tones were of course heard, but these too remained apolitical. George Thornbury's 'Spanish Hotels' warns of the danger and corruption which travelling Englishmen face abroad:

> I saw too many instances of how soon that subtle, demoralising climate saps the English pluck and energy, and reduces a man to the languid, lounging, smoking, idle, procrastinating Spaniard; whose energy is fitful, Eastern, and passionate, whose life is a sleepy dream, and can hardly be called a life at all [. . .].[193]

Percy Fitzgerald's 'Bogie Albion', which I have discussed in greater detail in chapter 2, expresses wonder at the tenacity with which the French continue to cling to their favourite stereotypes about the English, although Fitzgerald admits that 'every nation [must...] of necessity make to itself some sort of Bogie, which it may pillory and pelt with eggs'.[194]

Finally, Wilkie Collins delivered an article in 1859 on 'The Great (Forgotten) Invasion' in 1797, in which four French ships sailed up the Bristol Channel and landed on the Welsh coast, where the French were eventually overcome and captured. His choice of topic indicates that the idea of a French invasion was quite present to the public imagination at this time (after all, the *Illustrated London News* had already hinted at the possibility one and a half years previously). In the only vaguely political article on Europe during this period, Collins uses this historical event to comment on current affairs: Britain 'was just as miserably incapable of protecting itself on its own ground [. . .] at that day, as it is at the present time', while the French 'were even more densely ignorant of England and English institutions at that time than they are at this'.[195] The 'Moral to be drawn' from this incident, Collins states, is that 'if we are invaded again, and on a rather larger scale, let us not be so ill-prepared, this next time'.[196] Clearly, a foreign invasion had again become a possibility.

This chapter has sketched the developments in the British attitude to the rest of the European continent throughout the 1850s, both in the press at large and in *Household Words*. Britain's relationship with the European continent during this period was fraught with tension, alternately positing either France or Russia as the enemy. During the periods when Britain focused on France as its rival, it defined itself as distinct from 'the continent'; yet when Britain and France formed an alliance against Russia, it had no difficulty to see itself as an integral and important part of 'Europe'. Both discourses continued to exist throughout the decade, and both relied on an overriding sense of some essential shared characteristics that European nations shared, even though the actual definition of this essence varied.

In comparison to the daily and weekly news press, then, *Household Words* adopted a fairly moderate stance. Although influenced by the extremes between which *The Times* and *Illustrated London News* veered over the decade, *Household Words* usually followed those trends in a much more temperate line, effectively maintaining a (comparatively) affable, if somewhat detached, attitude to the continent. In this discourse, the journal tended to stick to non-political issues—for instance, those criticisms it makes within the framework of the Crimean War mostly relate to the British government alone, its inadequate decisions and short-sightedness. International politics featured very rarely.

One reason is, of course, that *Household Words* did not and could not make news coverage its primary aim due to the limitations placed on it. Its interest also lay less in official politics than in the nature of 'the people'. Despite the variety of its material, the frivolity which authors such as Sala or Murray brought to their writing, and its deep-seated patriotism, *Household Words* was nonetheless driven by an earnest desire to remain true to its chosen subjects, whereas much of contemporary travel-writing was too superficial, as James White humorously indicated:

> If a man can't make up his mind on any subject, or all subjects, in the course of seven days [. . .] don't let him attempt to compete with the really enlightened observers and travellers of the present day; gentlemen—and ladies, too—who settle the past and present and future of great states by means of a three months' tour, and in Glances at Europe, Glimpses of Asia, Peeps at Africa, and Squints at America, dispose of all the differences of manner, policy, religion, and government which have agitated the four quarters of the globe.[197]

This suggests that *Household Words* deliberately limited itself to smaller but more thorough portraits of the different places that it featured, rather than attempting to sketch all of a continent in its restricted scope and falsely eliminating all minor idiosyncrasies.

Yet, as series such as 'The Roving Englishman' showed, *Household Words* was not above some broad generalisations, especially in the service of humour and eccentricity. The audience that *Household Words* envisaged in those pieces rarely ventured beyond Britain's immediate neighbouring countries, if that, and typically read about Europe rather than visiting it, even though *Household Words* frequently presupposed a reasonable knowledge of French and German and the basics of European history. It remains to be seen how *Household Words'* attitude to such travelogues changed in the context of Britain's colonial possessions.

5 'Interlopers in the East'
Household Words and India

In dealing with *Household Words*' attitude to the colonies, I shall concentrate mainly on India, as it was not only the colony most frequently written about, but also makes for the most versatile and thus the most interesting case study. While Australia also featured relatively frequently, most articles tended to echo each other. Most articles were written by current or former emigrants, and most imagined Australia as an empty receptacle for British emigrants, gold-diggers, and opportunists. India, on the other hand, was so evidently populated that any attempts to imagine it as an empty source of material goods were doomed—its population had to be reckoned with. This became most evident during the so-called Indian Mutiny of 1857, when the native population turned in open revolt against their colonial 'masters'.

When news of the Mutiny broke in Britain, *Household Words* responded slowly and cautiously. Not until the publication of John Lang's series 'Wanderings in India', which appeared from November 1857 to February 1858, did the journal produce a consistent reaction to the Sepoy Rebellion. Set in 1848–9, the series of twelve instalments posed as a straightforward travelogue that retrospectively prophesied and explained the Rebellion, as it were. Although Lang's 'Wanderings' will form the focus of this chapter, it will take into account *Household Words*' coverage of India prior to the Rebellion of 1857 as well as other *Household Words* articles on the Rebellion and some responses in other publications. I argue that *Household Words* staff clearly felt the need to respond to the Rebellion but did not at first know what tone to take. 'Wanderings' offered a concerted and prolonged opportunity to make sense of 1857 in a 'safe' and indirect context.

INDIA BEFORE 1857

In the years between the Great Exhibition and the Sepoy Rebellion, *Household Words* was mostly interested in India as a source of (British) wealth. Articles concentrated on the production of cinnamon, coffee, cocoa, and opium, or discussed the possibilities to expand British trade in India.

Where *Household Words* does mention the population itself, it is often in anecdotal form rather than as a commentary on the existing state of affairs. Thus, John Lang's early contributions tell stories of a 'Mahommedan Mother', an orphaned half-caste boy, an 'Inundation in Bengal', and the difficulties of 'Starting a Paper in India'. In all four articles, he treats his subject as a curiosity and relates the misery and suffering that occurs in a detached, mildly curious fashion.

Of course, an occasional note of charitable concern for the native population crept into *Household Words*' early coverage of India, even though its key interest was economic gain, but this concern never translated into doubt about Britain's right to rule India—if anything, the rule was seen as not thorough enough. Thus, Samuel Sidney voiced the question, 'Have we done all we could for the welfare of the native population under our charge?' and found the answer unsatisfactory.[1] It would be in the natives' interest, Sidney stipulates, if they were encouraged to develop their agricultural resources—especially corn, cotton, and salt—in order to cater for British needs. The ultimate advantage of this would be that they could then trade with Britain and increase the turnover of British goods: 'The great mass of the Indian population are poor; but intelligent, willing to labour, and anxious to purchase British manufactures, if they had the means.'[2]

The same logic influences John Capper's concern for 'The Peasants of British India'. Capper criticised the rule of the East India Company more harshly than any other *Household Words* writer and showed a general respect for the Indian population that is not often rivalled in family journals of the time.[3] Britain's paternalist rule, he claimed, was responsible for allowing corruption and the ruthless exploitation of the poor labourers and tenants to become systemic, whereas it had been only sporadic before the British arrived. Under the circumstances, Sidney's wish seems ludicrous:

> Whilst the bulk of the Indian population remain thus degraded and helpless, it is worse than idle to expect them to undertake new agricultural projects. Why should these poor wretches grow cotton for our factories? What would they gain? [. . .] What is steam to them, who dare not eat the very food they grow?[4]

Capper's outrage at the miserable existence of the native population is genuine, yet he does not rely on humanitarian reasons alone to persuade his audience of the need to improve British rule in India. His final argument is, like Sidney's, economic: 'Yet these millions, if they took but half the goods from us which South Americans consume, would want each year not less than forty millions sterling worth beyond their present purchases.'[5] In other words, it is in Britain's own interest to care better for its Indian subjects in order to turn them into consumers of British produce.

The same self-interest is evident in other publications. *Chambers's Edinburgh Journal*, in contrast to Capper, believed that 'the steam engine is destined to do more for India than all her other teachers have yet effected', although the actual benefit from it is once again expected to go to Britain, who was in charge of European trade with India: 'The rich produce of Central India will be poured into Europe with a profusion and regularity never yet dreamed of.'[6] Simultaneously, *Chambers's* informed its younger readers that 'Indian Sweet-Meats' are quite tolerable, even though Indians are 'less civilised than we are', and laughed at the inefficiency of Indian labourers who prefer to carry wheelbarrows instead of pushing them and have not yet discovered chairs, 'one of those natural steps towards a higher civilisation'.[7] Although *Chambers's* also praised the 'Arts and Manufactures of India' as tasteful and yet realistic, their artistic achievement did not necessarily lift Indians up to a 'higher civilisation'; as my first chapter showed, it could in fact have the contrary effect.[8]

Most interesting in the years prior to 1857 is the various publications' judgement of the stability of the British regime in India. In 1850, *The Times* reported happily, if somewhat cautiously:

> If experience forbids us to place unqualified reliance on the permanency of the tranquillity reported from our Indian possessions, we have at least the satisfaction of observing that it is difficult to conjecture the quarter from which any disturbance is likely to ensue. Throughout the whole Peninsula all is profoundly tranquil.[9]

The complacent tone was even more prevalent in *Household Words* in the early 1850s. Despite Capper's repeated attacks on the East India Company's inefficiency, the journal never envisaged any serious difficulties in, let alone resistance to, British rule over India. Joachim Siddons, in describing 'Christmas in India', celebrated Europe as a civilising influence: 'The tide of European conquest, and, better still, the tide of European civilisation, has carried to the benighted land knowledge, and a large spirit of toleration'.[10] A few months later, Samuel Sidney announced proudly that

> less than ten thousand European military and civil officers rule and tax seventy millions of Mahomedans and Hindoos; fifty millions more are surrounded by our dominions, open to our commerce, and ready to submit to our rule, whenever we choose to accept their homage. India is at peace.[11]

Sidney did not view the relative numbers of European staff and Indian subjects as at all problematic, but saw it rather as an added reason for assuming that everything was under control. His use of the term 'homage' implies that the native population was virtually queuing up to come under British rule.

Chambers's Journal topped the sanguine predictions in an 1856 article on Britain's annexation of Oude, the very province where, less than a year later, the Sepoy Rebellion would begin:

> All persons [. . .] must rejoice that a country possessing a fertile soil, an industrious population, and which has produced two-thirds of the sepoys who have fought our battles for the last century, has been rescued from a state of anarchy and oppression [. . .] In Oude itself, all classes hail it as a boon.[12]

In order to win over those who are sceptical of 'our lust of territorial aggrandisement in the East', who may not believe that this is a charitable deed for the benefit of the inhabitants, the article concludes, in a by now familiar move, that 'in a financial point of view, the annexation is a profitable one'—profitable to Britain, that is.[13] As late as June 1857, *Chambers's* announced happily that the short overland route between India and Britain 'brings [an Englishman in India] home to re-Europeanise himself before he has become confirmed in the habits and tastes which the climate and custom of the country induce.'[14] While former 'unhappy individuals' who lived in India 'gradually subsided into native habits and amusements' and became morally corrupt, even giving up Christianity, 'the order of things is [now] reversed: instead of the European lowering himself to the level of the native, the latter endeavours to raise himself in the social scale by adopting civilised habits and conforming to European ideas.'[15]

WANDERINGS IN INDIA

At the time when *Chambers's* still rejoiced in the civilising influence of Europe on India, the Sepoy Rebellion had already been under way for nearly a month. On May 10, 1857, the Rebellion broke out in Meerut and Delhi simultaneously, the massacre at Meerut supposedly instigated by Nana Sahib, who subsequently became the single most infamous and reviled person in the British imagination.[16] News of the Rebellion reached Britain by the end of June, but *The Times* had already reported various smaller uprisings in the native units of the Indian army during the preceding months.[17] Although the scale of the Sepoy Rebellion must have come as a shock, Britain's surprise that it happened at all is in itself surprising and testifies to the faith Britain had in its own Empire's strength.

Initially, Britain struggled to make sense of the events, and the hardcore thirst for revenge for which the British response to the Rebellion has since become renowned was not evident in the first few weeks of reporting on events. Thus, some media initially blamed the Rebellion on Russian intrigues following the Crimean War. Although not sympathetic to the sepoys, the *Illustrated London News* did assign some blame to the British insensitivity to the local faiths in the affair of the greased cartridges and the general evangelising by British officers.[18] A few issues later, however, finer distinctions had disappeared, and now the *Illustrated London News* saw the Rebellion as a matter of European civilisation pitted against Asian barbarism.[19]

Other journals did not participate in the news at all. After events proved *Chambers's* recent optimism so disastrously and poignantly wrong, that journal hardly mentioned the Sepoy Rebellion or even India in the latter half of 1857. In fact, the only reference it made was in the description of 'instances [. . .] of fidelity and humanity' by those Indian domestic servants 'who have been brought into close home contact with the English', defiantly clinging to its former belief in the civilising influence of the British presence in India, even in the face of the Rebellion.[20]

Household Words was also relatively reluctant to respond, even if one takes its lengthy turnover time into account. While it published an article on Louis Napoleon's *coup d'état* only four weeks after the event, the first *Household Words* article that referred to 'A Mutiny in India', appeared only on August 15, 1857—a full six weeks after *The Times* reported the Meerut rebellion and several months after it first identified the disturbed state of India and reported various regiments' mutinies. This article took a relatively sympathetic stance in ascribing the cause of a native rebellion, which happened 'years ago', to the tyranny and insensitivity of some European officers who forced Muslim soldiers to shave off their beards; the current Rebellion was not mentioned in it.[21] There followed a few more relatively dry, informational articles that alluded in passing to the state of affairs in India. Only on September 5 did *Household Words* finally make the 1857 Rebellion the subject of an article in its own right, cautiously examining the history of 'Sepoy symbols' that were supposedly used to communicate in the run-up to the Rebellion.[22] *Household Words* slowly found its voice and outraged opinion in the form of John Capper's 'A Very Black Act', which chafed against the freshly imposed censorship of the British press in India as a means of 'levelling the white European to the depths of the black Asiatic'.[23] By the following week, some writers already expressed their fatigue of all things Indian:

> I really must protest against the bi-monthly irruption of barbaric words from dialects spoken by those hundred and eighty millions who eat rice and worship idols between the Himalayas and Cape Cormorin. [. . .] Indian news eclipses every other sort of intelligence.[24]

Dickens clearly felt the need for a more concerted and informative response, because he commissioned the Australian-born writer John Lang to write a series based on his own experience of India.[25] Lang's life was deeply implicated in the context of British imperialism and points towards a potential for ambiguous and conflicting identities. Since this ambiguity also informs 'Wanderings', I shall briefly sketch Lang's biography here.

John George Lang was born in Parramatta, New South Wales, in December 1816 and came from 'Jewish and emancipist backgrounds'; his mother was the offspring of two transported convicts, although she later denied her background and claimed to be the daughter of a British officer.[26] Lang received his schooling in Australia, then began a law degree at Cambridge, from where he was expelled 'for unspecified indiscretions'.[27] He continued his studies at the Middle Temple and proceeded to the bar in May 1841. Having married in 1839, he returned to Australia with his wife and child and practised as a barrister in Sydney, where 'his emancipist and Jewish background made it difficult for him to find acceptance'.[28] Lang 'was soon actively involved in emancipist affairs [and . . .] worked energetically for the Australian Patriotic Association which [. . .] press[ed] for responsible government'.[29] However, after only six months Lang and his family left Australia over 'some injudicious public statements about [. . .] colonial law' and moved to India.[30] Shortly afterwards, his marriage collapsed, and his wife and children returned to England.[31] Lang learnt Hindustani and Persian, and 'between 1843 and 1845 he practised law in Calcutta', where he also 'for a short time edited *The Optimist*'. 'In 1846 Lang moved to Meerut [. . .] where he founded the *Mofussilite*, an English language newspaper. In 1849 he became editor and later sole proprietor of the paper'.[32] These experiences served as the basis for his pre-1857 articles, in particular 'Starting a Paper in India'.

Lang continued to practice as a lawyer and fought 'two important and lucrative cases [. . .] first for Ajoodia Pershād against the East India Company in 1851, and then a case for the Ranee of Jhansi' in 1854.[33] While the Rani lost her case against the British government's annexation of her province on the death of her childless husband, Lang's defence of the banker Joti Prasad in 1851 was so successful that 'at the conclusion of the trial, crowds of Indians had carried him and his portly client out of the courthouse on their shoulders.'[34] Between 1853 and 1859 Lang returned to Europe and settled in London, travelled around Europe, and contributed new and rewritten sketches and short stories to *Fraser's* and *Welcome Guest* as well as *Household Words*.[35] By the time the 'Wanderings' began to appear, Lang was already an established writer for *Household Words*, in which he had published twelve articles, mostly about life in India and Australia, between February 1853 and August 1857. He continued to write for to *Household Words* until its very last issue, his contributions totalling twenty-two articles in addition to the twelve instalments of 'Wanderings'. In 1859, Lang returned to India, remarried, and 'succumbed to an insatiable craving for champagne at all hours of the day and night', of which he died 'a melancholy example of wasted talents and degraded abilities' in 1864.[36]

Most studies of John Lang have emphasised his Australian roots and choice of topics (his 'most significant Australian work was *Botany Bay: Or, True Tales of Early Australia* [1859]', some parts of which also appeared in

Household Words[37]), but the 'Wanderings' have been discussed less thoroughly. Keesing points out that Lang's 'fiction of Australia [was] all written in exile'.[38] The same is true of 'Wanderings', which was written during the second half of 1857, while Lang was a 'well-known and popular literary figure' in the metropolis.[39] Accordingly, the narrator emphasises his absence from India at the time of writing in the presupposition, 'should I again wander in India'.[40]

'At first appearance *Wanderings in India* seems to be accurately described as a travel book', which is the label *The Oxford Companion to Australian Literature* gives it.[41] Douglas Peers even refers to *Wanderings* as 'John Lang's autobiography'.[42] Amur's article, though allowing that 'at certain points Lang's narrative enters doubtful areas', assumes that the text is largely autobiographical in its inference that author and narrator are identical, and states that *Wanderings* 'is an account of a journey undertaken by the author in Northern India in 1847–48'.[43] Roderick claims that 'in substance [the 'Wanderings'] appear to be acceptable, if not as the naked truth, then as the truth adorned with few flowers of fancy'.[44] But Hosking proposes that 'it is clear that at least some of the pieces are not simply "history" or memoir', and it is occasionally difficult to judge where the borderline between fact and fiction lies.[45] I will try to avoid speculation about the 'truth content' of individual episodes and discuss Lang's representations of colonial India on their own merit, regardless of whether individual events or scenes stem from first-hand experience or not.

For a text that has widely been considered autobiographical, the narrator's identity remains remarkably vague throughout. Hosking suggests that although

> it is tempting to suggest that Lang's Jewish, emancipist [. . .] Australian background may have encouraged him to take a sceptical view of British imperialism [. . .] there are just as many moments when Lang presents [. . .] a Eurocentred, Anglophile view that [. . .] seems to deny his own colonial background.[46]

Although the narrator repeatedly criticises the British Raj, he nevertheless does so from the perspective of imperial Britain: 'It is devoutly to be hoped that, when *our* rule in India is completely re-established, these absurd concessions [. . .] will no longer be suffered to prevail'.[47] This monolithic 'we' appears most frequently in the context of comments on the 1857 rebellion: 'Without Jooteepersâd, we could not have held Agra'.[48] On the other hand, the narrator learns Hindi and Persian, develops 'a decent sun-tan and [initially] avoids contact with other Europeans' in an attempt to acquaint himself with 'native character' from the inside rather than from the 'blue books' most Englishmen seem to rely on.[49]

His national identity is not the only aspect of the narrator that remains vague. Apart from the fact that 'we discover [in instalment VIII] that he is thirty-two years old', hardly any biographical details are included that do not immediately concern the journey he describes.[50] His decision to 'become a wanderer in the East' seems to be a matter of having nothing else to do: 'I had no occupation, was my own master, and had a large tract of country to roam about in'.[51] Even the narrator's name is withheld throughout 'Wanderings'. All we can deduce is that 'the narrator is a mature male, experienced, cynical, laconic, an observer whose conversational prose style encourages readers to accept the validity of the narrative'.[52] His persona is thus remarkably similar to that of Grenville Murray's 'Roving Englishman'.

Most other 'witnesses' also remain unnamed, and many of them are reported to have died since their meeting with the narrator. Most of these observers, of both native and European origin, advocate a stricter rule of British India. The Indians tend to focus on native character, especially depravity and hypocrisy, lending the narrator's own commentary additional authority since they 'know [their] own countrymen better than you do'.[53] The European commentators often highlight inadequacies in the organisational structure of the Raj, though they too remark upon supposedly native characteristics. Neither native nor European observers question the propriety of British rule in India, but criticise only some of its practical aspects.

Considering the space these authoritative commentators take up in the narrative, it seems curious that so few of them are identified. Keesing states that

> Lang claimed a factual basis for all his tales; so far as one can check, his claim is correct [. . .] Lang also said he altered and suppressed material that might hurt people, or their descendants, who were alive when he wrote.[54]

However, most of the un- or renamed characters in 'Wanderings' appear in a positive light, and there seems to be no reason why they should remain anonymous if, indeed, they are 'factual'. One example is the Lieutenant with whom the narrator travels for several days between Cawnpore and Agra (instalments II to IV), and in whose 'eyes, the Hindoo, Mussulman, and the Christian, are all equal'.[55] Another native 'commentator' is named self-consciously: 'His name was—let us say—Nobinkissen'.[56] Nobinkissen, having been convicted for fraud but later released, 'could not face his countrymen in Bengal, and, therefore, retired to the upper provinces', so he has already been disgraced and could not be 'hurt' further by his inclusion in Lang's narrative, especially as the narrator has great respect for his opinions, which 'are, at the present time especially, entitled to the very gravest consideration'.[57]

In other places the narrator refers to a very talented actor who is 'a younger brother of an intelligent, influential, rich, and deservedly respected London tradesman, whose name is known in every quarter of the world where the English language is spoken', yet neither brother is named.[58] Neither is the keeper of a Meerut churchyard whose narrative takes up half of instalment VII. The narrator pre-emptively informs us that 'this old soldier and his family perished in the massacre at Meerut on the tenth of May. He was, in some way, related to, or connected by marriage with Mrs Courtenay, the keeper of the hotel, who, with her nieces, was so barbarously murdered on that occasion'.[59] Again, those connections that might help to identify the soldier are kept rather vague, though 'Mrs. Courtney, who helped to run the Meerut hotel' is named in Christopher Hibbert's *The Great Mutiny*, as 'she and her children were killed' during their attempted escape.[60]

Another initially nameless companion of the narrator is the assistant magistrate of Burnampore[61] who provides more explanations of the Brahmin caste in particular, as well as on the general ways of British India.[62] The assistant magistrate accompanies the narrator and two further unnamed friends, 'a German baron and a French gentleman' on a tour of the Himalayas.[63] In order to avoid confusion about the epithet 'my friend', the narrator decides that 'in future we will call [the assistant magistrate] Mr. West'.[64] Again, the implication is that this is not his 'real' name[65]. Besides, we have already learnt in instalment VII that Mr. West 'was accidentally drowned in the river Jumna, about two years ago', adding to the number of deceased 'witnesses'.[66]

Finally, the narrator stays with yet another nameless magistrate at Bijnore, who also discourses freely on the flaws in the imperial government of India, in particular in its corrupt judicial system. The narrator underlines the force of his strength as a witness: 'This statement, remember, was made by a magistrate who speaks as well as writes the native language as well as the natives themselves'.[67] His 'friend and distant connection' at Umballah, the final stage of the narrator's 'Wanderings', is only identified as 'an officer in one of her Majesty's regiments of foot then stationed' there; neither the regiment nor the officer are named in any more specific terms.[68] For an autobiographical text that is largely in praise of and in agreement with the persons it cites, then, 'Wanderings' keeps about the identity of both its narrator and his supposed witnesses very hazy indeed.

VENTRILOQUISING THE OTHER

Both European and native witnesses cited in 'Wanderings' serve the same purpose, namely to affirm and even improve on the narrator's own judgements. They all recommend a stricter rule and do not once challenge Britain's inherent right to India. Indeed, they often serve to justify it and to pre-empt any possible objections to it. For instance, one high-ranking sepoy declares that most of the natives' arguments about caste are 'a great many falsehoods'.[69] These words, supposedly from the horse's mouth, effectively defuse the reproach that the 1857 rebellion had been triggered by the insensitive attitude of the British to sepoys. This use of native witnesses in particular is a common device, as Patrick Brantlinger confirms:

> In most British writing about the Empire, English discourse and authority are imposed on imperialized peoples, often to the extent of denying them even imaginary voices (and what voices are occasionally granted support imperialism).[70]

What makes this device remarkable in 'Wanderings' are the respective roles that the narrator and his native interlocutors take: Lang's narrator often poses as the ignorant and mistakenly liberal 'interloper' who stands corrected by natives. For instance, when the narrator expresses his doubts about the alleged treachery of the Bengali zemindars (landholders), Nobinkissen retorts, 'Sir, I know my own countrymen better than you do'.[71] This serves the double purpose of letting the narrator appear unprejudiced and humble—after all, he is willing to learn from an Indian—and giving the native witnesses' statements added authority, especially as their views often relate implicitly to the events of 1857.

Nobinkissen is the most outspoken of native commentators and 'perhaps, the cleverest Hindoo whom I encountered'.[72] He suggests that the Europeans should 'resettle the whole of Bengal' and nonchalantly dismisses the possibility of any protests since it is 'only human—and certainly Asiatic—nature [not to . . .] like to behold our neighbours better off than ourselves'.[73] He underlines his faith in the British government by quoting Shakespeare's *Julius Caesar* III.1: 'Caesar never does wrong without just cause.'[74] Not surprisingly, the narrator finds in retrospect that 'Nobinkissen's prophecy has been fulfilled to the letter' and reformulates his views more radically:

> It is from the coffers of men of this stamp [Bengali zemindars] that large sums should be extracted annually towards keeping up a vast—an overwhelming—European force in India [. . .] What right [have they] to expect that we shall any longer forego [. . .] several millions annually [. . .] which, to every intent and purpose, is our just due?[75]

The same criticism of the zemindars—landholders—has already been made in Joachim Siddons's 1853 article 'Justice for Natives', which pointed out that the harshly underpaid and overtaxed natives could hardly help being corrupt. But where Lang suggests making the zemindars pay up ruthlessly, Siddons advocates a more egalitarian approach to resolve the situation for the benefit of the poorest victims of corruption:

> Give them, in promotion to the highest offices, a motive for integrity—reform the Hindoo and the Hindoo character by removing the

> broad distinctions between the European conqueror and the native subject; make their interests identical with ours, and they will become just administrators of the law, and originators of a vigilant and honest police.[76]

Naturally, Siddons' solution is directly opposed to Lang's own. In order to make his point, Lang enlists a second and more illustrious native, the 'late Maharajah Hindoo-Rao', 'the most remarkable native that I ever met'.[77] Hindoo-Rao's name was familiar to informed contemporary readers, as his house played a role in the Sepoy Rebellion and was 'famous throughout Europe as the position of one of our batteries'.[78] One of the rare times 'that the old chief could be induced to discuss politics' is 'the occasion of the Forty-first Regiment of Infantry having mutinied at Delhi'[79], upon which the Maharajah comments: 'Ah! if you go on humouring your native soldiers in this way, they will never be satisfied until they govern the country!'[80] Hindoo-Rao can be read as a parallel to Nobinkissen, as both scenes ventriloquise the 'other' and make it an authoritative advocate of a stricter imperial rule. Both natives have occupied respected positions in their time, and the narrator values their opinion because it happens to coincide with his own: like Nobinkissen, Hindoo-Rao implicitly recommends a more heavy-handed British government. If this recommendation comes from a native rather than a British imperialist, any potential claims that such a radical policy imposed from outside might be immoral are easily defused.

We have already seen the many European commentators whom Lang cites to underline the various shortcomings of the British Empire. Of these, the German baron is particularly intriguing, since he is native neither to India nor Britain and therefore occupies an ostensibly neutral position in the scramble for India. His aristocratic title aside, the narrator goes to some lengths to affirm the German baron's—and his French companion's—general credentials:

> [They] had seen a great deal of the world, and of the society at every court and capital in Europe. They were both possessed of considerable abilities, and of the most enviable dispositions; always good-natured and good-tempered; patient and cheerful [. . .] They were men of refined understanding, and [. . .] utterly devoid of vulgar nationalities—of any enthusiastic admiration of their own father-lands—and would just as soon ridicule the foibles peculiar to their own countries respectively, as the foibles of any other country.[81]

During the young men's ramble through the Himalayas, the German baron decides that the mountains of Italy and Switzerland are odious since 'the eyes of the vulgar, of all nations, have beheld' them. In contrast, the surrounding lands of the Himalaya 'remain uncultivated and unenjoyed'—by Europeans, that is. This glibly elides the native population that, presumably, *does* enjoy the land already.[82] The baron then fantasises about his own pet imperial project: 'What wine could be grown there! I will come out to this country with a few German peasants. I will have vineyards. I will make a [colossal] fortune'.[83] The German peasants would then be expected to instruct the natives in winemaking. The produce of this colony will be sold within India, for 'does not British India contain enough of Europeans to make a market?'[84] The objection that there are no roads is easily waived: 'True! But is there a scarcity of labour in India?'[85] Having acknowledged that there are in fact natives (though not their right to the 'superb' soil on which the baron builds his imaginary colony), they are transformed into 'labour' at the disposal of Europeans.[86] The baron then decides that he would grow tea as well:

> I would say to Mr. Chinaman, 'I thank you very much; but I do not want any more of your tea. You are insolent, overbearing, and insulting in your dealings with me, and now you may drink your own tea, and I will drink *my* own tea; and, if you like, you may stir yours with your own pigtail. We will bring China into our own dominions, for God has given to this climate and to this soil the same properties as your soil and climate possess.'[87]

In this passage the German baron voices a far more radical opinion than is uttered by any of the British, with whom he nevertheless claims allegiance in the phrase 'our own dominions' (which appear to be as 'God-given' as the soil and climate). While the officials of the British Raj have to maintain the idea that the agenda of the 'enlightened [British] government [is] to do for the people and the country, what they are unable to do for themselves', the foreign 'interloper' is free from such moral obligations and can express the true objectives behind the Empire, namely to amass 'a fortune so colossal that Rothschild [. . .] will have to write to me'.[88] He merely criticises the British government for its inefficiency:

> The result of my experience leads me to believe that the government of this country is, in all matters (save annexation), [slow . . .]. There is a listlessness and languor about its movements; a want of everything in the shape of society and enterprise, and seemingly such an earnest desire to discourage the efforts of those who would, in reality, develop the resources of India, that I am astonished any man unconnected with the services should persevere in the attempt to make a living in the Eastern British domains.[89]

Once more, the British Empire is attacked not for ruthlessly exploiting India, but for the failure to do so to its full potential, and for the restraints it places upon those who would appropriate Indian 'resources' more extensively. Predictably, the British magistrate in the company 'quite agree[s]' with the baron, and so of course does the narrator, who cites him at length without any further qualification.[90]

'ORIENTAL CHARACTER'

Despite the German baron's attempt to overlook the Indian natives, India is, of course, teeming with people, and it is these that are the narrator's main object: like the other 'interlopers in the East', he travels 'with a view to become acquainted with oriental character from personal observation' and to this end 'acquire[s] a knowledge of Hindoostanee and of Persian'.[91] His skin 'became far less fair than many natives of the country', and he makes 'a point of avoiding my own countrymen, and of associating only with the natives of India', even avoiding beef and pork out of respect for Hinduism and Islam.[92] He studiously turns himself into an expert on 'oriental character' and is in an ideal position to report back to his fellow-Europeans. According to Hosking, this

> suggest[s] that Lang consciously went out of his way to dissociate himself from the Imperial masters, and attempted to engage with the colonized in India in ways which tried to avoid the consequences of the British coloniser's essentialising and hegemonic will to dominate and rule.[93]

However, the experiences of 'eight months' in Tirhoot and 'five months in Oude' are compressed into the space of one column or half a page at the very beginning of 'Wanderings', and are limited to brief sketches of some native dignitaries who host the narrator. One of these shows 'small mental capacity [and . . .] immense cunning and inordinate vanity', while another's 'manners were refined, his address charming, and his bearing altogether that of a well-bred [. . .] learned and well-informed [gentle]man'.[94] This discrimination proves that 'Lang is not always so conventionally Eurocentric' but able to '"see" Indians as individuals, rather than represent[ing] them as homogenised into a collective "they", which is the typical imperial strategy'.[95] However, as I have suggested before, the narrator's distinction between different natives often coincides with his praise of those who support the imperial agenda, as in the case of Hindoo-Rao or Nobinkissen.

The most detailed description of any encounter with a single native is to be found in instalment I, where the narrator stays with the Maharajah 'Peishwa Bahadoor', better known as Nana Sahib, who was vilified as the arch enemy behind the Sepoy Rebellion. This episode has been analysed in some detail by G.S. Amur, therefore I shall keep it brief. The narrator is introduced to the Nana as 'a gentleman of distinction, a most intimate friend of the governor-general, and related by birth or marriage to every member of the council in Calcutta, as well as the constant guest of the Queen of England' and therefore receives a splendid welcome.[96]

The narrator, who has made no effort to disabuse the Nana of this misconception, then describes the mixture of European and native furniture and decorations which is characteristic of 'the house of a native gentleman', the former distributed 'indiscriminately' and without regard to use or value.[97] Later, the narrator is invited to an audience with his host, and type-casts (still in the 'ethnographic present tense') the dialogue as a role-play between 'Native Rajah' and 'Humble Sahib', the latter employing his knowledge of 'Asiatic manners and customs' which require him to 'eat [. . .] compliments with a good appetite' and to be 'childishly charmed' when the Rajah lets him win at billiards.[98] Amur finds that

> Lang's description of the incongruous European furniture in Nana Sahib's household and of the warm hospitality he received from the Peshwa carries conviction but the other details, like his conversations with Nana Sahib, are couched in general terms and create the impression of vagueness.[99]

Amur concludes that it is doubtful whether 'Lang [did] actually visit Nana Sahib at Bithur or was [. . .] only exploiting the tremendous popular interest in him in Britain during and after the days of the Mutiny' when Nana Sahib was popularly blamed as the perpetrator of the Cawnpore massacre.[100] The narrator's final verdict on Nana Sahib is full of negations and avoids any affirmative claims about his host: 'He appeared to be not a man of ability, nor a fool. He was selfish, but what native is not? He seemed to be far from a bigot in matters of religion'.[101] In contrast, Andrew Ward seems to have no doubt that Lang's narrative is truthful and cites it in great detail.[102]

The narrator's most assertive judgement on Nana Sahib concerns the latter's 'grievance':

> During my rambles in India, I have been the guest of some scores of rajahs, great and small; and I never knew one who had not a grievance. He had either been wronged by the government, or by some judge, whose decision had been against him. In the matter of the government, it was a sheer love of oppression that led to the evil of which he complained; in the matter of the judge, that functionary had been bribed by the other party.[103]

In order to cure his host of his preoccupation with that grievance, the narrator 'translated many sentiments of Juvenal and Horace [on the vanity of human wishes] into Hindoostanee; but, I regret to say, they had no effect on Nena Sahib'.[104] Like his house, the 'native rajah' remains impervious to improvement by the wholesome influence of Western culture. Ward points out, however, that Lang's lofty dismissal of such grievances was hypocritical, since they 'were Lang's bread and butter, and few princes would have put up with his pretensions except in order to sound him out. Nana carefully avoided discussing the matter directly with his other guests, even when the discussion turned to politics.' [105] Ward's discussion of this scene also throws some doubt over the time and occasion of this visit—he implies that Lang was treated with these honours following his victory against the East India Company on behalf of Joti Prasad in 1851.

The native obsession with grievances is by no means limited to rajahs. One of the Lieutenant's group is an 'almost imbecile native veteran' who habitually complains all day long.[106] The Lieutenant intimates that most natives are the same as the old officer: 'A native—especially a native commissioned officer—forget a grievance? [. . .] He will, it is true, forget his present grievance tomorrow, when he has a fresh one; but at the end of the journey they will be forthcoming in a lump'.[107] Even when the old man is dying, he nevertheless 'continued to gurgle forth a grievance'.[108] His farcical preoccupation with grievances thus becomes literally 'the end [. . .] of that old man's life'. [109] The Lieutenant informs the narrator that

> A grievance, real or imaginary, is quite necessary for that old man's existence [. . .] and if he can't find one for himself [. . .] he will concoct one for the sepoys. [. . .] I am sorry to say, that he is a perfect representative of the entire body of native commissioned officers.[110]

These native officers receive the implicit blame for the 1857 rebellion, which has already been alluded to two pages previously in the failed attempt to provoke a mutiny at Barruckpore: 'These native officers [are . . .] the curse of the native service. Many very clear-headed and experienced officers have recommended [. . .] appointing, in their stead, more European officers; but the advice has never been heeded, and never will be, I fear'.[111] Although the narrator refrains from any comment on Nana Sahib's involvement in the 1857 mutiny, the fixation with grievances which the Nana shares with this insubordinate old native commissioned officer places both of them, 'to every intent and purpose', in the context of the 1857 revolt.[112]

For the most part, the narrator adopts the stereotype of the 'mild Hindoo'.[113] This is particularly evident when the narrator passes through a village where he excites curiosity, though the villagers 'were not alarmed, and looked on simply with that stupidity which is characteristic of the cultivators of the soil in the upper provinces of India'.[114] In the same manner the village accepts the death of two children and an old man who are struck by lightning:

> The matter-of-fact way in which the natives of India regard the death of their relations or friends is something wonderful to behold. It is not that their affections are less strong than ours, or their feelings less acute. It is that fatality is the beginning and end of their creed.[115]

Ironically, the fatalistic attitude to death that the narrator diagnoses among the natives of India goes hand-in-hand with severe cruelty on many occasions. Within the first column of 'Wanderings' the narrator refers to 'Thugs' who were 'member[s] of a well-organized confederacy of professional assassins who traveled in gangs throughout India'[116]. Men, women and children are included among these 'domesticated demons' who relish the re-enactment of murder. Natives (Hindus and Muslims as well as Gurkhas) are shown abusing their animals and wives, immuring or hacking to pieces at the slightest suspicion of adultery.[117]. According to whether they support or oppose the British empire, native peoples are either condemned for their brutality or praised for their valiant services to Britain.

In addition to their discontent, passivity, and cruelty, Indians are habitually deceitful and dishonest: 'There are hypocrites in all countries, but India swarms with them more thickly than any other country in the world'.[118] On more than one occasion the narrator assures us that 'the Hindoos, and Mussulmans in India (like the Arabs), do not regard being guilty of a fraud or theft as a disgrace. The degrading part of the business is, being convicted'.[119] Worse, this duplicity can be passed on like a virus and corrupt the innocent:

> It is wonderful how rapidly the children of Europeans in India take a cue from a native servant [. . .] in very many cases, it is in deceit and falsehood that children are first schooled by the servants.[120]

Native perfidy is taken for granted, hence the narrator appears positively astonished if he accidentally comes across an honest native: '*Strange to say*, frequent as are the opportunities which the servants of these bungalows have of pilfering from travellers, they rarely or never avail themselves of such opportunities'.[121] This occasional honesty, however, has to be put into perspective: 'I moved entirely amongst [. . .] a very poor and very ignorant peasantry, but, *comparatively speaking*, civil and honest'.[122] The comparison is presumably being drawn between these and 'normal', deceitful natives, while European integrity and politeness remain superior to both. Such low expectations are embraced by (or rather projected back onto) natives themselves: 'I am a wandering dealer from Affghanistan [sic], *but* I am not destitute of good feeling and integrity, little as you may credit my assertions in this respect'.[123]

Most of the natives are fawning 'hypocrites' not only because of their innate dishonesty, but because the British 'foster hypocrisy'.[124] One example of this is the native doctor who heals the narrator's headache by 'mesmerism' and in return asks for a certificate, which he hoards along with the cheque for the treatment. The narrator draws a patronising comparison between the doctor's certificates and those of 'English charlatans', even though the doctor has just cured him of 'extreme agonies' in a matter of 'two or three minutes'.[125] Since the doctor does not cash the cheque but prefers to keep it as a recommendation 'by an European gentleman', the narrator concludes disdainfully: 'Such a strange people are the natives of India! Their cupidity is enormous, certainly, but their vanity (I am speaking of the better class) is even greater'.[126] Several natives, led by Nana Sahib, receive the narrator with presents, 'prostrated themselves at my feet, and in the most abject manner imaginable, craved my favour and protection' because they 'fancied that I was a sahib in authority'.[127] Although the narrator professes to be 'dismay[ed]' on all these occasions, he never clarifies the mistake but benevolently 'promised each and every one of them, with much sincerity, that if it ever lay in my power to do them a service, they might depend upon my exerting myself to the utmost'.[128] The worship and 'flattery', which 'every European guest of any real or supposed importance' receives from rajahs and peasants alike, is quite agreeable and 'not very tedious' after all.[129] In such scenes, it is quite possible to see how the Europeans might 'foster hypocrisy'.

Even the most harmless natives have some irritating attributes: 'A native of Hindostan can settle nothing without a noise'.[130] Several are described as 'childish'.[131] On a more physical level, natives are particularly 'black' when in disgrace, as indicated by the noisy 'black desputants' who put the narrator 'in a rage' and the 'sable cultivator of the soil' whom the government allegedly prefers over the British soldier.[132] By contrast, the narrator's servant Sham, who is 'so clever, so sharp, so intelligent, and so active a servant' that he is encouraged to vent his opinions, 'was, moreover, very good-looking and had, for a native of Hindoostan, a very fair complexion', which is however still distinct from Europeans who possess 'a skin as white as snow'.[133] Initially, the narrator is impressed by the cleanliness of the natives: 'It is impossible to witness and not to admire this part of the Hindoo and Mussulman religions'.[134] Later on, however, he witnesses a trial which takes place on the magistrate's veranda, 'for, a large number of half-clad natives, in a hot country, do not impart to a confined space an agreeable perfume, by any means'.[135]

While 'Wanderings' allows for exceptions on an individual basis, it nevertheless maintains a clear 'line of demarcation [. . .] between civilised man and savage'.[136] For all the shortcomings of the British Empire's administration (some of which are only the result of the bad 'material' available in India[137]), the overall impression remains that Europeans need to stick together in order to keep the natives in place and force them to obey and serve their 'superiors, the white man'.[138] Where Europeans are 'tolerant', natives cling to 'prejudices'.[139] The native 'stupidity' needs to be controlled by an 'enlightened government', and the 'true spirit of Oriental exaggeration' is counterbalanced by European rationality.[140] While it is 'Asiatic' nature not to like 'beholding our neighbours better off than ourselves', 'we (Christians) in India [readily] obliged one another (albeit utter strangers), and [. . .] gladly assist each other, whenever and wherever we meet'.[141]

THE (IM)POSSIBILITY OF RELIGIOUS CONVERSION

We have seen that Lang rewrites, to a degree, a pessimistic version of the more sanguine changes to Britain's rule of India that *Household Words* writers proposed before 1857. While Siddons proposed to solve corruption by removing the strict hierarchy and distinction between European and native, Lang wants to reinforce that distinction (although he also demands that European officers be trained properly, learn the languages of the people they are in charge of, and have a smattering of their cultural and religious habits). One area in which Lang's outlook is particularly bleak is the possibility of religious conversion. In his 1850 account of 'Christmas in India', Joachim Siddons announced that, after the wholesome influence of European colonisation, 'the cross is recognised by thousands who gladly accept its guarantee of salvation.'[142] Although Siddons found that the natives had become more tolerant as a result of prolonged European occupation, the Europeans themselves were less so:

> The British had been far more tolerant [in the eighteenth century . . .] It had been perfectly well understood that the obligations and restrictions that caste imposed upon a Hindu soldier's behaviour were all-important to him [. . .] But since then all had changed. Indian culture was less inclined to be respected than to be mocked by British officials.[143]

In the years prior to the Sepoy Rebellion, 'the insensitivity, disdain and lack of curiosity which characterized so many English residents in India [which would have been . . .] barely conceivable' a hundred years before, reached a new peak.[144] Lang alternates between condemning such intolerance on the part of the Europeans and advocating it. For instance, he demands that both military and civilian personnel should learn the languages they are likely to come into contact with, but his reason is that the British will find it easier to supervise their native staff's work and keep a tighter rule over them, as well as command their respect.

While missionaries had not been allowed to operate in India in the eighteenth century, by the middle of the nineteenth they

> spoke openly of the day when all men would embrace Christianity and turn against their heathen gods; and, though it was claimed that the missionaries were not paid by the Government [. . .] their activities were approved of, and in many cases supported by, the Government [. . .] Moreover, [. . .] there were plenty of British officers and officials who behaved as though they were missionaries themselves.[145]

Unsurprisingly, such behaviour aroused the fear of forcible conversion amongst the native soldiers, which was rife by 1856.[146] Although such religious fears were not the sole trigger of the Sepoy Rebellion, they certainly played a large part in it and prepared the ground for enduring and severe discontent.

Lang repeatedly demonstrates the futility of conversion. A good illustration is the case of an orphaned European boy who grows up with an Afghan dealer. He is recognised by a European party who are mesmerised by his beauty and his 'soft and silvery' voice that made 'even the guttural sounds that he uttered [. . .] like music'—clearly, his innate virtues shine through the 'mongrel Persian' identity he has acquired.[147] Although the boy considers himself a Muslim, the dealer explains that his charge 'is a Christian; for he is not a Mussulman. Though he thinks he is a Mussulman, and says his prayers, and is very constant to all the observances of the Mussulman faith.'[148] Religion and race are here used synonymously: one cannot acquire a faith but must be born into it, no matter how devoutly, enduringly, and sincerely one observes the creeds of that faith. Conversion thus becomes impossible.

Equally, Nobinkissen points out the futility of religious conversion, since the converters stem from

> the dregs of both Hindoos and Mussulmans. They are most debased and degraded of Indians—men who only assume Christianity in the hope of temporal advantage and preferment—and who fling aside their newly put-on faith [. . .] the moment they find their hope frustrated.[149]

Throughout this scene, Nobinkissen carries the authority over the narrator and is usually allowed the final word. He relates a few anecdotes to underline his point, which is backed up by a Roman Catholic priest who conveniently stops by at this instant to admit that 'we are [convinced] of the hopelessness of the task of converting the Hindoo and the Mussulman to Christianity.'[150] In the preceding discussion about religion, the narrator tells Nobinkissen that the British 'are a tolerant people, and wish to convince both creeds [Muslim and Hindu] that we have no desire to interfere with their religious prejudices in any way whatsoever.'[151] Not only does Nobinkissen reject this judgement as inconsistent with the encouragement Christian missionaries receive, but the term 'prejudice' itself undermines the very tolerance which the narrator is trying to ascertain, as it shows once again that, far from being 'tolerant', most Christians look down on the creeds which prevail 'in the land of heathens and idolators'.[152] The same word has occurred twice before in 'Wanderings': in instalment I, the narrator explains that although 'his Highness ['Nena Sahib'] was himself a strict Hindoo, he had no kind of prejudice' and allows beef to be served to his guests.[153] The second instance occurs in instalment II, when the Lieutenant praises his sepoys who, during the Afghan war, had shown 'themselves superior to prejudices most intimately connected with their religion—their caste' when they 'braved the [. . .] taunts of every Hindoo in the country, in order to pay respect to the memory of those officers whose dangers and privations they had cheerfully shared'.[154] In both cases the praise goes to those natives who are willing to forego their religious principles in the service of Europeans, though the praise for Nana Sahib's liberal attitude is almost annulled by the suggestion that he is in fact a hypocritical sensualist: 'He seemed to be far from a bigot in matters of religion; [. . .] I am quite satisfied that he drank brandy and smoked hemp in the chillum of his hookah'.[155]

Nobinkissen identifies the Brahmins as the source of much unnecessary trouble with the caste system. They 'incite the people' to protest against any transgressions by Europeans, while they 'say nothing' if a Muslim does the same.[156] The reason for this bias is that 'the Mahommedans are not the rulers of this country, but the Sahibs are; and hence the jealousy with which they are watched'.[157] Nobinkissen, himself 'a Brahmin of the highest caste', blames the British government for the arrogance of the Brahmins[158]: 'every concession on the part of the government leads those Brahmins to believe that they have great power, and leads the people also to believe it'.[159] Later on, the magistrate Mr West confirms that 'most of the diabolical crimes committed in this country are committed by Brahmins'.[160]

Nobinkissen therefore hopes that 'the Government of India will see the necessity of forbidding Hindoo festivals in the public streets—abolishing them—just as Suttee was abolished'.[161] Once again, Lang's preferred solution is not tolerance but strict suppression. In aligning the majority of Hindu festivals with the practice of burning widows on their husbands' funeral pyre, Nobinkissen depicts the recommended abolition of religious festivals as a necessary consequence of the moral superiority that Europeans profess as the basis of their rule over India. For

> it is only the dissolute rich and the rabble who take any delight in these festivals, many of which are indecent and disgusting. Sensible and respectable Hindoos [. . .] avoid them, and think them a nuisance. Hindooism will never become extinct, so long as this world lasts; but the British government has the power of doing away with those obnoxious observances [. . .] which only disfigure the religion.[162]

It goes without saying that throughout 'Wanderings' the 'sensible and respectable' natives are those who support the British government and who show no 'prejudice' in its service. A similar complaint is repeated in instalment IX, this time by the narrator himself: 'It is to be hoped that, when our rule in India is completely re-established, these absurd concessions—these mere pretexts for idleness—will no longer be suffered to prevail'.[163] The Lieutenant has already established in instalment II that

> more than four-fifths of what [the natives] talk about [caste] is pure nonsense [. . .] I don't mean to say that some Hindoos are not very strict. But I mean to say that a very small proportion live in accordance

> with the Shasters, and that when they cry out [. . .] it is nothing more than a rotten pretext for escaping some duty.[164]

Both native and European advisors agree, then, that the Indian caste system and religion needs to be moderated by the beneficial influence of a British government, for the natives' own good, just as suttee was abolished before. After all, 'it behoves an enlightened government to do for the people and the country, what they are unable to do for themselves'.[165] However, carrying out the white man's burden is continually hindered by the obstinate natives themselves, as the narrator discovers when he is told about the practice of immuring wives suspected of adultery:

> 'Hindoos as well as Mahommedans punish their wives in that way.'
> 'You mean that they used to do so in former times, previous to British rule in India. But such a thing could not occur in our time.'
> 'It does not occur so often as it did; but it does occur, sometimes, even in these days. How do you know what happens in the establishment of a wealthy native?' [166]

Clearly, the civilising mission which the 'enlightened' British government has taken upon itself in India needs yet stricter enforcement in order to abolish such native barbarism.

MUTINIES

The reason why the issues of religion and caste concern Lang so urgently is of course that these triggered the 1857 rebellion. Although 'Wanderings' is set in the late 1840s and therefore can only comment on the Sepoy Rebellion in passing, it features a whole range of smaller and concealed mutinies that provide a running commentary on 1857. In the 1840s, religious fears are still a cause for 'some merriment' amongst the sepoys, as the Lieutenant's sepoy Maun Sing states: 'The Mussulmans, when we laugh together about [the debate of which animal's hide their equipment is made of], say the cow. We protest that it is pigskin'.[167] But Maun Sing illustrates the dire consequences of taking such 'prejudices' seriously:

> When Pertab Sing came down to Barruckpore to corrupt the regiments of native infantry there stationed, in eighteen hundred and forty-eight, he wanted them to protest against wearing the [leather]. [. . .] Pertab [Sing's aim] was simply to excite the native troops to mutiny and to kill their officers.[168]

However, the Barruckpore sepoys report the plot, and the saboteur is arrested and ridiculed. Since 'the government deemed it best to treat the whole affair as a farce', it is not surprising that this particular mutiny is not to be found in any history books.[169] This affair appears like a rewriting of an uprising at Barrackpore in 1824 when 'a whole catalogue of grievances, aggravated by a fear that the sepoys might be ordered to travel by sea, resulted in another mutiny'.[170] In both the Pertab Sing episode and the 1824 uprising the threat of losing caste played a crucial role, which was also the issue at the heart of the infamous 'affair of the greased cartridges' that was assumed to have started the 1857 rebellion.[171] However, far from being considered a 'farce', the 1824 uprising at Barrackpore caused 'more deaths, more executions, and the disbandment of another regiment'.[172]

'Wanderings' is peppered with supposedly prophetic statements that form a subtext for the events of 1857, even though the reference is not always made explicit (given that news of the Rebellion were so ubiquitous, it was hardly necessary to spell the connection out in every instance). In a discussion about the differences between 'gorgeous [native] edifices' such as the Taj Mahal and the 'simple and economical structures of the British', the Lieutenant suggests that 'these monuments of folly, extravagance and superstition [lead . . .] the natives to draw prejudicial comparisons' about British supremacy: 'It looks as though we had no confidence in our hold of the country, and therefore would not go to any expense worth speaking of'.[173] A similar sentiment is expressed by the keeper of the Meerut churchyard who deplores the graves' rapid dilapidation and thinks that the government 'ought to expend a few hundred pounds every year on these yards, in order to avert such scandal and disgrace' and keep up appearances.[174] He mentions another graveyard that fell to ruin after the European forces were moved from there:

> Looking around me [. . .] it seemed to me as though the British had been turned out of the country by the natives, and that the most sacred spot in the cantonment had been desecrated out of spite or revenge. And it is just what they would do if ever they got the upper hand.[175]

As soon as this pessimistic statement has been recounted, the narrator adds that 'this old soldier and his family perished in the massacre at Meerut on the tenth of May'.[176] This last piece of information connects the theoretical possibility that Britain might lose the power struggle in India and the actual instance of this in 1857, and underlines the urgency of the soldier's vision.[177]

Another obscure mutiny, 'which, by the way, was hushed up', has taken place in Delhi, as Hindoo-Rao's advice that the British need to be more heavy-handed has already shown. This gruesome topic of conversation is counterpoised with a dinner that Hindoo-Rao gives for Sir Charles Napier, the former commander-in-chief of India. Napier 'made allusion to the pleasure it afforded him in seeing Christians, Hindoos and Mussulmen, on such good terms, and living together in such amity and concord'.[178] The narrator immediately bridles this pleasant impression with a snapshot from the present:

> What a change since that evening, which to me seems but as yesterday! Several of our party, on that occasion, have become chiefs of the recent rebellion, and were accessory to the massacre of English gentlemen and ladies.[179]

The narrator's host in Delhi is Joseph Skinner, 'the eldest son of [James Skinner . . .] the founder and commandant of the famous Skinner's Horse', who frequently entertains 'civilians and military men of every rank and grade [. . .] as well as native gentlemen of position in India—Hindoos and Mahommedans'.[180] The narrator mentions that Joseph Skinner died in 1855 and comments:

> I am rejoiced that he did not survive to be brutally massacred, as his brothers have been—or to see his house (near the Cashmere Gate) which was always the scene of good fellowship and good feeling, turned into a battery by the rebels—or the church, built by his father, burned and destroyed by the people who had for years and years paid, or affected to pay, unqualified respect and devotion to his family.[181]

In this passage the narrator evokes, posthumously as it were, the hypothetical fury Joseph Skinner would have felt if he had not died beforehand. But Lang is very selective with Skinner's biographical details. Hibbert notes that his father James Skinner 'was the son of a Scottish officer in the East India Company's army and a Rajput girl' and built not only 'St James's Church in Delhi [but also . . .] a mosque for one of his wives and a Hindu temple for his mother'.[182] However, Joseph Skinner's multiracial and multicultural background, which might complicate the simple justice of this outrage, is silenced in Lang's narrative.

A CRITIQUE OF EMPIRE

Great as his indignation is at the 1857 insurrection, the narrator blames not only the uncontrollable natives but also the British government of India. I have already discussed various suggestions towards a stricter rule and the suppression of native customs. However, it would be unfair to dismiss 'Wanderings' without entering into its more discriminate judgement of flaws in the colonial system, since 'there are moments when Lang presents a much more critical view of British imperialism'[183]. 'Wanderings' presents an ambivalent attitude to imperialism, on the one hand criticising the British Raj and its officials, on the other turning some of that criticism around to reflect on the natives which thwart the efforts of an 'enlightened government'.[184] One has to bear in mind that a critic of the Empire is not necessarily an anti-imperialist.

Lang frequently attacks the outdated system of promotion in the East India Company's army, which upgrades people not according to merit but to duration of service. In describing the mutiny that is supposed to have taken place in 1848 in Barruckpore, the narrator implicitly criticises the fact that the sepoys who reported the plot 'had no reward [. . .] beyond some expressions of praise from the authorities'.[185] While the natives who deserve a reward are overlooked, 'Wanderings' is full of European military men who have been promoted, 'albeit [they] had never been within range of an enemy's cannon in the whole course of [their] life'.[186] The Lieutenant sneers at one of these who

> knows nothing whatever of soldiering; having been in staff employ ever since he was an ensign. All the sepoys, as well as his officers, laugh at him as he comes on the parade ground, and attempts to handle the regiment; and after the farce is over, he laughs with them. For thirty years he was employed in commissariat duties [. . .] and then, according to the rules of the service, he was withdrawn from staff employ, and appointed to command a corps! [. . .] That is a part of our military system, sir.[187]

For all its humour, this description suggests that such incompetent officers pose a threat to British authority since native soldiers may ridicule and disrespect their commanders and, by extension, the government of which they are part. Another inept commander is 'General Sir Doodle Dudley', a deranged octogenarian who is in line for a promotion to the command of Bombay.[188] Dudley 'was quite childish before he relinquished his command' and, the narrator archly observes, not

> an average specimen of the General officers sent out [since . . .] some, though very old and inefficient, could, see, hear, and understand. But within the past ten years, some officers that I know of have been sent out, to Bengal alone, who were not one whit more efficient than General Sir Doodle Dudley.[189]

The criticism of such incompetent officers belongs to a wider criticism that accuses the British government in India of unnecessary bureaucracy. Instalment XII describes a court martial under Sir Doodle which draws a negligible incident between two drunk soldiers out into an inflated affair that lasts for several weeks, only to result in the 'severe reprimand' that had been recommended in the first place.[190] The narrator 'emphatically' asserts that this 'description [. . .] is a fair specimen of what usually transpires at these tribunals', based on his experience of 'no fewer than eighteen Courts Martial during my sojourn in the East Indies'.[191]

Another reason for the occasional incompetence of the British rule over India is illustrated in instalment IX of 'Wanderings', in which the narrator and Mr. West stay at the magistrate's house in Bijnore. Having got lost on his way to Meerut, a young lord chances upon the three men and informs them that he is 'travelling the country for a few months' in order to 'acquir[e] information concerning India' in preparation for his entrance into parliament.[192] This 'bird's-eye view of India, its people, its institutions, and so forth' only allows him to spend a few hours or days in any one place, which is enough to convince him that he 'knew all about them'.[193] In fact,

> in his own opinion, he knew all about India and its affairs long before he touched the soil, for he had read a good deal in blue books and newspapers [. . .] therefore when his lordship asked questions it was not so much with a view to obtain information as to test the accuracy of that already acquired by reading, over the fireside in the library, of his father's mansion in Bagdad Square.[194]

This bitterly sarcastic remark aims at the lack of interest in the 'real' India, which the narrator intends to disclose to his reader. Lord Jamleigh is led to some sweeping generalisations not only about the natives but also 'condemning all [Anglo-]Indian officials [as . . .] a parcel of sycophants'.[195] Ironically, though, the 'Wanderings' themselves belong to the kind of literature that the narrator condemns here, and may easily have the same effect, especially since the narrator continually reasserts his expertise and portrays himself as a reliable eye-witness and guide to any reader who travels India only from the comfort of their own armchair.

This episode also ridicules the government's preference for statistics as a reliable source of information. When Lord Jamleigh inquires about the crime rate in Bijnore, the magistrate informs him that 'we are going to reduce it during the ensuing half-year, exactly thirty-three and a-half per cent' by being 'less energetic by thirty-three and a-half per cent'.[196] He explains that the Court of Appeal bases its calculation of a crime rate on the work of some magistrates who 'only attend[] court once or twice a week', and that the 'figures in the official returns [are not . . .] to be taken as any criterion of the crime perpetrated in our respective districts'.[197] Statistics thus cover up the shortcomings of inefficient officials.

A minor point of criticism is the presence of European women in India, who complicate matters unnecessarily.[198] For instance, a minor question of etiquette between two military and civilian dignitaries erupts into a full-blown affair when their wives become involved, so the case is finally submitted to the authority of the government.

> At length, the decision of the Home Government came out to India; but, alas! they had only half done their work! They had given [the lieutenant] the precedence over the civilian of twenty years standing,

> but had been silent about their wives! So the matter was referred back. [. . .] When I left India, the question had not been decided.[199]

This petty dispute, though amusing to read, reveals a misogynist subtext in the assumption that the women exacerbate an affair that could otherwise have been amiably settled 'in a calmer spirit' between the men. Although (both European and native) women have only a marginal existence in 'Wanderings', they tend to make matters more complicated due to the increased care and chivalry that their presence demands. An interesting example is the narrator's claim that European women travel more safely 'on any dangerous road' than men.[200]

> This is not to be attributed to any ideas of gallantry, or chivalry, on the part of marauders in the East; but simply to the fact that they knew the perpetrators of an offence committed against a lady would be hunted down to the death, while the sympathies entertained for the sufferings of a Sahib, would be only those of an ordinary character, and soon 'blow over.'[201]

The need for defending helpless women and punishing those who commit a crime against them is thus projected onto and finally taken over by the natives from whom women have to be protected in the first place. A mildly reproachful undercurrent informs the allegation that an assault on a man would 'soon "blow over"'. Lang, it seems, is of an opinion with Grenville Murray's 'Roving Englishman': women complicate and aggravate virtually any situation and had best stay at home.

Another reason for the incompetence of the British administration is the Europeans' failure to learn the native languages:

> the order of the Governor-General in Council touching a knowledge of the Native languages is a mere sham; and [. . .] ignorance, clothed with interest, is—so far as advancement is concerned—far preferable to a well-stored and a steady character.[202]

This links back to the antiquated promotion system, which is based not on merit but on duration of service and nepotism or 'interest' in both the military and civilian sectors: 'not one civilian in a hundred [. . .] can read and write Hindoostanee or Persian', therefore they have to rely on 'their native officers' for an accurate translation of documents which they authorise and allow the natives to commit fraud by exploiting this widespread ignorance.[203]

But fraud is not the only danger of this ignorance—to drive the point home, Lang cites the example of a native newspaper editor who, due to the European authorities' linguistic incompetence, is able to infiltrate a European newspaper and to 'seize[] the views of his employers, views intended only for European eyes, and [give] his own version of them to his readers in the Hindoostanee language' as well as publishing 'quantities of matters which the conductor of the [European] Meerut paper thought proper to suppress'.[204] Another native editor 'never lost an opportunity of bringing British rule in India into disgrace, ridicule, and contempt amongst his countrymen [yet . . .] succeeded in obtaining an appointment under the government'.[205] In case the depravity were lost on the reader, the narrator adds that

> he is now aide-de-camp and military secretary to Bahadoor Khan, the rebel, who is at the head of a considerable army, and [. . .] in possession of the entire Bareilly district [. . .] Should I again wander in India, it will not [. . .] surprise me to find him in the service of the British government, and filling some office of considerable dignity and emolument.[206]

'The danger of permitting native newspapers to be published without any sort of supervision' leads on to a more ambiguous form of criticism that pervades 'Wanderings'.[207] Overtly, it targets the European institutions in India but implicitly blames the Indian rabble that necessitates stricter rule through their inherent unreliability and vice. This is best expressed by the magistrate of Bijnore who complains about the corruption of the legal system in India but blames it on the human 'material with which we have to deal': 'Where the great bulk of the people are corrupt, [the administration of justice] can scarcely be in anything like a perfect state'.[208] As a result of incompetent and ignorant European officers, several 'absurd general orders [. . .] frequently appear' which, among other things, demand mutual 'respect' between natives and Europeans.[209] Since these are 'copied into the newspapers, and were read by [. . .] every non-commissioned officer and private in Upper India, Native and European', this leads to abuse by 'bad and discontented sepoys [who] often take advantage' of them.[210] The only effect of such legislation is that 'those men who are willing to oblige their officers, laugh at it, while the disaffected will insolently quote it, if required only to pick up a glove or a walking-stick'.[211] The charge against European administration and staff is thus transformed into a criticism of the unruly natives. Perhaps the most obvious reproach in this context is the absence of 'an overwhelming [. . .] European force in India', which is needed in order to control the violent mob.[212] Nobinkissen's and Hindoo-Rao's accusations that the British 'humour' their native dependants too much fall under this heading.[213]

It is not only the natives but also the Europeans who flaunt such orders. For example, 'the order of government, forbidding civilians or military men corresponding with the press, was, to every intent and purpose, a perfect farce and a dead letter'.[214]

> Frequently the members of the staff of the governor-general and of the commander-in-chief would not only send items of news, but comments thereon; and [. . .] this practice was continued up to the date of the recent outbreak, and is still continued.[215]

The narrator claims that 'it was the press that introduced to the notice of the government many clever and able men' who were then 'placed in staff employ', 'not to silence' them but 'on the contrary, I know that they were expected—and, in some instances, requested—to use their pens in defence of certain government measures'.[216] If the press censure had been obeyed, the government would have missed out on competent and knowledgeable support.

This episode reverberates with an article on a similar press act published in *Household Words* four months earlier, John Capper's 'A Very Black Act'. Capper attacks the so-called 'Black Act', which censored the press during the Sepoy Rebellion, and is outraged at the 'general gagging of the press, British and native' in the government's attempt to achieve 'the equality of the subject [. . .] by dealing out the self-same treatment to the loyal British editor and the Mohammedan traitor'.[217] Both Capper and Lang treat the press act as another of those 'absurd general orders' that aim at 'the equality of the subject' and mutual respect between natives and Europeans, and that are best ignored.[218]

The government's desire for equality and fairness between natives and Europeans is also mocked in one of the extended extracts in which the narrator attacks the poor living conditions of European soldiers, a major point of criticism in 'Wanderings'. A colonel informs the narrator that he has tried to persuade his brother, an MP, to 'bring under the notice of the House of Commons, the condition of the British soldier in India'.[219] The MP informs him that the matter meets with utter indifference wherever he raises it:

> Find out some indigo-planter who has been, or is supposed to be, guilty of some sort of oppression towards a sable cultivator of the soil, and we will pretty soon grind his bones to make our bread, my boy; but, for Heaven's sake, and the sake of the House of Commons, don't inflict on us your British soldiers.[220]

Similar to the claim that an attack on a woman will be punished severely while that on a man will 'blow over', this passage indicates some resentment against the groups the government is trying to treat fairly, since this fairness is supposedly bought at the expense of the British man present in India.

However, in one instance the European government is guilty of an 'absurd, unjust, and shameful' unfairness against a native, the Lallah Jooteepersâd—the very case in which Lang himself had led the successful defence in 1851.[221] The 'Government had threatened to prosecute [Jooteepersâd ...] for an attempt to make an overcharge of forty-thousand rupees' when claiming back money he laid out for the government troops during the 'Seik campaigns'.[222] At this point, the Rajah Lall Singh, with whom the narrator stays during this episode, interjects that, in the event of such a suspicion, a native court would 'convict you, imprison you for life, and confiscate all your possession. But the Indian Government has not the courage to act in that way'.[223] The European government, although clearly in the wrong, is thus contrasted with a much more radical native one and implicitly condemned not so much for its unfairness but its liberality and tolerance. Jooteepersâd is merely ordered to remain in Agra while the case is being investigated, and the government finally acquits and pays him.

In his report of this episode, the narrator concentrates on the reaction of the natives who hold 'the firm belief [. . .] that these proceedings had been taken to evade payment of the contractor's just demands', even though Jooteepersâd himself 'was the first to deny this assertion'[224] The 'strict investigation', which the Governor-General demands in order to avoid all imputations of unfairness, unfortunately serves to convince 'the natives of India [to this day] that the object of the Government was to cheat their creditor'.[225] Jooteepersâd proves his loyalty to the imperial government and sportingly forgives

> the wrongs (involving disgrace and dishonour) which were heaped upon him; for it is he who has fed, since July last, the five thousand Christians during their incarceration in the fortress of Agra; and amongst the civilians there shut up, is the gentleman who conducted the prosecution on the behalf of the Government, and who [. . .] strove very hard indeed for a verdict of guilty. Without Jooteepersâd we could not have held Agra.[226]

Although the narrator is clearly on the side of Jooteepersâd and critical of the government's proceedings, the asides at the tenacious natives, who refuse to listen to better judgement from Jooteepersâd himself, guarantee that the justice of the British government is not questioned to quite the extent it might have been, while the natives receive a share of reproof.

Written after the Sepoy Rebellion but set before it, Lang's 'Wanderings' skilfully weaves a web of seemingly objective and prescient opinions about the state of India and forms a backdrop for commenting—both implicitly and explicitly—on the events of 1857. Rick Hosking, dealing with the printed 1859 volume *Wanderings in India*, finds that 'there are moments when Lang presents a much more critical view of British imperialism'.[227] Since that volume contained Lang's pre-1857 *Household Words* publications and some additional material, its overall message was more ambiguous than that of the initial series in *Household Words*. In the 'Wanderings' of 1857, Lang mostly condemns British colonial rule as too lenient and lackadaisical—Britain's worst fault lies in its very generosity and desire to do justice. Simultaneously, Lang pulls all the stops to give his narrative the utmost possible authority. Thus, the few instances where British authorities really are in the wrong only serve to make his account appear grounded and objective and thus all the more convincing, as do the various native and European witnesses whom Lang's narrator cites. In the aftermath of the Sepoy Rebellion, such an overall confirmation of British innocence and native perfidy must have been particularly gratifying to British readers. Even Dickens, renowned as the liberal champion of the oppressed, famously wrote to Angela Burdett Coutts:

> I wish I were commander-in-chief in India. The first thing I would do to strike that Oriental race with amazement [. . .] should be to proclaim to them, in their language, [. . .] that I should do my utmost to exterminate the Race upon which the stain of the late cruelties rested; and that I was [. . .] now proceeding, with all convenient dispatch and merciful swiftness of execution, to blot it out of mankind and raze it off the face of the Earth.[228]

At its best, then, India (once you've got rid of your wife and children) is a terrific place for sporting European gentlemen who 'love a drink, a gamble, the odd bit of shooting and fishing'.[229] At its worst, India is a 'penal country' in which Christians sacrifice themselves to carry out 'humane projects' for the good of ungrateful 'domesticated demons'.[230]

Conclusion

Now that this study has concluded its journey around the world in *Household Words*' eyes and examined the different categories into which it divides mankind, I would like to conclude by considering what the journal considers to be the very verge of humanity and focus, in particular, on Charles Dickens's notorious article 'The Noble Savage'.[1] Not only does this article neatly encapsulate *Household Words*' attitude to 'savages', but it also brings together the main strands of inquiry that this book has pursued: it illuminates *Household Words*' negotiation of civilisational and biological explanations for the different races of mankind and illustrates that a definition of Englishness can ultimately be reached only through exclusion and negation. Finally, the article reinforces *Household Words*' general sense of the respective worth and positions of Ireland, Europe, and 'savages' on the model of concentric circles that I introduced at the beginning.

Racial discourse in Britain changed dramatically from the 1830s, when abolitionism was at its height, to the 1850s, when Robert Knox's *Races of Men* came to propagate a much more rigid account of race.[2] In 1853, the climate had changed sufficiently for Carlyle to republish his 'Occasional Discourse on the Nigger Question' under his own name and with the derisive alteration in its title.[3] Under the guise of serving philanthropic interests, Carlyle's 'Occasional Discourse' argues that slavery was a more sensible system and more likely to bring 'some real benefit and victory for the poor negro' than any system aiming at or presupposing equality between the races, and that whites had every right to compel the negroes to work 'with beneficent whip', since they did not work on their own impulse.[4] Although monogenetic in his approach ('we poor united Human Species'), Carlyle is ambiguous on whether human races can evolve—while he can envisage that 'a manfuller class of cultivators, stronger, worthier [. . .], abler [. . .] shall make their appearance' and replace 'the Saxon British', 'quashee' seems destined to do the most basic of physical labour at his white masters' command and cannot be left to his own devices—indeed, an enlightened form of slavery was, in Carlyle's view, the only hope the 'nigger' had of reaching his full potential.[5] Carlyle thus mixes the 'racial determinism' of Knox, who had argued that, although all human races were of one origin, races had developed prehistorically 'into fixed, unalterable, unequal, and antagonistic types', with the civilisational model of mankind which had characterised the earlier, abolitionist discourses.[6] Like Knox's own work, Carlyle's was 'ideologically associated with the more ambiguously reactionary polygenist theories of the multiple and unequal creation of human races.'[7]

Catherine Hall has noted that Carlyle's rhetoric in the 'Occasional Discourse' was 'strongly evocative of Dickens', and the parallels between 'Occasional Discourse' and 'The Noble Savage' are particularly obvious.[8] While Carlyle consistently describes Africans as animals 'with their beautiful muzzles up to the ears in pumpkins, imbibing sweet pulps and juices; the grinder and incisor teeth ready for every new work', Dickens simply describes the 'noble savage' as 'a wild animal' and 'brute' throughout his piece.[9] Both pieces effusively object to the supposed sentimentalism in abolitionist and racial discourse:

> It is extraordinary to observe how some people will talk about [the noble savage], as they talk about the good old times; how they will regret his disappearance [. . .] It is not the miserable nature of the noble savage that is the new thing; it is the whimpering over him with maudlin admiration [. . .].[10]

In his disgust at this supposed softening of racial discourse, Dickens overlooks the fact that, on the contrary, only the hardening of the cultural climate in previous years had made publications such as Carlyle's and Dickens's possible in the first place.

Yet it is their differences as much as their similarities that make these two pieces enlightening to compare. While Carlyle predominantly focuses on 'the Demerara nigger' and thus maintains a definite racial argument on African races in particular, Dickens follows a more civilisational line throughout his piece. His aim in 'The Noble Savage' is, similar to Carlyle's, to debunk the 'enormous superstition' that there is anything noble in savages and to reassert Europe's place at the top of the global hierarchy.[11] But Dickens makes no difference between 'savages'—from Bushmen and Zulus to Native Americans, they are all manifestations of the same low stage of civilisation.[12] The distasteful racism of this piece is not in question: Dickens exerts his full powers of eloquence to ridicule all 'savages' and repeatedly—if facetiously—suggests that the extermination of the savages is 'an indispensable preparation for the sowing [. . .] of any influence that can exalt humanity'.[13] But while his demand for the physical eradication of savages is hyperbolic and (one hopes) facetious, his demand that the 'savage [. . .] be *civilised* off the face of the earth' is expressed in full earnestness.[14] This suggests that savageness is not so much an inborn, genetic tendency but a civilisational stage:

> We have no greater justification for being cruel to the miserable object, than for being cruel to a WILLIAM SHAKESPEARE or an ISAAC NEWTON; but he passes away before an immeasurably better and higher power than ever ran wild in any earthly woods, and the world will be all the better when his place knows him no more.[15]

What the savage shares with Shakespeare and Newton is their innate humanity, of course. Although savages on the one hand and Shakespeare on the other form the utmost extremes of the continuum of humanity that Dickens can conceive, they nonetheless belong to the same species and thus need to be accounted for in *Household Words'* model of the world and humanity, if at the outermost edges.[16] Where Carlyle effectively propagates a biological account of races, Dickens aligns himself firmly with a fluid, civilisational model. While Carlyle professes to write with a philanthropic interest in mind, Dickens declares nothing of the sort—yet in effect, Dickens's is the more philanthropic of the two pieces. Carlyle's solution is to keep the indolent, savage negro in line with the 'beneficent whip', making him as useful to the whites as his nature allows, while Dickens hopes to get rid of the savage state altogether by civilising them up the scale of mankind. Although Dickens's piece is extreme in its tone and, to modern sensibilities, highly offensive, its policies still embody *Household Words*' occasionally reluctant liberalism, especially in comparison to Carlyle's 'Occasional Discourse'.

Interestingly, Dickens has pieced together his information about 'savages' not only from the ethnological writings of the Comte de Buffon, George Catlin, and other contemporary writers (it would be surprising if he had not also read Knox and Prichard, like most other people of his class and standing), but also from various exhibitions and ethnographic displays. These reflected a particularly Anglocentric view of the world and catered directly for the viewers' scopophilia. After all, Englishmen paid to view these displays and enjoyed the simultaneous thrill and abhorrence they induced, and Dickens was more addicted to such entertainments than most people.[17] Human exhibits such as the Chinese family, Bushmen, Hottentots, Ojibways, and Kaffirs toured the country for years on end, sustaining a tolerable income from the desire to see such exotic aliens.[18] Yet such displays were staged deliberately in order to pander to Europeans' expectations of native life and to illustrate the 'savages' as exotic Others.[19] Dickens's response is thus to a substantial degree the result of an engineered and staged performance, designed precisely to allow Englishmen to draw favourable comparisons between themselves and the 'savages'. In the same way, the Great Exhibition of 1851 appeared to display the world realistically but in fact presented a highly biased view, which then confirmed the expectations of its equally biased audience. The coverage the Exhibition received both in *Household Words* and the media at large showed contemporary Britain's urgent need to order, structure, and contain discursively the 'heterogeneous masses' that the Exhibition brought into the 'capital of the world'.[20] On an international level, the model of the world in concentric circles was one way of maintaining such an order and ensuring that London remained firmly at the centre, at least in British eyes. Equally important, however, were 'endonational' discourses such as class, gender, profession, wealth, or education, all of which played a crucial role in the various responses that the Exhibition triggered.[21] These discourses enabled the educated, relatively wealthy middle-class men in charge of the nation to maintain their position at the top of the pack and to exclude other groups.

In *Household Words*' thinking about Englishness, it becomes clear that any attempt to define the national character invariably relies on excluding 'Others'—in the present instance, the 'savages'. Whenever *Household Words* attempts to formulate what constitutes Englishness, it takes recourse to 'foreigners' portraits of Englishmen' and of England merely in order to deny them—thus, it was much easier to define 'un-English' behaviour than to translate it into what 'English' characteristics actually were. Ironically, *Household Words* writers—and especially Dickens—were at times remarkably aware that 'un-Englishness' was an artificial construct without any factual basis. Yet it also testified to the compelling power that it nevertheless exerted over its subjects. Thus, *Household Words* held firmly on to the conviction that an essential Englishness did exist in the face of its own repeated failure to find out what it consisted of.

'The Noble Savage' also reveals the respective positions of the other categories in the model that formed the basis for this study. For Dickens, the 'European Powers' are at the head of the 'improving world'.[22] At a time when most British media still saw Europe as the embodiment of tyranny and only grudgingly reconciled themselves to the *coup d'état* that had recently taken place in France, Dickens finds that 'Paris is a civilised city' and the exact reverse of the 'despotism [that] is one great distinguishing mark of a savage always'. European and 'savage', then, are mutually exclusive in Dickens's terminology, and his sketch mirrors the thinking of *Household Words* at large that Europe is essentially, if not always, on a par with England. Although *Household Words* writers resort to some crude stereotyping if it promises added 'entertainment', *Household Words* generally maintains a friendly goodwill for Europe overall. Topics that other publications saw as cause for expecting the worst, are either missing entirely from *Household Words*, only dealt with in passing, or counterbalanced by surrounding positive accounts of life on the continent.

Ireland, however, is clearly a few steps below the civilisational perfection of Europe, both in *Household Words* at large and in 'The Noble Savage' in particular, as Dickens's nonchalant observation makes clear: 'Several of these scenes of savage life bear a strong generic resemblance to an Irish election, and I think would be extremely well received and understood at Cork.'[23] Once again, Irishmen are caught in an unstable middle-ground between European civilisation (as represented by elections) and non-European 'savages', between centre and periphery. In order to deal with the threat it posed to the order that *Household Words* envisages, the journal distinguishes clearly between the land and its population. *Household Words* repeatedly finds that it is the Irish people themselves who continually thwart Britain's efforts to 'develop' the land. To amend this situation, the journal recommends various schemes that were remarkably similar to the plans for large-scale colonisation in India and Australia. The crucial difference between such colonial natives and Irishmen, however, was that the Irish were physically and visually no different from the English themselves and even spoke the same language. Therefore, *Household Words* was all the more eager to emphasise what scant difference it could find, and this tendency is mirrored in Dickens's flippant equation of Irishmen and savages.

Household Words' treatment of India marks the transition of the concentric circles into a fully hierarchical model, as any ambiguities of skin colour and language are removed. Britain's relationship with India is clearly imagined as one of sovereign and subject, in both *Household Words* and other media. However, Britain's pride in its colonial management of India suffered a painful blow in the Sepoy Rebellion of 1857, which forced Britain to redefine that relationship and its ideas of 'the mild Hindoo'. John Lang's 'Wanderings in India' sets out to restore discursively the colonial order that the Rebellion threatened to sweep away, and rationalises the causes that were suspected to have triggered it. Endowing his narrative with authority through the use of both native and European 'witnesses', Lang invariably concludes that the British rule of India needs to become both more efficient and more ruthless.

Yet Britain still carried responsibility for its colonial subjects—a fact of which *Household Words* occasionally reminded its readers in articles such as 'Justice for "Natives"'. In comparison, Dickens's savage 'has no moral feelings of any kind, sort, or description; and his "mission" may be summed up as simply diabolical.'[24] Since he is such a hopeless case, Britain's own evangelical mission to bring morality and civilisation to the globe seems not to apply here. It is obvious throughout his article that Dickens wants to see 'savages' firmly at the outer edge of the concentric circles that surround the metropolitan centre. Yet their position in this model is precisely what is at stake in this article. What irks Dickens most and provokes him into writing this article in the first place is 'the drawing of any comparison of advantage between the blemishes of civilisation and the tenor of [the savage's] swinish life.'[25] The suggestion that 'savage' life may be equal or even superior in some respects to 'civilisation' forces together the core and furthest periphery of the concentric circles that structure *Household Words'* view of the world, and threatens to unhinge this order completely.[26] Dickens responds with a fierce denial and concludes: 'My position is that, if we have anything to learn from the Noble Savage, it is what to avoid.'[27]

In other words, the negative example of the savage allows Dickens to etch out what proper, civilised Englishness should consist of—after all, it is the 'paradox of Englishness [. . .] to define the national character against a colonial other that it must then disown', as Simon Gikandi has shown.[28] The very severity of Dickens's disavowal shows that the savage is intrinsically necessary to his—and *Household Words*'—definition of 'self'.[29]

Although an examination of other aspects—such as *Household Words*' relationship with North America and other British colonies—would help to refine this argument further, this investigation has proven that *Household Words* holds on to a world order that revolves around England. This order is not natural, however, but has to be maintained by a sustained conscious effort, as its individual components all have the potential to subvert and undermine it. *Household Words*' failure to offer a positive definition of Englishness opens the door to the possibility that the term may not actually mean anything. The same lack of definition attaches to *Household Words*' concept of Europe, whose boundaries and nature are not always clear, but which the journal yet assumes to be unified in some way. Ireland, meanwhile, is both a part of the United Kingdom and a colony, and the Irish both 'savage' and white, both different and the same. The developments in India during the 1850s showed that discursively stable categories can be brought down by actual events, and that the voiceless natives can rebel against their colonial rulers. And as strenuously as the journal tries to disavow 'savages' completely, they are essential to anchor its metropolitan centre. After all these efforts, the concentric circles turn out to be not a fixed model, but a relational and flexible one.

Notes

NOTES TO THE INTRODUCTION

1. Peter Ackroyd, *Dickens*, rec May 25, 2002, Television documentary, BBC2, 2002.
2. Charles Dickens, *Dombey and Son*, Oxford World's Classics, ed. by Alan Horsman (Oxford: Oxford University Press, 1999 [1846–48]), p.480.
3. [Charles Dickens], 'A Preliminary Word', in *Household Words*, 1:1 (March 30, 1850), 1–2, p.1. Since authors' names were not published alongside their material, but have been identified retrospectively with the help of the *Household Word*s office book, 'anonymous' contributors' names will be indicated in square brackets throughout.
4. Tore Rem, '*Little Dorrit*, *Pictures from Italy* and John Bull', in *Dickens, Europe and the New Worlds,* ed. by Anny Sadrin (Basingstoke: Macmillan Press Ltd, 1999), p.136.
5. Harold Frank Clark Jr., 'Dickensian Journalism: a Study of *Household Words*', (unpublished doctoral dissertation, Columbia University, 1967); *The Uncollected Writings of Charles Dickens: Household Words, 1850–1859,* ed. by Harry Stone, vol. 1, 2 vols. (Bloomington, London: Indiana University Press, 1968); *Household Words: a Weekly Journal, 1850–1859, Conducted by Charles Dickens: Table of Contents,* ed. by Anne Lohrli (Toronto: University of Toronto Press, 1973).
6. Lillian Nayder, *Unequal Partners: Charles Dickens, Wilkie Collins, & Victorian Authorship* (Ithaca: Cornell University Press, 2002); John M.L. Drew, *Dickens the Journalist* (London: Palgrave, 2003).
7. Cf. Peter D. Edwards, *Dickens's 'Young Men': George Augustus Sala, Edmund Yates and the World of Victorian Journalism*, Nineteenth Century (Aldershot: Scolar Press, 1997). Various shorter studies and essays consider particular topics in *Household Words* and *All the Year Round*, such as the metropolitan police or the railway.
8. Margaret Beetham, 'Towards a Theory of the Periodical as a Publishing Genre', in *Investigating Victorian Journalism,* ed. by Laurel Brake, Aled Jones and Lionel Madden (Basingstoke: Macmillan, 1990), p.20.
9. Cf. Shu-Fang Lai, 'Fact or Fancy: What Can we Learn about Dickens from His Periodicals *Household Words* and *All the Year Round*?' in *Victorian Periodicals Review*, 34:1 (Spring, 2001), 41–53.
10. [Mrs. Bell], 'The Longest Night in a Life', in *Household Words*, 9:205 (February 25, 1854), 21–25, p.21. It is not entirely evident whether this is due to the weather conditions that particular winter or the age in which the story is set. Arguably, it could even be a consequence of the story's

location (Scotland)—in a later piece on seventeenth-century Scotland, Henry Morley mentions that 'the whole of the English nation was solicitous to know what passed weekly in Germany, Poland, and other parts of Europe' and consulted its newspaper for this purpose, whereas Scotland didn't have a newspaper at all. [Henry Morley], 'The Thistle in Bud', in *Household Words*, 18:431 (June 26, 1858), 25–29, p.28.

11. [Elizabeth Gaskell], 'Modern Greek Songs', in *Household Words*, 9:205 (February 25, 1854), 25–32
12. [Henry Morley], 'Jack and the Union Jack', in *Household Words*, 9:205 (February 25, 1854), 32–33
13. The author, Miss Perrott, is not identified further. Anne Lohrli suspects that this may be a misspelling for Marianne Parrott, a 'writer of scripture stories and moral tales in verse and prose for children, and occasional contributor to periodicals.' *Household Words: Contents,* ed. by Lohrli, p.401. 'Died in India' is this writer's only contribution to *Household Words.*
14. [William Duthie], 'A Lift in a Cart', in *Household Words*, 9:205 (February 25, 1854), 34–37. Duthie, a London-based goldsmith, was one of the few working-class writers in *Household Words* and had extensively travelled and worked in Europe in the manner of German artisans, whom he describes in some of his other contributions.
15. [George Dodd], 'Moiré Antique', in *Household Words*, 9:205 (February 25, 1854), 37–38; [Leigh Hunt], 'Holland House (II)', in *Household Words*, 9:205 (February 25, 1854), 38–42.
16. [William Blanchard Jerrold], 'For the Benefit of the Cooks', in *Household Words*, 9:205 (February 25, 1854), 42–44.
17. Cf. the special Anderson issue of *Diacritics*, 29:4 (1999).
18. Benedict Anderson, *Imagined Communities*, 2nd edn (London, New York: Verso, 1991 [first published 1983]), p.35.
19. To use a modern example, most members of the British public would probably agree in their expectations of, say, *The Independent, The Sun, The Daily Mail*, or *The Guardian* (or, indeed, *Cosmopolitan, The New Scientist, Private Eye*, and *Newsweek*).
20. Anderson also claims that the emergence of a mass printing industry assigned a new significance to time itself. Before the advent of mass printing, events could be seen together due to a higher, vertical order of meaning ('Divine Providence'). The printing press substituted this by a horizontal, temporal connection as the main framework for simultaneity. Thus, the only factor that connects the various occurrences that form the content of a newspaper is the date on top of the page, their temporal (horizontal) simultaneity. Anderson, *Imagined Communities* , p.24.
21. Antony Easthope, *Englishness and National Culture* (London: Routledge, 1999), p.12. In this context, Easthope aims to dissolve the binary and frequently one-directional opposition between real (economic, social, political forces) and subjective manifestations (culture, identity), since the two are two sides of the same phenomenon, influencing each other.
22. In fact, the numbers came out on the preceding Wednesday.
23. Cf. *An Age of Equipoise? Reassessing Mid-Victorian Britain,* ed. by Martin Hewitt (Aldershot: Ashgate, 2000). The essays in this volume reassess the reception history that William L. Burn's 1964 book *The Age of Equipoise* underwent. Although Burn intended the term 'equipoise' to signify a precarious balance of many conflicting tensions, subsequent critics have often overlooked the fact that 'tension is fundamental to equipoise' and assumed that it indicated a period of peaceful prosperity. Martin Hewitt, 'Prologue, in *An Age of Equipoise?*, ed. by Hewitt, p.27.

24. For one, it implicitly forced a government change in 1846 when the Conservative Prime Minister Peel was forced out of office by his own party. Peel fought for a repeal of the Corn Laws, which kept the price of bread artificially high and further aggravated the miserable condition of Ireland, then in its second year of the potato famine. His bid could only succeed because it won the support of Liberal MPs, but it caused a rift in his own party. For this reason, many historians see 1846 as the beginning of a new political era of uncertainty and some volatility. Cf. K. Theodore Hoppen, *The Mid-Victorian Generation, 1846–1886*, The New Oxford History of England (Oxford: Oxford University Press, 1998).
25. Terence A. Jenkins, *Parliament, Party and Politics in Victorian Britain*, New Frontiers in History (Manchester: Manchester University Press, 1996), p.32.
26. Hoppen, *The Mid-Victorian Generation* , p.67.
27. Geoffrey Best, *Mid-Victorian Britain, 1851–75* (London: Fontana Press, 1979 [first published 1971]), p.100–103.
28. Hoppen, *The Mid-Victorian Generation* , p.71.
29. R.L.V. ffrench Blake, *The Crimean War* (London: Sphere Books, 1971), p.145.
30. Patrick Brantlinger, *Rule of Darkness: British Literature and Imperialism, 1830–1914* (Ithaca: Cornell University Press, 1988), p.14.
31. [Dickens], 'A Preliminary Word' , p.1.
32. *Household Words: Contents*, ed. by Lohrli, p.3.
33. Walter J. Graham, *English Literary Periodicals* (New York: Octagon Books, 1966 [first published 1930]), p.293.
34. *Uncollected Writings*, ed. by Stone, p.6.
35. *Uncollected Writings*, ed. by Stone, pp.6–7.
36. Clark Jr., 'Dickensian Journalism', pp.13–14.
37. *Uncollected Writings*, ed. by Stone, p.9; Clark Jr., 'Dickensian Journalism', p.17.
38. Robert L. Patten discusses some of these in 'Dickens as Serial Author: A Case of Multiple Identities', in Laurel Brake, Bill Bell and David Finkelstein (eds), *Nineteenth-Century Media and the Construction of Identities* (Basingstoke: Palgrave, 2000), pp. 137–153.
39. Clark Jr., 'Dickensian Journalism', p.17.
40. *Uncollected Writings*, ed. by Stone, p.10.
41. *Uncollected Writings*, ed. by Stone, p.11.
42. *Uncollected Writings*, ed. by Stone, p.11.
43. Dickens to John Forster, October 7th, 1849. *The Letters of Charles Dickens: Volume Five: 1847–1849*, ed. by Graham Storey and Kenneth J. Fielding, vol. 5 (Oxford: Clarendon Press, 1981), p.622.
44. *Letters V*, ed. by Storey and Fielding, p.623.
45. Dickens to John Forster, January 31, 1850. *The Letters of Charles Dickens: Volume Six: 1850–1852*, ed. by Graham Storey, Kathleen Tillotson and Nina Burgis, vol. 6 (Oxford: Clarendon Press, 1988), p.25.
46. *Uncollected Writings*, ed. by Stone, p.14. The final choice of title bridged the domestic, feminine sphere with the masculine subtext of its motto. The motto which appeared at the head of every title page—'Familiar in their Mouths as HOUSEHOLD WORDS'—is a slightly altered quotation from Shakespeare's Henry V, namely from Henry's rousing speech to his troops before the Battle of Agincourt (act IV, scene iii, line 52). Drew states that the motto:

    supplies a conflicting, masculine frame of reference to the domestic and feminine overtones of the title, in which death-defying valour and ambition

for fame and social advancement are uppermost. Just as the groundlings of Shakespeare's time were to be roused by the speech's anti-hierarchical concept of social betterment through military service, so Dickens might expect his readers to be inspired by its radical vision of social upward-mobility and self-improvement.
Drew, *Dickens the Journalist* , p.109.

47. *Household Words: Contents,* ed. by Lohrli, p.4.
48. *Uncollected Writings,* ed. by Stone, p.16. My emphasis.
49. *Household Words: Contents,* ed. by Lohrli, p.11.
50. A good example of this is the Great Exhibition of 1851. See chapter 1.
51. [Dickens], 'A Preliminary Word' , p.1.
52. The reverberations with Anderson's theory are particularly striking if one considers that the *Oxford English Dictionary* defines sympathy as 'fellow feeling' or affinity.
53. Clark Jr., 'Dickensian Journalism', p.341.
54. *Household Words: Contents,* ed. by Lohrli, p.4. Cf. Geoffrey A. Cranfield, *The Press and Society: from Caxton to Northcliffe,* Themes in British Social History, (London: Longman, 1978), p.170.
55. Dr. Maginn, 'Prologue.', in *Bentley's Miscellany,* 1:1 (January, 1837), 2–6.
56. 'Our "Confession of Faith"', in *Fraser's Magazine for Town and Country,* 1:1 (February, 1830), 1–7, p.7.
57. [William Chambers], 'The Editor's Address to his Readers', in *Chambers's Edinburgh Journal,* 1:1 (February 4, 1832), 1–2, p.1. Emphasis in the original.
58. [Chambers], 'The Editor's Address to his Readers' , p.1.
59. For instance, the sentence, 'we hope to be the comrade and friend of many thousands of people', clearly refers only to the producers, as opposed to the 'many thousands' who read the journal. A few lines on, the first person unites readers and producers in one moral aim: *Household Words* is 'not calculated to render any of us less ardently persevering in ourselves' etc. [Dickens], 'A Preliminary Word' , p.1.
60. In 1854, *Chambers's* changed its title to the more general *Chambers's Journal of Popular Literature, Science, and Arts,* possibly to appeal to a wider, pan-British readership.
61. See chapter 2 in particular.
62. The only exceptions are serial publications of longer novels. *Hard Times* is proclaimed to be 'by Charles Dickens', and *North and South* 'by the author of *Mary Barton*'.
63. *Uncollected Writings,* ed. by Stone, p.14. Most of these writers contributed only a few articles. Apart from Dickens himself, Lohrli identifies thirty-five 'regulars' among the *Household Words* writers who published more than twenty articles each, among them such well known names as Elizabeth Gaskell, Samuel Sidney, Harriet Martineau, James Payn, Caroline Norton, Adelaide Anne Procter, and Eliza Lynn Linton. A handful of these regulars comprised the staff of *Household Words,* among them Dickens's subeditor William Henry Wills, John Forster, Henry Morley, George Augustus Sala, Percy Fitzgerald, and Wilkie Collins. Lohrli points out that on the whole Dickens's 'established corps of contributors were well suited to [the . . .] purpose of providing entertainment and instruction for his middle-class audience' but were 'hardly what Percy Fitzgerald called [. . .] "a brilliant array of writers" [since] by its very nature, a "cheap weekly journal of general literature" did not attract thinkers or great writers as contributors'. *Household Words: Contents,* ed. by Lohrli, p.30, quoting from Percy Fitzgerald, *Recreations of a Literary Man, or Does Writing Pay?* (London: Chatto and Windus, 1883) pp. 37–38.

64. Cf. Anne Lohrli, '"With my Name on Every Page": Dickens References in *Household Words.*' in *Dickens Quarterly* (1992), vol. 9.
65. Nayder, *Unequal Partners* , p.9.
66. Bentley envisaged the juxtaposition of many different writers; Dickens aimed at unanimity.
67. The editorship of *Household Words* lay in the hands of Dickens himself and his sub-editor W.H. Wills. Clark points out that Wills was the 'best choice for the position of sub-editor' because of 'the very qualities which he did not share with Dickens. A thorough, quiet, efficient, unimaginative journalist, Wills provided the rudder and ballast for his tempestuous editor'. Dickens expected Wills to 'run the periodical completely, to deal with the staff and tell each member what he was required to do', while Dickens himself 'was unconcerned with business details or personal relations. He simply wanted a pleasant, harmonious atmosphere; the mechanics of how this atmosphere was to be achieved were Wills' responsibility'.

    Dickens's own editorial intervention was fairly hands-on and consisted mostly of 'cutting, tightening, compressing' articles for publication, sometimes rewriting them entirely. 'All articles were read by him. Many were heavily retouched or revised. Some were given new titles. Whenever practicable, all editorial decisions were made by Dickens, though their implementation sometimes had to be left' to members of his staff. This process continued even while Dickens was abroad, when Wills would send him a weekly parcel of suggested articles for publication. In addition to his editorial duties, Dickens was a prolific writer during the first two or three years, when *Household Words* was still finding its tone, but gradually turned his attention to other projects in later years. In 1850 he wrote some eighty articles, approximately thirty in 1851, between ten to fourteen each year between 1852 and 1857, eight in 1858 and three in 1859 (counting as one all pieces that appeared in more than one instalment). Clark Jr., 'Dickensian Journalism', , p.39–42, p.77; Edwards, *Dickens's 'Young Men'* , p.12.
68. *Household Words: Contents,* ed. by Lohrli, p.23. Cf. *Uncollected Writings,* ed. by Stone, p.23. However, 'the formula was modified for *All the Year Round* to include an instalment of a novel in the opening section of every number'. More significantly, 'Dickens had kept closer watch over *Household Words*' which consequently:

    > bore a greater imprint of his hand. As soon as he left the major responsibility completely to Wills, it became more and more a typical journal. The very things which hold *Household Words* together and make it interesting reading are missing altogether in *All the Year Round.* A unique thing died with *Household Words.*

    Clark Jr., 'Dickensian Journalism', pp.374–5.
69. Beetham, 'Theory of the Periodical', p.23.
70. Beetham, 'Theory of the Periodical', p.19.
71. Beetham, 'Theory of the Periodical', p.25.
72. *Uncollected Writings,* ed. by Stone, p.21.
73. N. Merrill Distad, 'Desiderata and Agenda for the Twenty-first Century', in *Victorian Periodicals: a Guide to Research,* ed. by J. Don Vann and Rosemary T. VanArsdel, vol. 2, 2 vols. (New York: Modern Language Association of America, 1989), p.125. The most influential of the newspapers was *The Times*, which by 1850 sold 'four times as many' copies every day 'as the *Chronicle, Herald* and *Morning Post* combined'. Cranfield attributes *The Times*' success to the fact that 'Britain was becoming the greatest industrial and trading country in the world: and *The Times* spoke for the industrial and mercantile classes.' *The Times* thus catered for the same audience that would

probably be interested in *Household Words*. Cranfield, *Press and Society* , p.159.

74. Cranfield, *Press and Society* , p.167.
75. Cranfield, *Press and Society* , p.167. Cf. Peter Ackroyd, *Dickens* (London: Vintage, 1990), p.622.
76. Cranfield, *Press and Society* , p.167. Emphasis in the original.
77. Dickens to W.H. Wills, February 11, 1850, *Letters VI,* ed. by Storey, Tillotson and Burgis, p.35.
78. Like *Chambers's*, *Household Words'* pages were covered by two columns of small print without illustrations, in a similar typeface. A typical number of *Chambers's* contained 16 pages, and its pages were a slightly larger format than *Household Words*', which usually ran to 24 pages.
79. Cf. Drew, *Dickens the Journalist* , p.110; *Dictionary of National Biography.*
80. Drew, *Dickens the Journalist* , p.110.
81. *Uncollected Writings,* ed. by Stone, p.21, p.19.
82. Cranfield, *Press and Society* , p.125. For more on the material presentation of *Household Words* and its place in the literary market place, readers are referred to the following excellent article: Lorna Huett, 'Among the Unknown Public: *Household Words, All the Year Round* and the Mass-Market Weekly Periodical in the Mid-Nineteenth Century', in *Victorian Periodicals Review,* 38:1 (Spring, 2005), 61–82.
83. Clark Jr., 'Dickensian Journalism', pp.35–6.
84. *Household Words: Contents,* ed. by Lohrli, p.4, p.15.
85. *Household Words: Contents,* ed. by Lohrli, pp.17–8. Although there is very little evidence of *Household Words*' actual readership, Cranfield speculates that the lower classes and readers 'on the fringe of literacy' found *Household Words* 'too heavy'; they resented the 'blatant didactic approach of many of the "family" magazines' and 'wanted not so much to keep up with the world as escape from it'. Cranfield, *Press and Society* , p.170.
86. *Household Words: Contents,* ed. by Lohrli, p.5.
87. Ackroyd, *Dickens* , p.627, emphasis in original; *Household Words: Contents,* ed. by Lohrli, p.7.
88. *Household Words: Contents,* ed. by Lohrli, p.9. Lohrli remarks that other *Household Words* writers' attempts at a light-hearted, humorous style in imitation of Dickens's own were 'at times distressing, in the inappropriateness and unsuitability of devices used, in the crudity and callousness displayed'. *Household Words: Contents,* ed. by Lohrli, p.10.
89. [Grenville Murray and Henry Morley], 'The Roving Englishman: A Masked Ball; Advertisements (3)', in *Household Words,* 4:93 (January 3, 1852), 358–360, p.359.
90. [W. H. Wills, Grenville Murray and Thomas Walker (prob.)], 'German Advertisements', in *Household Words,* 2:28 (October 5, 1850), 33–35.
91. Cf. [Grenville Murray], 'The Roving Englishman: A Greek Feast (25)', in *Household Words,* 8:196 (December 24, 1853), 393–397. The 'Roving Englishman' series will be considered in detail in chapter 4.
92. The very pervasiveness of this concern is both the chief attraction and difficulty in my research—to do the topic full justice, one would need to look at every single article. Yet the sheer mass of available material—*Household Words'* full run fills 19 volumes, each over 600 pages of small print—means that I have had to impose severe restrictions in my selection criteria. Where these are not self-evident, they will be pointed out in individual chapters.
93. This book does deliberately not seek to engage with Household Words' very diverse representation of North America, both the United States and

Canada, a complex topic that could in itself comprise a monograph. The reason for this omission is that Household Words's representation of North America is too diverse to allow for a reasonably comfortable generalisation in a relatively short study such as this. Its contributors alternately treat North America as a colony (in its natural resources, promise to emigrants, and the peculiarities of the 'savage' native population), as an extension of the British Empire and culture, as a projection of aspects of the English past or future, and as a degenerate carbon copy of or alternative reality to England. In effect, it is respectively seen as on a par to a British colony, to Britain's European neighbours, and occasionally to Britain itself.

94. [Charles Dickens], 'Why?' in *Household Words*, 13:310 (March 1, 1856), 145–148, p.145.
95. [Browne], 'The "Irish Difficulty" Solved by Con McNale', in *Household Words*, 1:9 (May 25, 1850), 207–210.
96. There is a small risk that I may have overlooked some pieces, as I selected my material according to titles and the brief summaries in Lohrli's *Table of Contents*. Conceivably, an article which mentions Ireland neither in title nor summary might slip through, but it is unlikely, as Lohrli's summaries, if not the titles themselves, are a reliable indication of the piece's content.
97. Dickens, *Dombey and Son* , p.417. Although the context of this quotation is one of social rather than geographical distinctions, it nevertheless applies to my analysis, since the 'circles' that *Household Words* sketches also suggest a hierarchy of relative worth.

NOTES TO CHAPTER 1

1. Much of this chapter has previously been published in an article. See Sabine Clemm, '"Amidst the Heterogeneous Masses": Charles Dickens's *Household Words* and the Great Exhibition of 1851', in *Nineteenth-Century Contexts*, 27:3 (September, 2005), 207–230.
2. [Richard Horne], 'The Wonders of 1851', in *Household Words*, 1:17 (July 20, 1850), 388–392, p.391.
3. [Horne], 'Wonders' , pp.389–391.
4. [Charles Knight], 'Three May-Days in London: III. The May Palace (1851)', in *Household Words*, 3:58 (May 3, 1851), 121–124, p.123.
5. 'A Glance at the Exhibition', in *Chambers's Edinburgh Journal*, 15:387 (n.s.) (May 31, 1851), 337–340, p.337.
6. Cf. William L. Burn, *The Age of Equipoise: a Study of the Mid-Victorian Generation* (London: George Allen & Unwin Ltd., 1964); Asa Briggs, *Victorian People* (Harmondsworth: Penguin Books, 1963); Geoffrey Best, *Mid-Victorian Britain, 1851–75* (London: Fontana Press, 1979 [first published 1971]). A recent re-assessment of Burn's *Age of Equipoise* stresses rightly that it cast 'tension [as] fundamental to equipoise. [. . .] We can now have little doubt that the mid-Victorian period was a period of considerable imbalances, but imbalances tied together by a complex series of centripetal forces. Far from being "a lull, a centre of indifference", as Kitson Clark put it in 1962, it was a period of conflict and contestation on an almost unprecedented scale.' *An Age of Equipoise? Reassessing Mid-Victorian Britain,* ed. by Martin Hewitt (Aldershot: Ashgate, 2000), p.27, quoting Kitson Clark, *The Making of Victorian England*, (London: Methuen, 1962), p.43. Britain's relationship with Europe during this decade will be examined in more detail in chapter 4.
7. 'The Morals of the Great Exhibition', in *Punch*, 20 (January—June, 1851), 233.

8. Cf. John R. Davis, *The Great Exhibition* (Stroud: Sutton, 1999); Jeffrey A. Auerbach, *The Great Exhibition of 1851: a Nation on Display* (New Haven: Yale University Press, 1999); *The Great Exhibition of 1851: New Interdisciplinary Essays,* ed. by Louise Purbrick (Manchester: Manchester University Press, 2001).
9. John Scott Russell, 'Statement of Proceedings Preliminary to the Exhibition of Industry of All Nations, 1851', in Auerbach, *A Nation on Display* , p.17.
10. Auerbach, *A Nation on Display* , p.29.
11. Auerbach, *A Nation on Display* , p.30.
12. Other accounts of the CWCC state that this was in fact William Makepeace Thackeray. Cf. Davis, *The Great Exhibition.*
13. Auerbach, *A Nation on Display* , p.130.
14. Auerbach, *A Nation on Display* , p.130.
15. Auerbach, *A Nation on Display* , p.128. For example, Dickens and Wills laugh at various 'horrible rumours' of 'the overthrow of the British Constitution'. Several people are 'of opinion that the time bids fair for a descent of Red Republicans on Manchester'. [Charles Dickens and W. H. Wills], 'The Metropolitan Protectives', in *Household Words*, 3:57 (April 26, 1851), 97–105, p.97.
16. Joseph Paxton even suggested in an open letter in *The Times* that there should be free admission, but *The Times*'s editor successfully undermined this proposal by informing the Commission beforehand and publishing a simultaneous retort. Auerbach, *A Nation on Display* , p.144.
17. '[Festivities in England and France]', in *The Times*, May 6, 1851).
18. Auerbach, *A Nation on Display* , p.128, quoting from *The Times*, May 23, 1851. The general suspicious aversion to the shilling days stood in stark relief to Dickens's policy in his public readings. His first readings, in 1853, were in benefit of charitable causes, notably 'on behalf of Mechanics' and Literary Institutes'. And even in the later readings he undertook 'for his own profit [. . .] Dickens insisted on keeping a portion of seats at modest prices, to enable working men and their families to enjoy entertainment within their means.' One may speculate that he must have found the hypocrisy that surrounded the debate about the shilling days deeply distasteful, and it may well have added to his general aversion to the Great Exhibition. Paul Schlicke, *Dickens and Popular Entertainment* (London: Unwin Hyman, 1988 [first published 1985]), pp.232–233.
19. 'London during the Great Exhibition', in *Illustrated London News*, 18:386 (May 17, 1851), 423–424.
20. 'The Crystal Palace—a National Reflection', in *Punch*, 20 (January—June, 1851), 111; 'Design for a Fountain: To Be Placed in the Transept on the Shilling Days', in *Punch*, 20 (January—June, 1851), 257.
21. For instance, *Punch* commented that 'One Shilling seems to make a better use of his time than Five'. 'The Morals of the Great Exhibition', in *Punch*, 20 (January—June, 1851), 233.
22. 'The Shilling Days at the Crystal Palace', in *Punch*, 20 (January—June, 1851), 240.
23. 'Opening of the Great Exhibition by the Queen', in *Northern Star*, April 19, 1851). The article prompted a response from the secretary of the Royal commission, printed in the next issue, declaring the Queen's desire to have the public present. 'Opening of the Great Exhibition on the First of May', in *Northern Star*, April 26, 1851).
24. 'Opening of the Great Exhibition by the Queen', in, April 19, 1851), *Northern Star.*

25. Malcolm Chase (University of Leeds), 'The Graphic Dimensions of the *Northern Star*' (unpublished conference paper), given at 'Image and Text, Image in Text', organised by Research Society for Victorian Periodicals, (Universiteit Gent, July 8–10, 2004).
26. The only exception was a collection of ethnographic models of Indian labourers, as Lara Kriegel points out. These models presented an idyllic, changeless image of Indians at work and caused a variety of reactions from utter disgust to nostalgic envy. Lara Kriegel, 'Narrating the Subcontinent in 1851: India at the Crystal Palace', in *The Great Exhibition of 1851: New Interdisciplinary Essays,* ed. by Louise Purbrick (Manchester: Manchester University Press, 2001), pp.164–165.
27. Auerbach, *A Nation on Display* , p.131.
28. 'The Exhibition of Industry.—A Hint.' in *Punch,* 18 (January—June, 1850), 141; 'Specimens from Mr. Punch's Industrial Exhibition of 1850. (To Be Improved in 1851)', in *Punch,* 18 (January—June, 1850), 145.
29. C. H. Gibbs-Smith, *The Great Exhibition of 1851* (London: H.M.S.O., 1950, 1964), p.33.
30. Auerbach, *A Nation on Display* , p.150–1.
31. 'Meditations in the Exhibition, by Mr. Doldrums', in *Punch,* 21 (July—December, 1851), 9.
32. Auerbach, *A Nation on Display* , p.150–1.
33. Auerbach, *A Nation on Display* , p.22–3.
34. Auerbach, *A Nation on Display* , p.24.
35. [George A. Sala], 'The Foreign Invasion', in *Household Words,* 4:81 (October 11, 1851), 60–64, p.64.
36. Gibbs-Smith, *The Great Exhibition of 1851* , p.33.
37. Kriegel, 'Narrating the Subcontinent', p.151.
38. Gibbs-Smith, *The Great Exhibition of 1851* , p.14.
39. Even the building itself 'traces its origins to a tale of travel, exploration and conquest'. According to one *Household Words* article, Paxton got the idea for the Palace from a South American lily which Sir Robert Schomburgk had brought back to England and renamed 'Victoria Regia'. Schomburgk then commissioned Paxton to 'manufactur[e] a Berbician climate in a tiny South America, under a class case'. Similarly, the Crystal Palace seemed to create a tiny world under glass, in the centre of London. Deborah Wynne, 'Responses to the 1851 Exhibition in *Household Words*', in *The Dickensian,* 97:3 (Winter, 2001), 228–234, p.230; [W. H. Wills], 'The Private History of the Palace of Glass', in *Household Words,* 2:43 (January 18, 1851), 385–391, p.385.
40. Kriegel, 'Narrating the Subcontinent'.
41. Kriegel, 'Narrating the Subcontinent', p.150.
42. Kriegel, 'Narrating the Subcontinent', p.161.
43. 'The East Indian Court', in *Illustrated London News,* 18:494 (June 14, 1851), 583–584, p.583. Previously, the *Illustrated London News* had grudgingly admitted that all modern agricultural technology had an equivalent in ancient Indian practices that had been around two thousand years before civilisation reached Europe. Simultaneously, it sneeringly invited its readers to compare 'what a world of intellect' lay between the native, manual production methods and the machinery that Western colonisers brought to India. 'A Guide to the Great Industrial Exhibition', in *Illustrated London News,* 18:484 (May 10, 1851), 392–404, p.392.
44. A later example of this logic is found in John Ruskin's 'The Two Paths'. Writing in the aftermath of the Sepoy Rebellion, John Ruskin tries to rationalise the fact that the Indians are 'a race rejoicing in art, and eminently and universally endowed with the gift of it':

All ornamentation of that lower kind is pre-eminently the gift [and . . .] the delight of the worst and cruellest [sic] nation [and individuals], Moorish, Indian, Chinese [. . .]. They are capable of doing this in a way which civilized nations cannot equal. The fancy and delicacy of eye [. . .] seems to be somehow an inheritance of ignorance and cruelty, belonging to men as spots to the tiger or hues to the snake.

The Complete Works of John Ruskin, ed. by E.T. Cook and Alexander Wedderburn, Library Edition, vol. 16, 39 vols. (London: George Allen, 1905), p.262, p.307fn.

45. Gibbs-Smith, *The Great Exhibition of 1851* , p.72. Original source is not referenced.
46. Auerbach, *A Nation on Display* , p.176.
47. C. P. Fitzgerald, *The Chinese View of their Place in the World*, Chatham House essays, (London: Oxford University Press, 1966 [first published 1964]), pp.33–35.
48. [Richard Horne and Charles Dickens], 'The Great Exhibition and the Little One', in *Household Words*, 3:67 (July 5, 1851), 356–360, p.358.
49. 'The Chinese Family', in *Illustrated London News*, 18:487 (May 24, 1851), 456.
50. T.W. Hill finds this 'an amusing comparison between Stoppage and Progress'. T.W. Hill, 'Dickens and the 1851 Exhibition, in *The Dickensian*, 47 (1951), 119–124, p. 122.
51. [Horne and Dickens], 'The Little Exhibition' , p.358. The owner of the Junk, posing as a Chinese mandarin, gatecrashed the opening ceremony in the Crystal Palace as a publicity stunt to promote his floating museum. Ironically, even this 'ridiculous abortion' thus proved that nineteenth-century Chinese entrepreneurs in Britain had a very clear sense of what the British market demanded—in this case, the spectacle of exotic nobility and mystery. Thus, the *Illustrated London News* stressed that the lady of the Chinese family was of noble descent—a claim which Horne and Dickens attacked respectively. Auerbach, *A Nation on Display* , p.178.
52. Information taken from a tour around the Chinese and Indian collections of the British Museum, April 13, 2000.
53. According to the *New Shorter Oxford English Dictionary* (1993), this usage dates back to the mid-17th century, which is also when tea was first imported into Britain. Susan Schoenbauer Thurin, *Victorian Travelers and the Opening of China, 1842–1907* (Athens, Ohio: Ohio University Press, 1999), p.6.
54. [Horne and Dickens], 'The Little Exhibition' , p.358.
55. Kriegel, 'Narrating the Subcontinent', p.153.
56. 'The Wanderer of the Crystal Palace', in *Punch*, 20 (January—June, 1851), 210; 'A Conversation at the Great Exhibition', in *Punch*, 21 (July—December, 1851), 19.
57. Gibbs-Smith, *The Great Exhibition of 1851* , p.34.
58. [Charles Dickens], 'The Last Words of the Old Year', in *Household Words*, 2:41 (January 4, 1851), 337–339, p.338.
59. *The Letters of Charles Dickens: Volume Six: 1850–1852,* ed. by Graham Storey, Kathleen Tillotson and Nina Burgis, vol. 6 (Oxford: Clarendon Press, 1988), p.392, my translation: 'Je ne puis soutenir le bruit, et la foule, de Londres—òu [sic] tout le monde est meme [sic] plus fou que l'ordinairement, apropos [sic] de l'Exposition. [. . .] Il n-y-a [sic] rien—rien—partout—excepté l'Exposition.'
60. Schlicke, *Dickens and Popular Entertainment* , p.216.
61. John Butt, '*Bleak House* in the Context of 1851', in *Nineteenth-Century Fiction*, 10:1 (June, 1955), 1–21, p.2.

62. Norman and Jeanne Mackenzie, *Dickens: a Life* (Oxford: Oxford University Press, 1979), p.248.
63. *The Collected Letters of Thomas and Jane Welsh Carlyle,* ed. by Clyde De L. Ryals and Kenneth J. Fielding (Durham: Duke University Press, 1997), p.48, March 14, 1850.
64. *Collected Letters of Carlyle,* ed. by Ryals and Fielding, pp.319–320, December 24, 1850.
65. David A. Wilson, *Carlyle at His Zenith (1840–1853)* (London: Kegan Paul, Trench, Trubner & Co., 1927), p.344.
66. *The Letters of Thomas Carlyle to his Brother Alexander,* ed. by Edwin W. Moors Jr. (Cambridge, Mass.: Belknap Press of Harvard UP, 1978), p. 684, October 10, 1851.
67. 'A Glance at the Exhibition' , *Chambers's Edinburgh Journal,* p.337.
68. Typically, the first number would cover its usual breadth of topics, while the extra number or supplement focused almost exclusively on the Exhibition.
69. 'London during the Great Exhibition' , *Illustrated London News*, p.423.
70. Richard D. Altick, *The Shows of London* (Cambridge, Mass.: Belknap Press, 1978), p.1.
71. Dickens to John Forster, January 31, 1850. *Letters VI,* ed. by Storey, Tillotson and Burgis, p.25.
72. [Charles Dickens], 'A Preliminary Word', in *Household Words*, 1:1 (March 30, 1850), 1–2, p.1.
73. [Dickens], 'A Preliminary Word' , p.1.
74. [Dickens], 'A Preliminary Word' , p.1.
75. Margaret Beetham, 'Towards a Theory of the Periodical as a Publishing Genre', in *Investigating Victorian Journalism,* ed. by Laurel Brake, Aled Jones and Lionel Madden (Basingstoke: Macmillan, 1990), p.26.
76. Beetham, 'Theory of the Periodical', p.26.
77. For example, some exhibits were chosen because they were unique, others because they were 'typical'.
78. Beetham, 'Theory of the Periodical', p.21.
79. Beetham, 'Theory of the Periodical', p.20.
80. Wynne, 'Responses' , p.228.
81. Wynne, 'Responses' , p.233.
82. Wynne, 'Responses' , p.231
83. Wynne, 'Responses' , p.231.
84. [George Meredith], 'Britain', in *Household Words*, 4:87 (November 22, 1851), 204. Cf. [Dora Greenwell], 'The Heart of England', in *Household Words*, 4:85 (November 8, 1851), 156. The classic fictional example is Mrs Jellyby in *Bleak House*, who neglects her own children in favour of the African mission in which she is engaged.
85. Wynne, 'Responses' , p.231.
86. One may also ask to which extent the joking tone of later pieces was not a result of the general facetious, in Elizabeth Gaskell's phrase 'Dickensy' tone, which *Household Words* writers often imitated, with varying success, in order to please their conductor. *Household Words: a Weekly Journal, 1850–1859, Conducted by Charles Dickens: Table of Contents,* ed. by Anne Lohrli (Toronto: University of Toronto Press, 1973), p.10.
87. Wynne, 'Responses' , p.230.
88. Wynne, 'Responses' , p.231; [Knight], 'The May Palace' , p.123.
89. [John C. Prince], 'A Voice from the Factory', in *Household Words*, 3:54 (April 5, 1851), 35–36. I return to this poem below.
90. [Horne and Dickens], 'The Little Exhibition' , p.356
91. [Horne and Dickens], 'The Little Exhibition' , p.356

92. As I pointed out earlier, Wynne finds that the very 'first article to appear in [*Household Words*] on the Crystal Palace traces its origins to a tale of travel, exploration and conquest'. Wynne, 'Responses' , p.230.
93. [Horne and Dickens], 'The Little Exhibition' , p.356
94. [Horne and Dickens], 'The Little Exhibition' , pp.356–7
95. [Horne], 'Wonders' , p.389.
96. Knight, a printer and publisher, had a personal lifelong interest in public education and the causes of the poor. From 1828 until its dissolution in 1846, he was the publisher of the 'Society for the Diffusion of Useful Knowledge', whose ideals *Household Words* shared and sought to improve on. 'Knight, Charles', in *Dictionary of National Biography.*
97. [Knight], 'The May Palace' , p.122.
98. [Horne and Dickens], 'The Little Exhibition' , p.357.
99. [W. H. Wills], 'The Invited Invasion', in *Household Words*, 2:46 (February 8, 1851), 475–477, p.475; [Horne and Dickens], 'The Little Exhibition' , p.358.
100. [Horne and Dickens], 'The Little Exhibition' , p.356.
101. [Knight], 'The May Palace' , p.123.
102. [Knight], 'The May Palace' , p.123.
103. [Knight], 'The May Palace' , p.123.
104. Cf. 'India', website, *The Columbia Encyclopaedia*, 2001, (http://www.xreferplus.com/entry.jsp?xrefid=797329&secid=.5.3.#s.5.3.-), accessed April 17, 2002; Kriegel, 'Narrating the Subcontinent'.
105. [Knight], 'The May Palace' , p.124.
106. [Knight], 'The May Palace' , p.124.
107. [Knight], 'The May Palace' , p.124.
108. After all, Britain's 'area is but a speck on the globe', therefore there *must* be a divine agency behind her success in colonising the rest of the planet.
109. [Knight], 'The May Palace' , pp.123–4.
110. [Knight], 'The May Palace' , p.124.
111. [Knight], 'The May Palace' , p.124. First emphasis mine, second in the original.
112. [Wills], 'The Invited Invasion' , p.477.
113. [William Howitt], 'A Pilgrimage to the Great Exhibition from Abroad', in *Household Words*, 3:66 (June 14, 1851), 321–324, p.322.
114. 'Prince, John Critchley', in *Dictionary of National Biography.*
115. [Prince], 'A Voice' , p.35.
116. I shall assume the narrator to be male.
117. [Prince], 'A Voice' , p.35.
118. [Prince], 'A Voice' , p.35.
119. [Prince], 'A Voice' , p.35.
120. [Prince], 'A Voice' , pp.34–35.
121. [Prince], 'A Voice' , p.35.
122. [Prince], 'A Voice' , p.35.
123. 'A Voice' , p.35.
124. 'The Exhibition of Industry.—A Hint.' , *Punch.*
125. 'While [Dickens] encouraged writers to embrace "the spirit of reform," he did not permit them to express views that he felt might put off middle-class readers.' Lillian Nayder, *Unequal Partners: Charles Dickens, Wilkie Collins, & Victorian Authorship* (Ithaca: Cornell University Press, 2002), p.19.
126. [Dickens], 'A Preliminary Word' , p.1.
127. [Dickens], 'A Preliminary Word' , p.1.

128. [Henry Morley], 'Mr. Bendigo Buster on the Model Cottages', in *Household Words*, 3:67 (July 5, 1851), 337–341.
129. [Henry Morley], 'What is not Clear about the Crystal Palace', in *Household Words*, 3:69 (July 19, 1851), 400–402.
130. [Horne], 'Wonders' , p.389.
131. [Horne], 'Wonders' , p.390
132. [Horne], 'Wonders' , p.390. Ironically, of course, this outlandish vision resembles the one finally adopted in Paxton's Crystal Palace, as does the 'series of cucumber-frames' that he mocks later (p.391).
133. [Horne], 'Wonders' , p.390.
134. [Knight], 'The May Palace' , p.123.
135. Catherine Hall, *White, Male and Middle-Class: Explorations in Feminism and History* (Cambridge: Polity, 1992), pp.256–257.
136. 'Horny-handed' seems to have been a familiar epithet to the Exhibition. *Punch*'s poem 'The Exhibition of Industry.—A Hint' uses the same term: 'One nation, horny-handed and strong-hearted', if only to point out the omission of the actual labourers. 'The Exhibition of Industry.—A Hint.' , *Punch*.
137. [Horne], 'Wonders' , p.389–391.
138. Some of these were echoed in the *Northern Star*'s concern about the exclusiveness of the opening ceremony. The *Northern Star* worried about the exclusivity and impact of the Exhibition in terms of class, rather than gender. 'Opening of the Great Exhibition by the Queen', in, *Northern Star*, April 19, 1851.
139. [Horne], 'Wonders' , pp.389–390.
140. [Morley], 'What is Not Clear' , p.400.
141. A similar debate continues about the future of the Millennium Dome, currently still standing in Greenwich.
142. [Morley], 'What is Not Clear' , p.400; Wynne, 'Responses' , p.232.
143. [Morley], 'What is Not Clear' , p.400.
144. Wynne, 'Responses' , p.232. Cf. Thomas Richards, *The Commodity Culture of Victorian England: Advertising and Spectacle, 1851–1914* (Stanford: Stanford University Press, 1990).
145. Wynne, 'Responses' , p.232.
146. [Horne], 'Wonders' , pp.389–390.
147. Incidentally, this is remarkably similar to a *Punch* article entitled 'Where are the Foreigners?' in *Punch*, 20 (January—June, 1851), 207.
148. [Horne], 'Wonders' , p.390; [Wills], 'The Invited Invasion' ; [Howitt], 'Pilgrimage' .
149. [Sala], 'The Foreign Invasion' , p.60.
150. [Sala], 'The Foreign Invasion' , pp.60–61
151. [Dickens and Wills], 'The Metropolitan Protectives' , p.97.
152. [Sala], 'The Foreign Invasion' , pp.61–62.
153. [Sala], 'The Foreign Invasion' , p.63, my emphasis.
154. [Sala], 'The Foreign Invasion' , pp.62–63
155. [Sala], 'The Foreign Invasion' , pp.63–64.
156. [Sala], 'The Foreign Invasion' , p.64. Emphasis in the original.
157. Wynne, 'Responses' , p.231.
158. Wynne, 'Responses' , p.231.
159. [Horne], 'Wonders' , p.391.
160. Louise Purbrick's *The Great Exhibition of 1851* offers a striking insight into some of the issues that complicated this search. *The Great Exhibition of 1851: New Interdisciplinary Essays*, ed. by Purbrick.
161. Wynne, 'Responses' , p.232.

NOTES TO CHAPTER 2

1. [Charles Dickens], 'Why?' in *Household Words*, 13:310 (March 1, 1856), 145–148, p.147.
2. Louis Althusser, 'Ideology and Ideological State Apparatuses', in *Literary theory: an anthology*, ed. by Julie Rivkin and Michael Ryan (Oxford: Blackwell, 1998).
3. Catherine Hall, *White, Male and Middle-Class: Explorations in Feminism and History* (Cambridge: Polity, 1992), p.26.
4. Ernest Renan, 'What is a Nation?' trans. Martin Thom, in *Nation and Narration*, ed. by Homi K. Bhabha (London: Routledge, 1990), p.20.
5. Cf Renan: 'Let me sum up Gentlemen. Man is a slave neither of his race nor his language, nor of his religion, nor of the course of rivers nor of the direction taken by mountain chains. A large aggregate of men, healthy in mind and warm of heart, creates the kind of moral conscience which we call a nation.' Renan, 'What is a Nation?', p20.
6. Paul Schlicke, *The Oxford Reader's Companion to Dickens* (Oxford: Oxford University Press, 1999), entry on 'Englishness', p.219, quoting from the *Quarterly Review*, June 1839.
7. Malcolm Andrews, *Dickens on England and the English* (Brighton: Harvester Press, 1979), p.xix.
8. Raphael Samuel dates the unity of the British Isles from 1746–1921, rather than the Act of Union of 1800, while Linda Colley argues that the formation of Great Britain as a single entity took place between 1707–1837. But even a century is a short time in the formation of a national identity—my subsequent analysis of *Household Words'* claims about other European peoples may serve to bring home the longevity of national stereotypes, which continue almost unaltered today. Raphael Samuel, 'Four Nations History', in *Island Stories: Unravelling Britain,* ed. by Alison Light, Sally Alexander and Gareth Jones, vol. 2, 2 vols. (London, New York: Verso, 1998); Linda Colley, *Britons : Forging the Nation, 1707–1837* (London: Vintage, 1992).
9. Moreover, the boundaries between those 'countries' have not always been the same as they are at the time of writing. Kearney points out that it may be misleading to speak of England, Wales, Scotland and Ireland as separate 'countries' or 'nations'. Hugh Kearney, *The British Isles: a History of Four Nations* (Cambridge: Cambridge University Press, 1995 [first published 1989]), 'Introduction'.
10. Catherine Hall, 'The Nation Within and Without', in *Defining the Victorian Nation: Class, Race, Gender and the British Reform Act of 1867,* ed. by Catherine Hall, Keith McClelland and Jane Rendall (Cambridge: Cambridge University Press, 2000), p.208. Linda Colley accounts for Ireland's outsider status by identifying religion, in particular Protestantism, as an important factor in the formation of British identity, which emerged against a common 'enemy' in the shape of Catholicism. Linda Colley, 'Britishness and Otherness: an Argument', in *Journal of British Studies*, 31:4 (October, 1992), 309–329, p.314.
11. For the purposes of this chapter, I will use 'English' to refer both to England as distinct from Wales or Scotland, and to the idea of a national character (which sometimes includes non-English members of the United Kingdom), while my use of 'British' will refer to Great Britain, consisting of England, Scotland, and Wales, and the British Empire. Some slippage between the different terms may be unavoidable because I am effectively dealing with two different concerns, namely the emotive issue of collective identity, and the political and geographical entities of the time.

12. Mary Poovey, 'Curing the "Social Body" in 1832: James Phillips Kay and the Irish in Manchester.' in *Gender and History*, 5:2 (1993), 196–211.
13. Stuart Hall, 'Cultural Identity and Diaspora', in *Identity: Community, Culture, Difference*, ed. by Jonathan Rutherford (London: Lawrence & Wishart, 1990), pp. 222–237.
14. [Charles Dickens], 'A Preliminary Word', in *Household Words*, 1:1 (March 30, 1850), 1–2, p.1.
15. Terry Eagleton, 'From *Literary Theory: an Introduction* (1983)', in *The Norton Anthology of Theory and Criticism*, ed. by Vincent B. Leitch, et al. (London: W.W. Norton & Company, 2001), pp. 2243–2249, p.2244.
16. Cf. [Dickens], 'A Preliminary Word' .
17. 'Morley, Henry', in *Dictionary of National Biography*.
18. Margaret Beetham describes the periodical genre in similar terms: A journal is a 'complex process in which writers, editors, publishers and readers engaged in [a struggle . . .] to make their world meaningful'. Margaret Beetham, 'Towards a Theory of the Periodical as a Publishing Genre', in *Investigating Victorian Journalism*, ed. by Laurel Brake, Aled Jones and Lionel Madden (Basingstoke: Macmillan, 1990), pp. 19–32, p.20.
19. Hall, 'Cultural identity', pp.229–230. Both Stuart Hall and Homi Bhabha apply Jacques Derrida's 'différance', the infinite postponement of meaning, to account for the slippage that inevitably occurs in national discourse. Along with Catherine Hall, however, I want to suggest here that meaning changes not only over time but simultaneously, according to who attempts to define it.
20. Homi K. Bhabha, *The Location of Culture* (London: Routledge, 1994), p.140.
21. Cf. the introduction of Bernard Porter, *Britain, Europe, and the World 1850–1986: Delusions of Grandeur* (London: Allen & Unwin, 1987); Lauren M.E. Goodlad, '"A Middle Class Cut into Two": Historiography and Victorian National Character', in *ELH*, 67:1 (Spring, 2000), 143–178; J.H. Grainger, 'The View from Britain II: the Moralizing Island', in *Intellectuals and Revolution: Socialism and the Experience of 1848*, ed. by Eugene Kamenka and F.B. Smith (London: Edward Arnold Ltd., 1979), pp. 121–130; Peter Mandler, '"Race" and "Nation" in Mid-Victorian Thought', in *History, Religion, and Culture: British Intellectual History 1750–1950*, ed. by Stefan Collini, Richard Whatmore and Brian W. Young (Cambridge: Cambridge University Press, 2000), pp. 224–244; Bernard Porter, '"Bureau and Barrack": Early Victorian Attitudes towards the Continent.' in *Victorian Studies*, 27 (1984), 407–433.
22. [Henry Morley], 'Views of the Country', in *Household Words*, 2:34 (November 16, 1850), 169–172, pp.169–70.
23. Cf. Beetham, 'Theory of the Periodical'.
24. Cf. Shu-Fang Lai, 'Fact or Fancy: What Can we Learn about Dickens from His Periodicals *Household Words* and *All the Year Round*?' in *Victorian Periodicals Review*, 34:1 (Spring, 2001), 41–53.
25. [Morley], 'Views of the Country' , p.169.
26. [Wilkie Collins], 'The Unknown Public', in *Household Words*, 18:439 (August 21, 1858), 217–222, p.217.
27. [Collins], 'The Unknown Public' , p.218.
28. [Collins], 'The Unknown Public' , p.222.
29. Hall, *White, male and middle-class* , p.26.
30. Goodlad, 'Victorian national character' , p.145. It is noteworthy that Goodlad sees the contrast of continental Europe as the main comparator of Englishness, while Gikandi and Stuart Hall focus on the British colonies respectively.

31. '"National identity" [. . .] only becomes available as a salient cultural concept at certain historical conjunctures. Such historical moments are often marked by explicit conflict with another country or by enhanced imperial ambitions'. Poovey, 'Curing the "Social Body"', p.196.
32. Hall, *White, male and middle-class* , chapters 9 and 10.
33. Mandler, 'Race and Nation'. Mandler finds that critics such as Catherine Hall simplify the case too much by disregarding the civilisational context in which arguments of race were often made.
34. Hall, *White, male and middle-class* , p.269.
35. Catherine Hall notes that Carlyle's 'Occasional Discourse' stylistically echoed Dickens: 'Using a combination of characters with metaphorical names, proverbs, folk-tales, biblical references and social commentary, he held the polemic together with an acerbic humour strongly evocative of Dickens.' Hall, *White, male and middle-class* , p.270.
36. Mandler, 'Race and Nation', p.224.
37. Mandler, 'Race and Nation', p.230.
38. Lauren Goodlad suggests that the middle classes is further 'cut in two' by the distinction of professionalism and entrepreneurialism, which further complicated the argument. Goodlad, 'Victorian national character'.
39. John Robertson's work will be discussed later in this chapter, while Dickens's 'The Noble Savage' forms part of the conclusion of this book.
40. Benedict Anderson, *Imagined Communities*, 2nd edn (London, New York: Verso, 1991 [first published 1983]), p.7.
41. Only one article appeared on foreign ideas about Scotland, while an occasional anecdote concerned Ireland. Cf. [Grenville Murray], 'A German Picture of the Scotch', in *Household Words*, 2:29 (October 12, 1850), 71–72
42. [Sidney L. Blanchard], 'More Modern Munchausens', in *Household Words*, 7:170 (June 25, 1853), 402–405, p.403.
43. [Henry Morley], 'British Phenomena', in *Household Words*, 9:220 (June 10, 1854), 386–390, p.386.
44. [Charles Dickens, W. H. Wills and Grenville Murray], 'Foreigners' Portraits of Englishmen', in *Household Words*, 1:26 (September 21, 1850), 601–604, p.601.
45. [Percy Fitzgerald], 'Bogie Albion', in *Household Words*, 19:465 (February 19, 1859), 263–269, p.265.
46. [E. Townsend and Alexander Hamilton], 'Indian Recruits and Indian English', in *Household Words*, 16:393 (October 3, 1857), 319–322, p.321.
47. [Edmund S. Dixon], 'Literal Claims', in *Household Words*, 12:297 (December 1, 1855), 420–422, p.421.
48. [Charles Dickens], 'Insularities', in *Household Words*, 13:304 (January 19, 1856), 1–4, p.1.
49. [Dickens], 'Insularities' , p.1.
50. [Dickens], 'Insularities' , p.1.
51. [Dickens], 'Why?' , pp.147–8, my emphasis.
52. [Dickens, Wills, and Murray], 'Foreigners' Portraits' , p.603.
53. For the sake of clarity, one should remark that whenever *Household Words* mentions 'foreigners' as a generic group, these usually turn out to be European. This is certainly the case in the articles discussed in this chapter.
54. [Blanchard], 'More Modern Munchausens' , p.403.
55. [John Robertson], 'English Coast Folk', in *Household Words*, 14:333 (August 9, 1856), 81–85.
56. [Blanchard], 'More Modern Munchausens' , pp.403–4.
57. [Dickens], 'Insularities' , p.2.

58. [Sidney L. Blanchard], 'Munchausen Modernised', in *Household Words*, 6:152 (February 19, 1853), 533–538, p.533.
59. For example in Sala's 'Perfidious Patmos', which appeared three weeks after 'Munchausen Modernised'. Other examples include William Thomas's 'An Englishman's Castle', Sala's 'Foreign Invasion' and 'Music in Paving Stones', Dickens's 'Insularities' (which, however, is in favour of beards) and his, Murray's, and Wills's 'Foreigners' Portraits of Englishmen', and William Duthie's 'What my Landlord Believed'.
60. [Blanchard], 'More Modern Munchausens' , p.402.
61. [Blanchard], 'More Modern Munchausens' , p.402. This is probably Blanchard's own expression rather than the German original's. Britain's rule in India and its struggle for semi-control over China in the Opium Wars was frequently expressed in terms of benevolently bringing progress and innovation to a nation stuck in ancient and outdated ways. Hence the metaphor of the Chinaman as the epitome of pointless tradition and resistance to progress of any kind would have been more accessible and current in British than German culture in the 1850s. *Household Words* repeats the same association in other places. Cf. [Richard Horne and Charles Dickens], 'The Great Exhibition and the Little One', in *Household Words*, 3:67 (July 5, 1851), 356–360; [Robertson], 'English Coast Folk' ; [Eliza Lynn Linton], 'National Contrasts', in *Household Words*, 18:449 (October 30, 1858), 472–476.
62. [Charles Dickens], 'Proposals for a National Jest-Book', in *Household Words*, 13:319 (May 3, 1856), 361–364, p.362.
63. [William Blanchard Jerrold], 'An Old Portrait from The Hague', in *Household Words*, 9:227 (July 29, 1854), 569–572.
64. [Jerrold], 'An Old Portrait' , p.572.
65. [Edmund S. Dixon], 'Paris on London', in *Household Words*, 16:402 (December 5, 1857), 540–545, p.540.
66. [Morley], 'British Phenomena' .
67. Charles Dickens, *David Copperfield* (London: Penguin Popular Classics, 1994[first published 1849–50]), p.714.
68. [Otto von Wenckstern], 'English Cookery', in *Household Words*, 13:308 (February 16, 1856), 116.
69. Cf. [Eliza Lynn and W. H. Wills], 'Common Cookery', in *Household Words*, 13:305 (January 26, 1856), 42–46.
70. [Dixon], 'Paris on London' , p.540. Ironically, Wey also finds the English 'neither greedy of flattery from foreign visitors, nor over-sensitive to a little sharp criticism from the same', yet Dixon reacts quite snappily to some of the points brought forward, and pokes fun at Wey's misspellings of English words.
71. [Lynn], 'Common Cookery' , p.540.
72. Raphael Samuel, for example, proposes that Scottish nationalism blossomed amongst Scots in colonial diasporas, rather than in Scotland itself. Samuel, 'Four Nations History', p.35.
73. [Lynn], 'Common Cookery' , p.544.
74. [W. H. Wills], 'Christopher Shrimble on the "Decline of England"', in *Household Words*, 1:15 (July 6, 1850), 358–360, p.359.
75. [Wills], 'Christopher Shrimble' , p.560.
76. [Wills], 'Christopher Shrimble' , p.560.
77. In 'Christopher Shrimble', it is not clear whether this characteristic stems from Ledru-Rollin or is Wills's own addition.
78. [Horne and Dickens], 'The Little Exhibition' , p.357.
79. [Blanchard], 'Munchausen Modernised' , p.536.

80. [Blanchard], 'Munchausen Modernised' , p.536.
81. [Morley], 'Views of the Country' , p.170, my emphasis.
82. [Dickens], 'Proposals for a National Jest-Book' , p.363. From the immediate power of the condemnation, we can surmise that 'revolutionary' is on a par with 'un-English'.
83. [Morley], 'Views of the Country' , p.169.
84. [George A. Sala], 'Music in Paving Stones', in *Household Words*, 10:231 (August 26, 1854), 37–43, p.38.
85. This belonged to the ideal of Englishness revolving around authority and mastery that was on the rise in the 1850s, exemplified by Thomas Carlyle:

    The England he evoked [. . .] was a nation which hated anarchy and loved order. Its epitome was to be found in John Bull, who might not be clever with words but who knew what was what when it came to deeds. [they were] born conservatives [. . .] a noble, silent, peaceable people but one that could be roused to terrible rage.

    Hall, *White, male and middle-class* , p.287.
86. [Blanchard], 'More Modern Munchausens' , p.403.
87. [Morley], 'British Phenomena' , p.388.
88. [Dixon], 'Paris on London' , p.541.
89. Hall, *White, male and middle-class* , p.257.
90. Lauren Goodlad's article on 'Victorian national character' complicates the class division and the question of the gentleman in the light of conflicting ideologies of entrepreneurialism and professionalism. Goodlad, 'Victorian national character' .
91. [Dickens], 'Insularities' , p.2.
92. [Blanchard], 'Munchausen Modernised' , p.537.
93. [Dixon], 'Paris on London' , p.543, my emphasis.
94. For an account of gendered Englishness, see Elizabeth Langland, 'Nation and Nationality: Queen Victoria in the Developing Narrative of Englishness', in *Remaking Queen Victoria,* ed. by Margaret Homans and Adrienne Munich (Cambridge: Cambridge University Press, 1997). Langland finds that women often embody passive virtues such as purity and self-sacrifice, while men show active ones such as courage and honesty.
95. [Charles Dickens], 'The Household Narrative', in *Household Words*, 1:3 (April 13, 1850), 49, p.1. I have included articles which refer to England or Britain (in general terms, rather than to a specific aspect of either) in the title, or which address these according to Lohrli's *Table of Contents.* Within those parameters, I deal with those pieces that do not (primarily) rely on another nation or foreign observer as contrast but attempt to define it in positive terms or 'in a vacuum' instead. This process leaves about fifteen articles.
96. Anderson, *Imagined Communities* , p.5.
97. [Morley], 'Views of the Country' ; [W.H. Wills], 'Cheerful Arithmetic', in *Household Words*, 1:23 (August 31, 1850), 531–534; [Richard Horne], 'A Time for All Things', in *Household Words*, 2:52 (March 22, 1851), 615–617; [Dora Greenwell], 'The Heart of England', in *Household Words*, 4:85 (November 8, 1851), 156; [George Meredith], 'Britain', in *Household Words*, 4:87 (November 22, 1851), 204.
98. [Charles Dickens], 'The Toady-Tree', in *Household Words*, 11:270 (May 26, 1855), 385–387; [Charles Dickens], 'Cheap Patriotism', in *Household Words*, 11:272 (June 9, 1855), 433–435; [Dickens], 'Insularities' ; [Dickens], 'Why?' ; [Dickens], 'Proposals for a National Jest-Book' ; [Browne and Henry Morley], 'Perfectly Contented', in *Household Words*, 14:338 (September 13, 1856), 213–216.

99. In the same period Dickens published three articles on the mismanagement of the Crimean War in *Household Words*, with such revealing titles as 'Gone to the Dogs'.
100. [Wills], 'Cheerful Arithmetic' , pp.531–2.
101. [Browne], 'Perfectly Contented' , p.214.
102. [Morley], 'Views of the Country' , p.169
103. [Horne], 'A Time for All Things' , p.616.
104. [Collins], 'The Unknown Public' , p.217.
105. [Wills], 'Cheerful Arithmetic' , p.533.
106. [Browne], 'Perfectly Contented' , pp.214–5.
107. [Greenwell], 'The Heart of England' . Cf. Hall, *White, male and middle-class* .
108. Cf. Mrs Jellyby's neglect of her own children in Bleak House, or Dickens's letters on the Crimean War.
109. [Meredith], 'Britain' .
110. During his years as British consul in Barcelona, Hannay frequently published his letters 'From an Englishman in Spain' in the *Pall Mall Gazette*. 'James Hannay', 2004, website, (http://90.1911encyclopedia.org/H/HA/HANNAY_JAMES.htm), accessed August 27, 2004.
111. [James Hannay], 'English Songs', in *Household Words*, 4:86 (November 15, 1851), 173–178.
112. [Hannay], 'English Songs' , p.177.
113. 'Hannay, James', in *Dictionary of National Biography*.
114. [Hannay], 'English Songs' , p.177.
115. Dibdin himself did not go to sea, although he had an older brother who did. 'The Contemplator's Short Biography of Charles Dibdin', website, (http://www.contemplator.com/history/dibdin.html), accessed June 22, 2004.
116. [Hannay], 'English Songs' , p.177.
117. Eagleton, 'From *Literary Theory: an Introduction* (1983)', p.2244.
118. [Meredith], 'Britain' .
119. [Meredith], 'Britain' .
120. [Greenwell], 'The Heart of England' .
121. [Dickens], 'Why?' , pp.147–8.
122. [Dickens], 'Why?' , p.147.
123. The same is true of his fiction: 'Without losing his Englishness, Dickens emerges as a European in his comic treatment of his own countrymen.' Tore Rem, '*Little Dorrit, Pictures from Italy* and John Bull', in *Dickens, Europe and the New Worlds,* ed. by Anny Sadrin (Basingstoke: Macmillan Press Ltd, 1999), pp.134–5.
124. [Dickens], 'Insularities' , p.1.
125. Significantly, it is in exhibitions and stage displays that Dickens encounters the savage 'strangers' that make him feel so uncomfortable and provoke one of the most racist articles in all of *Household Words*. [Charles Dickens], 'The Noble Savage', in *Household Words*, 7:168 (June 11, 1853), 337–339, p.338.
126. [Dickens], 'Insularities' , pp.1–2.
127. [Dickens], 'Proposals for a National Jest-Book' .
128. [Dickens], 'The Toady-Tree' , p.386. The same question is raised in 'Why?' and alluded to in 'Proposals to a National Jest-Book'
129. [Dickens], 'Insularities' , p.2.
130. [Robertson], 'English Coast Folk' , p.82. I discuss Robertson's theories in detail in the following section.
131. [Dickens], 'The Toady-Tree' , p.387.

132. For added complication, the lion is also an English symbol as opposed to the Scottish unicorn.
133. [Henry Morley], 'Britannia's Figures', in *Household Words*, 19:454 (December 4, 1858), 13–16.
134. [John Robertson], 'Scotch Coast Folk', in *Household Words*, 13:328 (July 5, 1856), 585–590.
135. As far as the title is an indication, for every article about Britain there are ten about England.
136. Raphael Samuel, 'Unravelling Britain', in *Island Stories: Unravelling Britain*, ed. by Alison Light, Sally Alexander and Gareth Jones, vol. 2, 2 vols. (London, New York: Verso, 1998), p.48.
137. Colley, *Britons* . Cf. Simon Gikandi, *Maps of Englishness: Writing Identity in the Culture of Colonialism* (New York: Columbia University Press, 1996); Catherine Hall, *Civilising Subjects: Metropole and Colony in the English Imagination, 1830–1867* (Cambridge: Polity, 2002); Goodlad, 'Victorian national character' .
138. Colley, 'Britishness and Otherness' , p.316. What they did have in common, of course, was the Empire, which Gikandi calls Britain's *raison d'être.* Gikandi, *Maps of Englishness* .
139. Colley, 'Britishness and Otherness' , p.315.
140. Eric J. Evans, 'Englishness and Britishness: National Identities, c.1790-c.1870', in *Uniting the Kingdom? The Making of British History*, ed. by Alexander Grant and Keith J. Stringer (London: Routledge, 1995), p.233.
141. Eric Evans offers an excellent discussion of the ambiguities of Englishness and Britishness and finds that 'neither [. . .] is a separately identifiable phenomenon', precisely because the two terms were used largely interchangeably and across the political spectrum. Evans, 'Englishness and Britishness 1790–1870', p.243.
142. The term 'ethnicity' is so loaded that it deserves some clarification here. Catherine Hall uses it to signify a cultural identity rather than a racial, genetic one. Yet the word has changed quite dramatically since the publication of *White, male, and middle class* in 1992 and has effectively come to mean 'non-European', as every-day occurrences such as 'ethnic festivals' or 'ethnic clothing' prove. In 2001, Gerry Kearns used the term to distinguish between 'ethnic nationalism', which 'delimits citizenship in terms of rules of descent', and 'civic nationalism', which 'treats it in terms of residence'. In other words, it has turned into the opposite meaning of that which Hall intended. I use the term in a neutral sense as an equivalent of 'national identity', without wishing to suggest whether this identity is conceived of in biological or cultural terms. Cf. Gerry Kearns, 'Time and Some Citizenship: Nationalism and Thomas Davis', in *Bullàn: an Irish Studies Journal*, 5:2 (Winter/Spring, 2001), 23–55, p.24.
143. Hall, *White, male and middle-class* , p.206.
144. The Duke of Wellington, born and bred in Ireland, is another example.
145. Gikandi, *Maps of Englishness* , p.29.
146. Samuel, 'Four Nations History', p.22.
147. Samuel, 'Four Nations History', p.24.
148. [Mrs. Wyley], 'A Welsh Wedding', in *Household Words*, 2:47 (February 15, 1851), 492–493, p.493.
149. [James Payn], 'Miss Davies', in *Household Words*, 12:297 (December 1, 1855), 429–432, p.429.
150. [Payn], 'Miss Davies' , p.430.
151. [Wilkie Collins], 'The Great (Forgotten) Invasion', in *Household Words*, 19:468 (March 12, 1859), 337–341, p.337.

152. [Murray], 'A German Picture of the Scotch' ; [Henry Morley], 'Highland Emigration', in *Household Words*, 5:117 (June 19, 1852), 324–325.
153. [Eliza Lynn], 'The Witches of Scotland', in *Household Words*, 16:383 (July 25, 1857), 75–83; [Henry Morley], 'The Thistle in Bud', in *Household Words*, 18:431 (June 26, 1858), 25–29.
154. [Lynn], 'The Witches of Scotland' , p.81.
155. [Eliza Lynn], 'The Witches of England', in *Household Words*, 16:385 (August 8, 1857), 138–141, p.139.
156. [Lynn], 'The Witches of England' , p.141. Her 'National Contrasts' ends on a similarly disparaging note, citing various shortcomings of modern England—such as its social mismanagement and ludicrous fashion requirements—and asking 'whether Chinaman or Hindu submits to more absurdities than the Englishman of the nineteenth century does.' [Lynn], 'National Contrasts' , p.476.
157. [Lynn], 'The Witches of England' , p.138.
158. [Morley], 'The Thistle in Bud' , p.25.
159. [Morley], 'The Thistle in Bud' , p.29.
160. [Morley], 'The Thistle in Bud' , p.26.
161. In comparison, there are some thirty articles dealing with Germany, not counting the individual instalments of serials, some of which ran to eight parts.
162. [Morley], 'The Thistle in Bud' , p.28.
163. Eric Evans notes that this was not unusual: 'The theme of "backward" Scots and Welsh holding back "advanced" England in an unprecedently [sic] prosperous Great Britain was also heard, though less stridently than in the case of the Irish.' Evans, 'Englishness and Britishness 1790–1870', p.240.
164. [Morley], 'Highland Emigration' , p.325.
165. [Morley], 'Highland Emigration' , pp.324–5.
166. Gikandi, *Maps of Englishness* , p.29.
167. [Morley], 'The Thistle in Bud' , p.25.
168. [William Chambers], 'The Editor's Address to his Readers', in *Chambers's Edinburgh Journal*, 1:1 (February 4, 1832), 1–2, p.1. Emphasis in the original.
169. Colley, 'Britishness and Otherness' , p.315.
170. [John Robertson], 'Coast Folk', in *Household Words*, 13:326 (June 21, 1856), 550–552, p.552.
171. [Robertson], 'Coast Folk' , p.552.
172. [Robertson], 'Scotch Coast Folk' , p.589. Reason, of course, is also a major ingredient of Englishness, as all the accounts of the steady, not easily incensed, revolution-hating population have shown.
173. [Robertson], 'Scotch Coast Folk' , p.587.
174. [Robertson], 'Scotch Coast Folk' , p.589.
175. [Robertson], 'English Coast Folk' , pp.82–4.
176. [Robertson], 'Coast Folk' , p.552; [Robertson], 'English Coast Folk' , p.84.
177. [Robertson], 'English Coast Folk' , p.82–4.
178. [John Robertson], 'Notes on the Fishers of the Scotch East Coast', in *Blackwood's Edinburgh Magazine*, 51:317 (March, 1842), 296–305, pp.296–7.
179. [Robertson], 'Scotch Coast Folk' , p.587.
180. Gikandi, *Maps of Englishness* , p.29.
181. [Robertson], 'Scotch Coast Folk' , pp.589–90
182. [Robertson], 'English Coast Folk' , p.81.
183. [Robertson], 'English Coast Folk' , pp.82–4.
184. [Robertson], 'English Coast Folk' , pp.84–5.
185. [Robertson], 'English Coast Folk' , p.81.

186. [Robertson], 'English Coast Folk' , pp.81–2. Presumably, the other nations Robertson cites built their empires for the same reason, i.e. their refusal to be ruled by anyone else.
187. [Robertson], 'English Coast Folk' , p.81.
188. [Robertson], 'Scotch Coast Folk' , p.590.
189. Elizabeth Langland describes an English equivalent of Robertson's Scottish myth of origin. She writes that Prince Albert, who was formerly seen as a foreign influence, was gradually reworked into an Anglo-Saxon, especially in conjunction with Victoria in a series of paintings of the 1850s and 1860s. England now remembered that the Anglo-Saxons were, after all German, and that 'the very essence of Englishness' lay in Anglo-Saxon roots. Langland, 'Nation and Nationality', p.16.
190. Colley, *Britons* , p.162.
191. [Blanchard], 'More Modern Munchausens' , p.403.
192. [Dickens], 'Why?' , p.147.

NOTES TO CHAPTER 3

1. Pete McCarthy, *McCarthy's Bar: a Journey of Discovery in Ireland* (London: Hodder and Stoughton, 2000), p.4.
2. [Browne], 'The "Irish Difficulty" Solved by Con McNale', in *Household Words*, 1:9 (May 25, 1850), 207–210.
3. Cf. Edward W. Said, *Orientalism* (Harmondsworth: Penguin, 1991 [first published 1978]), 'Introduction'.
4. Karen Corrigan, 'Demythologizing Migration and Language Shift in Postcolonial Ireland' in *'(Re)Visioning the World: Travelling in "Old" and "New" Empires'*, University of Newcastle (2003),.
5. L. Perry Curtis's study of the simianisation of the Irish identifies the middle decades of the nineteenth century as the key period. The large-scale immigration of Irishmen to Britain in the 1840s served to establish the 'prognathous' face as specifically 'Irish', while the cartoons of the late 1850s and 1860s increasingly transformed the cartoon Irishman into an ape. 'The transformation of peasant paddy into an ape-man or simianized Caliban was completed by the 1860s and 1870s.' L. Perry Curtis Jr, *Apes and Angels: the Irishman in Victorian Caricature*, revised edition (Washington and London: Smithsonian Institution Press, 1997 [first published 1971]), p.2. Kavita Philip maps the wider trajectory of racial language in reference to the Irish (as well as the London poor and natives of India). Philip, 'Race, Class and the Imperial Politics of Ethnography in India, Ireland, and London, 1850–1910', in *Irish Studies Review*, 10:3 (Winter, 2002), 289–302.
6. '[Celts in Ireland]', in *The Times*, Issue, Date 1852)
7. Cora Kaplan, 'White, Black, and Green: Racialising Irishness in Victorian England', in *Victoria's Ireland? Irishness and Britishness, 1837–1901,* ed. by Peter Gray (Dublin: Four Courts Press, 2004), p.53.
8. Kaplan, 'White, Black, and Green', p.54.
9. [Henry Morley], 'The Irish Use of the Globe, in One Lesson', in *Household Words*, 2:29 (October 12, 1850), 51–56.
10. Catherine Hall, 'The Nation Within and Without', in *Defining the Victorian Nation: Class, Race, Gender and the British Reform Act of 1867,* ed. by Catherine Hall, Keith McClelland and Jane Rendall (Cambridge: Cambridge University Press, 2000), p.210.

11. [Grenville Murray], 'The Roving Englishman: A Few More Hints (14)', in *Household Words*, 6:144 (December 25, 1852), 358–360 p.359.
12. [Grenville Murray], 'The Roving Englishman: Dolma Bakjah; A Turkish Bath (42)', in *Household Words*, 10:245 (December 2, 1854), 369–373; [Grenville Murray], 'The Roving Englishman: On Horseback (12)', in *Household Words*, 6:142 (December 11, 1852), 309–312; [Grenville Murray], 'The Roving Englishman: Travelling Servants (15)', in *Household Words*, 6:148 (January 8, 1853), 453–456.
13. Eric J. Evans, 'Englishness and Britishness: National Identities, c.1790-c.1870', in *Uniting the Kingdom? The Making of British History*, ed. by Alexander Grant and Keith J. Stringer (London: Routledge, 1995), p.233.
14. Mary Poovey, 'Curing the "Social Body" in 1832: James Phillips Kay and the Irish in Manchester' in *Gender and History*, (1993), p.209.
15. Hall, 'Defining the Victorian Nation', p.182.
16. John Barrell, *The Infection of Thomas De Quincey: a Psychopathology of Imperialism* (New Haven, London: Yale University Press, 1991), p.10.
17. Barrell, *Thomas DeQuincey* , p.11.
18. Leon Litvack, 'Exhibiting Ireland, 1851–3: Colonial Mimicry in London, Cork and Dublin', in *Ireland in the Nineteenth Century: Regional Identity*, ed. by Glenn Hooper and Leon Litvack (Dublin: Four Courts Press, 2000), p.23, quoting from Homi K. Bhabha, *The Location of Culture* (London: Routledge, 1994), pp.70–71.
19. Litvack, 'Exhibiting Ireland', p.22. Pete McCarthy diagnoses the same bias in today's media:

    > The English press, of course, have got this nationality business down to a fine art. If you win an Olympic medal, an Oscar, or the George Cross, then you're British; unless you're involved in a sex scandal, a drugs deal, or a court case, in which case you're once again Scottish, Welsh, Northern Irish, or black.

    McCarthy, *McCarthy's Bar* , p.254.
20. [Morley], 'The Irish Globe' , p.54. Cf.[William Howitt], 'Two Aspects of Ireland. The Second Aspect.' in *Household Words*, 4:80 (October 4, 1851), 27–32. For an excellent exploration of the racial discourse on the English and Irish, i.e. Anglo-Saxons and Celts, see Hall, 'Defining the Victorian Nation'.
21. Naturally, many contributors are unidentified, and the biographies of several more remain incomplete—fourteen is the bare, ascertainable minimum, on the basis of Anne Lohrli's *Table of Contents*. A number of others studied at Trinity College, Dublin.
22. The poem which Allingham considered his most important, 'Laurence Bloomfield in Ireland', describes a young English-educated Irishman's return to Ireland and his efforts to 'raise the society to which he comes to the level of the society he has left'. 'Allingham, William', in *Dictionary of National Biography*; *Household Words: a Weekly Journal, 1850–1859, Conducted by Charles Dickens: Table of Contents*, ed. by Anne Lohrli (Toronto: University of Toronto Press, 1973).
23. Kevin Whelan, 'Writing Ireland: Reading England', in *Ireland in the Nineteenth Century: Regional Identity*, ed. by Glenn Hooper and Leon Litvack (Dublin: Four Courts Press, 2000), p.189. For the concept of auto-ethnography see Mary Louise Pratt, *Imperial Eyes: Travel Writing and Transculturation* (London, New York: Routledge, 1992), p.7.
24. [E. Townsend and Alexander Hamilton], 'Indian Recruits and Indian English', in *Household Words*, 16:393 (October 3, 1857), 319–322, p.321.
25. Hall, 'Defining the Victorian Nation', p.214.

26. *Harriet Martineau: Letters from Ireland,* ed. by Glenn Hooper (Dublin: Irish Academic Press, 2001), p.13.
27. *Martineau: Letters from Ireland,* ed. by Hooper, pp.12–13, 16.
28. [Harriet Martineau], 'Peatal Aggression', in *Household Words*, 6:130 (September 18, 1852), 13–18, p.16.
29. [Harriet Martineau], 'Hope with a Slate Anchor', in *Household Words*, 6:136 (October 30, 1852), 156–161, p.161.
30. [Martineau], 'Peatal Aggression' , p.16.
31. [Martineau], 'Slate' , p.161.
32. [Martineau], 'Slate' , p.159, my emphasis. The corresponding 'Letter' does not see this as a contradiction but as a necessary consequence of good pay and training. *Martineau: Letters from Ireland,* ed. by Hooper, pp.138–141.
33. [Harriet Martineau], 'The Irish Union', in *Household Words*, 6:137 (November 6, 1852), 169–175, p.170.
34. [Martineau], 'The Irish Union' , p.169.
35. [Martineau], 'The Irish Union' , p.170, pp.172–3. Hooper's remarks on this claim in the corresponding 'Letter from Ireland' that it was 'highly dubious', since most 'ophthalmic victims were children'. *Martineau: Letters from Ireland,* ed. by Hooper, p.187.
36. [Harriet Martineau], 'The Famine Time', in *Household Words*, 6:138 (November 13, 1852), 214–216, p.214.
37. [Martineau], 'The Irish Union' , p.172.
38. [Martineau], 'Slate' , p.161.
39. [Martineau], 'The Irish Union' , p.174.
40. [Martineau], 'The Irish Union' , p.171.
41. *Martineau: Letters from Ireland,* ed. by Hooper, p.147.
42. K. Theodore Hoppen, *Ireland since 1800: Conflict and Conformity*, Studies in Modern History, ed. by John Morrill and David Cannadine (London, New York: Longman, 1989), p.58.
43. [T.M. Thomas], 'A Suburban Connemara', in *Household Words*, 2:50 (March 8, 1851), 562–565, pp.564–565.
44. [Eliza Lynn and W. H. Wills], 'Common Cookery', in *Household Words*, 13:305 (January 26, 1856), 42–46, p.42. Cf. also [Martineau], 'The Irish Union' , p.171: "Too many of [the Famine victims] had fancied that they could not live on the diet of the [workhouse], and had held out until they sank for want of any kind of food whatever.' Hoppen states that, on the contrary, poor Irish people relied on Indian meal as a staple part of their diet. Hoppen, *Ireland since 1800* , p.54.
45. [Browne], 'The "Irish Difficulty"' , p.207.
46. [Browne], 'The "Irish Difficulty"' , p.210.
47. Hoppen, *Ireland since 1800* , pp. 35–38.
48. [Morley], 'The Irish Globe' , p.55.
49. '[State of Ireland]', in *The Times*, October 29, 1852, 4.
50. Cf. [Martineau], 'Slate' ; [Howitt], 'The Second Aspect of Ireland' ; [Anna S. Grey and W. H. Wills], 'Ballinglen', in *Household Words*, 3:71 (August 2, 1851), 450–451; [Browne], 'The "Irish Difficulty"' ; [Morley], 'The Irish Globe' .
51. [Howitt], 'The Second Aspect of Ireland' , p.29.
52. Hoppen, *Ireland since 1800* , p.56.
53. Hoppen, *Ireland since 1800* , p.54.
54. '[Agriculture in Ireland]', in *The Times*, August 12, 1850, 4.
55. [Howitt], 'The Second Aspect of Ireland' , p.32.

56. Hooper cites a number of works from the 1850s which 'systematically endorsed the notion of Irish resettlement potential'. *Martineau: Letters from Ireland,* ed. by Hooper, p.17.
57. [Grey], 'Ballinglen' ; [Percival Leigh], 'The Latest Intelligence from the Irish California', in *Household Words*, 3:77 (September 13, 1851), 595; [Martineau], 'Slate' .
58. [Howitt], 'The Second Aspect of Ireland' , p.29.
59. [Howitt], 'The Second Aspect of Ireland' , p.29.
60. [Howitt], 'The Second Aspect of Ireland' , p.27.
61. [E. Mitchell], 'An Encumbered Estate', in *Household Words*, 16:383 (July 25, 1857), 84–89, p.89.
62. Hoppen, *Ireland since 1800* , p.56. Cf. also Martineau's 'The Famine Time' and 'The Irish Union', as discussed above.
63. Catherine Hall notes that anti-Catholicism abounded after Catholic emancipation in 1829 and peaked in the 1860s. Cf. Hall, 'Defining the Victorian Nation', pp.210–220.
64. '[Papal Aggression in Ireland]', in *The Times*, January 22, 1851, 4.
65. '[The Irish]', in *The Times*, October 24, 1851, 4.
66. '[Difficulties in Ireland]', in *The Times*, June 17, 1850, 4.
67. [Charles Dickens], 'A Crisis in the Affairs of Mr. John Bull', in *Household Words*, 2:35 (November 23, 1850), 193–196, pp.194–195.
68. [Dickens], 'A Crisis' , pp.194–195.
69. The movement only ended in 1848 with the conviction and transportation of its main leaders.
70. [Grey], 'Ballinglen' , p.451.
71. [Martineau], 'Peatal Aggression' . It is not known whether this title was Martineau's choice or that of *Household Words'* editors.
72. [Martineau], 'The Irish Union' , p.171.
73. Pete McCarthy's *McCarthy's Bar* dedicates a chapter to the same pilgrimage, virtually unchanged since Allingham published his piece in 1850.
74. [William Allingham], 'The Irish "Stationers"', in *Household Words*, 2:28 (October 5, 1850), 29–33, p.33.
75. [Browne], 'The "Irish Difficulty"' , p.207.
76. [Morley], 'The Irish Globe' , p.54.
77. [Mrs. Hoare], 'An Irish Peculiarity', in *Household Words*, 1:25 (September 14, 1850), 594–596, p.594.
78. [Hoare], 'An Irish Peculiarity' , p.595.
79. Pratt, *Imperial Eyes* , p.64.
80. [Hoare], 'An Irish Peculiarity' , p.596.
81. [Hoare], 'An Irish Peculiarity' , p.596.
82. [William Howitt], 'Two Aspects of Ireland. The First Aspect.' in *Household Words*, 4:79 (September 27, 1851), 6–10, p.7. The 'black tint of skin' is particularly interesting in the light of racial discourse on the Irish and especially the desire to 'black-lead' them. See Kaplan, 'White, Black, and Green'.
83. [Grey], 'Ballinglen' , p.451.
84. [Harriet Martineau], 'Triumphant Carriages', in *Household Words*, 6:135 (October 23, 1852), 121–125; [George A. Sala], 'An Irish Stew', in *Household Words*, 7:179 (August 27, 1853), 617–620.
85. [Browne], 'The "Irish Difficulty"' , p.208–209.
86. [Howitt], 'The First Aspect of Ireland' , p.8.
87. [Hoare], 'An Irish Peculiarity' , p.595.
88. [Allingham], 'The Irish "Stationers"' ; [Grey], 'Ballinglen' ; [Mitchell], 'An Encumbered Estate' .

89. [Howitt], 'The Second Aspect of Ireland' ; [Mrs. Hoare], 'Barryhooraghan Post-Office', in *Household Words*, 6:150 (February 5, 1853), 503–504; [William Allingham], 'Round the Midsummer Fire', in *Household Words*, 5:121 (July 17, 1852), 426–428.
90. [Martineau], 'The Famine Time' ; [Eyre Evans Crowe], 'The Golden Vale', in *Household Words*, 6:145 (January 1, 1853), 377–381; [Miss French], 'Number Five, Hanbury Terrace', in *Household Words*, 16:403 (December 12, 1857), 568–572.
91. [William M. Thomas], 'The Last Howley of Killowen', in *Household Words*, 9:225 (July 15, 1854), 513–519; 'An Encumbered Estate' ; [Mrs. Hoare], 'Father and Son', in *Household Words*, 1:9 (May 25, 1850), 213–216.
92. [Howitt], 'The First Aspect of Ireland' ; [Leigh], 'The Latest Intelligence' ; [Hoare], 'An Irish Peculiarity' ; [Crowe], 'The Golden Vale' ; [Mitchell], 'An Encumbered Estate' ; [Allingham], 'Round the Midsummer Fire' .
93. [Crowe], 'The Golden Vale' ; [Sala], 'An Irish Stew' ; [William Allingham], 'Irish Ballad Singers and Irish Street Ballads', in *Household Words*, 4:94 (January 10, 1852), 361–368; [William Allingham], 'Saint Patrick', in *Household Words*, 13:315 (April 5, 1856), 279–283.
94. [Dickens], 'A Crisis' ; [Eliza Lynn Linton], 'National Contrasts', in *Household Words*, 18:449 (October 30, 1858), 472–476; [Martineau], 'Triumphant Carriages' .
95. [Martineau], 'The Irish Union' ; [Martineau], 'The Famine Time' ; [Sala], 'An Irish Stew' ; [George A. Sala], 'The Length of the Quays', in *Household Words*, 7:178 (August 20, 1853), 582–586; [Browne], 'The "Irish Difficulty"'.
96. [Martineau], 'The Irish Union' ; [Morley], 'The Irish Globe' ; [Sala], 'An Irish Stew' ; [Lynn], 'National Contrasts' ; [Howitt], 'The Second Aspect of Ireland' .
97. [Morley], 'The Irish Globe' , p.54.
98. [Mitchell], 'An Encumbered Estate' ; [Hoare], 'Barryhooraghan Post-Office'.
99. [Grey], 'Ballinglen' .
100. [Allingham], 'Irish Ballads' , p.362.
101. [Sala], 'The Length of the Quays' , p.582.
102. [Martineau], 'Slate' , p.159, my emphasis.
103. [Morley], 'The Irish Globe' ; [Howitt], 'The Second Aspect of Ireland' ; [Grey], 'Ballinglen' ; [Edmund S. Dixon], 'More Work for the Ladies', in *Household Words*, 6:130 (September 18, 1852), 18–22.
104. [Sala], 'The Length of the Quays' , p.583.
105. [Sala], 'The Length of the Quays' , p.583.
106. [Sala], 'An Irish Stew' , p.617.
107. [Sala], 'An Irish Stew' , p.620.
108. [Howitt], 'The Second Aspect of Ireland' , p.31. Martineau also repeatedly refers to the Irish habit of sharing their accommodation with their pigs. Cf. [Martineau], 'The Irish Union', [Martineau], 'Triumphant Carriages'.
109. [Martineau], 'The Irish Union' , p.170.
110. [Martineau], 'Slate' , p.161.
111. [Thomas], 'Killowen' ; [Hoare], 'Father and Son' .
112. [Martineau], 'Triumphant Carriages' .
113. [Mrs. Hoare], 'Little Mary. A Tale of the Black Year', in *Household Words*, 1:17 (July 20, 1850), 392–396, p.393.
114. [Allingham], 'Round the Midsummer Fire' , p.427.
115. [Allingham], 'Irish Ballads' , p.362.
116. [Allingham], 'Irish Ballads' , p.365.

117. Although *Household Words* occasionally uses the term 'race' in the Irish context, it is usually to be taken as 'people'. *Household Words* typically assumes that Irish characteristics are a matter of (lacking) culture, education, morality, and habit, all of which can be improved by beneficial English influence. The only exceptions are William Howitt's 'Celtic physiognomy' and the highly contradictory 'Coast folk' articles of John Robertson.
118. [Martineau], 'The Irish Union' , p.172.
119. [Leigh], 'The Latest Intelligence' , p.595.
120. [Richard Horne and Charles Dickens], 'The Great Exhibition and the Little One', in *Household Words*, 3:67 (July 5, 1851), 356–360, p.357.
121. [Hoare], 'An Irish Peculiarity' , p.595.

NOTES TO CHAPTER 4

1. See, for example, the essays by Dominic Rainsford, Michael Hollington, and Tore Rem in *Dickens, Europe and the New Worlds,* ed. by Anny Sadrin (Basingstoke: Macmillan Press Ltd, 1999).
2. Most instalments were reprinted in independent volumes in 1854–5 and quite widely read. For example, Frances Duberly, the wife of an officer taking part in the Crimean war, writes in her diary entry for August 24, 1855: 'I cannot refrain from mentioning a brilliant little work entitled "The Roving Englishman in Turkey," and from thanking the author for the pleasure he has afforded me in its perusal. It was put into my hands a short time ago, and since then it has sparkled on my table like a gem.' Frances Duberly, 'Diary', 1855, website (http://www.silverwhistle.co.uk/crimea/duberly6.html), accessed February 18, 2004.
3. *An Age of Equipoise? Reassessing Mid-Victorian Britain,* ed. by Martin Hewitt (Aldershot: Ashgate, 2000), p.27, quoting from Kitson Clark, *The Making of Victorian England,* (London: Methuen, 1962), p.43.
4. Eric J. Hobsbawm, *The Age of Capital, 1848–1875*, History of Civilisation (London: Weidenfeld and Nicolson, 1975), p.2
5. [George A. Sala], 'Perfidious Patmos', in *Household Words*, 7:155 (March 12, 1853), 25–29; [George A. Sala], 'Music in Paving Stones', in *Household Words*, 10:231 (August 26, 1854), 37–43.
6. Bernard Porter, *Britain, Europe, and the World 1850–1986: Delusions of Grandeur* (London: Allen & Unwin, 1987), p.1–2.
7. Cf., for instance, Dickens and Horne's vision of 'Old England' as the benign, patient teacher of hot-headed European nations. [Richard Horne and Charles Dickens], 'The Great Exhibition and the Little One', in *Household Words*, 3:67 (July 5, 1851), 356–360.
8. Porter, *Britain, Europe, and the world* , p.3. Peter Mandler makes a similar case, by offsetting the 'forces allegedly "racialising" and "nationalising" English self-consciousness after 1848 [. . .] against the backdrop of [a] flexible and adaptive civilisational perspective'. Peter Mandler, '"Race" and "Nation" in Mid-Victorian Thought', in *History, Religion, and Culture: British Intellectual History 1750–1950,* ed. by Stefan Collini, Richard Whatmore and Brian W. Young (Cambridge: Cambridge University Press, 2000), p.229.
9. In actual fact, *The Times* persistently uses 'England' in relation to European affairs and 'Britain' in relation to non-European/colonial ones, such as the Indian Revolt. However, I shall adhere to my own usage of 'English' as the emotive identity and 'British' as the political state, in as far as this is possible.

10. 'The Defence of the Country', in *Illustrated London News*, 31:884 (October 24, 1857), 401–402.
11. R.L.V. ffrench Blake, *The Crimean War* (London: Sphere Books, 1971), p.145.
12. '[Map Of Europe In 1860]', *The Times*, February 14, 1859, 10; '[France and Europe]', *The Times*, January 18, 1859, 6.
13. '[Alliance between France and Russia]', *The Times*, April 27, 1859, 8.
14. Cf. Bernard Porter, '"Bureau and Barrack": Early Victorian Attitudes towards the Continent' in *Victorian Studies*, 27 (1984), 407–433.
15. Cf. Hobsbawm, *Age of Capital* , p.33.
16. [Charles Dickens], 'A Flight', in *Household Words*, 3:75 (August 30, 1851), 529–533.
17. 'A Glance at Continental Railways', in *Chambers's Edinburgh Journal*, 18:455 (n.s.) (September 18, 1852), 177–180, p.77.
18. One might add to these the Great Exhibition of 1851, although it is debatable whether this was cause or symptom of the 'shrinking' of Europe.
19. Maria P. Bakardjieva, 'The Electric Telegraph', website, December 1, 2000, (http://www.ucalgary.ca/~bakardji/ElectricComm/takeoff.html), accessed November 24, 2003. Cf. Tom Standage, *The Victorian Internet: the Remarkable Story of the Telegraph and the Nineteenth Century's Online Pioneers* (London: Weidenfeld and Nicholson, 1998).
20. 'The Continental "Bradshaw" in 1852', in *Chambers's Edinburgh Journal*, 18:452 (n.s.) (August 28, 1852), 133–136, p.133.
21. [Grenville Murray], 'The Roving Englishman: His Hints to Travellers (10)', in *Household Words*, 6:138 (November 13, 1852), 211–214, p.211.
22. Mary Louise Pratt, *Imperial Eyes: Travel Writing and Transculturation* (London, New York: Routledge, 1992), p.38.
23. Linda Colley repeatedly stresses that France helped to define Britain as everything that France was not. Linda Colley, *Britons : Forging the Nation, 1707–1837* (London: Vintage, 1992). Cf. Dominic Rainsford, 'Crossing the Channel with Dickens', in *Dickens, Europe and the New Worlds*, ed. by Anny Sadrin (Basingstoke: Macmillan Press Ltd, 1999).
24. Jonathan Philip Parry, 'The Impact of Napoleon III on British Politics, 1851–1880' in *Transactions of the Royal Historical Society*, 6th series, 11 (2001), 147–175.
25. Cf. Parry, 'The impact of Napoleon III.' Porter, *Britain, Europe, and the world* .
26. [Malcolm R.L. Meason], 'French and English Staff Officers', in *Household Words*, 13:307 (February 9, 1856), 84–88; [W.H. Wills], 'The Schoolmaster at Home and Abroad', in *Household Words*, 1:4 (April 20, 1850), 82–84.
27. [George A. Sala], 'The Great Hotel Question (I)', in *Household Words*, 13:308 (February 16, 1856), 97–103; [Grenville Murray], 'The Roving Englishman: Messina (59)', in *Household Words*, 13:312 (March 15, 1856), 214–216; [Wilkie Collins], 'My Black Mirror', in *Household Words*, 14:337 (September 6, 1856), 169–175; [George Thornbury], 'Spanish Hotels', in *Household Words*, 19:459 (January 8, 1859), 132–137; [Eliza Lynn Linton], 'National Contrasts', in *Household Words*, 18:449 (October 30, 1858), 472–476.
28. Murray's series 'The Roving Englishman' is particularly outspoken on these two countries.
29. Charles Dickens, *Bleak House*, ed. by Stephen Gill, Oxford World's Classics, (Oxford: Oxford University Press, 1996 [first published 1852–3]), p.188 (chp.13).

30. Tore Rem, '*Little Dorrit, Pictures from Italy* and John Bull', in *Dickens, Europe and the New Worlds,* ed. by Anny Sadrin (Basingstoke: Macmillan Press Ltd, 1999), p.131.
31. Malcolm Andrews, *Dickens on England and the English* (Brighton: Harvester Press, 1979), p.159.
32. However, Dickens's correspondence during his spells abroad often reveals an underlying restlessness and anxiety to be back in England. Part of his motivation for taking up residence abroad was financial.
33. In comparison, *Blackwood's* published in-depth analyses and reviews of Crimean affairs, Russian and Turkish religion, culture, economy, and politics, and the 'Eastern Question' in virtually every number during the war.
34. [Sidney L. Blanchard], 'Munchausen Modernised', in *Household Words,* 6:152 (February 19, 1853), 533–538, p. 538.
35. [George A. Sala], 'The Foreign Invasion', in *Household Words,* 4:81 (October 11, 1851), 60–64; [Sala], 'Music in Paving Stones' .
36. [William Duthie], 'What my Landlord Believed', in *Household Words,* 11:271 (June 2, 1855), 418–420.
37. [Dickens], 'A Flight' , p.532.
38. [Charles Dickens], 'Insularities', in *Household Words,* 13:304 (January 19, 1856), 1–4, p.2.
39. [William M. Thomas], 'An Englishman's Castle', in *Household Words,* 4:92 (December 27, 1851), 321–324, p.321; Fred Kaplan, *Thomas Carlyle: a Biography* (Cambridge: Cambridge University Press, 1983), p.405. I suggest below that 'foreign' is usually synonymous with 'European' in *Household Words*' terminology.
40. [Collins], 'My Black Mirror' , p. 173.
41. [Collins], 'My Black Mirror' , p.170.
42. [Collins], 'My Black Mirror' , p.173.
43. [Collins], 'My Black Mirror' , p.173.
44. Porter, 'Bureau and Barrack' , p.426, quoting from Charles Lever's *A Day's Ride.*
45. [Collins], 'My Black Mirror' , p.174.
46. [Lynn Linton] 'National Contrasts' , p.474.
47. Cf. Catherine Hall, 'The Nation Within and Without', in *Defining the Victorian Nation: Class, Race, Gender and the British Reform Act of 1867,* ed. by Catherine Hall, Keith McClelland and Jane Rendall (Cambridge: Cambridge University Press, 2000), p.196fn.
48. Cf., for example, [Charles Dickens, W. H. Wills and Grenville Murray], 'Foreigners' Portraits of Englishmen', in *Household Words,* 1:26 (September 21, 1850), 601–604; 'The Foreign Invasion' ; 'Music in Paving Stones' ; 'An Englishman's Castle' .
49. Porter, *Britain, Europe, and the world* , p.11.
50. [Lynn Linton], 'National Contrasts' , p.475.
51. [Lynn Linton], 'National Contrasts' , p.476.
52. At the time of publication, Turkey occupied most of what is today northern Greece, and from the identifiable place-names that the narrator mentions—Constantinople, Lesbos, Mytilene—he seems to have spent his time on Turkish territory. This indicates that 'Greek' and 'Turkish' are not to be understood as political or national distinctions, but as expressions of cultural and ethnic identity.
53. *Household Words: a Weekly Journal, 1850–1859, Conducted by Charles Dickens: Table of Contents,* ed. by Anne Lohrli (Toronto: University of Toronto Press, 1973), p.381.

54. [Grenville Murray and Henry Morley], 'A Roving Englishman: Benighted; Out Shooting (1)', in *Household Words*, 4:88 (November 29, 1851), 221–224, p.223.
55. [Grenville Murray], 'The Roving Englishman: Greek Waters (35)', in *Household Words*, 9:221 (June 10, 1854), 402–404, p.403. The assertion is tongue-in-cheek, though—he claims that due to his age he is not interested in women any more, only to praise the Mytilene ladies' beauty in the very next sentence. His taxing look at women throughout the series further casts this assertion into doubt.
56. For example, the narrator states in his description of a pasha that 'my Pasha is not a portrait. He is the type of a class' that exists throughout Turkey. [Grenville Murray], 'The Roving Englishman: The Pasha (36)', in *Household Words*, 9:223 (July 1, 1854), 462–464, p.463.
57. Dickens, in fact, found Murray 'too slovenly' and sometimes wanting in accuracy of information. *The Letters of Charles Dickens: Volume Seven: 1853–1855,* ed. by Graham Storey, Kathleen Tillotson and Angus Easson, vol. 7 (Oxford: Clarendon Press, 1993), p.110. Cf. *Household Words: Contents,* ed. by Lohrli, p.382.
58. [Murray], 'The Roving Englishman (10)' , p.212.
59. [Murray], 'The Roving Englishman (10)' , p.212.
60. [Grenville Murray], 'The Roving Englishman: On Horseback (12)', in *Household Words*, 6:142 (December 11, 1852), 309–312, p.309.
61. [Grenville Murray and Henry Morley], 'A Roving Englishman: The Apple-Green Spencer; Gastein Baths (2)', in *Household Words*, 4:91 (December 20, 1851), 299–301, p. 300.
62. Elsewhere, the narrator sees women in similarly mercenary and ruthless terms, out on 'matrimonial speculation' and inevitably keeping the upper hand in a marriage. [Grenville Murray], 'The Roving Englishman at the Pera Theatre (44)', in *Household Words*, 10:253 (January 27, 1855), 570–572, p.570; [Grenville Murray], 'The Roving Englishman: Very Cold at Bucharest; The Theatre; The Terrible Officer (45)', in *Household Words*, 11:257 (February 24, 1855), 82–85.
63. [Grenville Murray], 'The Roving Englishman: Greek Fire (29)', in *Household Words*, 9:209 (March 25, 1854), 132–134, p.132.
64. [Grenville Murray], 'The Roving Englishman: A Greek Feast (25)', in *Household Words*, 8:196 (December 24, 1853), 393–397, p.396. Cf. 'A Greek Girl', which gives a thoroughly disgusting portrait of the average Greek girl as stupid, uneducated, malicious, shy, garish, and promiscuous. Both articles, and some others, suggest that this is the outcome of a patriarchal culture, yet the narrator remains ambiguous as to the balance of nature and nurture—the claim that Greek women are 'without mind, or heart' seems to go beyond their upbringing alone. [Grenville Murray], 'The Roving Englishman: A Greek Girl (32)', in *Household Words*, 9:217 (May 20, 1854), 321–323; [Grenville Murray], 'The Roving Englishman: The Cadi; Britons in Turkey (31)', in *Household Words*, 9:214 (April 29, 1854), 254–257.
65. [Murray], 'The Roving Englishman (25)' , p.396.
66. [Grenville Murray], 'The Roving Englishman: Regular Turks (33)', in *Household Words*, 9:218 (May 27, 1854), 349–352, p.403.
67. [Grenville Murray], 'The Roving Englishman: A Few More Hints (14)', in *Household Words*, 6:144 (December 25, 1852), 358–360, p.358.
68. [Murray], 'The Roving Englishman (14)' , p.359.
69. [Murray], 'The Roving Englishman (14)' , p.359; [Murray], 'The Roving Englishman (10)' , p.213.

70. [Murray], 'The Roving Englishman (10)' , p.214, 212.
71. [Grenville Murray], 'The Roving Englishman: From Varna to Rustchuk (49)', in *Household Words*, 11:266 (April 28, 1855), 307–308, p.308.
72. [Murray], 'The Roving Englishman (29)' , p.132–3.
73. [Murray], 'The Roving Englishman (29)' , p.133.
74. [Murray], 'The Roving Englishman (14)' , p.359.
75. [Murray], 'The Roving Englishman (25)' , p.396–7.
76. Smith does acknowledge that this may be the result of Turkish rule, and that 'the Greek is naturally clean in his dress, his person, and his house', and also 'naturally polite'. For the most part, however, Smith has very little positive to say of the Greeks, in this instalment or any other.
77. [Murray], 'The Roving Englishman (29)' , p.133.
78. [Murray], 'The Roving Englishman (29)' , p.133.
79. [Murray], 'The Roving Englishman (29)' , p.133.
80. [Grenville Murray], 'The Roving Englishman: From Kraiova to London (55)', in *Household Words*, 12:291 (October 20, 1855), 282–284, p.283.
81. [Murray], 'The Roving Englishman (59)' , p.216.
82. Cf. [Murray], 'The Roving Englishman (36)' .
83. [Grenville Murray], 'The Roving Englishman; and the Prince de Vendome (24)', in *Household Words*, 8:194 (December 10, 1853), 355–360, p.358.
84. [Murray], 'The Roving Englishman (25)' , p.396–7.
85. [Grenville Murray], 'The Roving Englishman: From Bucharest to Kraiova (54)', in *Household Words*, 12:284 (September 1, 1855), 109–112, p.110.
86. Inderpal Grewal, *Home and Harem: Nation, Gender, Empire and the Cultures of Travel* (London: Leicester University Press, 1996), p.1.
87. [Grenville Murray], 'The Roving Englishman: Rustchuk (51)', in *Household Words*, 11:271 (June 2, 1855), 427–429, p.429.
88. [Grenville Murray], 'The Roving Englishman: Dolma Bakjah; A Turkish Bath (42)', in *Household Words*, 10:245 (December 2, 1854), 369–373, p.371.
89. [Murray], 'The Roving Englishman (33)' .
90. Grewal, *Home and Harem* , p.1.
91. [Grenville Murray], 'The Roving Englishman: Diplomacy (21)', in *Household Words*, 7:169 (June 18, 1853), 373–375, p.374.
92. 'Russia and the European Crisis' in *Bentley's Miscellany*, 27 (1850), p.497.
93. 'Russia and the European Crisis' in *Bentley's Miscellany*, 27 (1850), pp.497–501.
94. 'Russia and the European Crisis' in *Bentley's Miscellany*, 28 (1850), pp.172–179.
95. [Henry Morley], 'Views of the Country', in *Household Words*, 2:34 (November 16, 1850), 169–172, p.170–1.
96. [Wills], 'The Schoolmaster' , p.82.
97. [Charles Dickens and Henry Morley], 'Mr. Bendigo Buster on Our National Defences Against Education', in *Household Words*, 2:40 (December 28, 1850), 313–319, p.313.
98. [Charles J. Lever], 'Continental Ways and Means', in *Household Words*, 4:99 (February 14, 1852), 490–492. The difference may well be that Lever is thinking about a wealthier class than Wills, Dickens, and Morley—Lever evaluates precisely the kind of education that is available for money, while the others are discussing education for the broad masses' offspring, focusing on essentials such as reading and writing.
99. [Eliza Lynn], 'The Workmen of Europe', in *Household Words*, 12:296 (November 24, 1855), 390–394.
100. [Grenville Murray], 'The Roving Englishman: His Philosophy of Dining (11)', in *Household Words*, 6:139 (November 20, 1852), 231–233, p.233.

101. [Grenville Murray], 'The Roving Englishman: Free Quarters; A Saint's Brother (30)', in *Household Words*, 9:212 (April 15, 1854), 206–209, p.206.
102. Even *The Times* tried to reassure its readers that there was nothing wrong with 'the unconstrained movements of a free people', even though recent French history made the association between a crowd of people and revolution inevitable. '[Festivities in England and France]', *The Times*, May 6, 1851, 5.
103. '[France and England]', *The Times*, July 10, 1851, 4.
104. 'The Liberties of Europe', in *Illustrated London News*, 19:511 (August 23, 1851), 225–226.
105. '[Probability of War with France]', *The Times*, February 12, 1853, 8.
106. 'The Prospects of Europe', in *Illustrated London News*, 19:536 (December 20, 1851), 721–722.
107. '[France and the Great Powers of Europe]', *The Times*, June 1, 1852, 4;
108. '[European Monarchs and Despots]', *The Times*, October 6, 1853, 8. The only exception that *The Times* allowed for was Belgium, which *Chambers's Edinburgh Journal* in turn terms 'a kind of little England'. Cf. 'A Glance at Continental Railways' , p.177.
109. [George A. Sala], 'Liberty, Equality, Fraternity, and Musketry', in *Household Words*, 4:92 (December 27, 1851), 313–318.
110. [Lever], 'Continental Ways and Means' , p.490.
111. Lever's usage of those words mirrors that of the journal as a whole.
112. [Lever], 'Continental Ways and Means' , p.491–2.
113. [Lever], 'Continental Ways and Means' , p.492.
114. [Grenville Murray], 'The Roving Englishman: Concerning a Pair of Demons (6)', in *Household Words*, 4:100 (February 21, 1852), 514–517, p.514.
115. [Grenville Murray], 'The Roving Englishman: A Golden Wedding (8)', in *Household Words*, 6:131 (September 25, 1852), 46–48, p.48.
116. [Murray], 'The Roving Englishman (8)' , p.47.
117. Pratt, *Imperial Eyes* , p.7.
118. [Grenville Murray and Henry Morley], 'The Roving Englishman: A Brace of Blunders (5)', in *Household Words*, 4:96 (January 24, 1852), 431–432. Cf. [Grenville Murray], 'The Roving Englishman: The Great Do (18)', in *Household Words*, 7:156 (March 19, 1853), 67–72.
119. Since Germany was not a nation state then but a collection of motley independent states, it is usually used as an ethnic and cultural term rather than a political one. In most media's usage at the time, Prussia and Austria are both 'German', not only linguistically, but also culturally.
120. [Murray], 'The Roving Englishman (8)' , p.46.
121. [Murray], 'The Roving Englishman (14)' , p.359. Cf.: 'I had never before known [. . .] what an odd, singing, dancing, saving, dreaming, stuffing, love-making, visiting, lazy, gossipping, speculating, friendshippy [. . .] maudlin, smoking, soaking life the Germans lead.' [Grenville Murray], 'The Roving Englishman: Travelling Servants (15)', in *Household Words*, 6:148 (January 8, 1853), 453–456, p. 456
122. [Murray], 'The Roving Englishman (15)' , p.454. Cf. [Murray], 'The Roving Englishman (21)' .
123. For example, Sala's discovery of the hopeless, impoverished, and squalid underbelly of Dublin leads him to term the city 'continental' and comments on its 'semi-continental picturesqueness', the latter a term that repeatedly crops up in connection to the continent. [George A. Sala], 'An Irish Stew', in *Household Words*, 7:179 (August 27, 1853), 617–620, p.617.
124. 'A Glance at Continental Railways' , p.177.
125. 'A Glance at Continental Railways' , p.179.

126. '[France and Louis Napoleon 2]', *The Times*, May 21, 1852, 5.
127. '[France and England on Turkey]', *The Times*, October 29, 1853, 6.
128. 'European Powers in Crimean War', *The Times*, November 21, 1854, 6
129. 'Christians in Turkey', *The Times*, July 11, 1853, 5.
130. '[Greek Insurrection against Turkey]', *The Times*, May 18, 1854, 10.
131. 'Peoples and Prospects of Eastern Europe. Second Article', in *Chambers's Journal of Popular Literature, Science, and Arts*, 2:28 (July 15, 1854), 44–46, p.45.
132. '[Greek Insurrection against Turkey]', , *The Times*, May 18, 1854, p.10.
133. Porter, *Britain, Europe, and the world* , p.26.
134. 'The Duties of the Allies to themselves and to Europe', in *Illustrated London News*, 25:714 (November 25, 1854), 525–526. Interestingly, Nicholas was termed 'the emperor' while Britain approved of him, but became 'the czar' as soon as he fell out of favour.
135. Not entirely, of course—occasional articles still appeared that compared Britain to other European countries and found it superior to them. Cf. '[British and Continental Governments Compared', *The Times*, August 15, 1856, 6.
136. 'Extension of the War', in *Illustrated London News*, 26:741 (May 5, 1855), 425–426
137. Although the first design for it dates back to 1802, the Channel tunnel was not completed until 1994. Eurotunnel, 'History', website, 2004, 2003, (http://www.eurotunnel.com/ukcMain/ukcCompany/ukcAboutUs/ukpAboutUsHistory), accessed September 28, 2004.
138. 'An Extraordinary Scheme', *The Times*, October 24, 1855, 6.
139. 'Alarm of a French Invasion', in *Chambers's Journal of Popular Literature, Science, and Arts*, 1:10 (March 11, 1854), 151–152.
140. 'Cravens in Council', in *Illustrated London News*, 26:742 (May 12, 1855), 449.
141. [Lynn], 'The Workmen of Europe' , p.394.
142. [Edmund S. Dixon], 'Wheel within Wheel', in *Household Words*, 10:250 (January 6, 1855), 481–483, p.481.
143. [Dixon], 'Wheel within Wheel' , p.483.
144. Cf. Edward W. Said, *Orientalism* (Harmondsworth: Penguin, 1991 [first published 1978]).
145. [Murray], 'The Roving Englishman (33)' , p.351.
146. [Grenville Murray], 'The Roving Englishman at Constantinople (23)', in *Household Words*, 8:188 (October 29, 1853), 204–207, pp. 204, 206.
147. [Murray], 'The Roving Englishman (24)' , p.358.
148. [Murray], 'The Roving Englishman (42)'
149. Indeed, laziness—and women—are at the root of all of Turkey's problems. [Murray], 'The Roving Englishman (32)' ; [Murray], 'The Roving Englishman (33)' .
150. [Murray], 'The Roving Englishman (44)' ; [Murray], 'The Roving Englishman (51)' .
151. [Grenville Murray], 'The Roving Englishman: A Turkish Auctioneer (34)', in *Household Words*, 9:219 (June 3, 1854), 362–364.
152. Smith advises 'travellers to the East' to buy 'a good European saddle and bridle at the last place on their way where such a thing can be got'. [Murray], 'The Roving Englishman (10)' , p.211.
153. Steven S. Sowards, '"Asia Begins at the *Landstrasse*:" Comparing Eastern European and European Histories', December 2003 website (http://www.lib.msu.edu/sowards/balkan/lecture2.html), accessed February 24, 2004.
154. 'istanbul.com—Official City Guide' (website), last update February 2004. Available at http://english.istanbul.com/ (accessed February 25, 2004). This

aspect was again emphasised at the Eurovision Song Contest, staged in Istanbul on May 15, 2004. One is also reminded of the continuing debate on whether Turkey should be allowed to join the European Union.

155. [Murray], 'The Roving Englishman (11)' , p.232.
156. [Murray], 'The Roving Englishman (23)' , p.205.
157. [Murray], 'The Roving Englishman (25)' , p.395.
158. [Murray], 'The Roving Englishman (44)' , p.570.
159. [Murray], 'The Roving Englishman (33)' .
160. [Grenville Murray], 'The Roving Englishman: Greek Easter at Constantinople; A Defense of Fleas (26)', in *Household Words*, 8:197 (December 31, 1853), 415–418.
161. [Murray], 'The Roving Englishman (33)' .
162. [Murray], 'The Roving Englishman (42)' .
163. [Grenville Murray], 'Turkish Contrasts', in *Household Words*, 12:314 (March 29, 1856), 263–264.
164. [William Blanchard Jerrold], 'The Turk at Home', in *Household Words*, 9:206 (March 4, 1854), 56–61, p.57.
165. [Murray], 'Turkish Contrasts' , p.264.
166. [Murray], 'Turkish Contrasts' , p.264.
167. For instance, an article on the 'Ethnology of Europe' in *Blackwood's* expresses its conviction that, 'Whatever the issue of the present contest, [. . .] the contagion of Western ideas, disseminated in the most imposing ways by the presence of the armies of England and France, cannot fail to impress itself on the slumbering but awakening Ottomans, and not only expand their stereotyped civilisation into a wider and freer form, but possibly to strike also from their religion the more faulty and obstructive of its tenets.' 'Ethnology of Europe', in *Blackwood's Edinburgh Magazine*, 76:456 (August, 1854), 165–182, p.180.
168. 'The present generation of Europeans seem almost to have been ignorant of [the Turks] until lately.' [Murray], 'The Roving Englishman (33)' , p.351.
169. [Murray], 'The Roving Englishman (23)' , p.207.
170. [Murray], 'The Roving Englishman (33)' , p.352.
171. [Murray], 'The Roving Englishman (23)' , p.207.
172. Other examples are Dickens and Horne's image of the 'newly turned-up furrows of the earth', which gratefully receive the seed of civilisation that England bestows on them, or William Howitt's and Harriet Martineau's sanguine prediction that the Irish population would take kindly to English investors who buy up and 'improve' Irish soil. [Horne and Dickens], 'The Little Exhibition' , p.356; [William Howitt], 'Two Aspects of Ireland. The Second Aspect.' in *Household Words*, 4:80 (October 4, 1851), 27–32; [Harriet Martineau], 'Hope with a Slate Anchor', in *Household Words*, 6:136 (October 30, 1852), 156–161.
173. [Murray], 'The Roving Englishman (34)' .
174. [Murray], 'The Roving Englishman (29)' , p.206.
175. [Murray], 'The Roving Englishman (55)' , p.282.
176. [Sala], 'The Great Hotel Question (I)' ; [George A. Sala], 'The Great Hotel Question (II)', in *Household Words*, 13:309 (February 23, 1856), 141–144; [George A. Sala], 'The Great Hotel Question (III)', in *Household Words*, 13:310 (March 1, 1856), 148–154; [Wilkie Collins], 'Laid up in Two Lodgings (I): My Paris Lodgings', in *Household Words*, 13:324 (June 7, 1856), 481–486; [Wilkie Collins], 'Laid up in Two Lodgings (II): My London Lodgings', in *Household Words*, 13:325 (June 14, 1856), 517–523.
177. [William Duthie], 'Some German Sundays', in *Household Words*, 13:317 (April 19, 1856), 320–325; [William Duthie], 'More Sundays Abroad', in *Household Words*, 13:320 (May 10, 1856), 400–404.

178. [Grenville Murray], 'Army Interpreters', in *Household Words*, 10:247 (December 16, 1854), 431–432; [William Jerdan], 'The Gift of Tongues', in *Household Words*, 15:355 (January 10, 1857), 41–43; [Reeves], 'Promotion, French and English', in *Household Words*, 15:357 (January 24, 1857), 90–92.
179. [Charles Dickens], 'Proposals for a National Jest-Book', in *Household Words*, 13:319 (May 3, 1856), 361–364, p.363. Importantly, he did not see France as a threat (as other journals had before and after him), but as a positive case in point.
180. 'The Mutiny in India', in *Illustrated London News*, 31:867 (July 4, 1857), 1–2.
181. 'British Ideas in India', in *Illustrated London News*, 31:878 (September 12, 1857), 251–252.
182. 'The Defence of the Country' , in *Illustrated London News*.
183. 'The Defence of the Country' , in *Illustrated London News*.
184. '[England and France]', *The Times*, September 5, 1857, 6.
185. '[French Reaction to Indian Mutiny]', *The Times*, November 20, 1857, 6.
186. '[French Reaction to Indian Mutiny]', *The Times*, November 20, 1857, 6.
187. '[England and France]', *The Times*, March 29, 1858, 8; '[Protestants in France]', *The Times*, January 9, 1858, 8.
188. '[France and Europe]', *The Times*, January 18, 1859, 6.
189. '[Alliance between France and Russia]' *The Times*, April 27, 1854, 8; '[The State of Europe]', *The Times*, February 23, 1859.
190. [Lynn], 'National Contrasts' . It is not clear which reports she is alluding to.
191. These titles stand in marked contrast to the domesticity implied in 'Household Words'. Murray's narrator finds an actual 'Café de l'Europe' in Naples. [Grenville Murray], 'The Roving Englishman: Beautiful Naples (20)', in *Household Words*, 7:166 (May 28, 1853), 302–305.
192. [Edmund S. Dixon], 'Literary Small Change', in *Household Words*, 18:446 (October 9, 1858), 404–408, p.406.
193. [Thornbury], 'Spanish Hotels' , p. 135–136.
194. [Percy Fitzgerald], 'Bogie Albion', in *Household Words*, 19:465 (February 19, 1859), 263–269, p.265.
195. [Wilkie Collins], 'The Great (Forgotten) Invasion', in *Household Words*, 19:468 (March 12, 1859), 337–341, 340.
196. [Collins], 'The Great (Forgotten) Invasion' , p.341.
197. [Rev. James White], 'A Testimony in Praise of Testimonials', in *Household Words*, 15:359 (February 7, 1857), 121–124, p.121.

NOTES TO CHAPTER 5

1. [Samuel Sidney], 'Indian Railroads and British Commerce', in *Household Words*, 2:51 (March 15, 1851), 590–595, p.591.
2. [Sidney], 'Indian Railroads' , p.591.
3. Cf. [John Capper], 'Monsters of Faith', in *Household Words*, 5:125 (August 19, 1852), 506–508; [John Capper], 'The Great Indian Bean-Stalk', in *Household Words*, 8:182 (September 17, 1853), 60–64; [John Capper], 'Honourable John', in *Household Words*, 7:175 (July 30, 1853), 516–518. 'Monsters of Faith' describes the voluntary tortures that believers undergo at Indian religious festivals. In spite of the horror these brutal acts inspire in him, Capper also emphasises, with a certain respect, that nobody is coerced into them, and that the victims willingly submit to the torture as an act of gratitude after a prayer has been fulfilled, rather than as an attempt to 'blackmail' a deity beforehand into the granting of a wish.

4. [John Capper], 'The Peasants of British India', in *Household Words*, 4:95 (January 17, 1852), 389–393, p.393.
5. [Capper], 'The Peasants' , p.393.
6. 'Indian Handicrafts', in *Chambers's Edinburgh Journal*, 15:387 (n.s.) (May 31, 1851), 342–345, p.345.
7. 'Indian Sweet-Meats', in *Chambers's Edinburgh Journal*, 16:399 (n.s.) (August 23, 1851), 126–127, p.126; 'Indian Handicrafts' , *Chambers's*, p.343. I would like to thank Bill Emery from the British Library, who helped me identify one of these references at very short notice.
8. 'Arts and Manufactures of India', in *Chambers's Edinburgh Journal*, 20:498 (n.s.) (July 16, 1853), 45–47.
9. '[Tranquility in Indian Possessions]', *The Times*, February 26, 1850, 4.
10. [Joachim H. Siddons], 'Christmas in India', in *Household Words*, 2:39 (December 21, 1850), 305–306, p.305.
11. [Sidney], 'Indian Railroads' , p.591.
12. 'An Indian Pageant', in *Chambers's Journal of Popular Literature, Science, and Arts*, 5:129 (June 21, 1856), 385–389, p.385.
13. 'An Indian Pageant' , *Chambers's*, p.389.
14. 'Past and Present of India', in *Chambers's Journal of Popular Literature, Science, and Arts*, 7:179 (June 6, 1857), 355–358, p.355.
15. 'Past and Present of India' , pp.355–6.
16. It was in fact the electric telegraph which allowed the British in Meerut and Delhi to give its troops elsewhere early warning and come to their aid. Saul David, *The Indian Mutiny* (London: Penguin Books, 2003), 'Prologue'.
17. The news of the Meerut massacre, which started on May 10, made *The Times* on June 29, 1857.
18. 'The Mutiny in India', in *Illustrated London News*, 31:867 (July 4, 1857), 1–2, p.1.
19. 'British Ideas in India', in *Illustrated London News*, 31:878 (September 12, 1857), 251–252.
20. 'Indian Servants', in *Chambers's Journal of Popular Literature, Science, and Arts*, 8:197 (October 10, 1857), 229–231, p.229.
21. [E. Townsend], 'A Mutiny in India', in *Household Words*, 16:386 (August 15, 1857), 154–156, p.154. Townsend attributes the guilt to a tyrannical commander who whimsically orders his brigade, comprised of men 'of a class far superior to that which furnishes the sepoy', to shave off their beards and faces stern but reasonable refusal. Through his determination to punish this refusal, the commander causes a bloody escalation of violence. 'The regiment was disbanded, its name was blotted out [. . .] and the matter was hushed up'. [Townsend], 'A Mutiny' , pp.155–6.
22. [John Robertson], 'Sepoy Symbols of Mutiny', in *Household Words*, 16:389 (September 5, 1857), 228–232.
23. [John Capper], 'A Very Black Act', in *Household Words*, 16:392 (September 26, 1857), 293–294, p.203.
24. [E. Townsend and Alexander Hamilton], 'Indian Recruits and Indian English', in *Household Words*, 16:393 (October 3, 1857), 319–322, pp.321–322.
25. According to Roderick and Earnshaw, the series 'was written [to order] for Dickens, who no doubt believed that the Indian Mutiny of 1857–8 would have created a desire in many minds to know more of the country in which it had occurred.' Colin Roderick and John Earnshaw, 'John Lang (1816–1864): First Australian-born Novelist', in *Royal Australian Historical Society Journal*, 49:2 (July, 1963), 100–135, p.128.
26. *The Oxford Companion to Australian Literature,* ed. by William H. Wilde, Joy W. Hooton and Barry G. Andrews (Melbourne: Oxford University Press,

1985), p.400. G. F. J. Bergman and John S. Levi, *Australian Genesis: Jewish Convicts and Settlers, 1788–1850* (London: Hale, 1974), p.38.

27. *The Oxford Companion to Australian Literature,* ed. by Wilde, Hooton and Andrews, p.400.
28. Rick Hosking, 'Magnetic Amalgams? John Lang's *Wanderings in India* (1859), Rudyard Kipling and Henry Lawson', in *Journal of British Studies*, 23:2, 1995), 59–80, pp.61–2. I am very much indebted to Rick Hosking for his prompt and enthusiastic help in pointing me towards other materials on Lang.
29. Nancy Keesing, *John Lang & 'The Forger's Wife': a True Tale of Early Australia* (Sydney: John Ferguson, 1979), p.43.
30. Hosking, 'Magnetic Amalgams' , p.62. *The Oxford Companion to Australian Literature,* ed. by Wilde, Hooton and Andrews, p.400.
31. 'His wife left him somewhere between 1843 and 1845 and returned to England with their children'. The official marriage certificate of his second marriages 'gives Lang's condition as [. . .] "divorcer"', although 'no record of this divorce appears to exist in England or in the records of [. . .] the India Office'. Hosking, 'Magnetic Amalgams' , p.62; Roderick and Earnshaw, 'John Lang' , pp. 129–130.
32. Hosking, 'Magnetic Amalgams' , p.62–3.
33. Hosking, 'Magnetic Amalgams' , p.63. The Rani, a childhood playmate of Nana Sahib, was a notorious name in 1857. When the British annexed Jhansi in 1854, she tried her utmost to stop the British government, enlisting Lang's professional services. Those attempts being unsuccessful, 'there is good reason to suspect that she was in contact with other disgruntled princes prior to the rebellion of 1857', and she later took a leading role in the Rebellion, commanding rebel troops. David, *The Indian Mutiny* , pp.350ff. David's source for the description of the Rani is Lang himself, supposedly a 'Briton'.
34. Andrew Ward, *Our Bones are Shattered: The Cawnpore Massacres and the Indian Mutiny of 1857* (London: John Murray, 2004 [first published 1996]), p.53.
35. Hosking, 'Magnetic Amalgams' , p.63. Lohrli, p.337.
36. Hosking, 'Magnetic Amalgams' , p.64. Henry Vizetelly, *Glances Back through Seventy Years: Autobiographical and Other Reminiscences* vol. 2, 2 vols. (London: Kegan Paul, Trench, Trübner & Co, 1893), p.9. *Madras Times* (29th August 1864), quoted in Keesing, *The Forger's Wife* , p.62.
37. *The Oxford Companion to Australian Literature,* ed. by Wilde, Hooton and Andrews, p.400.
38. Keesing, *The Forger's Wife* , p.57.
39. *The Oxford Companion to Australian Literature,* ed. by Wilde, Hooton and Andrews, p.400.
40. [John Lang], 'Wanderings in India (VI)', in *Household Words*, 17:408 (January 16, 1858), 112–118, p.115.
41. Hosking, 'Magnetic Amalgams' , p.65. *The Oxford Companion to Australian Literature,* ed. by Wilde, Hooton and Andrews, p.400.
42. Douglas M. Peers, '"Those Noble Exemplars of the True Military Tradition": Constructions of the Indian Army in the Mid-Victorian Press', in *Modern Asian Studies*, 31:1, (1997), 109–142, p.119.
43. G.S. Amur, 'In Search of the Picturesque: John Lang's Wanderings in India and other Sketches of Life in Hindostan', in *The Colonial and the Neo-Colonial Encounters in Commonwealth Literature,* ed. by H. H. Anniah Gowda (Mysore: Prasaranga University of Mysore, 1983), p.52, p.50.
44. Roderick and Earnshaw, 'John Lang' , p. 122.

45. Hosking, 'Magnetic Amalgams' , p.65.
46. Hosking, 'Magnetic Amalgams' , pp.65–6.
47. [John Lang], 'Wanderings in India (IX)', in *Household Words*, 17:411 (February 6, 1858), 179–186, p.181, my emphasis.
48. [John Lang], 'Wanderings in India (IV)', in *Household Words*, 17:406 (January 2, 1858), 64–70, p.69.
49. Hosking, 'Magnetic Amalgams' , p.74; [John Lang], 'Wanderings in India (I)', in *Household Words*, 16:399 (November 14, 1857), 457–463, p.461; [Lang], 'Wanderings (IX)' , p.182.
50. Hosking, 'Magnetic Amalgams' , p.66.
51. [Lang], 'Wanderings (I)' , p.457.
52. Hosking, 'Magnetic Amalgams' , p.78.
53. [John Lang], 'Wanderings in India (V)', in *Household Words*, 17:407 (January 9, 1858), 87–94, p.92.
54. Keesing, *The Forger's Wife* , p.x.
55. [John Lang], 'Wanderings in India (II)', in *Household Words*, 16:401 (November 28, 1857), 505–511, p.509.
56. [Lang], 'Wanderings (V)' , p.91.
57. [Lang], 'Wanderings (V)' , p.91–92.
58. [Lang], 'Wanderings (VI)' , p.116.
59. [John Lang], 'Wanderings in India (VII)', in *Household Words*, 17:409 (January 23, 1858), 134–144, p.138.
60. Christopher Hibbert, *The Great Mutiny, India 1857* (Harmondsworth: Penguin Books, 1980), p.84.
61. At the beginning of instalment VIII, this appears as 'Barnapore'. [John Lang], 'Wanderings in India (VIII)', in *Household Words*, 17:410 (January 30, 1858), 148–156, p.148.
62. [Lang], 'Wanderings (VII)' , p.140.
63. [Lang], 'Wanderings (VIII)' , p.148.
64. [Lang], 'Wanderings (VIII)' , p.149.
65. Perhaps 'West' is chosen to make a clear distinction between the Europeans and their object of study, 'the East'.
66. [Lang], 'Wanderings (VII)' , p.144.
67. [Lang], 'Wanderings (IX)' , p.181.
68. [John Lang], 'Wanderings in India (XI)', in *Household Words*, 17:413 (February 20, 1858), 220–224, p.220.
69. [John Lang], 'Wanderings in India (III)', in *Household Words*, 17:404 (December 19, 1857), 12–20, p.13.
70. Patrick Brantlinger, *Rule of Darkness: British Literature and Imperialism, 1830–1914* (Ithaca: Cornell University Press, 1988), p.88.
71. [Lang], 'Wanderings (V)' , p.92.
72. [Lang], 'Wanderings (V)' , p.91.
73. [Lang], 'Wanderings (V)' , p.92.
74. [Lang], 'Wanderings (V)' , p.93.
75. [Lang], 'Wanderings (V)' , pp.92–3.
76. [Joachim Heyward Siddons], 'Justice for "Natives"', in *Household Words*, 7:170 (June 25, 1853), 397–402, p.402.
77. [Lang], 'Wanderings (VI)' , p.112.
78. [Lang], 'Wanderings (VI)' , p.112.
79. Neither Hibbert nor Peter Stanley, *White Mutiny: British Military Culture in India, 1825–1875* (London: Hurst & Co., 1998) mention any mutiny in Delhi before 1857. Hibbert, however, refers to 'Hindu Rao's house' in the context of the 1857 rebellion and adds in a footnote that 'Hindu Rao was a Mahratta nobleman, "of frank, bluff manners and genial tempera-

ment". His house had been built probably by Sir Edward Colebroke [. . .] It was sold to Hindu Rao in 1835; but since his death in 1855 it had been left empty [. . .] It is now a hospital'. Hibbert, *India 1857* , p.284, p.422, quoting from Sir John William Kaye, *History of the Sepoy War in India, 1857–1858*, 9th edn., 3 vols. (London, 1880). 'Wanderings' claims that 'Hindoo-Rao died in eighteen hundred and fifty-four'. [Lang], 'Wanderings (VI)' , p.113.

80. [Lang], 'Wanderings (VI)' , p.112.
81. [Lang], 'Wanderings (VIII)' , p.148.
82. [Lang], 'Wanderings (VIII)' , p.151.
83. [Lang], 'Wanderings (VIII)' , p.151.
84. [Lang], 'Wanderings (VIII)' , p.151.
85. [Lang], 'Wanderings (VIII)' , p.152.
86. [Lang], 'Wanderings (VIII)' , p.152.
87. [Lang], 'Wanderings (VIII)' , p.152, emphasis in the original.
88. [John Lang], 'Wanderings in India (X)', in *Household Words*, 17:412 (February 13, 1858), 212–216, p.215; [Lang], 'Wanderings (VIII)' , p.151.
89. [Lang], 'Wanderings (VIII)' , p.152.
90. [Lang], 'Wanderings (VIII)' , p.152. The four Europeans on their Himalayan expedition, however, are hardly in any danger of incurring such judgement, as they treat their surroundings like a gigantic playground, requiring an astonishing 'one hundred and fifty' coolies 'to carry our baggage and stores' and shooting animals for sport: 'All we bagged was ghooral, which we did not stop to look at even'. [Lang], 'Wanderings (VIII)' , pp.151–2.
91. [Lang], 'Wanderings (V)' , p.88; [Lang], 'Wanderings (VIII)' , p.148; [Lang], 'Wanderings (I)' , p.457.
92. [Lang], 'Wanderings (I)' , pp.458–9.
93. Hosking, 'Magnetic Amalgams' , p.66.
94. [Lang], 'Wanderings (I)' , p.458.
95. Hosking, 'Magnetic Amalgams' , p.75.
96. [Lang], 'Wanderings (I)' , p.458.
97. [Lang], 'Wanderings (I)' , p.459.
98. [Lang], 'Wanderings (I)' , pp.460–1.
99. Amur, 'In Search of the Picturesque', p.53.
100. Amur, 'In Search of the Picturesque', p.54.
101. [Lang], 'Wanderings (I)' , p.462.
102. Ward, *Our Bones Are Shattered* , pp.53–57.
103. [Lang], 'Wanderings (I)' , p.461.
104. [Lang], 'Wanderings (I)' , p.463.
105. Ward, *Our Bones Are Shattered* , p.57.
106. [Lang], 'Wanderings (III)' , p.15.
107. [Lang], 'Wanderings (IV)' , p.65.
108. [Lang], 'Wanderings (IV)' , p.65.
109. [Lang], 'Wanderings (III)' , p.15.
110. [Lang], 'Wanderings (III)' , p.15.
111. [Lang], 'Wanderings (III)' , p.15.
112. [Lang], 'Wanderings (V)' , p.92.
113. Jenny Sharpe, *Allegories of Empire: the Figure of Woman in the Colonial Text* (Minneapolis: University of Minnesota Press, 1993), p.58.
114. [Lang], 'Wanderings (II)' , p.508.
115. [Lang], 'Wanderings (II)' , p.508–9.
116. 'Thug', *Encyclopaedia Britannica Online*. Available at http://www.britannica.com/eb/article?eu=74198&tocid=0 (accessed June 28, 2001).

117. Cf. [Lang], 'Wanderings (IX)' , p.155. However, 'when [European] ladies in India fall, they deserve far more of pity than of blame'. [Lang], 'Wanderings (VII)' , p.144. It is not made clear exactly why this should be the case in India and not Britain, but later the narrator offers a possible analogy when he suggests that European servants who start drinking in India are 'much more deserving of pity than of condemnation' since they 'can talk to no one' and become 'perfectly miserable'. [Lang], 'Wanderings (IX)' , p.186.
118. [Lang], 'Wanderings (II)' , p.510.
119. [Lang], 'Wanderings (V)' , p.91.
120. [Lang], 'Wanderings (VII)' , p.142.
121. [Lang], 'Wanderings (VII)' , p.142, my emphasis. A similar astonishment informs the narrator's description of the Gurkhas as 'a very odd race' because they are 'wonderfully honest, even amongst themselves [. . .] obedient and respectful, without cringing to fawning or flattering their superiors, the white man.' [Lang], 'Wanderings (VIII)' , p.155. One is also reminded of Martineau's patronising surprise that the Irish quarry workers are neither sullen nor dishonest (see chapter 3).
122. [Lang], 'Wanderings (XI)' , p.220.
123. [Lang], 'Wanderings (III)' , p.18, my emphasis.
124. [Lang], 'Wanderings (II)' , p.510.
125. [Lang], 'Wanderings (X)' , pp.212–3.
126. [Lang], 'Wanderings (X)' , p.213.
127. [Lang], 'Wanderings (X)' , p.216.
128. [Lang], 'Wanderings (X)' , p.216.
129. [Lang], 'Wanderings (I)' , p.461.
130. [Lang], 'Wanderings (II)' , p.506.
131. [Lang], 'Wanderings (VI)' , p.112; [Lang], 'Wanderings (IX)' , p.155.
132. [Lang], 'Wanderings (II)' , p.506; [Lang], 'Wanderings (VI)' , p.117.
133. [Lang], 'Wanderings (X)' , p.214; [Lang], 'Wanderings (VII)' , p.143.
134. [Lang], 'Wanderings (III)' , p.14.
135. [Lang], 'Wanderings (IX)' , p.179. One dreads to think of the 'perfume' emitted by the Europeans in their stifling suits and dresses.
136. [Lang], 'Wanderings (IX)' , p.184.
137. [Lang], 'Wanderings (IX)' , p.181.
138. [Lang], 'Wanderings (VIII)' , p.155.
139. [Lang], 'Wanderings (V)' , p.93; [Lang], 'Wanderings (II)' , p.510.
140. [Lang], 'Wanderings (II)' , p.508; [Lang], 'Wanderings (X)' , p.215; [Lang], 'Wanderings (VII)' , p.142.
141. [Lang], 'Wanderings (V)' , p.93; [Lang], 'Wanderings (II)' , p.507. The parenthesis 'we (Christians)' is interesting in this context, as the same point is made two pages before in slightly different form: 'How readily, to be sure, do people in India accommodate each other'. [Lang], 'Wanderings (II)' , p.505. Evidently the narrator finds it necessary to exclude non-Christians from 'people'—and we have already seen that 'Christian' is more or less synonymous with 'white'.
142. [Siddons], 'Christmas in India' , p.305.
143. Hibbert, *India 1857* , pp.50–1.
144. Hibbert, *India 1857* , p.37.
145. Hibbert, *India 1857* , p.51.
146. Hibbert, *India 1857* , p.53.
147. [Lang], 'Wanderings (III)' , p.16.
148. [Lang], 'Wanderings (III)' , p.18.
149. [Lang], 'Wanderings (V)' , p.94.
150. [Lang], 'Wanderings (V)' , p.94.

151. [Lang], 'Wanderings (V)' , p.93.
152. [Lang], 'Wanderings (VII)' , p.136.
153. [Lang], 'Wanderings (I)' , p.459.
154. [Lang], 'Wanderings (II)' , p.510.
155. [Lang], 'Wanderings (I)' , p.462.
156. [Lang], 'Wanderings (V)' , p.93.
157. [Lang], 'Wanderings (V)' , p.93.
158. [Lang], 'Wanderings (V)' , p.91.
159. [Lang], 'Wanderings (V)' , p.93.
160. [Lang], 'Wanderings (VII)' , p.141.
161. [Lang], 'Wanderings (V)' , p.93.
162. [Lang], 'Wanderings (V)' , p.93.
163. [Lang], 'Wanderings (IX)' , p.181.
164. [Lang], 'Wanderings (II)' , p.510.
165. [Lang], 'Wanderings (X)' , p.215.
166. [Lang], 'Wanderings (IV)' , p.70.
167. [Lang], 'Wanderings (III)' , p.13.
168. [Lang], 'Wanderings (III)' , p.13.
169. Hibbert writes that prior to the 1857 rebellion 'there had been other mutinies less publicized, some actually concealed from the public by the authorities'. Therefore this scene seems to be plausible, whether it rests on a historical event or not. Hibbert, *India 1857* , p.62.
170. Hibbert, *India 1857* , p.62.
171. Michael Edwardes, 'Introduction', in William Howard Russell and Michael Edwardes, *My Indian Mutiny Diary* (London: Cassell, 1957 [1857] [first published 1857]), pp.xiii-xXVII, p.xiii. The 'affair' emerged over the introduction of new Enfield rifles, which were loaded with greased cartridges, whose end had to be bitten or nipped off. Rumours emerged that the grease used for these cartridges was composed of beef and pig fat, rendering them 'degrading to Hindus and [. . .] offensive to Mohammedans'. 'Since beef and pig fat were the cheapest animal fats available, the sepoys' suspicion [. . .] was far from unreasonable'. Hibbert, *India 1857* , p.55. Most critics agree that the cartridges were only the last straw in a whole range of professional and other grievances that prepared the ground for such widespread discontent. Cf. David, *The Indian Mutiny* ; Hibbert, *India 1857.*
172. Hibbert, *India 1857* , p.62.
173. [Lang], 'Wanderings (IV)' , p.65. He opines that 'these stupendous and costly edifices' should be 'pull[ed] down [and . . .] convert[ed] into useful buildings [. . .] splendid barracks for our British and native troops; hospitals [. . .] courthouses, churches, magazines, and so forth'.
174. [Lang], 'Wanderings (VII)' , p.137.
175. [Lang], 'Wanderings (VII)' , p.138.
176. [Lang], 'Wanderings (VII)' , p.138.
177. One of the graves that the soldier elaborates on belongs to 'the officer that the Duke of Wellington fixed upon to bring the Fifty-third Foot into good order, when they ran riot in Gibraltar, some years ago'—the possibility of mutiny evidently exists elsewhere in the British army. [Lang], 'Wanderings (VII)' , p.137.
178. [Lang], 'Wanderings (VI)' , p.112.
179. [Lang], 'Wanderings (VI)' , pp.112–3.
180. [Lang], 'Wanderings (VI)' , p.112.
181. [Lang], 'Wanderings (VI)' , p.113.
182. Hibbert, *India 1857* , pp.406–7.
183. Hosking, 'Magnetic Amalgams' , p.74.

184. [Lang], 'Wanderings (X)' , p.215.
185. [Lang], 'Wanderings (III)' , p.13.
186. [Lang], 'Wanderings (V)' , p.89.
187. [Lang], 'Wanderings (III)' , p.15.
188. [Lang], 'Wanderings (XI)' , p.221.
189. [Lang], 'Wanderings (XI)' , p.224.
190. [John Lang], 'Wanderings in India (XII)', in *Household Words*, 17:414 (February 27, 1858), 254–260, p.255.
191. [Lang], 'Wanderings (XII)' , p.260.
192. [Lang], 'Wanderings (IX)' , p.182.
193. [Lang], 'Wanderings (IX)' , p.182.
194. [Lang], 'Wanderings (IX)' , p.182.
195. [Lang], 'Wanderings (IX)' , p.182.
196. [Lang], 'Wanderings (IX)' , p.183.
197. [Lang], 'Wanderings (IX)' , p.183.
198. Hibbert notes that there is some justification in this: 'It was not until the 1830s and 1840s, when marriage to white women became more common, that living with a native mistress was considered to be rather disreputable.' Consequently, the separation between European and Indian reached much deeper: previously, officers who had lived with a native mistress or wife had shown more respect and understanding for their cultures—now, everything 'native' became a source of mockery. Hibbert, *India 1857* , pp.57–8.
199. [Lang], 'Wanderings (V)' , p.90.
200. [Lang], 'Wanderings (II)' , p.507.
201. [Lang], 'Wanderings (II)' , p.507.
202. [Lang], 'Wanderings (XI)' , p.224.
203. [Lang], 'Wanderings (V)' , p.91. In January 1857, William Jerdan had already commented in *Household Words* on the need for the British to learn more foreign languages. Although his point of reference is the Crimean War, Jerdan also finds that the British cannot rule their Indian Empire effectively through interpreters and should be encouraged to extend their command of languages in which Britain has a direct interest. [William Jerdan], 'The Gift of Tongues', in *Household Words*, 15:355 (January 10, 1857), 41–43.
204. [Lang], 'Wanderings (VI)' , p.114. The European newspaper at Meerut was, most likely, Lang's own—he had founded the *Mofussilite* there in 1846 and later became its editor and proprietor. Hosking, 'Magnetic Amalgams' , pp.62–3.
205. [Lang], 'Wanderings (VI)' , p.115.
206. [Lang], 'Wanderings (VI)' , p.115.
207. [Lang], 'Wanderings (VI)' , p.115.
208. [Lang], 'Wanderings (IX)' , p.181.
209. [Lang], 'Wanderings (III)' , p.14.
210. [Lang], 'Wanderings (XII)' , p.260; [Lang], 'Wanderings (III)' , p.14.
211. [Lang], 'Wanderings (III)' , p.14.
212. [Lang], 'Wanderings (V)' , p.92.
213. [Lang], 'Wanderings (VI)' , p.112.
214. [Lang], 'Wanderings (VI)' , pp.113–4.
215. [Lang], 'Wanderings (VI)' , p.114.
216. [Lang], 'Wanderings (VI)' , p.114.
217. [Capper], 'A Very Black Act' , p.204.
218. [Lang], 'Wanderings (III)' , p.14.
219. [Lang], 'Wanderings (VI)' , p.117.
220. [Lang], 'Wanderings (VI)' , p.117.

221. [Lang], 'Wanderings (IV)' , p.69. Cf. Amur, 'In Search of the Picturesque', p.55.
222. [Lang], 'Wanderings (IV)' , p.68.
223. [Lang], 'Wanderings (IV)' , p.68.
224. [Lang], 'Wanderings (IV)' , p.68.
225. [Lang], 'Wanderings (IV)' , p.68.
226. [Lang], 'Wanderings (IV)' , p.69.
227. Hosking, 'Magnetic Amalgams' , p.74.
228. *The Letters of Charles Dickens: Volume Eight 1856–1858,* ed. by Graham Storey and Kathleen Tillotson, vol. 8 (Oxford: Clarendon Press, 1995), October 4, 1857.
229. Hosking, 'Magnetic Amalgams' , p.71.
230. [Lang], 'Wanderings (IX)' , p.183; [Lang], 'Wanderings (VIII)' , p.154; [Lang], 'Wanderings (I)' , p.457.

NOTES TO THE CONCLUSION

1. A number of other *Household Words* articles also examine 'savage' tribes—for instance George Hogarth's 'Heathen and Christian Burial', Dudley Costello's 'Called to the Savage Bar', Henry Morley's 'A Group of Noble Savages', Henry R.F. Bourne's 'Fire-Worshippers', Eliza Lynn's 'Devil Worshippers', Sidney L. Blanchard's 'The Santals', or John Lang's 'The Abors'.
2. Cf. Catherine Hall, *White, Male and Middle-Class: Explorations in Feminism and History* (Cambridge: Polity, 1992), chapter 10: 'Competing Masculinities: Thomas Carlyle, John Stuart Mill and the case of Governor Eyre'; Catherine Hall, Keith McClelland and Jane Rendall, *Defining the Victorian Nation: Class, Race, Gender and the British Reform Act of 1867* (Cambridge: Cambridge University Press, 2000); Simon Gikandi, *Maps of Englishness: Writing Identity in the Culture of Colonialism* (New York: Columbia University Press, 1996), pp.57–69; Cora Kaplan, '"A Heterogeneous Thing": Female Childhood and the Rise of Racial Thinking in Victorian Britain', in *Human, All Too Human,* ed. by Diana Fuss (New York: Routledge, 1995).
3. It was originally published anonymously in *Fraser's* in 1848–49 as 'Occasional Discourse on the Negro Question'.
4. Thomas Carlyle, 'Occasional Discourse on the Nigger Question', 1853 website, 1853, (http://cepa.newschool.edu/het/texts/carlyle/odnqbk.htm), accessed April 11, 2008, p.371, p.374. This electronic version is taken from the version reprinted in America under the title 'Fifteen Years of Emancipation in the West Indies' in three installments in *The Old Guard*, (ed. C. Chauncey Burr, New York), 1866, Volume 4, Issue 4 (April), pp. 239–245, Issue 5 (May), pp. 308–311, and Issue 6 (June), pp. 372–377. In referencing this, I shall follow the page numbers indicated on this website.
5. Carlyle, 'Occasional Discourse on the Nigger Question', p. 373.
6. Kaplan, '"A Heterogeneous Thing"', p.176.
7. Kaplan, '"A Heterogeneous Thing"', p.177.
8. Hall, *White, male and middle-class* , p.270. Dickens professed deep admiration for Carlyle and dedicated *Hard Times* to him, which began its publication in April 1854. Cf. also Hall's discussion of the Governor Eyre controversy in the mid-1860s. Catherine Hall, *Civilising Subjects: Metropole and Colony in the English Imagination, 1830–1867* (Cambridge: Polity, 2002), 'Prologue'.

9. Carlyle, 'Occasional Discourse on the Nigger Question', p. 240; [Charles Dickens], 'The Noble Savage', in *Household Words*, 7:168 (June 11, 1853), 337–339.
10. [Dickens], 'The Noble Savage' , p.337.
11. [Dickens,] 'The Noble Savage' , p.337. On the history of this trope, see Stelio Cro, 'The Noble Savage: Myth and Reality', in *Romance Languages Annual*, 4 (1992), 216–226.
12. [Dickens], 'The Noble Savage' , p.337. This contrasts heavily with chapter 12 of *American Notes*, published eleven years earlier, in which Dickens had portrayed a Native American chief in respectful terms and allowed him the last, wistful word on the onslaught of 'civilisation':

    On my telling him that I regretted not to see him in his own attire, he [. . .] [answered [. . .] that his race were losing many things besides their dress and would soon be seen upon the earth no more [. . .] Their number were decreasing every day. A few of his brother chiefs had been obliged to become civilised, and to make themselves acquainted with what the whites knew, for it was their only chance of existence. But they were not many; and the rest were as they always had been. He dwelt on this: and said several times that unless they tried to assimilate themselves to their conquerors, they must be swept away before the strides of civilised society [. . .] [When Dickens invites him to England,] He rejoined with a good-humoured smile and an arch shake of his head, that the English used to be very fond of the Red Men when they wanted their help, but had not cared much for them, since.

    Charles Dickens, *American Notes and Pictures from Italy* (London: Oxford University Press, 1957 [first published 1842]), pp.165–167.
13. [Dickens], 'The Noble Savage' , p.337.
14. [Dickens], 'The Noble Savage' , p.337, my emphasis. Throughout the article Dickens remains noncommittal on whether he wants the savage races to die out physically or to be improved and transformed by the civilising influence of Western imperialism—it would be possible to see the hyperbole merely as a disguise covering up his actual beliefs, a form of irony that masks a serious point, especially when compared to his extreme reaction to the Sepoy Rebellion (see chapter 5).
15. [Dickens], 'The Noble Savage' , p.339. The fact that Dickens uses two dead 'heroes' to mark the difference between civilisation and savage also implies that he sees the savages' passing away as a natural, biological fact.
16. Anthony Chennells finds that the same mixture of racism and liberalism is to be found in Dickens's fiction:

    Any reader of Dickens has to confront the conventional prejudice with which he regards people of colour in his narratives, although the extent of this prejudice can be exaggerated. Whenever Dickens writes on Africa or slavery he affirms the common humanity of blacks and whites despite the influential theories of contemporary polygenecists who believed blacks were a separate species.

    Anthony Chennells, 'Savages and Settlers in Dickens: Reading Multiple Centres', in *Dickens and the Children of Empire,* ed. by Wendy S. Jacobson (Houndmills, Basingstoke: Palgrave, 2000), p.164.
17. Cf. Paul Schlicke, *Dickens and Popular Entertainment* (London: Unwin Hyman, 1988 [first published 1985]).
18. Cf.Richard D. Altick, *The Shows of London* (Cambridge, Mass.: Belknap Press, 1978), chapters 19 and 20.
19. In a conference paper, Randal Rogers gave an account of the 'racial insubordination' especially of the 'pygmies' displayed at the St Louis World's Fair of 1904, which shows clearly the staged nature of such events. With the

help of original photographs, Rogers showed that the individuals were self-consciously enacting the 'exotic' behaviour that was expected of them, yet they had simultaneously 'become aware of the power of photography and, importantly, of their role within the spectacle' and undermined the supposed truthfulness of the exhibit by mimicking and parodying the very expectations they had been intended to confirm. Randal Rogers (Concordia University Canada), 'Colonial Imitation and Racial Insubordination: on Some Photographs from St. Louis, 1904' (unpublished conference paper), given at 'Cultural Imperialism and Competition: Travel, World's Fairs and National/ Colonial Image', organised by The Nineteenth Century Studies Association, St Louis, Missouri, March 11–13, 2004.

20. [Richard Horne], 'The Wonders of 1851', in *Household Words*, 1:17 (July 20, 1850), 388–392.391; [Knight], [Charles Knight], 'Three May-Days in London: III. The May Palace (1851)', in *Household Words*, 3:58 (May 3, 1851), 121–124, p.122.
21. Interestingly, these also take effect on the level of Dickens's savages—throughout his piece, the savage is male and has some power amongst his people. Part of Dickens's disgust stems from the fact that he is 'a sulky tyrant [. . .] to his women'. [Dickens], 'The Noble Savage' , p.337.
22. [Dickens], 'The Noble Savage' , p.339.
23. [Dickens], 'The Noble Savage' , p.339. Cf. Cora Kaplan, 'White, Black, and Green: Racialising Irishness in Victorian England', in *Victoria's Ireland? Irishness and Britishness, 1837–1901,* ed. by Peter Gray (Dublin: Four Courts Press, 2004), pp. 51–68.
24. [Dickens], 'The Noble Savage' , p.338.
25. [Dickens], 'The Noble Savage' , p.337.
26. As my introduction showed, *Dombey and Son* had already prefigured the possibility of such a collapse:

    In this round world of many circles within circles, do we make a weary journey from the high grade to the low, to find at last that they lie close together, that the two extremes touch, and that our journey's end is but our starting place?

    Charles Dickens, *Dombey and Son*, Oxford World's Classics, (Oxford: Oxford University Press, 1999 [first published 1846–48]), p.417.
27. [Dickens], 'The Noble Savage' , p.339.
28. Gikandi, *Maps of Englishness* , pp.55–6.
29. Anthony Chennells shows that the savage other is also at the centre of Dickens's later novels, often as a reproach to Britain itself: 'In *Dombey and Son* the name Native is invariably part of an oxymoron suggesting that Britain in centering large parts of the world on itself de-centres everyone else', while the crossing-sweeper Jo in *Bleak House* is another victim of 'the centre which denies its own heart'. Chennells, 'Savages and Settlers', pp.162–164.

Bibliography

1. PRIMARY WORKS

1.1. Material published in Household Words

Although *Household Words* published articles anonymously, Anne Lohrli's work on the journal's office book has identified most contributors. To indicate the anonymous publication of material, authors' names are given in square brackets.

———, 'An English Wife', in *Household Words*, 12:300 (December 22, 1855), 489–490

———, 'Sorrow and My Heart', in *Household Words*, 13:307 (February 9, 1856), 84

———, 'Books for the Indian Army', in *Household Words*, 18:448 (October 23, 1858), 437–438

[Allingham, William], 'The Irish "Stationers"', in *Household Words*, 2:28 (October 5, 1850), 29–33

[Allingham, William], 'Irish Ballad Singers and Irish Street Ballads', in *Household Words*, 4:94 (January 10, 1852), 361–368

[Allingham, William], 'Round the Midsummer Fire', in *Household Words*, 5:121 (July 17, 1852), 426–428

[Allingham, William], 'The Bright Little Girl. Song to an Irish Tune', in *Household Words*, 8:193 (December 3, 1853), 325

[Allingham, William], 'Saint Patrick', in *Household Words*, 13:315 (April 5, 1856), 279–283

[Arnold, Edwin], 'Mine Host', in *Household Words*, 9:229 (August 12, 1854), 608

[Bell, Mrs.], 'The Longest Night in a Life', in *Household Words*, 9:205 (February 25, 1854), 21–25

[Blanchard, Sidney L.], 'Munchausen Modernised', in *Household Words*, 6:152 (February 19, 1853), 533–538

[Blanchard, Sidney L.], 'More Modern Munchausens', in *Household Words*, 7:170 (June 25, 1853), 402–405

[Blanchard, Sidney L.], 'The Santals', in *Household Words*, 12:294 (November 10, 1855), 347–349

[Blanchard, Sidney L.], 'The Road in India', in *Household Words*, 12:301 (December 29, 1855), 517–521

[Bourne, Henry R.F.], 'The Hero of a Hundred Plays', in *Household Words*, 18:443 (September 18, 1858), 324–327

[Bourne, Henry R.F., and Henry Morley], 'Fire-Worshippers', in *Household Words*, 19:465 (February 19, 1859), 286–288

[Brockedon, William], 'Chamouny', in *Household Words*, 3:71 (August 2, 1851), 451–452
[Browne], 'The "Irish Difficulty" Solved by Con Mcnale', in *Household Words*, 1:9 (May 25, 1850), 207–210
[Browne and Henry Morley], 'Perfectly Contented', in *Household Words*, 14:338 (September 13, 1856), 213–216
[Capper, John], 'A Cinnamon Garden', in *Household Words*, 2:49 (March 1, 1851), 546–548
[Capper, John], 'The Cocoa-Nut Palm', in *Household Words*, 2:51 (March 15, 1851), 585–589
[Capper, John], 'A Dutch Family Picture', in *Household Words*, 4:94 (January 10, 1852), 372–376
[Capper, John], 'The Peasants of British India', in *Household Words*, 4:95 (January 17, 1852), 389–393
[Capper, John], 'Monsters of Faith', in *Household Words*, 5:125 (August 19, 1852), 506–508
[Capper, John], 'Honourable John', in *Household Words*, 7:175 (July 30, 1853), 516–518
[Capper, John], 'The Great Indian Bean-Stalk', in *Household Words*, 8:182 (September 17, 1853), 60–64
[Capper, John], 'Our Russian Relations', in *Household Words*, 10:243 (November 18, 1854), 333
[Capper, John], 'A Very Black Act', in *Household Words*, 16:392 (September 26, 1857), 293–294
[Capper, John], 'Calcutta', in *Household Words*, 16:396 (October 24, 1857), 393–397
[Carter, Robert B.], 'King Missirie', in *Household Words*, 14:353 (December 27, 1856), 553–556
[Cayley, George J.], 'The Poisoner of Springs', in *Household Words*, 15:357 (January 24, 1857), 92–96
[Chisholm, Caroline, and Richard H. Horne], 'Pictures of Life in Australia', in *Household Words*, 1:13 (June 22, 1850), 307–310
[Clark], 'By Dawk to Delhi', in *Household Words*, 8:195 (December 17, 1853), 365–370
[Collins, Wilkie], 'Laid up in Two Lodgings (I): My Paris Lodgings', in *Household Words*, 13:324 (June 7, 1856), 481–486
[Collins, Wilkie], 'Laid up in Two Lodgings (II): My London Lodgings', in *Household Words*, 13:325 (June 14, 1856), 517–523
[Collins, Wilkie], 'My Black Mirror', in *Household Words*, 14:337 (September 6, 1856), 169–175
[Collins, Wilkie], 'A Sermon for Sepoys', in *Household Words*, 17:414 (February 27, 1858), 244–247
[Collins, Wilkie], 'The Unknown Public', in *Household Words*, 18:439 (August 21, 1858), 217–222
[Collins, Wilkie], 'The Great (Forgotten) Invasion', in *Household Words*, 19:468 (March 12, 1859), 337–341
[Costello, Dudley], 'Called to the Savage Bar', in *Household Words*, 9:226 (July 22, 1854), 531–533
[Craig, George], 'Blown Away!' in *Household Words*, 17:418 (March 27, 1858), 348–350
[Crowe, Eyre E.], 'The Golden Vale', in *Household Words*, 6:145 (January 1, 1853), 377–381
[Dickens, Charles], 'A Preliminary Word', in *Household Words*, 1:1 (March 30, 1850), 1–2

[Dickens, Charles, and Caroline Chisholm], 'A Bundle of Emigrants' Letters', in *Household Words*, 1:1 (March 30, 1850), 19–24
[Dickens, Charles], 'The Household Narrative', in *Household Words*, 1:3 (April 13, 1850), 49
[Dickens, Charles, W. H. Wills and Grenville Murray], 'Foreigners' Portraits of Englishmen', in *Household Words*, 1:26 (September 21, 1850), 601–604
[Dickens, Charles], 'A Crisis in the Affairs of Mr. John Bull', in *Household Words*, 2:35 (November 23, 1850), 193–196
[Dickens, Charles, and Henry Morley], 'Mr. Bendigo Buster on Our National Defences against Education', in *Household Words*, 2:40 (December 28, 1850), 313–319
[Dickens, Charles], 'The Last Words of the Old Year', in *Household Words*, 2:41 (January 4, 1851), 337–339
[Dickens, Charles, and W. H. Wills], 'The Metropolitan Protectives', in *Household Words*, 3:57 (April 26, 1851), 97–105
[Dickens, Charles], 'A Flight', in *Household Words*, 3:75 (August 30, 1851), 529–533
[Dickens, Charles], 'Sucking Pigs', in *Household Words*, 4:85 (November 8, 1851), 145–147
[Dickens, Charles, and Henry Morley], 'H.W.' in *Household Words*, 7:160 (April 16, 1853), 145–149
[Dickens, Charles], 'The Noble Savage', in *Household Words*, 7:168 (June 11, 1853), 337–339
[Dickens, Charles], 'Gone to the Dogs', in *Household Words*, 11:259 (March 10, 1855), 121–124
[Dickens, Charles], 'Fast and Loose', in *Household Words*, 11:261 (March 24, 1855), 169–170
[Dickens, Charles], 'Thousand and One Humbugs (1)', in *Household Words*, 11:265 (April 21, 1855), 265–267
[Dickens, Charles], 'Thousand and One Humbugs (2)', in *Household Words*, 11:266 (April 28, 1855), 289–292
[Dickens, Charles], 'The Toady-Tree', in *Household Words*, 11:270 (May 26, 1855), 385–387
[Dickens, Charles], 'Cheap Patriotism', in *Household Words*, 11:272 (June 9, 1855), 433–435
[Dickens, Charles], 'Insularities', in *Household Words*, 13:304 (January 19, 1856), 1–4
[Dickens, Charles], 'Why?' in *Household Words*, 13:310 (March 1, 1856), 145–148
[Dickens, Charles], 'Proposals for a National Jest-Book', in *Household Words*, 13:319 (May 3, 1856), 361–364
[Dickens, Charles], 'Personal', in *Household Words*, 17:429 (June 12, 1858), 601
[Dixon, Edmund S.], 'The Rights of French Women', in *Household Words*, 5:113 (May 22, 1852), 218–221
[Dixon, Edmund S.], 'More Work for the Ladies', in *Household Words*, 6:130 (September 18, 1852), 18–22
[Dixon, Edmund S.], 'African Zephyrs', in *Household Words*, 8:186 (October 15, 1853), 145–150
[Dixon, Edmund S.], 'Wheel within Wheel', in *Household Words*, 10:250 (January 6, 1855), 481–483
[Dixon, Edmund S.], 'Literal Claims', in *Household Words*, 12:297 (December 1, 1855), 420–422
[Dixon, Edmund S.], 'Paris on London', in *Household Words*, 16:402 (December 5, 1857), 540–545

[Dixon, Edmund S.], 'Literary Small Change', in *Household Words*, 18:446 (October 9, 1858), 404–408
[Dodd, George], 'Moiré Antique', in *Household Words*, 9:205 (February 25, 1854), 37–38
[Dodd, George], 'Opium, Chap.I: India', in *Household Words*, 16:384 (August 1, 1857), 104–108
[Dodd, George], 'Opium, chap.ii: China', in *Household Words*, 16:387 (August 22, 1857), 181–185
[Dowdall, P.], 'An Anecdote of the Irish Poor Law', in *Household Words*, 2:30 (October 19, 1850), 94
[Duthie, William], 'A Taste of Austrian Jails', in *Household Words*, 4:94 (January 10, 1852), 368–372
[Duthie, William], 'The German Workman', in *Household Words*, 5:121 (July 17, 1852), 410–415
[Duthie, William, and Henry Morley], 'Travel on Tramp in Germany (I): Hamburgh to Lubeck', in *Household Words*, 6:147 (January 15, 1853), 420–422
[Duthie, William, and Henry Morley], 'Travel on Tramp in Germany (II): Lübeck to Berlin', in *Household Words*, 6:150 (February 5, 1853), 492–496
[Duthie, William, and Henry Morley], 'The French Workman', in *Household Words*, 8:188 (October 29, 1853), 199–204
[Duthie, William], 'A Lift in a Cart', in *Household Words*, 9:205 (February 25, 1854), 34–37
[Duthie, William], 'What My Landlord Believed', in *Household Words*, 11:271 (June 2, 1855), 418–420
[Duthie, William], 'Some German Sundays', in *Household Words*, 13:317 (April 19, 1856), 320–325
[Duthie, William], 'More Sundays Abroad', in *Household Words*, 13:320 (May 10, 1856), 400–404
[Fitzgerald, Percy], 'Home Again!' in *Household Words*, 19:457 (December 25, 1858), 73–80
[Fitzgerald, Percy], 'Bogie Albion', in *Household Words*, 19:465 (February 19, 1859), 263–269
[French, Miss], 'Number Five, Hanbury Terrace', in *Household Words*, 16:403 (December 12, 1857), 568–572
[Gaskell, Elizabeth], 'My French Master (I)', in *Household Words*, 8:195 (December 17, 1853), 361–365
[Gaskell, Elizabeth], 'My French Master (II)', in *Household Words*, 8:196 (December 24, 1853), 388–393
[Gaskell, Elizabeth], 'Modern Greek Songs', in *Household Words*, 9:205 (February 25, 1854), 25–32
[Greenwell, Dora], 'The Heart of England', in *Household Words*, 4:85 (November 8, 1851), 156
[Grey, Anna S., and W. H. Wills], 'Ballinglen', in *Household Words*, 3:71 (August 2, 1851), 450–451
[Grumride?, Mrs.], 'New Year's Day in China', in *Household Words*, 19:464 (February 12, 1859), 258–260
[Gwynne, Francis, and W.H. Wills], 'Two Letters from Australia', in *Household Words*, 1:20 (August 10, 1850), 475–480
[Hannay, James], 'English Songs', in *Household Words*, 4:86 (November 15, 1851), 173–178
[Harper], 'A Vagrant's Deathbed', in *Household Words*, 3:53 (March 29, 1851), 13
[Harper], 'The Claims of Labour', in *Household Words*, 3:67 (July 5, 1851), 356
[Harper], 'The Voice of Cheer', in *Household Words*, 4:92 (December 27, 1851), 324

[Hoare, Mrs.], 'Father and Son', in *Household Words*, 1:9 (May 25, 1850), 213–216

[Hoare, Mrs.], 'Little Mary. A Tale of the Black Year', in *Household Words*, 1:17 (July 20, 1850), 392–396

[Hoare, Mrs.], 'An Irish Peculiarity', in *Household Words*, 1:25 (September 14, 1850), 594–596

[Hoare, Mrs.], 'Barryhooraghan Post-Office', in *Household Words*, 6:150 (February 5, 1853), 503–504

[Hoare, Mrs.], 'The Irish Letter-Writer', in *Household Words*, 10:237 (October 7, 1854), 190–192

[Hogarth, George, and W. H. Wills], 'Heathen and Christian Burial', in *Household Words*, 1:2 (April 6, 1850), 43–48

[Horne, Richard H.], 'The Wonders of 1851', in *Household Words*, 1:17 (July 20, 1850), 388–392

[Horne, Richard H.], 'A Time for All Things', in *Household Words*, 2:52 (March 22, 1851), 615–617

[Horne, Richard H. and Charles Dickens], 'The Great Exhibition and the Little One', in *Household Words*, 3:67 (July 5, 1851), 356–360

[Horne, Richard H.], 'A Penitent Confession', in *Household Words*, 3:71 (August 2, 1851), 436–445

[Horne, Richard H., and Hogarth Jr.], 'Look before You Leap', in *Household Words*, 6:150 (February 5, 1853), 497–499

[Howitt, Anna M.], 'Bits of Life in Munich (I)', in *Household Words*, 2:32 (November 2, 1850), 133–137

[Howitt, Anna M.], 'Bits of Life in Munich (II)', in *Household Words*, 2:41 (January 4, 1851), 358–359

[Howitt, Anna M.], 'Bits of Life in Munich (III)', in *Household Words*, 2:43 (January 18, 1851), 395–397

[Howitt, Anna M.], 'Bits of Life in Munich (IV)', in *Household Words*, 2:49 (March 1, 1851), 535–540

[Howitt, Anna M.], 'Bits of Life in Munich (V)', in *Household Words*, 3:53 (March 29, 1851), 9–13

[Howitt, Anna M.], 'Bits of Life in Munich (VI)', in *Household Words*, 3:54 (April 5, 1851), 43–46

[Howitt, Anna M.], 'Bits of Life in Munich (VII)', in *Household Words*, 3:61 (May 24, 1851), 209–211

[Howitt, Anna M.], 'Bits of Life in Munich (VIII)', in *Household Words*, 3:63 (June 7, 1851), 261–264

[Howitt, William], 'A Pilgrimage to the Great Exhibition from Abroad', in *Household Words*, 3:66 (June 14, 1851), 321–324

[Howitt, William], 'Two Aspects of Ireland. The First Aspect.' in *Household Words*, 4:79 (September 27, 1851), 6–10

[Howitt, William], 'Two Aspects of Ireland. The Second Aspect.' in *Household Words*, 4:80 (October 4, 1851), 27–32

[Hunt, Leigh], 'The Trumpets of Doolkarnein', in *Household Words*, 6:130 (September 18, 1852), 12–13

[Hunt, Leigh], 'Holland House (1)', in *Household Words*, 9:204 (February 18, 1854), 8–15

[Hunt, Leigh], 'Holland House (2)', in *Household Words*, 9:205 (February 25, 1854), 38–42

[Jerdan, William], 'The Gift of Tongues', in *Household Words*, 15:355 (January 10, 1857), 41–43

[Jerrold, William B.], 'For the Benefit of the Cooks', in *Household Words*, 9:205 (February 25, 1854), 42–44

[Jerrold, William B.], 'The Turk at Home', in *Household Words*, 9:206 (March 4, 1854), 56–61

[Jerrold, William B.], 'An Old Portrait from the Hague', in *Household Words*, 9:227 (July 29, 1854), 569–572

[Jewsbury], 'Gold Mines at Home', in *Household Words*, 13:312 (March 15, 1856), 203–204

[Knight, Charles], 'Three May-Days in London: Iii. The May Palace (1851)', in *Household Words*, 3:58 (May 3, 1851), 121–124

[Lang, John], 'Wedding Bells', in *Household Words*, 6:152 (February 19, 1853), 551–552

[Lang, John], 'Wolf Nurses', in *Household Words*, 6:153 (February 26, 1853), 562–563

[Lang, John], 'Fisher's Ghost', in *Household Words*, 7:154 (March 5, 1853), 6–9

[Lang, John], 'An Inundation in Bengal', in *Household Words*, 7:156 (March 19, 1853), 53–54

[Lang, John], 'Starting a Paper in India', in *Household Words*, 7:157 (March 26, 1853), 94–96

[Lang, John], 'The Mahommedan Mother', in *Household Words*, 7:168 (June 11, 1853), 339–346

[Lang, John], 'Black and Blue', in *Household Words*, 14:341 (October 4, 1856), 276–282

[Lang, John], 'Hovelling', in *Household Words*, 15:359 (February 7, 1857), 139–142

[Lang, John], 'The Himalaya Club', in *Household Words*, 15:365 (March 21, 1857), 265–272

[Lang, John], 'An Experience of Austria', in *Household Words*, 15:369 (April 18, 1857), 381–384

[Lang, John], 'Tracks in the Bush', in *Household Words*, 16:383 (July 25, 1857), 93–96

[Lang, John], 'Invisible Ghosts', in *Household Words*, 16:384 (August 1, 1857), 109–111

[Lang, John], 'Wanderings in India (I)', in *Household Words*, 16:399 (November 14, 1857), 457–463

[Lang, John], 'Wanderings in India (II)', in *Household Words*, 16:401 (November 28, 1857), 505–511

[Lang, John], 'Wanderings in India (III)', in *Household Words*, 17:404 (December 19, 1857), 12–20

[Lang, John], 'Wanderings in India (IV)', in *Household Words*, 17:406 (January 2, 1858), 64–70

[Lang, John], 'Wanderings in India (V)', in *Household Words*, 17:407 (January 9, 1858), 87–94

[Lang, John], 'Wanderings in India (VI)', in *Household Words*, 17:408 (January 16, 1858), 112–118

[Lang, John], 'Wanderings in India (VII)', in *Household Words*, 17:409 (January 23, 1858), 134–144

[Lang, John], 'Wanderings in India (VIII)', in *Household Words*, 17:410 (January 30, 1858), 148–156

[Lang, John], 'Wanderings in India (IX)', in *Household Words*, 17:411 (February 6, 1858), 179–186

[Lang, John], 'Wanderings in India (X)', in *Household Words*, 17:412 (February 13, 1858), 212–216

[Lang, John], 'Wanderings in India (XI)', in *Household Words*, 17:413 (February 20, 1858), 220–224

[Lang, John], 'Wanderings in India (XII)', in *Household Words*, 17:414 (February 27, 1858), 254–260
[Lang, John], 'Chips: A Human Waif', in *Household Words*, 17:428 (June 5, 1858), 595–597
[Lang, John], 'The Abors', in *Household Words*, 18:438 (August 14, 1858), 204–205
[Lang, John], 'An Illustrious Exile', in *Household Words*, 19:472 (April 9, 1859), 454–456
[Lang, John], 'A Bad Name', in *Household Words*, 19:473 (April 16, 1859), 477–480
[Lang, John], 'A Special Convict', in *Household Words*, 19:474 (April 23, 1859), 489–491
[Lang, John], 'Baron Wald', in *Household Words*, 19:476 (May 7, 1859), 537–541
[Lang, John], 'Three Celebrities', in *Household Words*, 19:477 (May 14, 1859), 553–557
[Lang, John], 'Kate Crawford', in *Household Words*, 19:478 (May 21, 1859), 596–600
[Lang, John], 'Bad Bargains', in *Household Words*, 19:479 (May 28, 1859), 610–613
[Lang, John], 'Miss Saint Felix', in *Household Words*, 19:479 (May 28, 1859), 613–617
[Leigh, Percival], 'The Irish California', in *Household Words*, 2:41 (January 4, 1851), 348–353
[Leigh, Percival], 'The Latest Intelligence from the Irish California', in *Household Words*, 3:77 (September 13, 1851), 595
[Lever, Charles J.], 'Continental Ways and Means', in *Household Words*, 4:99 (February 14, 1852), 490–492
[Lynn, Eliza], 'Devil Worshippers', in *Household Words*, 10:232 (September 2, 1854), 57–61
[Lynn, Eliza], 'The Workmen of Europe', in *Household Words*, 12:296 (November 24, 1855), 390–394
[Lynn, Eliza, and W. H. Wills], 'Common Cookery', in *Household Words*, 13:305 (January 26, 1856), 42–46
[Lynn, Eliza, and W. H. Wills], 'Duelling in England', in *Household Words*, 15:378 (June 20, 1857), 596–600
[Lynn, Eliza, and W. H. Wills], 'Duelling in France', in *Household Words*, 15:379 (June 27, 1857), 614–620
[Lynn, Eliza], 'The Witches of Scotland', in *Household Words*, 16:383 (July 25, 1857), 75–83
[Lynn, Eliza], 'The Witches of England', in *Household Words*, 16:385 (August 8, 1857), 138–141
[Lynn Linton, Eliza], 'National Contrasts', in *Household Words*, 18:449 (October 30, 1858), 472–476
[MacCabe, William B.], 'The Six Giants of Lehon', in *Household Words*, 17:425 (May 15, 1858), 509–518
[Markham, Clements R.], 'The First Sack of Delhi', in *Household Words*, 16:391 (September 19, 1857), 276–279
[Martineau, Harriet], 'The Forbidden Land', in *Household Words*, 5:122 (July 24, 1852), 431–436
[Martineau, Harriet], 'Peatal Aggression', in *Household Words*, 6:130 (September 18, 1852), 13–18
[Martineau, Harriet], 'Triumphant Carriages', in *Household Words*, 6:135 (October 23, 1852), 121–125

[Martineau, Harriet], 'Hope with a Slate Anchor', in *Household Words*, 6:136 (October 30, 1852), 156–161
[Martineau, Harriet], 'The Irish Union', in *Household Words*, 6:137 (November 6, 1852), 169–175
[Martineau, Harriet], 'The Famine Time', in *Household Words*, 6:138 (November 13, 1852), 214–216
[Meason, Malcolm R.L.], 'Regulars and Irregulars', in *Household Words*, 12:282 (August 18, 1855), 58–60
[Meason, Malcolm R.L.], 'French and English Staff Officers', in *Household Words*, 13:307 (February 9, 1856), 84–88
[Meredith, George], 'The Congress of Nations', in *Household Words*, 2:50 (March 8, 1851), 572
[Meredith, George], 'Britain', in *Household Words*, 4:87 (November 22, 1851), 204
[Meredith, George], 'The Linnet-Hawker', in *Household Words*, 4:94 (January 10, 1852), 372
[Michelsen, Edward H.], 'Chinese Players', in *Household Words*, 8:191 (November 19, 1853), 281–283
[Milne, William C.], 'Francis Moore in China', in *Household Words*, 10:238 (October 14, 1854), 203–204
[Milne, William C.], 'The Chinese Adam', in *Household Words*, 11:256 (February 17, 1855), 67–68
[Milne, William C.], 'The Chinaman's Parson', in *Household Words*, 11:262 (March 31, 1855), 202–204
[Milne, William C.], 'The Chinese Postman', in *Household Words*, 11:264 (April 14, 1855), 259–261
[Milne, William C.], 'Chinese Charms', in *Household Words*, 17:419 (April 3, 1858), 370–372
[Mitchell, E.], 'An Encumbered Estate', in *Household Words*, 16:383 (July 25, 1857), 84–89
[Morley, Henry], 'The Irish Use of the Globe, in One Lesson', in *Household Words*, 2:29 (October 12, 1850), 51–56
[Morley, Henry], 'Views of the Country', in *Household Words*, 2:34 (November 16, 1850), 169–172
[Morley, Henry], 'Our Phantom Ship: China', in *Household Words*, 3:66 (June 28, 1851), 325–331
[Morley, Henry], 'Mr. Bendigo Buster on the Model Cottages', in *Household Words*, 3:67 (July 5, 1851), 337–341
[Morley, Henry], 'What is not Clear about the Crystal Palace', in *Household Words*, 3:69 (July 19, 1851), 400–402
[Morley, Henry], 'Foreign Airs and Native Places', in *Household Words*, 3:71 (August 2, 1851), 446–450
[Morley, Henry], 'The Catalogue's Account of Itself', in *Household Words*, 3:74 (August 23, 1851), 519–523
[Morley, Henry], 'Little Red Working Coat', in *Household Words*, 4:92 (December 27, 1851), 324–325
[Morley, Henry], 'Highland Emigration', in *Household Words*, 5:117 (June 19, 1852), 324–325
[Morley, Henry], 'China with a Flaw in It', in *Household Words*, 5:119 (July 3, 1852), 368–374
[Morley, Henry], 'Jack and the Union Jack', in *Household Words*, 9:205 (February 25, 1854), 32–33
[Morley, Henry], 'British Phenomena', in *Household Words*, 9:220 (June 10, 1854), 386–390

[Morley, Henry], 'At Home with the Russians', in *Household Words*, 10:252 (January 20, 1855), 533–538

[Morley, Henry], 'Tinder from a Californian Fire', in *Household Words*, 11:257 (February 24, 1855), 88–93

[Morley, Henry], 'Far East', in *Household Words*, 13:310 (March 1, 1856), 154–157

[Morley, Henry], 'Weeds', in *Household Words*, 15:355 (January 10, 1857), 32–35

[Morley, Henry], 'Celtic Bards', in *Household Words*, 17:419 (April 3, 1858), 379–384

[Morley, Henry], 'The Thistle in Bud', in *Household Words*, 18:431 (June 26, 1858), 25–29

[Morley, Henry], 'Britannia's Figures', in *Household Words*, 19:454 (December 4, 1858), 13–16

[Morley, Henry], 'Perils in India', in *Household Words*, 19:461 (January 22, 1859), 174–179

[Morley, Henry], 'A Group of Noble Savages', in *Household Words*, 19:470 (March 26, 1859), 385–390

[Murray, Grenville], 'A German Picture of the Scotch', in *Household Words*, 2:29 (October 12, 1850), 71–72

[Murray, Grenville], 'Domestic Servants in Austria', in *Household Words*, 3:54 (April 5, 1851), 42–43

[Murray, Grenville, and Henry Morley], 'A Roving Englishman: Benighted; Out Shooting (1)', in *Household Words*, 4:88 (November 29, 1851), 221–224

[Murray, Grenville, and Henry Morley], 'A Roving Englishman: The Apple-Green Spencer; Gastein Baths (2)', in *Household Words*, 4:91 (December 20, 1851), 299–301

[Murray, Grenville, and Henry Morley], 'The Roving Englishman: A Masked Ball; Advertisements (3)', in *Household Words*, 4:93 (January 3, 1852), 358–360

[Murray, Grenville, and Henry Morley], 'The Roving Englishman: In Praise of Salad (4)', in *Household Words*, 4:95 (January 17, 1852), 406–408

[Murray, Grenville, and Henry Morley], 'The Roving Englishman: A Brace of Blunders (5)', in *Household Words*, 4:96 (January 24, 1852), 431–432

[Murray, Grenville], 'The Roving Englishman: Concerning a Pair of Demons (6)', in *Household Words*, 4:100 (February 21, 1852), 514–517

[Murray, Grenville], 'The Roving Englishman: A Ramble to Rehburg (7)', in *Household Words*, 5:125 (August 14, 1852), 522–524

[Murray, Grenville], 'The Roving Englishman: A Golden Wedding (8)', in *Household Words*, 6:131 (September 25, 1852), 46–48

[Murray, Grenville], 'The Roving Englishman: A German Joe Miller (9)', in *Household Words*, 6:135 (October 23, 1852), 142–144

[Murray, Grenville], 'The Roving Englishman: His Hints to Travellers (10)', in *Household Words*, 6:138 (November 13, 1852), 211–214

[Murray, Grenville], 'The Roving Englishman: His Philosophy of Dining (11)', in *Household Words*, 6:139 (November 20, 1852), 231–233

[Murray, Grenville], 'The Roving Englishman: On Horseback (12)', in *Household Words*, 6:142 (December 11, 1852), 309–312

[Murray, Grenville], 'The Roving Englishman: With a Baron Much Interested in Him (13)', in *Household Words*, 6:143 (December 18, 1852), 333–336

[Murray, Grenville], 'The Roving Englishman: A Few More Hints (14)', in *Household Words*, 6:144 (December 25, 1852), 358–360

[Murray, Grenville], 'The Roving Englishman: Travelling Servants (15)', in *Household Words*, 6:148 (January 8, 1853), 453–456

[Murray, Grenville], 'The Roving Englishman: Cares of State (16)', in *Household Words*, 6:149 (January 29, 1853), 478–480

[Murray, Grenville], 'The Roving Englishman: Monsieur le Curé; Ma Sœur, the Governess (17)', in *Household Words*, 7:154 (March 5, 1853), 20–22
[Murray, Grenville], 'The Roving Englishman: The Great Do (18)', in *Household Words*, 7:156 (March 19, 1853), 67–72
[Murray, Grenville], 'The Roving Englishman: After the Boars (19)', in *Household Words*, 7:158 (April 2, 1853), 118–120
[Murray, Grenville], 'The Roving Englishman: Beautiful Naples (20)', in *Household Words*, 7:166 (May 28, 1853), 302–305
[Murray, Grenville], 'The Roving Englishman: Diplomacy (21)', in *Household Words*, 7:169 (June 18, 1853), 373–375
[Murray, Grenville], 'The Roving Englishman: A Canter with Polychronopulos (22)', in *Household Words*, 7:173 (July 16, 1853), 472–475
[Murray, Grenville], 'The Roving Englishman at Constantinople (23)', in *Household Words*, 8:188 (October 29, 1853), 204–207
[Murray, Grenville], 'The Roving Englishman; and the Prince de Vendome (24)', in *Household Words*, 8:194 (December 10, 1853), 355–360
[Murray, Grenville], 'The Roving Englishman: A Greek Feast (25)', in *Household Words*, 8:196 (December 24, 1853), 393–397
[Murray, Grenville], 'The Roving Englishman: Greek Easter at Constantinople, A Defense of Fleas (26)', in *Household Words*, 8:197 (December 31, 1853), 415–418
[Murray, Grenville], 'The Roving Englishman: Education in Turkey (27)', in *Household Words*, 9:207 (March 11, 1854), 79–80
[Murray, Grenville], 'The Roving Englishman: Captain Jorgey (28)', in *Household Words*, 9:208 (March 18, 1854), 102–104
[Murray, Grenville], 'The Roving Englishman: Greek Fire (29)', in *Household Words*, 9:209 (March 25, 1854), 132–134
[Murray, Grenville], 'The Roving Englishman: Free Quarters; A Saint's Brother (30)', in *Household Words*, 9:212 (April 15, 1854), 206–209
[Murray, Grenville], 'The Roving Englishman: The Cadi; Britons in Turkey (31)', in *Household Words*, 9:214 (April 29, 1854), 254–257
[Murray, Grenville], 'The Roving Englishman: A Greek Girl (32)', in *Household Words*, 9:217 (May 20, 1854), 321–323
[Murray, Grenville], 'The Roving Englishman: Regular Turks (33)', in *Household Words*, 9:218 (May 27, 1854), 349–352
[Murray, Grenville], 'The Roving Englishman: A Turkish Auctioneer (34)', in *Household Words*, 9:219 (June 3, 1854), 362–364
[Murray, Grenville], 'The Roving Englishman: Greek Waters (35)', in *Household Words*, 9:221 (June 10, 1854), 402–404
[Murray, Grenville], 'The Roving Englishman: The Pasha (36)', in *Household Words*, 9:223 (July 1, 1854), 462–464
[Murray, Grenville], 'The Roving Englishman: Village Diplomatists; The Schoolmaster and His Lesson (37)', in *Household Words*, 9:225 (July 15, 1854), 510–513
[Murray, Grenville], 'The Roving Englishman: The Bin-Bashee (38)', in *Household Words*, 9:226 (July 22, 1854), 542–543
[Murray, Grenville], 'The Roving Englishman: Hadji Hassan (39)', in *Household Words*, 9:227 (July 29, 1854), 556–558
[Murray, Grenville and George A. Sala], 'The Roving Englishman: The Sea Captain and His Ship (40)', in *Household Words*, 9:229 (August 12, 1854), 606–608
[Murray, Grenville], 'The Roving Englishman: A Greek Carnival (41)', in *Household Words*, 10:233 (September 9, 1854), 77–79
[Murray, Grenville], 'The Roving Englishman: Dolma Bakjah; A Turkish Bath (42)', in *Household Words*, 10:245 (December 2, 1854), 369–373

[Murray, Grenville], 'Army interpreters', in *Household Words*, 10:247 (December 16, 1854), 431–432
[Murray, Grenville], 'The Roving Englishman: A Roadside Picture; Locusts (43)', in *Household Words*, 10:249 (December 30, 1854), 477–480
[Murray, Grenville], 'The Roving Englishman at the Pera Theatre (44)', in *Household Words*, 10:253 (January 27, 1855), 570–572
[Murray, Grenville], 'The Roving Englishman: Very Cold at Bucharest; the Theatre; the Terrible Officer (45)', in *Household Words*, 11:257 (February 24, 1855), 82–85
[Murray, Grenville], 'The Roving Englishman: From Constantinople to Varna (46)', in *Household Words*, 11:259 (March 10, 1855), 142–144
[Murray, Grenville], 'The Roving Englishman: From Varna to Balaklava (47)', in *Household Words*, 11:260 (March 17, 1855), 153–157
[Murray, Grenville], 'The Roving Englishman: A Dinner in Camp (48)', in *Household Words*, 11:261 (March 24, 1855), 191–192
[Murray, Grenville], 'The Roving Englishman: From Varna to Rustchuk (49)', in *Household Words*, 11:266 (April 28, 1855), 307–308
[Murray, Grenville], 'The Roving Englishman: A Bulgarian Post-House (50)', in *Household Words*, 11:267 (May 5, 1855), 335–336
[Murray, Grenville], 'The Roving Englishman: Rustchuk (51)', in *Household Words*, 11:271 (June 2, 1855), 427–429
[Murray, Grenville], 'The Roving Englishman: The Passage of the Danube (52)', in *Household Words*, 11:273 (June 16, 1855), 465–468
[Murray, Grenville], 'The Roving Englishman: From Giurgevo to Bucharest (53)', in *Household Words*, 11:277 (July 14, 1855), 558–561
[Murray, Grenville], 'The Roving Englishman: From Bucharest to Kraiova (54)', in *Household Words*, 12:284 (September 1, 1855), 109–112
[Murray, Grenville], 'The Roving Englishman: From Kraiova to London (55)', in *Household Words*, 12:291 (October 20, 1855), 282–284
[Murray, Grenville], 'The Roving Englishman in Belgium (56)', in *Household Words*, 12:292 (October 27, 1855), 309–312
[Murray, Grenville], 'The Roving Englishman: Down the Danube (57)', in *Household Words*, 12:300 (December 22, 1855), 502–504
[Murray, Grenville], 'The Roving Englishman: The Show Officer (58)', in *Household Words*, 13:304 (January 19, 1856), 22–24
[Murray, Grenville], 'The Sulina Mouth of the Danube', in *Household Words*, 12:307 (February 9, 1856), 73–77
[Murray, Grenville], 'The Roving Englishman: Messina (59)', in *Household Words*, 13:312 (March 15, 1856), 214–216
[Murray, Grenville], 'Turkish Contrasts', in *Household Words*, 12:314 (March 29, 1856), 263–264
[Ollier, Edmund], 'A Vision of Old Babylon', in *Household Words*, 13:310 (March 1, 1856), 157
[Payn, James], 'Back from the Crimea', in *Household Words*, 11:258 (March 3, 1855), 119–120
[Payn, James], 'Embarkation', in *Household Words*, 11:268 (May 12, 1855), 354–356
[Payn, James], 'Miss Davies', in *Household Words*, 12:297 (December 1, 1855), 429–432
[Payn, James], 'The Savage Muse', in *Household Words*, 18:437 (August 7, 1858), 181–184
[Peppé], 'The Crocodile Battery', in *Household Words*, 2:49 (March 1, 1851), 540–543

[Perrott, Miss], 'Died in India', in *Household Words*, 9:205 (February 25, 1854), 33–34
[Prince, John C.], 'A Voice from the Factory', in *Household Words*, 3:54 (April 5, 1851), 35–36
[Procter, Adelaide A.], 'The Voice of the Wind', in *Household Words*, 9:207 (March 11, 1854), 80–81
[Procter, Adelaide A], 'Home-Sickness', in *Household Words*, 9:208 (March 18, 1854), 104–105
[Reeves], 'Promotion, French and English', in *Household Words*, 15:357 (January 24, 1857), 90–92
[Robertson, John], 'Coast Folk', in *Household Words*, 13:326 (June 21, 1856), 550–552
[Robertson, John], 'Scotch Coast Folk', in *Household Words*, 13:328 (July 5, 1856), 585–590
[Robertson, John], 'Scotch Coast Folk: Footdee in the Last Century', in *Household Words*, 14:330 (July 19, 1856), 16–20
[Robertson, John], 'English Coast Folk', in *Household Words*, 14:333 (August 9, 1856), 81–85
[Robertson, John], 'Sepoy Symbols of Mutiny', in *Household Words*, 16:389 (September 5, 1857), 228–232
[Ross, Thomasina], 'The "Mouth" of China', in *Household Words*, 3:67 (July 5, 1851), 348–353
[Sala, George A.], 'The Foreign Invasion', in *Household Words*, 4:81 (October 11, 1851), 60–64
[Sala, George A.], 'Liberty, Equality, Fraternity, and Musketry', in *Household Words*, 4:92 (December 27, 1851), 313–318
[Sala, George A.], 'Cities in Plain Clothes', in *Household Words*, 5:121 (July 17, 1852), 417–422
[Sala, George A.], 'A Handful of Foreign Money', in *Household Words*, 5:128 (September 4, 1852), 573–577
[Sala, George A.], 'Perfidious Patmos', in *Household Words*, 7:155 (March 12, 1853), 25–29
[Sala, George A.], 'English Milords', in *Household Words*, 7:165 (May 21, 1853), 270–273
[Sala, George A.], 'The Length of the Quays', in *Household Words*, 7:178 (August 20, 1853), 582–586
[Sala, George A.], 'An Irish Stew', in *Household Words*, 7:179 (August 27, 1853), 617–620
[Sala, George A.], 'Some Amenities of War', in *Household Words*, 9:225 (July 15, 1854), 521–524
[Sala, George A.], 'Music in Paving Stones', in *Household Words*, 10:231 (August 26, 1854), 37–43
[Sala, George A.], 'Convicts, English and French', in *Household Words*, 11:257 (February 24, 1855), 85–88
[Sala, George A.], 'The Great Hotel Question (I)', in *Household Words*, 13:308 (February 16, 1856), 97–103
[Sala, George A.], 'The Great Hotel Question (II)', in *Household Words*, 13:309 (February 23, 1856), 141–144
[Sala, George A.], 'The Great Hotel Question (III)', in *Household Words*, 13:310 (March 1, 1856), 148–154
[Sala, George A.], 'English Hotels', in *Household Words*, 13:311 (March 8, 1856), 172–178
[Siddons, Joachim H.], 'Christmas in India', in *Household Words*, 2:39 (December 21, 1850), 305–306

[Siddons, Joachim H.], 'Justice for "Natives"', in *Household Words*, 7:170 (June 25, 1853), 397–402
[Siddons, Miss], 'The Burial of the Old Year', in *Household Words*, 2:41 (January 4, 1851), 348
[Sidney, Samuel], 'An Australian Ploughman's Story', in *Household Words*, 1:2 (April 6, 1850), 39–43
[Sidney, Samuel], 'Two-Handed Dick the Stockman. An Adventure in the Bush', in *Household Words*, 1:6 (May 4, 1850), 141–144
[Sidney, Samuel], 'An Exploring Adventure', in *Household Words*, 1:18 (July 27, 1850), 418–420
[Sidney, Samuel], 'Family Colonisation Loan Society', in *Household Words*, 1:22 (August 24, 1850), 514–515
[Sidney, Samuel], 'Father Gabriel; or, The Fortunes of a Farmer', in *Household Words*, 2:29 (October 12, 1850), 67–71
[Sidney, Samuel], 'Father Gabriel's Story', in *Household Words*, 2:30 (October 19, 1850), 85–90
[Sidney, Samuel], 'Two Adventures at Sea', in *Household Words*, 2:31 (October 26, 1850), 104–108
[Sidney, Samuel], 'Letters of Introduction to Sydney', in *Household Words*, 2:34 (November 16, 1850), 187–188
[Sidney, Samuel], 'Land Ho!—Port Jackson', in *Household Words*, 2:38 (December 14, 1850), 276–277
[Sidney, Samuel], 'Christmas Day in the Bush', in *Household Words*, 2:39 (December 21, 1850), 309–310
[Sidney, Samuel], 'Indian Railroads and British Commerce', in *Household Words*, 2:51 (March 15, 1851), 590–595
[Sidney, Samuel], 'Three Colonial Epochs', in *Household Words*, 4:97 (January 31, 1852), 433–438
[Sidney, Samuel], 'Travellers' Contrivances', in *Household Words*, 12:301 (December 29, 1855), 505–511
[Sidney, Samuel], 'Feudal Fetters for Farmers', in *Household Words*, 13:311 (March 8, 1856), 178–181
[Sidney, Samuel], 'French and English', in *Household Words*, 15:376 (June 6, 1857), 529–534
[Smith, Sidney], 'The Spade in Ireland', in *Household Words*, 3:57 (April 26, 1851), 114–115
[Soutar, Keys and Henry Morley], 'The Jews in China', in *Household Words*, 3:71 (August 2, 1851), 452–456
[St. John, James Augustus], 'A Chinaman's Ball', in *Household Words*, 5:117 (June 19, 1852), 331–332
[Thomas, T. M.], 'A Suburban Connemara', in *Household Words*, 2:50 (March 8, 1851), 562–565
[Thomas, William M.], 'An Englishman's Castle', in *Household Words*, 4:92 (December 27, 1851), 321–324
[Thomas, William M.], 'Sentimental Journalism', in *Household Words*, 4:101 (February 28, 1852), 550–552
[Thomas, William M.], 'The Last Howley of Killowen', in *Household Words*, 9:225 (July 15, 1854), 513–519
[Thornbury, George], 'Spanish Hotels', in *Household Words*, 19:459 (January 8, 1859), 132–137
[Tomkins, Mary J.], 'Before Sebastopol', in *Household Words*, 11:257 (February 24, 1855), 85
[Townsend, E.], 'A Mutiny in India', in *Household Words*, 16:386 (August 15, 1857), 154–156

[Townsend, E.], 'Indian Irregulars', in *Household Words*, 16:390 (September 12, 1857), 244–246
[Townsend, E.], 'Lutfullah Khan', in *Household Words*, 16:400 (November 21, 1857), 490–496
[Townsend, E.], 'Indian Hill Stations', in *Household Words*, 17:417 (March 20, 1858), 316–319
[Townsend, E., and Alexander Hamilton], 'Indian Recruits and Indian English', in *Household Words*, 16:393 (October 3, 1857), 319–322
[Vincent, Frank, and Henry Morley], 'John Chinaman in Australia', in *Household Words*, 17:421 (April 17, 1858), 416–420
[Wenckstern, Otto von], 'The German Exile's New Year's Eve', in *Household Words*, 4:92 (December 27, 1851), 325–329
[Wenckstern, Otto von], 'English Cookery', in *Household Words*, 13:308 (February 16, 1856), 116
[White, Rev. James], 'Spanish Romance', in *Household Words*, 5:121 (July 17, 1852), 415–417
[White, Rev. James], 'A Testimony in Praise of Testimonials', in *Household Words*, 15:359 (February 7, 1857), 121–124
[Wills, W.H.], 'The Schoolmaster at Home and Abroad', in *Household Words*, 1:4 (April 20, 1850), 82–84
[Wills, W.H.], 'Christopher Shrimble on the "Decline of England"', in *Household Words*, 1:15 (July 6, 1850), 358–360
[Wills, W.H.], 'Cheerful Arithmetic', in *Household Words*, 1:23 (August 31, 1850), 531–534
[Wills, W.H.], 'The Private History of the Palace of Glass', in *Household Words*, 2:43 (January 18, 1851), 385–391
[Wills, W.H.], 'The Invited Invasion', in *Household Words*, 2:46 (February 8, 1851), 475–477
[Wills, W.H.], 'For India Direct', in *Household Words*, 5:110 (May 1, 1852), 141–145
[Wills, W.H.], 'An Oriental Firman', in *Household Words*, 6:138 (November 13, 1852), 210–211
[Wills, W.H., and Henry Morley], 'Improving a Bull', in *Household Words*, 1:19 (August 3, 1850), 450–451
[Wills, W.H., Grenville Murray and Thomas (prob.) Walker], 'German Advertisements', in *Household Words*, 2:28 (October 5, 1850), 33–35
[Wood], 'Progress', in *Household Words*, 9:223 (July 1, 1854), 464
[Wyley, Mrs.], 'A Welsh Wedding', in *Household Words*, 2:47 (February 15, 1851), 492–493

1.2 Material published in other periodical publications (identified authors)

[Chambers, William], 'The Editor's Address to His Readers', in *Chambers's Edinburgh Journal*, 1:1 (February 4, 1832), repr.1834 (7th edn.), 1–2
Maginn, Dr., 'Prologue', in *Bentley's Miscellany*, 1:1, (1837), 2–6
Hartmann, Karl, 'A Story of the Crimea. In Four Chapters', in *Chambers's Journal of Popular Literature, Science, and Arts*, 3:75 (June 9, 1855), 353–357
Hartmann, Karl, 'A Story of the Crimea. In Four Chapters', in *Chambers's Journal of Popular Literature, Science, and Arts*, 3:76 (June 16, 1855), 379–385
Hartmann, Karl, 'A Story of the Crimea. In Four Chapters', in *Chambers's Journal of Popular Literature, Science, and Arts*, 3:77 (June 23, 1855), 387–390
Hartmann, Karl, 'A Story of the Crimea. In Four Chapters', in *Chambers's Journal of Popular Literature, Science, and Arts*, 3:78 (June 30, 1855), 410–413

Jerrold, William Blanchard, 'The History of Industrial Exhibition', in *Illustrated London News*, 18:482 (May 3, 1851), 372
[Robertson, John], 'Notes on the Fishers of the Scotch East Coast', in *Blackwood's Edinburgh Magazine*, 51:317 (March, 1842), 296–305

1.3. Material published in other periodical publications (anonymous)

'1851', in *Punch*, 20 (January—June, 1851), 60
'Alarm of a French Invasion', in *Chambers's Journal of Popular Literature, Science, and Arts*, 1:10 (March 11, 1854), 151–152
'America and the War', in *Illustrated London News*, 26:724 (January 20, 1855), 49–50
'America in Crystal', in *Punch*, 20 (January—June, 1851), 209
'Amusements for the People', in *Chambers's Edinburgh Journal*, 18:449 (n.s.) (August 7, 1852), 95–96
'An Englishman in Ireland', in *Chambers's Edinburgh Journal*, 19:495 (n.s.) (June 25, 1853), 409–412
'An Indian Pageant', in *Chambers's Journal of Popular Literature, Science, and Arts*, 5:129 (June 21, 1856), 385–389
'Arts and Manufactures of India', in *Chambers's Edinburgh Journal*, 20:498 (n.s.) (July 16, 1853), 45–47
'The Bathhurst Diggings', in *Chambers's Edinburgh Journal*, 16:410 (n.s.) (November 8, 1851), 291–294
'Beggars in the Far East', in *Chambers's Edinburgh Journal*, 17:419 (n.s.) (January 10, 1852), 29–30
'British Ideas in India', in *Illustrated London News*, 31:878 (September 12, 1857), 251–252
'The Bushrangers', in *Chambers's Edinburgh Journal*, 16:400 (n.s.) (August 30, 1851), 134–138
'Celestial Agriculture', in *Chambers's Journal of Popular Literature, Science, and Arts*, 11:285 (June 18, 1859), 398–400
'China-Ism in All Countries', in *Chambers's Edinburgh Journal*, 20:500 (n.s.) (July 30, 1853), 65–66
'The Chinese Family', in *Illustrated London News*, 18:487 (May 24, 1851), 456
'A Chinese Monastery', in *Chambers's Journal of Popular Literature, Science, and Arts*, 11:281 (May 21, 1859), 323–327
'A Chinese Puzzle', in *Punch*, 21 (January—June, 1851), 19
'Chinese Socialism', in *Chambers's Journal of Popular Literature, Science, and Arts*, 4:84 (August 11, 1855), 93–95
'Climate and Health in Australia', in *Chambers's Edinburgh Journal*, 19:475 (n.s.) (February 5, 1853), 89–92
'Condition of England Question', in *Chambers's Edinburgh Journal*, 14:348 (n.s.) (August 31, 1850), 129–132
'The Conference of Vienna', in *Illustrated London News*, 23:638 (August 13, 1853), 119
'The Continental "Bradshaw" in 1852', in *Chambers's Edinburgh Journal*, 18:452 (n.s.) (August 28, 1852), 133–136
'A Conversation at the Exhibition, between an Anxious Mother and a Policeman', in *Punch*, 21 (January—June, 1851), 19
'A Conversation at the Great Exhibition', in *Punch*, 21 (July—December, 1851), 19
'Conversations in Chinese', in *Punch*, 20 (January—June, 1851), 232
'The Cosmopolitan before and after the Exhibition', in *Punch*, 21 (January—June, 1851), 44

'Cravens in Council', in *Illustrated London News*, 26:742 (May 12, 1855), 449
'The Crystal Palace—a National Reflection', in *Punch*, 20 (January—June, 1851), 111
'Curiosities of China', in *Chambers's Journal of Popular Literature, Science, and Arts*, 3:70 (May 5, 1855), 283–286
'The Danubian Principalities', in *Illustrated London News*, 31:873 (August 15, 1857), 153–154
'Death of the Emperor Nicholas', in *Illustrated London News*, 26:731 (March 10, 1855), 217–218
'The Defence of the Country', in *Illustrated London News*, 31:884 (October 24, 1857), 401–402
'The Depopulation of Ireland', in *Illustrated London News*, 18:483 (May 10, 1851), 386–388
'Design for a Fountain: To Be Placed in the Transept on the Shilling Days', in *Punch*, 20 (January—June, 1851), 257
'Dibdin's Songs', in *Chambers's Edinburgh Journal*, 17:425 (n.s.) (February 21, 1852), 124–125
'The Duties of the Allies to Themselves and to Europe', in *Illustrated London News*, 25:714 (November 25, 1854), 525–526
'The East Indian Court', in *Illustrated London News*, 18:494 (June 14, 1851), 583–584
'The Eastern Crisis', in *Illustrated London News*, 23:646 (Supplement) (September 24, 1853), 261–276
'Emigrant Ship "Washington"', in *Chambers's Edinburgh Journal*, 16:393 (n.s.) (July 12, 1851), 27–30
'Emigration to Ireland', in *Chambers's Edinburgh Journal*, 19:489 (n.s.) (May 14, 1853), 308–311
'Emigration', in *Chambers's Edinburgh Journal*, 1:1 (February 4, 1832), repr.1834 (7th edn.), 3–4
'England and India', in *Illustrated London News*, 31:880 (September 26, 1857), 305–306
'England and the English. By a Chinese', in *Chambers's Journal of Popular Literature, Science, and Arts*, 3:62 (March 10, 1855), 153–155
'The English at Home', in *Blackwood's Edinburgh Magazine*, 75:449 (January, 1854), 37–54
'Ethnology of Europe', in *Blackwood's Edinburgh Magazine*, 76:456 (August, 1854), 165–182
'The Exhibition as It Myght Have Been in the Days of Yore', in *Punch*, 20 (January—June, 1851), 208
'The Exhibition of Industry.—a Hint.' in *Punch*, 18 (January—June, 1850), 141
'The Exhibition', *Northern Star*, April 12, 1851, 8
'The Exhibition', *Northern Star*, May 3, 1851, 5
'Extension of the War', in *Illustrated London News*, 26:741 (May 5, 1855), 425–426
'Facts and Incidents of the Great Exhibition', *Northern Star*, May 17, 1851, 5
'Facts and Incidents of the Great Exhibition', *Northern Star*, May 31, 1851, 6
'Family Physic for 1851', in *Punch*, 20 (January—June, 1851), 206
'A Farewell Banquet', in *Chambers's Edinburgh Journal*, 15:388 (n.s.) (June 7, 1851), 360–362
'Foundling-Hospitals in China', in *Chambers's Journal of Popular Literature, Science, and Arts*, 6:135 (August 2, 1856), 78–79
'Freaks of the English Abroad', in *Chambers's Edinburgh Journal*, 16:414 (n.s.) (December 6, 1851), 363–364

'The French Press', in *Chambers's Edinburgh Journal*, 16:402 (n.s.) (September 13, 1851), 169–170
'A Geographical Guide for the Foreign Visitors in 1851', in *Punch*, 20 (January—June, 1851), 42
'German Gastronomy', in *Chambers's Journal of Popular Literature, Science, and Arts*, 12:313 (December 31, 1859), 417–419
'A Glance at Continental Railways', in *Chambers's Edinburgh Journal*, 18:455 (n.s.) (September 18, 1852), 177–180
'A Glance at the Exhibition', in *Chambers's Edinburgh Journal*, 15:387 (n.s.) (May 31, 1851), 337–340
'Glances at the Crystal Palace and Its Content', *Northern Star*, May 10, 1851, 5
'Glances at the Crystal Palace and Its Content', *Northern Star*, May 31, 1851, 6
'The Gold-Fever in Australia', in *Chambers's Edinburgh Journal*, 17:435 (n.s.) (May 1, 1852), 282–284
'A Great Day for Ireland', in *Chambers's Edinburgh Journal*, 19:493 (n.s.) (June 11, 1853), 369–372
'The Great Derby Race for Eighteen Hundred and Fifty-One', in *Punch*, 20 (January—June, 1851), 214–215
'The Great Exhibition', in *Illustrated London News*, 18:481 (May 3, 1851), 343–344
'The Great International Exhibition', in *Illustrated London News*, 18:484 (May 10, 1851), 391–392
'A Guide to the Great Exhibition of Industry', in *Illustrated London News*, 18:482 (May 3, 1851),
'A Guide to the Great Industrial Exhibition', in *Illustrated London News*, 18:484 (May 10, 1851), 392–404
'The Happy Family in Hyde-Park', in *Punch*, 21 (January—June, 1851), 38
'Her Majesty, as She Appeared on the First of May, Surrounded by "Horrible Conspirators and Assassins."', in *Punch*, 20 (January—June, 1851), 193
'The Hindoo Funeral', in *Chambers's Edinburgh Journal*, 16:401 (n.s.) (September 6, 1851), 157–158
'A Hint for the American Non-Exhibitors', in *Punch*, 20 (January—June, 1851), 246
'Indian Handicrafts', in *Chambers's Edinburgh Journal*, 15:387 (n.s.) (May 31, 1851), 342–345
'Indian Servants', in *Chambers's Journal of Popular Literature, Science, and Arts*, 8:197 (October 10, 1857), 229–231
'Indian Sweet-Meats', in *Chambers's Edinburgh Journal*, 16:399 (n.s.) (August 23, 1851), 126–127
'Irish Travelling', in *Chambers's Edinburgh Journal*, 14:349 (n.s.) (September 7, 1850), 157–160
'Jhellâbore', in *Chambers's Edinburgh Journal*, 16:392 (n.s.) (July 5, 1851), 13–14
'John Bull at the Fountain in the Crystal Palace', in *Punch*, 20 (January—June, 1851), 256
'The Ladies and the Police.—the Battle of the Crystal Palace', in *Punch*, 20 (January—June, 1851), 202
'Letters on the War and the Eastern Question (No.1)', in *Illustrated London News*, 26:734 (March 31, 1855), 289–290
'The Liberties of Europe', in *Illustrated London News*, 19:511 (August 23, 1851), 225–226
'Life in Turkey', *Chambers's Journal of Popular Literature, Science, and Arts*, April 28, 1855, p.262–265

'London During the Great Exhibition', in *Illustrated London News*, 18:386 (May 17, 1851), 423–424
'London with a Clean Front On', in *Punch*, 20 (January—June, 1851), 83
'Magic in India', in *Chambers's Edinburgh Journal*, 18:457 (n.s.) (October 2, 1852), 217–219
'The Marvellous Shilling', in *Punch*, 20 (January—June, 1851), 241
'May Day, Eighteen Hundred and Fifty-One', in *Punch*, 20 (January—June, 1851), 180–181
'Meditations in the Exhibition, by Mr. Doldrums', in *Punch*, 21 (July—December, 1851), 9
'Meeting of Exhibitors', *Northern Star*, May 17, 1851, 5
'The Morals of the Great Exhibition', in *Punch*, 20 (January—June, 1851), 233
'More Life in Turkey', in *Chambers's Journal of Popular Literature, Science, and Arts*, 4:83 (August 4, 1855), 71–74
'Mrs Chisholm', *Chambers's Edinburgh Journal*, September 25, 1852, p.193–196
'The Mutiny in India', in *Illustrated London News*, 31:867 (July 4, 1857), 1–2
'The New Convict Establishment in Western Australia', in *Chambers's Edinburgh Journal*, 18:450 (n.s.) (August 14, 1852), 106–108
'The New Land System', in *Chambers's Edinburgh Journal*, 16:397 (n.s.) (August 9, 1851), 88–90
'A New Result of the Great Exhibition', in *Illustrated London News*, 18:497 (June 28, 1851), 607–608
'Noble Instance of Turkish Generosity and Honesty', in *Chambers's Edinburgh Journal*, 18:444 (n.s.) (July 3, 1852), 15
'Notes from Australia', in *Chambers's Edinburgh Journal*, 17:421 (n.s.) (January 24, 1852), 62–63
'The Old and New Holy Alliance', in *Illustrated London News*, 18:491 (June 7, 1851), 503–504
'On the Formation of Scottish Society', in *Chambers's Edinburgh Journal*, 1:1 (February 4, 1832), repr.1834 (7th edn.), 2–3
'Open House at the Crystal Palace', in *Punch*, 20 (January—June, 1851), 43
'Opening of the Great Exhibition by the Queen', Northern Star, April 19, 1851, 4.
'Opening of the Great Exhibition by the Queen', Northern Star, April 26, 1851, 3.
'Our "Confession of Faith"', in *Fraser's Magazine for Town and Country*, 1:1 (February, 1830), 1–7
'Our Opening Chant', in *Bentley's Miscellany*, 1:1, (1837), 6
'Paper-Money and Banking in China', in *Chambers's Edinburgh Journal*, 17:439 (n.s.) (May 29, 1852), 347–349
'Past and Present of India', in *Chambers's Journal of Popular Literature, Science, and Arts*, 7:179 (June 6, 1857), 355–358
'Past and Present State of France', in *Bentley's Miscellany*, 28 (1850), 172–179
'The Pattern Nation', in *Chambers's Edinburgh Journal*, 17:424 (n.s.) (February 14, 1852), 97–99
'The Peace of Europe and the Balance of Power', in *Bentley's Miscellany*, 27 (1853), 208–221
'Peasant Proverbs of Northern Germany', in *Chambers's Journal of Popular Literature, Science, and Arts*, 4:89 (September 15, 1855), 170–172
'The People and the War', in *Illustrated London News*, 26:728 (February 17, 1855), 145–146
'Peoples and Prospects of Eastern Europe. First Article', in *Chambers's Journal of Popular Literature, Science, and Arts*, 2:27 (July 8, 1854), 24–26
'Peoples and Prospects of Eastern Europe. Second Article', in *Chambers's Journal of Popular Literature, Science, and Arts*, 2:28 (July 15, 1854), 44–46

'Phantoms of the Far East', in *Chambers's Edinburgh Journal*, 17:437 (n.s.) (May 15, 1852), 314–316
'Pictures for the Exhibition of Industry', in *Punch*, 20 (January—June, 1851), 42
'The Position of Prussia and Austria', in *Illustrated London News*, 26:732 (March 17, 1855), 241–242
'The Pound and the Shilling. "Whoever Thought of Meeting You Here?"', in *Punch*, 20 (January—June, 1851), 247
'The Prospects of Europe', in *Illustrated London News*, 19:536 (December 20, 1851), 721–722
'Russia, and the European Crisis', in *Bentley's Miscellany*, 27 (1850), 497–501
'Schooling in India', in *Chambers's Journal of Popular Literature, Science, and Arts*, 10:243 (August 28, 1858), 131–134
'The Sheep-Farmer in Australia', in *Chambers's Edinburgh Journal*, 15:385 (n.s.) (May 17, 1851), 317–319
'The Shilling Days at the Crystal Palace', in *Punch*, 20 (January—June, 1851), 240
'The Slave-Trade in Turkey', in *Chambers's Journal of Popular Literature, Science, and Arts*, 9:225 (April 24, 1858), 264–266
'Specimens from Mr. Punch's Industrial Exhibition of 1850. (to Be Improved in 1851)', in *Punch*, 18 (January—June, 1850), 145
'The Tea-Countries of China', in *Chambers's Edinburgh Journal*, 17:442 (n.s.) (June 19, 1852), 395–397
'The Turkish Gentry at Home', in *Chambers's Journal of Popular Literature, Science, and Arts*, 4:92 (October 6, 1855), 221–223
'The Turkish Question', in *Illustrated London News*, 22:625 (June 4, 1853), 433–434
'Turkey, Its Hopes and Perils', in *Bentley's Miscellany*, 34 (1853), 70–88
'Turkish Railways', in *Chambers's Journal of Popular Literature, Science, and Arts*, 9:233 (June 19, 1858), 387–389
'Two Exhibitions in One', in *Punch*, 20 (January—June, 1851), 232
'Village Life in France. In Two Parts—Part I', in *Chambers's Journal of Popular Literature, Science, and Arts*, 5:113 (March 1, 1856), 140–144
'Village Life in France. In Two Parts—Part II', in *Chambers's Journal of Popular Literature, Science, and Arts*, 5:114 (March 8, 1856), 157–160
'A Voice on Emigration to Australia. By a Colonist.' in *Chambers's Edinburgh Journal*, 19:483 (n.s.) (April 2, 1853), 210–212
'The Wanderer of the Crystal Palace', in *Punch*, 20 (January—June, 1851), 210
'Where Are the Foreigners?' in *Punch*, 20 (January—June, 1851), 207
'Workings of the Great Exhibition', in *Punch*, 20 (January—June, 1851), 227

1.4. Material published in newspapers

'[Tranquility in Indian Possessions]', *The Times*, February 26, 1850, p.4
'[Irish Expenditures]', *The Times*, February 26, 1850, p.4
'[Papacy and Socialism in France]', *The Times*, May 2, 1850, p.5
'[France and England]', *The Times*, May 21, 1850, p.4
'[Difficulties in Ireland]', *The Times*, June 17, 1850, p.4
'[Condition of Ireland]', *The Times*, July 26, 1850, p.4
'[Agriculture in Ireland]', *The Times*, August 12, 1850, p.4
'[Military States of Europe]', *The Times*, November 18, 1850, p.4
'[Papal Aggression in Ireland]', *The Times*, January 22, 1851, p.4
'Tour through Europe', *The Times*, February 19, 1851, p.5
'Official Return of the Number of English Residents in France in 1851', *The Times*, April 28, 1851, p.8

'[Festivities in England and France]', *The Times*, May 6, 1851, p.5
'Continental Statistics', *The Times*, June 9, 1851, p.8
'[France and England]', *The Times*, July 10, 1851, p.4
'Hints to Travellers in France and Italy', *The Times*, July 25, 1851, p.5
'[French Army in the Vatican]', *The Times*, August 2, 1851, p.4
'[The Irish]', *The Times*, October 24, 1851, p.4
'[French Revolution]', *The Times*, December 3, 1851, p.4
'[France and Universal Suffrage]', *The Times*, December 20, 1851, p.4
'[France and Louis Napoleon]', *The Times*, April 22, 1852, p.4
'[France and Louis Napoleon]', *The Times*, May 15, 1852, p.5
'[France and the Great Powers of Europe]', *The Times*, June 1, 1852, p.4
'[Celts in Ireland]', *The Times*, October 7, 1852, p.4
'[Turkey]', *The Times*, October 27, 1852, p.4
'[State of Ireland]', *The Times*, October 29, 1852, p.4
'[Recognition of the Empire of France by the Great Powers]', *The Times*, January 4, 1853, p.4
'[London Cheapest European Capital]', *The Times*, January 10, 1853, p.4
'[Probability of War with France]', *The Times*, February 12, 1853, p.8
'[Probability of War with France]', *The Times*, February 21, 1853, p.4
'Christians in Turkey', *The Times*, July 4, 1853, p.8
'Christians in Turkey', *The Times*, July 11, 1853, p.5
'Christians in Turkey', *The Times*, July 18, 1853, p.2
'Christians in Turkey', *The Times*, July 25, 1853, p.6
'[European Monarchs and Despots]', *The Times*, October 6, 1853, p.8
'[France and England on Turkey]', *The Times*, October 29, 1853, p.6
'[Liberation of Christian Population of Turkey]', *The Times*, March 1, 1854, p.9
'[Greek Insurrection against Turkey]', *The Times*, May 18, 1854, p.10
'European Powers in Crimean War', *The Times*, November 21, 1854, p.6
'[Admission of Turkey into Western Powers]', *The Times*, September 28, 1855, p.6
'An Extraordinary Scheme', *The Times*, October 24, 1855, p.6
'[British and Continental Governments Compared', *The Times*, August 15, 1856, p.6
'[British and Continental Governments Compared]', *The Times*, August 18, 1856, p.6
'[England and France]', *The Times*, September 5, 1857, p.6
'[England and France]', *The Times*, September 30, 1857, p.8
'[French Reaction to Indian Mutiny]', *The Times*, November 20, 1857, p.6
'[Protestants in France]', *The Times*, January 9, 1858, p.8
'Turkey', *The Times*, March 27, 1858, p.10
'[England and France]', *The Times*, March 29, 1858, p.8
'Continental Winter Quarters', *The Times*, October 13, 1858, p.10
'[France and Europe]', *The Times*, January 18, 1859, p.6
'[Map of Europe in 1860]', *The Times*, February 14, 1859, p.10
'[The State of Europe]', *The Times*, February 23, 1859, p.8
'[Alliance between France and Russia]', *The Times*, April 27, 1859, p.8

1.5. Material published in independent volumes

Baker, Nicholson, *The Fermata* (London: Chatto & Windus, 1994)
Dickens, Charles, *American Notes and Pictures from Italy* (London: Oxford University Press, 1957 [first published 1842])
Dickens, Charles, *Dombey and Son*, ed. by Alan Horsman, Oxford World's Classics (Oxford: Oxford University Press, 1999 [first published 1846–8])

Dickens, Charles, *David Copperfield*, Penguin Popular Classics (London: Penguin, 1994 [first published 1849–50])
Dickens, Charles, *Bleak House*, ed. by Stephen Gill, Oxford World's Classics (Oxford: Oxford University Press, 1996 [first published 1852–3])
Martineau, Harriet, *Letters from Ireland*, ed. by Glenn Hooper (Dublin: Irish Academic Press, 2001 [first published 1852])
McCarthy, Pete, *McCarthy's Bar: A Journey of Discovery in Ireland* (London: Hodder and Stoughton, 2000)

2. SECONDARY LITERATURE

2.1. Material in print

Achebe, Chinua, 'An Image of Africa: Racism in Conrad's *Heart of Darkness*'', in Vincent B. Leitch, and others (eds.), *The Norton Anthology of Theory and Criticism* (London; New York: W.W. Norton & Company, 2001), pp. 1783–1794
Ackroyd, Peter, *Dickens* (London: Vintage, 1990)
Allwood, John, *The Great Exhibitions* (London: Studio Vista, 1977)
Althusser, Louis, 'Ideology and Ideological State Apparatuses', in Julie Rivkin and Michael Ryan (eds.), *Literary Theory: An Anthology* (Oxford: Blackwell, 1998), pp. 294–304
Altick, Richard D., *The English Common Reader: A Social History of the Mass Reading Public, 1800–1900* (Chicago: University of Chicago Press, 1963)
Altick, Richard D., *Victorian People and Ideas* (London: Dent, 1974)
Altick, Richard D., *The Shows of London* (Cambridge, Mass.: Belknap Press, 1978)
Amur, G.S., 'In Search of the Picturesque: John Lang's *Wanderings in India and Other Sketches of Life in Hindostan*', in H. H. Anniah Gowda (ed.), *The Colonial and the Neo-Colonial Encounters in Commonwealth Literature* (Mysore: Prasaranga University of Mysore, 1983), pp. 49–62
Anderson, Benedict, *Imagined Communities*, second edition (London, New York: Verso, 1991 [first published 1983])
Anderson, Olive, *A Liberal State at War: English Politics and Economics During the Crimean War* (London: Macmillan, 1967)
Andrews, Malcolm, *Dickens on England and the English* (Brighton: Harvester Press, 1979)
Auerbach, Jeffrey A., *The Great Exhibition of 1851: A Nation on Display* (New Haven: Yale University Press, 1999)
Augstein, Hannah F. (ed.), *Race: The Origins of an Idea, 1760–1850*, Key Issues (Bristol: Thoemmes Press, 1996)
Barrell, John, *The Infection of Thomas De Quincey: A Psychopathology of Imperialism* (New Haven, London: Yale University Press, 1991)
Baucom, Ian, *Out of Place: Englishness, Empire, and the Locations of Identity* (Princeton, N.J.: Princeton University Press, 1999)
Beer, Gillian, 'Writing Darwin's Islands: England and the Insular Condition', in Timothy Lenoir (ed.), *Inscribing Science: Scientific Texts and the Materiality of Communication* (Stanford: Stanford University Press, 1998), pp. 119–139
Beetham, Margaret, 'Towards a Theory of the Periodical as a Publishing Genre', in Laurel Brake, Aled Jones, and Lionel Madden (eds.), *Investigating Victorian Journalism* (Basingstoke: Macmillan, 1990), pp. 19–32
Belchem, John, 'Nationalism, Republicanism and Exile: Irish Emigrants and the Revolutions of 1848', in *Past & Present*, 146 (February, 1995), 103–135
Bennett, Scott, 'Revolutions in Thought: Serial Publication and the Mass Market for Reading', in Joanne Shattock and Michael Wolff (eds.), *The Victorian*

Periodical Press: Samplings and Soundings (Leicester: Leicester University Press, 1982), pp. 225–257
Bergman, G. F. J., and John S. Levi, *Australian Genesis: Jewish Convicts and Settlers, 1788–1850* (London: Hale, 1974)
Best, Geoffrey, *Mid-Victorian Britain, 1851–75* (London: Fontana Press, 1979 [first published 1971])
Bhabha, Homi K., *Nation and Narration* (London: Routledge, 1990)
Bhabha, Homi K., *The Location of Culture* (London: Routledge, 1994)
Black, Jeremy, *A History of the British Isles* (Basingstoke: Macmillan, 1996)
Blake, Andrew, 'Writing on the Edge: Britishness and Its European Other', in Andrew Blake and Jopi Nyman (eds.), *Text and Nation: Essays on Post-Colonial Cultural Politics* (Joensuu, Finland: Faculty of Humanities, University of Joensuu, 2001), pp. 14–28
Blake, R.L.V. ffrench, *The Crimean War* (London: Sphere Books, 1971)
Blunt, Alison, 'Embodying War: British Women and Domestic Defilement in the Indian "Mutiny", 1857–8', in *Journal of Historical Geography*, 26:3 (2000), 403–428
Borm, Jan, 'In-Betweeners? On the Travel Book and Ethnographies', in *Studies in Travel Writing*, 4 (2000), 78–105
Bosbach, Franz, and John R. Davis (eds.), *Die Weltausstellung von 1851 und ihre Folgen* (München: K.G. Caur, 2002)
Bradford, Sarah, *Disraeli* (London: Weidenfeld and Nicholson, 1982)
Brake, Laurel, Aled Jones, and Lionel Madden (eds.), *Investigating Victorian Journalism* (Basingstoke: Macmillan, 1990)
Brake, Laurel, *Subjugated Knowledges: Journalism, Gender and Literature in the Nineteenth Century* (Houndmills, Basingstoke: Macmillan, 1994)
Brake, Laurel, Bill Bell, and David Finkelstein (eds.), *Nineteenth-Century Media and the Construction of Identities* (Basingstoke: Palgrave, 2000)
Brake, Laurel, *Print in Transition, 1850–1910: Studies in Media and Book History* (Basingstoke: Palgrave, 2001)
Brantlinger, Patrick, *Rule of Darkness: British Literature and Imperialism, 1830–1914* (Ithaca, N.Y.: Cornell University Press, 1988)
Bratton, J.S., 'Of England, Home, and Duty: The Image of England in Victorian and Edwardian Juvenile Fiction', in John Mackenzie (ed.), *Imperialism and Popular Culture* (Manchester: Manchester University Press, 1986), pp. 73–93
Brennan, Timothy, 'The National Longing for Form', in Homi K. Bhabha (ed.), *Nation and Narration* (London: Routledge, 1990), pp. 44–70
Briggs, Asa, *Victorian People* (Harmondsworth: Penguin Books, 1963)
Briggs, Asa, 'Exhibiting the Nation' in *History Today*, January 2000, 16–25
Brody, Jennifer DeVere, *Impossible Purities: Blackness, Femininity, and Victorian Culture* (Durham, N.C.: Duke University Press, 1998)
Broinowski, Alison, *The Yellow Lady: Australian Impressions of Asia* (Melbourne, New York: Oxford University Press, 1992)
Brown, Richard H., 'Cultural Representation and Ideological Domination', in *Social Forces*, 71:3 (March, 1993), 657–676
Burn, William L., *The Age of Equipoise: A Study of the Mid-Victorian Generation* (London: George Allen & Unwin Ltd., 1964)
Burton, Antoinette M., *Burdens of History: British Feminists, Indian Women, and Imperial Culture, 1865–1915* (Chapel Hill: University of North Carolina Press, 1994)
Butt, John, '*Bleak House* in the Context of 1851', in *Nineteenth-Century Fiction*, 10:1 (June, 1955), 1–21
Buzard, James, '"Anywhere's Nowhere": Dickens on the Move', in Anny Sadrin (ed.), *Dickens, Europe and the New Worlds* (Basingstoke: Macmillan Press Ltd, 1999), pp. 113–127

Campbell, Kate, 'Journalistic Discourses and Constructions of Modern Knowledge', in Laurel Brake, Bill Bell, and David Finkelstein (eds.), *Nineteenth-Century Media and the Construction of Identities* (Basingstoke: Palgrave, 2000), pp. 40–53

Casey, Ellen, '"That Specially Trying Mode of Publication": Dickens as Editor of the Weekly Serial', in *Victorian Periodicals Review*, 14:3 (Fall, 1981), 93–101

Chatterjee, Partha, 'Anderson's Utopia', in *Diacritics*, 29:4 (1999), 128–134

Cheadle, Brian, 'Despatched to the Periphery: The Changing Play of Centre and Periphery in Dickens's Work', in Anny Sadrin (ed.), *Dickens, Europe and the New Worlds* (Basingstoke: Macmillan Press Ltd, 1999), pp. 100–112

Cheah, Pheng, 'Grounds of Comparison', in *Diacritics*, 29:4 (1999), 3–18

Chennells, Anthony, 'Savages and Settlers in Dickens: Reading Multiple Centres', in Wendy Jacobson (ed.), *Dickens and the Children of Empire* (Houndmills, Basingstoke: Palgrave, 2000), pp. 153–172

Chesneaux, Jean, Marie C. Bergere, and Marianne Bastid, *China from the Opium Wars to the 1911 revolution* (Hassocks, Sussex: Harvester Press, 1977)

Childs, Peter (ed.), *Post-Colonial Theory and English Literature: A Reader* (Edinburgh: Edinburgh University Press, 1999)

Clark, Jonathan, 'Protestantism, Nationalism, and National Identity, 1660–1832', in *The Historical Journal*, 43:1 (2000), 249–276

Clemm, Sabine, '"Amidst the Heterogeneous Masses": Charles Dickens's *Household Words* and the Great Exhibition of 1851', in *Nineteenth-Century Contexts*, 27:3 (September, 2005), 207–230

Cohen, Michele, 'The Grand Tour: Language, National Identity and Masculinity', in *Changing English: Studies in Reading and Culture*, 8:2 (October, 2001), 129–141

Cohen, Robin, *Frontiers of Identity: The British and the Others* (London: Longman, 1994)

Colley, Linda, 'Britishness and Otherness: An Argument', in *Journal of British Studies*, 31:4 (October, 1992), 309–329

Colley, Linda, *Britons : Forging the Nation, 1707–1837* (London: Vintage, 1992)

Collini, Stefan, Richard Whatmore, and Brian W. Young (eds.), *History, Religion, and Culture: British Intellectual History 1750–1950* (Cambridge: Cambridge University Press, 2000)

Collins, Philip, '"Inky Fishnets": Dickens as Editor', in *The Dickensian*, 61 (1965), 120–125

Collinson, Susan, 'Robert Knox, Anatomy of Race' in *History Today*, December 1990, 44–49

Colls, Robert, *Identity of England* (Oxford: Oxford University Press, 2002)

Colls, Robert, and Philip Dodd (ed.), *Englishness: Politics and Culture 1880–1920* (London: Croom Helm, 1986)

Conacher, J.B., *Britain and the Crimea, 1855/56: Problems of War and Peace* (Basingstoke: Macmillan Press Ltd, 1987)

Cook, E.T., and Alexander Wedderburn, *The Complete Works of John Ruskin*, Library Edition, 39 vols. (London, George Allen, 1904-)

Cotsell, Michael, *Creditable Warriors, 1830–1876*, English Literature and the Wider World (London: Ashfield Press, 1990)

Cranfield, Geoffrey A., *The Press and Society: From Caxton to Northcliffe*, Themes in British Social History (London: Longman, 1978)

Cro, Stelio, 'The Noble Savage: Myth and Reality', in *Romance Languages Annual*, 4 (1992), 216–226

Culler, Jonathan, 'Anderson and the Novel', in *Diacritics*, 29:4 (1999), 20–39

Curtin, Philip D., *The Image of Africa: British Ideas and Action, 1780–1850* (Madison, London: University of Wisconsin Press, 1964)

Curtis Jr, L. Perry, *Apes and Angels: The Irishman in Victorian Caricature*, revised edition (Washington and London: Smithsonian Institution Press, 1997 [first published 1971])

David, Deirdre, 'Children of Empire: Victorian Imperialism and Sexual Politics in Dickens and Kipling', in *Gender and Discourse in Victorian Literature*, 18 (1992), 124–142

David, Saul, *The Indian Mutiny* (London: Penguin Books, 2003)

Davis, John R., *The Great Exhibition* (Stroud: Sutton, 1999)

Davis, Leith, '*Allegories of Union in Irish and English Writing, 1790–1870: Politics, History, and the Family from Edgeworth to Arnold*, by Mary Jean Corbett', in *Victorian Studies*, 44:4 (2002), 684–686

Dennis, Rutledge M., 'Social Darwinism, Scientific Racism, and the Metaphysics of Race', in *Journal of Negro Education*, 64:3 (Summer, 1995), 243–252

Distad, N. Merrill, 'Desiderata and Agenda for the Twenty-First Century', in J. Don Vann and Rosemary T. VanArsdel (eds.), *Victorian Periodicals: A Guide to Research*, vol. 2, 2 vols. (New York: Modern Language Association of America, 1989), pp. 124–136

Donoghue, Denis, 'The English Dickens and *Dombey and Son*', in *Nineteenth-Century Fiction*, 24:4 (March, 1970), 383–403

Doyle, Brian, *English and Englishness*, New Accents (London: Routledge, 1989)

Drew, John M.L., *Dickens the Journalist* (London: Palgrave, 2003)

During, Simon, 'Literature—Nationalism's Other? The Case for Revision', in Homi K. Bhabha (ed.), *Nation and Narration* (London: Routledge, 1990), pp. 138–153

Eagleton, Terry, 'From *Literary Theory: An Introduction* (1983)', in Vincent B. Leitch, and others (eds.), *The Norton Anthology of Theory and Criticism* (London: W.W. Norton & Company, 2001), pp. 2243–2249

Eagleton, Terry, '*England's Disgrace: J.S. Mill and the Irish Question*, by Bruce L. Kinzer', in *Victorian Studies*, 44:4 (2002), 682–684

Early, Julie English, 'Susan Schoenbauer Thurin, *Victorian Travellers and the Opening of China 1842–1907* (review)', in *Victorian Studies*, 43:3 (Spring, 2001), 524–526

Easley, Alexis, 'Authorship, Gender and Power in Victorian Culture: Harriet Martineau and the Periodical Press', in Laurel Brake, Bill Bell, and David Finkelstein (eds.), *Nineteenth-Century Media and the Construction of Identities* (Basingstoke: Palgrave, 2000), pp. 154–164

Easson, Angus, 'Dickens, *Household Words* and a Double Standard', in *The Dickensian*, 60 (1964), 104–114

Easthope, Antony, *Englishness and National Culture* (London: Routledge, 1999)

Edwardes, Michael, *Battles of the Indian Mutiny* (London: Pan Books Ltd, 1963)

Edwards, Peter D., *Dickens's 'Young Men': George Augustus Sala, Edmund Yates and the World of Victorian Journalism*, Nineteenth Century (Aldershot: Scolar Press, 1997)

Eldridge, C. C., *Victorian Imperialism* (London: Hodder and Stoughton, 1978)

Eldridge, C. C., *The Imperial Experience : from Carlyle to Forster*, Context and Commentary (Houndmills, Basingstoke: Macmillan Press Ltd., 1996)

Ellegård, Alvar, 'The Readership of the Periodical Press in Mid-Victorian Britain II. Directory', in *Victorian Periodicals Newsletter*, 13 (1971), 3–22

Engler, Balz, 'Englishness and English Studies', in Balz Engler and Renate Haas (eds.), *European English Studies: Contributions Towards the History of a Discipline* (Leicester: English Association, for European Society for the Study of English, 2000), pp. 335–348

English, Barbara, 'The Kanpur Massacres in India in the Revolt of 1857', in *Past & Present*, 142 (1994), 169–178

Ermath, Elizabeth Deeds, *The English Novel in History 1840–1895* (London: Hodder and Stoughton, 1997)

Evans, Eric J., 'Englishness and Britishness: National Identities, c.1790-c.1870', in Alexander Grant and Keith J. Stringer (eds.), *Uniting the Kingdom? The Making of British History* (London & New York: Routledge, 1995), pp. 223–243

Fairbank, John King, *Trade and Diplomacy on the China Coast: The Opening of the Treaty Ports, 1842–1854*, Harvard Historical Studies, 2 vols. (Cambridge: Harvard University Press, 1964)

Fanon, Frantz, *The Wretched of the Earth* (Grove Press, 1968)

Fitzgerald, C. P., *The Chinese View of Their Place in the World*, Chatham House Essays (London: Oxford University Press, 1966 [first published 1964])

Foley, Tadhg, and Séan Ryder (eds.), *Ideology and Ireland in the Nineteenth Century* (Dublin: Four Courts Press, 1998)

Freedgood, Elaine, *Victorian Writing about Risk: Imagining a Safe England in a Dangerous World*, Cambridge Studies in Nineteenth-Century Literature and Culture (New York: Cambridge University Press, 2000)

Gates, Barbara T., '*Solitary Travelers: Nineteenth-Century Women's Travel Narratives and the Scientific Vocation*, by Lila Marz Harper', in *Victorian Studies*, 44:4 (2002), 716–717

Gervais, David, *Literary Englands: Versions of 'Englishness' in Modern Writing* (Cambridge: Cambridge University Press, 1993)

Gervais, David, 'Englands of the Mind', in *Cambridge Quarterly*, 30:2 (2001), 151–169

Gibbons, Luke, 'Identity Without a Centre: Allegory, History and Irish Nationalism', in *Cultural Studies*, 6:3 (1992), 358–378

Gibbs-Smith, C. H., *The Great Exhibition of 1851* (London: H.M.S.O., 1964 [first published 1950])

Gikandi, Simon, 'Englishness, Travel, and Theory: Writing the West Indies in the Nineteenth Century', in *Nineteenth-Century Contexts*, 18:1 (1994), 49–70

Gikandi, Simon, *Maps of Englishness: Writing Identity in the Culture of Colonialism* (New York: Columbia University Press, 1996)

Gikandi, Simon, 'The Embarrassment of Victorianism: Colonial Subjects and the Lure of Englishness', in John Kucich and Dianne Sadoff (eds.), *Victorian Afterlife: Postmodern Culture Rewrites the Nineteenth Century* (Minnesota: University of Minnesota Press, 2000), pp. 157–185

Gilmour, Robin, *The Victorian Period: The Intellectual and Cultural Context of English Literature, 1830–1890*, Longman Literature in English Series (London, New York: Longman, 1993)

Girvin, Brian, 'Making Nations: O'connell, Religion and the Creation of Political Identity', in Maurice R. O'Donnell (ed.), *Daniel O'connell: Political Pioneer* (Dublin: IPA, 1991), pp. 13–34

Gittings, Christopher E. (ed.), *Imperialism and Gender: Constructions of Masculinity* (New Lambton, N.S.W.; Hebden Bridge: Dangaroo Press, 1996)

Gleason, John H., *The Genesis of Russophobia in Great Britain* (Cambridge, Mass.: Harvard University Press, 1950)

Golby, John M. (ed.), *Culture and Society in Britain 1850–1890: A Source Book of Contemporary Writings* (Oxford, New York: Oxford University Press, 1986)

Goodlad, Lauren M.E., '"A Middle Class Cut into Two": Historiography and Victorian National Character', in *ELH*, 67:1 (Spring, 2000), 143–178

Graham, Walter J., *English Literary Periodicals* (New York: Octagon Books, 1966 [first published 1930])

Grainger, J.H., 'The View from Britain Ii: The Moralizing Island', in Eugene Kamenka and F.B. Smith (eds.), *Intellectuals and Revolution: Socialism and the Experience of 1848* (London: Edward Arnold Ltd., 1979), pp. 121–130
Gray, Peter (ed.), *Victoria's Ireland? Irishness and Britishness, 1837–1901* (Dublin: Four Courts Press, 2004)
Green, Martin, *Dreams of Adventure, Deeds of Empire* (New York: Basic Books, 1979)
Greet, Annie, S.C. Harrex, and Susan Hosking (eds.), *Raj Nostalgia: Some Literary and Critical Implications* (Adelaide: CRNLE, 1992)
Grewal, Inderpal, *Home and Harem: Nation, Gender, Empire and the Cultures of Travel* (London: Leicester University Press, 1996)
Grubb, Gerald G., 'The Editorial Policies of Charles Dickens', in *PMLA*, 58:4 (December, 1943), 1094–1109
Hall, Catherine, *White, Male and Middle-Class: Explorations in Feminism and History* (Cambridge: Polity, 1992)
Hall, Catherine, *Cultures of Empire: A Reader: Colonisers in Britain and the Empire in the Nineteenth and Twentieth Centuries* (Manchester: Manchester University Press, 2000)
Hall, Catherine, Keith McClelland, and, Jane Rendall, *Defining the Victorian Nation: Class, Race, Gender and the British Reform Act of 1867* (Cambridge: Cambridge University Press, 2000)
Hall, Catherine, *Civilising Subjects: Metropole and Colony in the English Imagination, 1830–1867* (Cambridge: Polity, 2002)
Hall, Stuart, 'New Ethnicities', *ICA Documents* (1989)
Hall, Stuart, 'Cultural Identity and Diaspora', in Jonathan Rutherford (ed.), *Identity: Community, Culture, Difference* (London: Lawrence & Wishart, 1990), pp. 222–237
Harrison, Brian, 'Press and Pressure Group in Modern Britain', in Joanne Shattock and Michael Wolff (eds.), *The Victorian Periodical Press: Samplings and Soundings* (Leicester: Leicester University Press, 1982), pp. 261–295
Harvie, Christopher, 'Uncool Britannia: Linda Colley's *Britons* Reconsidered', *Times Literary Supplement*, January 8, 1999, p.12
Hawkins, Angus, 'British Parliamentary Alignment and the Indian Issue, 1857–1858', in *Journal of British Studies*, 23:2 (1984), 79–105
Heilman, Robert B., 'The New World in Dickens's Writings. Part Two', in *Trollopian*, 1:4 (March, 1947), 11–26
Helsinger, Elizabeth K., *Rural Scenes and National Representation: Britain, 1815–1850*, Literature in History (Princeton: Princeton University Press, 1997)
Hewitt, Martin (ed.), *An Age of Equipoise? Reassessing Mid-Victorian Britain* (Aldershot: Ashgate, 2000)
Hibbert, Christopher, *The Great Mutiny, India 1857* (Harmondsworth: Penguin Books, 1980)
Hill, T.W., 'Dickens and the 1851 Exhibition', in *The Dickensian*, 47 (1951), 119–124
Hobhouse, Hermione, *The Crystal Palace and the Great Exhibition : Art, Science and Productive Industry : A History of the Royal Commission for the Exhibition of 1851* (London: Athlone Press, 2002)
Hobsbawm, Eric J., *The Age of Capital, 1848–1875*, History of Civilisation (London: Weidenfeld and Nicolson, 1975)
Hobsbawm, Eric J., *Nations and Nationalism Since 1760: Programme, Myth, Reality* (Cambridge: Cambridge University Press, 1990)
Hollington, Michael, 'Dickens, *Household Words* and the Paris Boulevards', in Anny Sadrin (ed.), *Dickens, Europe and the New Worlds* (Basingstoke: Macmillan Press Ltd, 1999), pp. 22–33

Homans, Margaret, and Adrienne Munich, *Remaking Queen Victoria*, Cambridge Studies in Nineteenth-Century Literature and Culture (Cambridge: Cambridge University Press, 1997)

Hooper, Glenn, and Leon Litvack (ed.), *Ireland in the Nineteenth Century: Regional Identity* (Dublin: Four Courts Press, 2000)

Hoppen, K. Theodore, *Ireland since 1800: Conflict and Conformity*, Studies in Modern History (London, New York: Longman, 1989)

Hoppen, K. Theodore, *The Mid-Victorian Generation, 1846–1886*, The New Oxford History of England (New York: Oxford University Press, 1998)

Hosking, Rick, 'Magnetic Amalgams? John Lang's *Wanderings in India* (1859), Rudyard Kipling and Henry Lawson', in *Journal of British Studies*, 23:2 (1995), 59–80

Houghton, Walter E., *The Victorian Frame of Mind* (New Haven: Yale University Press, 1957)

Houghton, Walter E., 'Periodical Literature and the Articulate Classes', in Joanne Shattock and Michael Wolff (eds.), *The Victorian Periodical Press: Samplings and Soundings* (Leicester: Leicester University Press, 1982), pp. 3–27

Hughes, Linda K., '*Serializing Fiction in the Victorian Press*, by Graham Law', in *Victorian Studies*, 44:4 (2002), 688–690

Hulme, Peter, 'Travel and Travel Writing: Some Recent Collections of Essays', in *Studies in Travel Writing*, 4 (2000), 184–188

Jacobson, Wendy S. (ed.), *Dickens and the Children of Empire* (Houndmills, Basingstoke: Palgrave, 2000)

Jenkins, Terence A., *The Liberal Ascendancy, 1830–1886* (Basingstoke, London: Macmillan, 1994)

Jenkins, Terence A., *Parliament, Party and Politics in Victorian Britain*, New Frontiers in History (Manchester: Manchester University Press, 1996)

Jordan, John O., and Robert L. Patten, *Literature in the Marketplace: Nineteenth-Century British Publishing and the Circulation of Books*, Cambridge Studies in Nineteenth-Century Literature and Culture (Cambridge: Cambridge University Press, 1995)

Judd, Denis, *Empire: the British Imperial Experience, from 1765 to the Present* (London: Fontana, 1997)

Kanter, 'Robert Peel and the Waning of the "Influence of the Crown" in Ireland, 1812–1818', in *New Hibernia Review*, 5:2 (Summer, 2001), 54–71

Kaplan, Cora, '"Like a Housemaid's Fancies": The Representation of Working-Class Women in Nineteenth-Century Writing', in Susan Sheridan (ed.), *Grafts: Feminist Cultural Criticism* (London, New York: Verso, 1988), pp. 55–75

Kaplan, Cora, '"A Heterogeneous Thing": Female Childhood and the Rise of Racial Thinking in Victorian Britain', in Diana Fuss (ed.), *Human, All Too Human* (New York: Routledge, 1995), pp. 169–202

Kaplan, Cora, 'White, Black, and Green: Racialising Irishness in Victorian England', in Peter Gray (ed.), *Victoria's Ireland? Irishness and Britishness, 1837–1901* (Dublin: Four Courts Press, 2004), pp. 51–68

Kaplan, Fred, *Thomas Carlyle: A Biography* (Cambridge: Cambridge University Press, 1983)

Kearney, Hugh, *The British Isles: A History of Four Nations* (Cambridge: Cambridge University Press, 1989; repr. 1995)

Keesing, Nancy, *John Lang & 'the Forger's Wife': A True Tale of Early Australia* (Sydney: John Ferguson, 1979)

Kennedy, Paul, *The Realities Behind Diplomacy: Background Influences on British External Policy, 1865–1980* (London: George Allen & Unwin, 1981)

Kent, Christopher A., 'Victorian Periodicals and the Constructing of Victorian Reality', in J. Don Vann and Rosemary T. VanArsdel (eds.), *Victorian Periodicals: A*

Guide to Research, vol. 2, 2 vols. (New York: Modern Language Association of America, 1989), pp. 1–12
Khan, Sayyid Ahmad and Francis Robinson, *The Causes of the Indian Revolt*, Oxford in Asia Historical Reprints (Oxford: Oxford University Press, 2000 [first published 1873])
Kidd, Colin, 'Gaelic Antiquity and National Identity in Enlightenment Ireland and Scotland', in *The English Historical Review*, 109:434 (November, 1994), 1197–1214
Koditschek, Theodore, 'The Making of British Nationality', in *Victorian Studies*, 44:3 (Spring, 2002), 389–398
Kranidis, Rita S. (ed.), *Imperial Objects: Essays on Victorian Women's Emigration and the Unauthorized Imperial Experience* (New York, London: Twayne Publishers, 1998)
Kriegel, Lara, 'Narrating the Subcontinent in 1851: India at the Crystal Palace', in Louise Purbrick (ed.), *The Great Exhibition of 1851: New Interdisciplinary Essays* (Manchester: Manchester University Press, 2001), pp. 146–178
Lai, Shu-Fang, 'Fact or Fancy: What Can We Learn about Dickens from His Periodicals *Household Words* and *All the Year Round?*' in *Victorian Periodicals Review*, 34:1 (Spring, 2001), 41–53
Langford, Paul, and Martin Rowson, *Englishness Identified: Manners and Character, 1650–1850* (Oxford: Oxford University Press, 2000)
Langland, Elizabeth, 'Nation and Nationality: Queen Victoria in the Developing Narrative of Englishness', in Margaret Homans and Adrienne Munich (eds.), *Remaking Queen Victoria* (Cambridge: Cambridge University Press, 1997), pp. 13–32
Law, Graham, '*Nineteenth-Century Media and the Construction of Identities*, edited by Laurel Brake, Bill Bell, and David Finkelstein', in *Victorian Studies*, 44:4 (2002), 690–692
Leapman, Michael, *The World for a Shilling : How the Great Exhibition of 1851 Shaped a Nation* (London: Headline, 2001)
Lebow, Richard, *White Britain and Black Ireland: The Influence of Stereotypes on Colonial Policy* (Philadelphia: Institute for the Study of Human Issues, 1976)
Lehmann, R.C., *Charles Dickens as Editor* (Smith, Elder & Co. London, 1912)
Levy, Anita, *Other Women: The Writing of Class, Race, and Gender, 1832–1898* (Princeton, N.J.: Princeton University Press, 1991)
Lewandowski, Ken, 'A New Transportation for the Penitentiary Era: Some Household Words on Free Emigration', in *Victorian Periodicals Review*, 26:1 (1993), 8–18
Li, Chien-nung, Ssu-Yu Teng, and Jeremy Ingalls, *The Political History of China, 1840–1928* (Princeton, N.J.: D. Van Nostrand Co., 1956)
Linehan, Katherine Bailey, 'Mixed Politics: The Critique of Imperialism in Daniel Deronda', in *Texas Studies in Literature and Language*, 34:3 (Fall, 1992), 323–346
Litvack, Leon, 'Dickens, Australia and Magwitch Part I: The Colonial Context', in *The Dickensian*, 95:1 (Spring, 1999), 24–50
Litvack, Leon, 'Dickens, Australia and Magwitch Part II: The Search for *Le Cas Magwitch*', in *The Dickensian*, 95:2 (Summer, 1999), 101–127
Litvack, Leon, 'Exhibiting Ireland, 1851–3: Colonial Mimicry in London, Cork and Dublin', in Glenn Hooper and Leon Litvack (eds.), *Ireland in the Nineteenth Century: Regional Identity* (Dublin: Four Courts Press, 2000), pp. 15–57
Lloyd, David, *Nationalism and Minor Literature: James Clarence Mangan and the Emergence of Irish Cultural Nationalism* (Berkeley, London: University of California Press, 1987)

Lohrli, Anne (ed.), *Household Words: A Weekly Journal, 1850–1859, Conducted by Charles Dickens: Table of Contents* (Toronto: University of Toronto Press, 1973)

Lohrli, Anne, '*Household Words*: Its Editor and its Sub-Editor', in *The Dickensian*, 74 (1978), 30–32

Lohrli, Anne, 'Securing Fame in *Household Words*', in *Victorian Periodicals Review*, 12:4 (Winter, 1989), 162–163

Lohrli, Anne, '"With my Name on Every Page": Dickens References in *Household Words*', in *Dickens Quarterly*, 9:1 (1992), 7–19

Mackenzie, Norman and Jeanne, *Dickens: A Life* (Oxford: Oxford University Press, 1979)

Maidment, Brian E., 'Victorian Periodicals and Academic Discourse', in Laurel Brake, Aled Jones and Lionel Madden (eds.), *Investigating Victorian Journalism* (Basingstoke: Macmillan, 1990), pp. 143–154

Mandler, Peter, 'Against "Englishness": English Culture and the Limits to Rural Nostalgia, 1850–1940', in *Transactions of the Royal Historical Society*, 6th series, 7 (1997), 155–175

Mandler, Peter, '"Race" and "Nation" in Mid-Victorian Thought', in Stefan Collini, Richard Whatmore and Brian William Young (eds.), *History, Religion, and Culture: British Intellectual History 1750–1950* (Cambridge: Cambridge University Press, 2000), pp. 224–244

Marshall, P. J., and Glyndwr Williams, *The Great Map of Mankind: British Perceptions of the World in the Age of Enlightenment* (Cambridge, Mass.: Harvard University Press, 1982)

McClintock, Anne, *Imperial Leather: Race, Gender, and Sexuality in the Colonial Conquest* (New York, London: Routledge, 1995)

McKenzie, Judy, *Letters of George Augustus Sala to Edmund Yates*, Victorian Fiction Research Guides (Department of English, University of Queensland, 1993)

Moors Jr., Edwin W. (ed.), *The Letters of Thomas Carlyle to His Brother Alexander* (Cambridge, Mass.: Belknap Press of Harvard UP, 1978)

Mosse, George L., *The Image of Man: The Creation of Modern Masculinity*, Studies in the History of Sexuality (Oxford: Oxford University Press, 1996)

Mukherjee, Rudrangshu, 'Reply to Barbara English, "The Kanpur Massacres in India in the Revolt of 1857"', in *Past & Present*, 142 (1994), 178–189

Nayder, Lillian, 'Class Consciousness and the Indian Mutiny in Dickens's "The Perils of Certain English Prisoners"', in *Studies in English Literature*, 32:4 (Autumn, 1992), 689–705

Nayder, Lillian, 'Dickens and "Gold Rush Fever": Colonial Contagion in *Household Words*', in Wendy S. Jacobson (ed.), *Dickens and the Children of Empire* (Houndmills, Basingstoke: Palgrave, 2000), pp. 67–77

Nayder, Lillian, *Unequal Partners: Charles Dickens, Wilkie Collins, & Victorian Authorship* (Ithaca, NY: Cornell University Press, 2002)

Neff, D.S., '*The Times*, the Crimean War, and "Stanzas from the Grande Chartreuse"', in *Papers on Language and Literature*, 33:2 (Spring, 1997), 169–181

Newsome, David, *The Victorian World Picture: Perceptions and Introspections in an Age of Change* (London: John Murray, 1997)

Panayi, Panikos (ed.), *Racial Violence in Britain, 1840–1950* (Leicester: Leicester University Press, 1996)

Parker, Andrew, 'Bogeyman: Benedict Anderson's "Derivative" Discourse', in *Diacritics*, 29:4 (1999), 40–57

Parry, Jonathan Philip, 'The Impact of Napoleon III on British Politics, 1851–1880', in *Transactions of the Royal Historical Society*, 6th series, 11 (2001), 147–175

Patten, Robert L., 'Dickens as Serial Author: A Case of Multiple Identities', in Laurel Brake, Bill Bell and David Finkelstein (eds.), *Nineteenth-Century Media and the Construction of Identities* (Basingstoke: Palgrave, 2000), pp. 137–153
Paxman, Jeremy, *The English: A Portrait of a People* (London: Penguin, 1999)
Paxton, Nancy L., 'Mobilizing Chivalry: Rape in British Novels About the Indian Uprising of 1857', in *Victorian Studies*, 36:1 (Fall, 1992), 5–30
Peers, Douglas M., '"Those Noble Exemplars of the True Military Tradition": Constructions of the Indian Army in the Mid-Victorian Press', in *Modern Asian Studies*, 31:1 (1997), 109–142
Pemble, John, *The Mediterranean Passion: Victorians and Edwardians in the South* (Oxford: Clarendon, 1987)
Philip, Jim, 'Journeywork', in *Studies in Travel Writing*, 1 (1997), 199–215
Philip, Kativa, 'Race, Class and the Imperial Politics of Ethnography in India, Ireland, and London, 1850–1910', in *Irish Studies Review*, 10:3 (Winter, 2002), 289–302
Pocock, J.G.A, 'British History: A Plea for a New Subject', in *Journal of Modern History*, 47:4 (December, 1975), 601–621
Pocock, J.G.A, 'The Limits and Divisions of British History: In Search of the Unknown Subject', in *American Historical Review*, 87:2 (April, 1982), 311–336
Pocock, J.G.A, 'The New British History in Atlantic Perspective: An Antipodean Commentary', in *American Historical Review*, 104:2 (April, 1999), 490–500
Poovey, Mary, *Uneven Developments: The Ideological Work of Gender in Mid-Victorian England* (London: Virago, 1989)
Poovey, Mary, 'Curing the "Social Body" in 1832: James Phillips Kay and the Irish in Manchester', in *Gender and History*, 5:2 (1993), 196–211
Poovey, Mary, *Making a Social Body : British Cultural Formation, 1830–1864* (Chicago: Chicago University Press, 1995)
Porter, Bernard, *The Lion's Share: A Short History of British Imperialism, 1850–1995*, third edition (London, New York: Addison Wesley Longman, 1996 [first published 1975])
Porter, Bernard, '"Bureau and Barrack": Early Victorian Attitudes Towards the Continent', in *Victorian Studies*, 27 (1984), 407–433
Porter, Bernard, *Britain, Europe, and the World 1850–1986: Delusions of Grandeur* (London: Allen & Unwin, 1987)
Pratt, Mary Louise, *Imperial Eyes: Travel Writing and Transculturation* (London, New York: Routledge, 1992)
Price, Roger, *The Revolutions of 1848*, Studies in European History (London: Macmillan Education, 1988)
Purbrick, Louise (ed.), *The Great Exhibition of 1851: New Interdisciplinary Essays*, Texts in Culture (Manchester: Manchester University Press, 2001)
Pykett, Lyn, 'Reading the Periodical Press: Text and Context', in *Victorian Periodicals Review*, 22:3 (Fall, 1989), 100–108
Pykett, Lyn, *Charles Dickens*, Critical Issues (Basingstoke: Palgrave, 2002)
Quinn, John F., *Father Mathew's Crusade: Temperance in Nineteenth-Century Ireland and Irish America* (Massachusetts: University of Massachusetts Press, 2002)
Rainsford, Dominic, 'Crossing the Channel with Dickens', in Anny Sadrin (ed.), *Dickens, Europe and the New Worlds* (Basingstoke: Macmillan Press Ltd, 1999), pp. 3–13
Redfield, Marc, 'Imagi-Nation: The Imagined Community and the Aesthetics of Mourning', in *Diacritics*, 29:4 (1999), 58–83
Rem, Tore, '*Little Dorrit*, *Pictures from Italy* and John Bull', in Anny Sadrin (ed.), *Dickens, Europe and the New Worlds* (Basingstoke: Macmillan Press Ltd, 1999), pp. 131–145

Renan, Ernest, 'What Is a Nation?' (1882), trans. Martin Thom, in Homi K. Bhabha (ed.), *Nation and Narration* (London: Routledge, 1990), pp. 8–22

Reynolds, Stephen, 'Dickens and *the Times*', in *Dickens Quarterly*, 2:2 (June, 1985), 57–58

Rich, Paul B., 'The Quest for Englishness', in *Victorian Values: Personalities and Perspectives in Nineteenth-Century Society*, ed. by Gordon Marsden (London and New York: Longman, 1990), pp. 211–225

Richards, Thomas, *The Commodity Culture of Victorian England: Advertising and Spectacle, 1851–1914* (Stanford, Calif.: Stanford University Press, 1990)

Robbins, Bruce, 'Telescopic Philanthropy: Professionalism and Responsibility in *Bleak House*', in *Nation and Narration*, ed. by Homi K. Bhabha (London: Routledge, 1990), pp. 213–230

Robbins, Keith, 'An Imperial and Multinational Polity: The "Scene from the Centre", 1832–1922', in Alexander Grant and Keith J. Stringer (eds.), *Uniting the Kingdom?: The Making of British History* (London & New York: Routledge, 1995), pp. 223–243

Robbins, Keith, *Great Britain : Identities, Institutions and the Idea of Britishness*, The Present and the Past (London: Longman, 1998)

Robbins, Ruth, and Julian Wolfreys (eds.), *Victorian Identities: Social and Cultural Formations in Nineteenth-Century Literature* (Houndmills, Basingstoke: Macmillan Press, 1996)

Roderick, Colin, and John Earnshaw, 'John Lang (1816–1864): First Australian-Born Novelist', in *Royal Australian Historical Society Journal*, 49:2 (July, 1963), 100–135

Russell, William Howard, *My Indian Mutiny Diary*, ed. by Michael Edwardes (London: Cassell, 1957 [first published 1857])

Rutherford, Jonathan, *Forever England: Reflections on Race, Masculinity and Empire* (London: Lawrence & Wishart, 1997)

Ryals, Clyde De L., and Kenneth J. Fielding (eds.), *The Collected Letters of Thomas and Jane Welsh Carlyle* (Durham: Duke University Press, 1997)

Ryan, J.S., 'The Australian Materials in *Household Words*', in Marion Adams (ed.), *AULLA: Proceedings of the Ninth Congress Melbourne 19–26 August*, 1964, pp. 57–59

Sadrin, Anny (ed.), *Dickens, Europe and the New Worlds* (Basingstoke: Macmillan Press Ltd, 1999)

Said, Edward W., *Orientalism* (Harmondsworth: Penguin, 1991 [first published 1978])

Said, Edward W., *Culture and Imperialism* (London: Vintage, 1994 [first published 1993])

Salmon, Richard, '"a Simulacrum of Power": Intimacy and Abstraction in the Rhetoric of the New Journalism', in Laurel Brake, Bill Bell and David Finkelstein (eds.), *Nineteenth-Century Media and the Construction of Identities* (Basingstoke: Palgrave, 2000), pp. 27–39

Samuel, Raphael (ed.), *Patriotism: The Making and Unmaking of British National Identity,* 3 vols. (London: Routledge, 1989)

Samuel, Raphael, *Island Stories: Unravelling Britain*, ed. by Alison Light, Sally Alexander and Gareth Jones, 2 vols (London, New York: Verso, 1998)

Sanders, Andrew, 'The Dickens World', in Michael Cotsell (ed.), *Creditable Warriors, 1830–1876* (London: Ashfield Press, 1990)

Schlicke, Paul, *Dickens and Popular Entertainment* (London: Unwin Hyman, 1988 [first published 1985])

Schlicke, Paul, *The Oxford Reader's Companion to Dickens* (Oxford: Oxford University Press, 1999)

Schmitt, Cannon, 'Alien Nation: Gender, Genre, and English Nationality in Wilkie Collins's the Woman in White', in *Genre: Forms of Discourse and Culture*, 26:2–3 (Summer-Fall, 1993), 283–310

Sharpe, Jenny, *Allegories of Empire: The Figure of Woman in the Colonial Text* (Minneapolis: University of Minnesota Press, 1993)

Shattock, Joanne, and Michael Wolff (ed.), *The Victorian Periodical Press: Samplings and Soundings* (Leicester: Leicester University Press, 1982)

Shuttleworth, Sally, Gowan Dawson and Richard Noakes, 'Women, Science and Culture: Science in the Nineteenth-Century Periodical', in *Women: A Cultural Review*, 12:1 (Spring, 2001), 57–70

Simmons, Clare A., '*The Vikings and the Victorians: Inventing the Old North in Nineteenth-Century Britain*, by Andrew Wawn', in *Victorian Studies*, 44:4 (2002), 721–723

Sinha, Mrinalini, *Colonial Masculinity: The 'Manly Englishman' and the 'Effeminate Bengali' in the Late Nineteenth Century*, Studies in Imperialism (Manchester: Manchester University Press, 1995)

Stanley, Peter, *White Mutiny: British Military Culture in India, 1825–1875* (London: Hurst & Co., 1998)

Stapleton, Julia, 'Political Thought and National Identity, 1850–1950', in Stefan Collini, Richard Whatmore and Brian W. Young (eds.), *History, Religion, and Culture: British Intellectual History 1750–1950* (Cambridge: Cambridge University Press, 2000), pp. 245–269

Stepan, Nancy, *The Idea of Race in Science : Great Britain, 1800–1960* (London: Macmillan, 1982)

Stocking, George W., *Victorian Anthropology* (New York: Maxwell Macmillan, 1987)

Stone, Harry, 'Dickens "Conducts" *Household Words*', in *The Dickensian*, 64 (1968), 71–85

Stone, Harry (ed.), *The Uncollected Writings of Charles Dickens: Household Words, 1850–1859*, 2 vols. (Bloomington, London: Indiana University Press, 1968)

Storey, Graham, Kathleen Tillotson and Nina Burgis (eds.), *The Pilgrim Edition of the Letters of Charles Dickens* (Oxford: Clarendon Press, 1965-)

Taylor, Brandon, *Art for the Nation: Exhibitions and the London Public, 1747–2001* (Brunswick, N.J.: Rutgers University Press, 1999)

Taylor, Jenny Bourne, and Sally Shuttleworth (eds.), *Embodied Selves: An Anthology of Psychological Texts, 1830–1890* (Oxford: Clarendon Press, 1998)

Thurin, Susan Schoenbauer, *Victorian Travelers and the Opening of China, 1842–1907* (Athens, Ohio: Ohio University Press, 1999)

Tomlin, Eric W. F., 'The Englishness of Dickens', in *Etudes Anglaises: Grande Bretagne, Etats Unis*, 23 (1970), 113–124

Tracy, Robert, 'Lighthousekeeping: *Bleak House* and the Crystal Palace', in *Dickens Studies Annual: Essays on Victorian Fiction*, 33 (2003), 25–53

Turner, Mark W., 'Periodical Time in the Nineteenth Century', in *Media History*, 8:2 (2002), 183–196

Vann, J. Don, and Rosemary T. VanArsdel (eds.), *Victorian Periodicals: A Guide to Research*, Reviews of Research, 2 vols. (New York: Modern Language Association of America, 1989)

Vizetelly, Henry, *Glances back through Seventy Years: Autobiographical and Other Reminiscences*, 2 vols. (London: Kegan Paul, Trench, Trübner & Co, 1893)

Ward, Andrew, *Our Bones Are Shattered: The Cawnpore Massacres and the Indian Mutiny of 1857* (London: John Murray, 2004 [first published 1996])

Watson, Tim, 'Maps of Englishness', in *Contemporary Literature*, 41:4 (Winter, 2000), 726–739

Watts, Lan, 'Dickens and Immigrant Ships: A Matter of Whitewashing', in *The Dickensian*, 85:3 (419) (1989), 167–175
Wee, C.J.W.-L., 'Christian Manliness and National Identity: The Problematic Construction of a Racially "Pure" Nation', in Donald Hall (ed.), *Muscular Christianity: Embodying the Victorian Age* (Cambridge: Cambridge University Press, 1994), pp. 66–88
West, Shearer (ed.), *The Victorians and Race* (Aldershot: Ashgate, 1996)
Whelan, Kevin, 'Writing Ireland: Reading England', in Glenn Hooper and Leon Litvack (eds.), *Ireland in the Nineteenth Century: Regional Identity* (Dublin: Four Courts Press, 2000), pp. 185–198
Wilde, William H., Joy W. Hooton and Barry G. Andrews (eds.), *The Oxford Companion to Australian Literature* (Melbourne: Oxford University Press, 1985)
Wilson, Angus, *The World of Charles Dickens* (London: Martin Secker & Warburg Limited, 1970)
Wilson, Kathleen, *The Island Race: Englishness, Empire, and Gender in the Eighteenth Century* (London: Routledge, 2002)
Wilson, Kathleen, *Nations, Empires and Identities in the Eighteenth Century* (London: Routledge, 2003)
Winter, Alison, *Mesmerized: Powers of Mind in Victorian Britain* (Chicago: University of Chicago Press, 1998)
Wynne, Deborah, 'Responses to the 1851 Exhibition in *Household Words*', in *The Dickensian*, 97:3 (Winter, 2001), 228–234
Wynne, Deborah, *The Sensation Novel and the Victorian Family Magazine* (Basingstoke: Palgrave, 2001)
Young, Robert, *Colonial Desire: Hybridity in Theory, Culture, and Race* (London, New York: Routledge, 1995)
Žižek, Slavoj, 'The Sublime Object of Ideology', in Julie Rivkin and Michael Ryan (eds.), *Literary Theory: An Anthology* (Oxford: Blackwell, 1998), pp. 312–325

2.2. Electronic and audiovisual resources

'The Contemplator's Short Biography of Charles Dibdin' (website). Available at http://www.contemplator.com/history/dibdin.html (accessed June 22, 2004)
'Eurotunnel: History' (website), last update 2004. Available at http://www.eurotunnel.com/ukcMain/ukcCompany/ukcAboutUs/ukpAboutUsHistory (accessed September 28, 2004)
'In Our Time', July 12, 2001. Radio magazine, BBC Radio 4, 2001
'India' (website), The Columbia Encyclopaedia. Available at http://www.xreferplus.com/entry.jsp?xrefid=797329&secid=.5.3.#s.5.3.- (accessed April 17, 2002)
'James Hannay' (website). Available at http://90.1911encyclopedia.org/H/HA/HANNAY_JAMES.htm (accessed August 27, 2004)
'Thug' (website). Available at http://www.britannica.com/eb/article?eu=74198&tocid=0 (accessed June 28, 2001)
Ackroyd, Peter, 'Dickens', May 2002. Television documentary, 3 parts, BBC2, 2002
Bakardjieva, Maria P., 'The Electric Telegraph' (website), last update December 1, 2000. Available at http://www.ucalgary.ca/~bakardji/ElectricComm/takeoff.html (accessed November 24, 2003)
Sowards, Steven S., 'Twenty-five lectures on modern Balkan history' (website), last update December 2003. Available at http://www.lib.msu.edu/sowards/balkan/ (accessed February 24, 2004)

2.3. Unpublished material

Chase, Malcolm (University of Leeds), 'The Graphic Dimensions of the *Northern Star*' (unpublished conference paper), given at 'Image and Text, Image in Text', organised by Research Society for Victorian Periodicals, Universiteit Gent, July 8–10, 2004

Clark Jr., Harold Frank, 'Dickensian Journalism: A Study of *Household Words*' (unpublished doctoral dissertation, New York, Columbia University, 1967)

Corrigan, Karen (University of Newcastle), 'Demythologizing Migration and Language Shift in Postcolonial Ireland' (unpublished conference paper), given at '(Re)Visioning the World: Travelling in "Old" and "New" Empires', University of Newcastle, 23–24 May, 2003

Rogers, Randal (Concordia University Canada), 'Colonial Imitation and Racial Insubordination: On Some Photographs from St. Louis, 1904' (unpublished conference paper), given at 'Cultural Imperialism and Competition: Travel, World's Fairs and National/Colonial Image', organised by The Nineteenth Century Studies Association, St Louis, Missouri, March 11–13, 2004

Index